looking back to the future

essays on art, life and death

Critical Voices in Art, Theory and Culture
A series edited by Saul Ostrow

Now Available

Seams: Art as a Philosophical Context
Essays by Stephen Melville. Edited and Introduced by Jeremy Gilbert-Rolfe

Capacity: History, the World, and the Self in Contemporary Art and Criticism
Essays by Thomas McEvilley. Commentary by G. Roger Denson

Media Research: Technology, Art, Communication
Essays by Marshall McLuhan. Edited and with a Commentary by Michel A. Moos

Literature, Media, Information Systems
Essays by Friedrich A. Kittler. Edited and Introduced by John Johnston

England and Its Aesthetes: Biography and Taste
Essays by John Ruskin, Walter Pater and Adrian Stokes. Commentary by David Carrier

The Wake of Art: Criticism, Philosophy, and the Ends of Taste
Essays by Arthur C. Danto
Selected and with a Critical Introduction by Gregg Horowitz and Tom Huhn

Beauty is Nowhere: Ethical Issues in Art and Design
Edited and Introduced by Richard Roth and Susan King Roth

Music/Ideology: Resisting the Aesthetic
Edited and Introduced by Adam Krims. Commentary by Henry Klumpenhouwer

Footnotes: Six Choreographers Inscribe the Page
Essays by Douglas Dunn, Marjorie Gamso, Ishmael Houston-Jones,
Kenneth King, Yvonne Meier, Sarah Skaggs
Text and Commentary by Elena Alexander. Foreword by Jill Johnston

Difference/Indifference: Musings on Postmodernism, Marcel Duchamp and John Cage
Introduction and Text by Moira Roth. Commentary by Jonathan D. Katz

Looking Back to the Future: Essays on Art, Life and Death
Essays by Griselda Pollock. Introduction and Commentary by Penny Florence

Forthcoming Titles

Critical Vices: The Myths of Postmodern Theory
Essays by Nicholas Zurbrugg. Commentary by Warren Burt

When Down Is Up: The Desublimating Impulse
Essays by John Miller. Commentary by Roger Denson

See the back of this book for other forthcoming titles in the Critical Voices series.

**griselda
pollock**

essays

looking back to the future
essays on art, life and death

introduction and
commentary

**penny
florence**

Australia · Canada · France · Germany · India · Japan · Luxembourg · Malaysia ·
The Netherlands · Russia · Singapore · Switzerland

G+B
ARTS
INTERNATIONAL

Copyright © 2001 OPA
(Overseas Publishers Association) N. V.
Published by license under the G+B Arts International imprint,
part of The Gordon and Breach Publishing Group.

Amsteldijk 166
1st Floor
1079 LH Amsterdam
The Netherlands

British Library Cataloguing in Publication Data
A catalogue record for this book is available from
the British Library

ISSN 1025-9325
ISBN 90-5701-132-8

contents

Introduction to the Series   *vii*

Introduction: *1*   Penny Florence
Looking Back to the Future

Essays   Griselda Pollock

**Part I   Critical Positions:
Addressing the Now**

Critical Positions   *11*

Trouble in the Archives   *23*

Femwatching in the 1990s   *41*

**Part II   Feminism, History, and
Contemporary Practice in the
Visual Arts**

~~Feminist~~ Interventions in History: *53*
On the Historical, the Subjective,
and the Textual

Painting, Feminism, History   *73*

Abandoned at the Mouth of Hell   *113*
or A Second Look That Does Not
Kill: The Uncanny Coming to
Matrixial Memory

Part III   Historical Re-Visions

Proximity and the Color of Desire: *177*
The Laboring Body and Its Sex

On Mary Cassatt's *Reading Le Figaro* or The Case of the Missing Women   *227*

Part IV   Cinematic Moments

Crows, Blossoms and Lust for Death—Cinema and the Myth of Van Gogh the Modern Artist   *277*

Empire, Identity, and Place: Masculinities in *Greystoke: The Legend of Tarzan*   *311*

Part V   Autohistories

Territories of Desire: Reconsiderations of an African Childhood   *339*

Deadly Tales   *371*

Commentary: Griselda Pollock and Feminist Critique: Post/Modernism in the Fourth Dimension   *391*   Penny Florence

introduction to the series

CRITICAL VOICES IN ART, THEORY AND Culture is a response to the changing perspectives that have resulted from the continuing application of structural and poststructural methodologies and interpretations to the cultural sphere. From the ongoing processes of deconstruction and reorganization of the traditional canon, new forms of speculative, intellectual inquiry and academic practices have emerged that are premised on the realization that insights into differing aspects of the disciplines that make up this realm are best provided by an interdisciplinary approach that follows a discursive, rather than a dialectic, model.

In recognition of these changes, and of the view that the histories and practices that form our present circumstances are in turn transformed by the social, economic, and political requirements of our lives, this series will publish not only those authors who already are prominent in their field—or those who are now emerging—but also those writers who had previously been acknowledged, then passed over, only now to become relevant once more. This multigenerational approach will give many writers an opportunity to analyze and reevaluate the position of those thinkers who have influenced their own practices, or to present responses to the themes and writings that are significant to their own research.

In emphasizing dialogue, self-reflective critiques, and exegesis, the Critical Voices series not only acknowledges the deterritorialized nature of our present intellectual environment, but also extends the challenge to the traditional supremacy of the authorial voice by literally relocating it within a discursive network. This approach to text breaks with the current practice of speaking of multiplicity, while continuing to construct a singularly linear vision of discourse that retains the characteristics of dialectics. In an age when subjects are conceived of as acting upon one another, each within the context of its own history and without contradiction, the ideal of a totalizing system does not seem to suffice. I have come to realize that the near collapse of the endeavor to produce homogeneous terms, practices, and histories—once thought to be an essential aspect of defining the practices of art, theory, and culture—reopened each of these subjects to new interpretations and methods.

My intent as editor of Critical Voices in Art, Theory and Culture is to make available to our readers heterogeneous texts that provide a view that looks ahead to new and differing approaches, and back toward those views that make the dialogues and debates developing within the areas of cultural studies, art history, and critical theory possible and necessary. In this manner we hope to contribute to the expanding map not only of the borderlands of modernism, but also of those newly opened territories now identified with postmodernism.

Saul Ostrow

introduction
looking back to the
future

penny florence

penny florence

READERS ACQUAINTED WITH GRISELDA Pollock's work will find in this volume an important selection of her recent essays full of insight into major areas of contemporary theory, especially at the interface between sexed subjectivities, post-colonialism and Marxist-informed history. Anyone who may still believe Griselda Pollock's thought is adequately exemplified by *Old Mistresses*—and there are indeed many who do not think about modern feminism beyond its infancy—should most certainly read it, because Pollock has remained fully engaged with radical theoretical, art-historical and feminist debates. Both kinds of reader, together with whoever might be new to her work, will discover continuities on many, intersecting levels that are in themselves illuminating at a time when so many write as if the production of the new were possible "ex nihilo." The idea of "History" is fundamental to this texture of writing.

Old Mistresses (1981) is "art history" in that it is now an indispensable part of the recent revisioning of the history of art for anyone seriously interested in the discipline, and it remains a reference point for feminist and/or sexed art history. Co-written with Roszika Parker it is also recognizably of the art-historical genre; radical for its time, especially in its definitional refusal of a neutrality exposed as spurious, constantly interrogative and challenging, yet rooted in the best traditions of art historical inquiry. The unique collection *Framing Feminism* (1987) is in its own right a primary document of British art in an international perspective. Its importance will become clearer still as the generation of women whose art it documents passes. *Vision and Difference* (1988) may perhaps be taken to mark the shift towards a greater emphasis on psychoanalytic concepts, signalled also in her essays and articles, and in her work on the editorial boards of several of the most important journals in art and cultural history, including *Screen* and *Block*, as well as the specifically feminist.

Taken together, these interventions and innovative writings make Griselda Pollock the most important voice in feminist art history in Britain. This has been true now for twenty years, and it remains so today; only Lisa Tickner (who was also a member of the 1972 Women's Art History Collective) is comparable in having consistently published groundbreaking work over such a long period. Pollock is also among the most significant writers on art internationally, and one of the few art historians—let alone female and/or feminist art historians—who is also read as a cultural theorist by those outside her immediate discipline. This much is well enough known perhaps, in academic circles. But it may not be very widely known that Pollock has remained an activist working for women's cultural expression in and beyond "the establishment" in exemplary, contentious and antihierarchical ways, networking and supporting local feminist initiatives. The formation and promotion of the British Feminist Arts and Histories Network is one recent example. In an age when the term "feminism" has been made highly problematic, she can be relied upon to stand up and be counted at the same time as recognizing all the contradictions and difficulties both theoretical and actual that this entails. Nor has she feared those other debates so crucial to our time, those around Marxism and the crisis of the Left, insisting that the relevance of feminism be seen on the level of underlying conceptualization and structures.

Feminist revisionings of subjectivity are indeed inseparable from the historical developments which have seen a crisis in the Left. As with post-modern theory, however, it is all too easy to submerge its contribution, perpetuating the marginalization of issues of sex when it comes to human rights and "universals." The invention of revisioned universals and collectivities is vitally at stake in this process—signalled by what Rosi Braidotti has called the Female Universal, and paralleled, for example, by writers including Homi Bhaba and Salman Rushdie with regard to race.

All oppositional politics are necessarily conceived with a contradiction at heart: they must work for their own redundancy. This is true both of means and end. They begin in the relative darkness of reaction and must move forward without knowing, at least at first, where the paths will lead. This makes it inevitable that they must undergo more or less radical change, both in ideas and in strategies, as their achievements make visible new possibilities. Success in specific areas will often mean a kind of dissolution, rather than arrival and the consolidation of forming permanent institutions. This inherently performative and anticonservative process is bound to be controversial and to excite internal antagonism, and the careful reflection it can provoke may be no bad thing. The current naming of this process as concerning postmodernism is often reductive, and it continues the depoliticizing gesture of so much late capitalist cultural commentary; modernism was born complete with antidote. So was feminism. Those now grappling with the problematics of "post-Enlightenment" sex and subjectivity (encompassing a whole range of issues consequent to breaking down the model of a neuter, masterful and achieved idea of rational selfhood) are frequently perceived as having "sold out" to a well-rewarded careerism, but it would be a grave mistake to think that changing the underlying philosophy of a system is necessarily losing touch with lived reality. Griselda Pollock's work participates fully in what can be sometimes a thankless dynamic, especially for those whose business it is to be understood. Legible in her writings since the 1970s is an analytic awareness of the major concerns of the feminism of their time, the Marxism of their time, the art-history of their time. This is very far from the work of one who has turned her back on social commitment for some easy and sequestered option, away from the so-called real world.

"Art History" as a discipline has lagged behind others in its evolution since the 1960s. This is not the place for a full analysis of complex developments; but among the reasons for this are its relation to capital and, in ways that require differentiation between the U.S. and U.K., class, multicultural and racial issues (since these last are not always identical). Paintings are circulated as part of the economics of exchange, material and symbolic, in ways whose specificity affect their sexed interpretation quite differently from other cultural forms. Film studies was, with literature, the main engine of essential change, at least from within the academy, and film, too, has a special relation to capital, this time also more particularly at the level of production as well as distribution or dissemination. It also has a special relation to psychoanalysis with which it is roughly contemporaneous. The semiotic and psychoanalytic debates, which in the U.K. focused around the journal *Screen*, were in some senses also among the variform crucibles of feminism.

It will be clear even from this merest outline sketch that to be a feminist art historian during the 1970s, 1980s and 1990s required fluency in several political and cultural discourses, some highly developed and some born kicking into a contested and hostile milieu; and this without even a mention of the discipline of history itself. While this volume focuses on the 1990s it locates itself in the longer trajectory of feminism and in the flexuous temporality of what has been called woman's time; but this naming should not be understood as essentialist, for reasons that Pollock's long-term historical project make clear. Her work in this volume always seeks to locate the feminist thinking that underlies it in the broader and interrelated artistic, philosophical and critical debates of our time. It is near-scandalous that it is impossible to take for granted that such an enterprize is indispensable to many other "-isms" and near-isms than feminism, including modernism, postmodernism, deconstructionism and post-colonialism.

the backlash in borrowed clothes

The 1990s was a decade of backlash against work of this kind both intellectually and in the wider political arena, a backlash characterized by a conservatism that has learned the language of opposition and revolution. Let me illustrate this with an anecdote about Pollock, who was the keynote speaker at the 1990 conference of the American Women's Caucus for Art, which met in New York in February of that year. In April, an anonymous article was published by *The New Criterion*, claiming that Pollock, monolithic feminism incarnate, substitutes a battery of political tests for questions about truth and quality, rendering such issues off limits. Like those who accuse the advocates of change of a static political correctness, this misapprehends a fixed projection as the opposing stance, which is of a different order. In this scrutiny of its own reflection, *The New Criterion* practices a kind of catoptromancy, or divination by mirrors, and is about as reliable. Feminism, like most of the significant contemporary epistemologies, not only takes questions of truth and quality very seriously indeed, but it starts at least one step back to ask about what truth and quality are and where they might inhere. A problem for those who believe concepts, signs or texts are transparent is that feminism conducts its inquiries in such a way as to change them beyond the range of previous conceptualizations. Feminist thought grows because it is alive. The actual process of this change is indispensable. It is at least in part the lack of insight into this essentially dynamic and reticulated intelligence that renders feminism opaque to the *New Criterion* inheritors of a deathly tradition of cultural guardianship and preservation. This is how it is possible on the one hand to lament that "intellectual probity is scarcely a memory" (p. 1) and on the other to mock as "ritual self-criticism" Griselda Pollock's self-identification as "white, middle class and heterosexual" (p. 2). That reflexivity might be vital to intellectual probity is imperceptible to the monocultural. It is not at all the case that, in the *New Criterion's* words, "terms like 'art' and 'quality' have absolutely no meaning" (p. 2) for the feminist art historians of the Women's Caucus for Art or for Griselda Pollock. They are crucial. But they are not transparent in meaning and they are neither the center nor the goal because centrality and teleology themselves are disputed.

The attack is instructive to consider and not only because it characterizes the nascent decade's neoconservativism in its guise as antifeminist backlash: it trots out several persistent misconceptions without any consciousness of its ignorance, and exposes what I might call structural incomprehension; that is to say the kind of misreading that occurs when one epistemological position renders another invisible. This in itself is exemplary; feminism suffers acutely from the characteristic assumption of the entrenched and the validated that their own intellectual position is adequate to deal with developments which are not only radical but of a kind which makes the otherwise straightforward matter of making yourself informed strange and new.

Caricaturing an individual like Pollock who dares to try and speak difficult truths in an original voice is, of course, a strategy that has a long and scurrilous tradition in political journalism, but its appearance in an article arguing for disinterestedness is symptomatic; the establishment is being forced to betray the politicization it denies. This kind of move is singularly inappropriate when it comes to feminism, however. No philosophy is as difficult to situate in relation to its exponents as feminism. There is no founding individual, no equivalent to Marx or Derrida or Freud, to take some random names from a possible list of the relevant or even imperfectly equivalent. Whether this is A Good Thing or a problem exemplifying culture's obliteration of the Mother is a moot point. The relationship of any given feminist to feminism is never either straightforward or single; and yet to name oneself a feminist is to be seen to become a Representative of feminism. This awkward and distorting conflation of individual and representative voice has been particularly burdensome for feminists of color, whose earliest articulations were hungrily consumed by a guiltily well-meaning white readership wishing to "include" "the Black experience." All those who in their different ways forged contemporary feminism were put in a similarly impossible position, which reflects the reason why feminists so bitterly dispute modernism and postmodernism; in the political climate just indicated, only the naive would easily abandon their claim to some kind of representable self. Making any kind of evaluation of the contribution of prominent feminists requires due attention to the issues of collectivity and anti-individualism which form one of its constituent nodes. It is an instructive difficulty, a crucial but tricky indicator. Like all symptoms it is a structured displacement of an underlying and suppressed problem.

Because symptoms are not random they can be read. Pollock's text, and this commentary on it, may be read on one level as an elaboration of the problematic involved in such a task, one which draws on the work that has been done over the last quarter or a century to bring the unspoken symptoms of cultures in transition into the light of day. (Already the reader attuned to the problematic will sense areas of hotly contested debate; my metaphor of the symptom implies a model of scientific rationalism, surely, an acceptance of the arch-Father-figure, Sigmund Freud. Perhaps—and up to a point. But the puzzle has multiple answers. Pollock's work evidences how reasoned ways of knowing are embedded in all the pathways of unknowing. And what lies in that plural "cultures"? Again, we, whoever "we" are, shall see.)

Griselda Pollock's position evinces issues of these kinds endemic both to feminism and to cultural criticism. She is a trailblazer who has been taken, certainly in the UK, to "represent" feminist art criticism. She is also, as I say, an activist whose work at grass roots levels inflects her theoretical work with the strategic aims that are sharpened by direct engagement. She would be among the first to acknowledge that such a politic is definitional in dealing with "art," its practices, philosophies and institutions.

Those familiar with recent debates around feminist-postmodernist-modernist intersections will know that "subjectivity" is a central issue. How is it, one feminist interrogation runs, that as soon as women challenge the masculinism of dominant philosophies, those philosophies shift to declare the death of the embodied voice and the obsolescence of sexed distinctions? Yet how vulnerable feminism is to this murderous intent—at least equality feminism—in its assertion of women's rights and capacities as regards the traditionally male. This is clear in the outlines of another argument about how it is that theories of postmodernism have come to be circulated apart from the current of feminism to which it clearly owes so much, to the extent that feminist sympathizers can ponder why women have not "contributed" to the contemporary adventure they name postmodernist.

What I take to be one sign of her strategic self-positioning in the shape-shifting force that is the Women's Movement is that Pollock does not exemplify the (possibly entirely respectable) type of thinker whose life work is the elaboration of one governing theory or stance. Many feminists of this kind have refused to be either mocked or defined out of existence, and some of them should be applauded and supported, especially since the work of reiteration is so much less glamorous than that of discovery. But fewer have been at the same time as fully responsive as Pollock to the rapid social and political developments of the past twenty-five years. Of course, her response is mediated through academe, but it has been a near-fatal error for feminists to lose sight of the imbrication of all sites of power with semiosis: the legal, social, institutional and political arenas which impact directly on women's lives all try to define what women are and what they mean. Feminist academics have to continue to dialogue, particularly with women active in other spheres and particularly with a new generation: many women critical of what they see as over-abstract and difficult feminist theory resulting from opting out of "real" problems are often astonished to learn what a hostile place women academics generally inhabit.

This change is the more apparent if they take in the magnitude of changing the discipline of old-style, *New Criterion*-style "Art History" and the ways it is entrenched in wider regimes of power. The vicious backlash against feminism from those who can afford to sit out the battles should alert exponents of the variform "New Art History" to remain vigilant. Two very high-profile TV series in Britain are a case in point: Andrew Graham-Dixon's *History of British Art* (1996) and *The Renaissance* (1999) are virtually pre-feminist and prestructuralist. Yet one eminent critic has compared the former with John Berger's *Ways of Seeing* (1972, also a TV series and book) apparently without any awareness of the irony. Such is the signifying power in Britain of the BBC that the BBC itself is perceived as the most significant point of comparison between two cultural productions that signify such different moments and histories. I mean this with as little irony and rather more political seriousness. The pretence that there can ever be a "return" is an historical delusion that equally affects the USA, as it must, because it is very probably endemic to recorded cultures. This book evidences much that is conflicted and demands the capacity to hold contradiction in tension with conviction. The obliteration of histories has a long and disgraceful history in dominant cultures, one in which the history of art is complicit. Whether or not you accept what feminism might have to say to you, what Pollock's feminism has to say about history you disregard at your peril. Whoever "you" are—or might become—and whatever alliances you may wish to forge across the gap between "you" and "me."

part I
critical positions: addressing the now

griselda pollock

I AM NOT AN ART CRITIC. BY PROFESSION, I do not intend to write art criticism. Yet I find myself compelled to write about the art being made now.

The coming of the Women's Movement in the early 1970s, however, made all the difference to writing about art. The difference cannot be reduced to adding the auxiliary characters of *feminist* artist, *feminist* critic and *feminist* art historian. "Feminist interventions in art's histories"—my 1988 neologism—redefine the key characters in the processes of artistic production and consumption—the Artist, the Critic and the Reader/Viewer.

I have taken the abstract figures of Author [Artist], Critic and Reader [Viewer] from Roland Barthes's overused and misread essay, "The Death of the Author," published in 1968, in which Barthes theorised how the textual system of "modernist writing" that had replaced the "classic realist text" effectively destroyed the idea of literature as the utterance of an authoritative subject. Barthes argued that modernist writing presents itself to the Reader as a fragmented text whose momentary coherence is only achieved at the destined site called the Reader. Replacing notions of a work of art as expressive, the "text" is no longer conceived as a "single line of words releasing as a single "theological" meaning the message of the Author God but it is a multidimensional space in which a variety of writings, none of them original, blend and clash."[1] Text makes writing (or any other creative activity) a productive space that does not communicate preformed meaning. Text is the play of a writer with the social processes of signification. Abdicating authority, writing acknowledges that subjectivity itself is an effect of signification and textuality.[2]

It is obvious that women, never admitted fully as candidates for the God-like space of The Author-Subject, have not mourned his passing. Yet Barthes' system posits the now enhanced Reader as "without history, biography or psychology," merely a destination toward which the writing works, where "all traces by which the writing is constituted" are momentarily held together.[3] The Reader is thus the bearer of the culture, the site of the play of the multiplicities of which the writing is the parody, citation, contestation. Should we query, in the name of the nameless women, such an abstraction and argue instead that it does matter, always, who is reading, and what structures of power privilege certain readings to the repression of others that are equally possible.

A second fatality of the demise of the Author is the demotion of the Critic, who was, according to Barthes, the chief ideologue and beneficiary of the Author system. Claiming merely to decipher the meanings inherent in the text through the direct deposit of the Author's presence—the author who served as the "limit on a text, a final signified"—the Critic, in fact, invested the text with his/her own meaning, thus generating his/her authority as the mirror of that borrowed from the Author that the Critic has in effect created. In Barthes's anatomy of the modernist text, we are all Readers now.

The history of modernism in the visual arts (and in literature too for that matter) has not exactly followed this course. The Critic continues to play a significant role in the determination of preferred or authoritative readings of works of art. We need a more social and historical framework than Barthes's structural abstractions allow in order to understand this apparent paradox.

Commodification of cultural production in the nineteenth century eroded the public sphere of culture by privatizing it. The typical "private individual" producer, the producer in a capitalist economy always being a private individual, working in the private space of the studio, produced for the competitive market. Distribution was mediated by dealer, curator and gallery, and this gave rise to a modern form of the author system even while the cultural practices being distributed moved towards a modern textual system at the level of their work on representation. The role of the individual producer's name and career strategy that secured its status as Author became a vital part of brand identity when art entered the open market of cultural commodities. Yet the modernist initiatives had a supra-individual project that created collaborations and a sense of collective identity that we call the avant-garde. Criticism was radically altered in this conjuncture.

At first, artists such as the informal and internally dissonant Impressionist grouping went public by soliciting commentary from the existing critical profession doing their rounds for dailies and periodicals. Soon, however, specialist advocacy emerged, with partisan or specialist journals established, and reasoned, often historically based apologia for this group's desire both to renovate the great tradition and innovate in order to articulate a sense of modernity. In this new space, the partisan intellectual as critic emerged and set about creating the new terms for recognizing and valorizing the artists' new programs. A growing stress on formal over communicative or narrative concerns and an emphasis on individuality signalled by singular stylistic signatures developed into the major but contradictory strategies. With the proliferation of factions, the avant-garde became internally competitive and the critic's new function developed even more into a form of advocacy, advertizing and publicizing a select tendency amidst those vying for leadership within, and status beyond, the subcultural fraction of the avant-garde minority.

When this subcultural formation was appropriated to become the dominant cultural tendency of modernizing Western bourgeoisies in the early twentieth century, criticism functioned to secure the equation between a particular interpretation of the pre-history and trajectory of the modernist project and Modern Art (as in the founding of and publishing activities of the Museum of Modern Art). The writings of the interwar period exhibit a strongly historicist and teleological tendency, while framing modernism in highly individuated forms denoted by the proper Author names, Picasso, Matisse, Pollock. Clement Greenberg clearly stated the case, concluding his review of the history of modern painting from Courbet to the late 1930s by saying that he found himself merely producing a historical apology for abstract art—the logical rather than historically inevitable conclusion to its own pre-history.[4]

I would not wish to suggest that so magisterial a critic as Greenberg should be dismissed with easy skepticism. In the end, I might find that his strategy may also be my own.[5] To engage with contemporary practice from the inevitably Baudelairean position of partisanship is always to engage with questions of historical possibility and contemporary significance. Any writing about contemporary practices will find itself structurally defined by the conditions of marketable artistic production and the power of the institutions and discourses which define artistic practice's social spaces and cultural valuations. The important point is that these never exhaust the meanings or effects of any one of culture's products.[6]

Museums and magazines serve, as the Vancouver Art Gallery so bravely stated in its mission statement in the early 1990s, "the purposes of art." They are not merely fooling themselves that they are concerned with making a "living culture." But making culture, like history, does not occur in circumstances of our own choosing, but in "circumstances directly encountered, given and transmitted from the past."[7] Those who write about this process find themselves forced in two directions at once—advocacy and perspective, appreciation and analysis, partisanship and explanation.

If modernism can be understood as the coming of a radical yet creative doubt about the possibility of meaning, throwing off the fixity of authority for the pleasures of reading, the critical management of modernism has, however, confidently re-attributed meaning and recreated canonical authorities. Raymond Williams named this process the making of a "selective tradition," "an intentionally selective version of a shaping past and a pre-shaped present, which is then powerfully operative in the process of social and cultural definition and identification."[8] The selective tradition based upon a litany of proper names that singularize and Westernize the complex and diverse projects of modernity in culture becomes through this re-fathering of the Author an element in the constitution of domination, of cultural hegemony, working always in the interests of a specific constituency, "the privileged male of the white race."[9]

The Women's Movement involved a commitment to the critique of that dominance and the contestation of those interests. As a feminist, working on and against the discourses of art and artist which figure symbolically in that hegemony, I look back to recover forgotten and effaced histories of artists who were women in order to position and understand the stakes for women as artists in practice today. I have learned from the work of women artists in the present what might have been the stakes for those working at the initiation of the modernist project and before, in other configurations of sexual difference, power and representation. The main difference is the stories I tell are not, cannot be teleological. They do not add up to what Williams defined as "a sense of predisposed continuity." They are the contribution to the production of a counterhegemony.

The result is a certain irony. To achieve discursive and theoretical space in which to speak of that which has been repressed in modernist critical and art historical discourse, I have utilized the writings of Roland Barthes that effectively assassinate the Author and the Critic. Yet the urgency of the situation for women artists requires a highly articulated advocacy of the work of named individuals. To survive in a market economy, artists who are women need publicity and the legitimation of a supportive discourse that creates a social image of their intervention. Yet the work in question may in fact propose a critique of social, economic and cultural power vicariously sustained in the symbolic realm of culture by the very practices they need in order to be heard or seen as artists. These artist are engaged in a struggle that has to take place in the arenas of culture, determined but never entirely defined by its capitalist economics.

Let me be clearer. Such a project as I am envisaging is not merely the invention of a compensatory, all-women canon. It does not imply discovering a "single, theological meaning" in the statements made by artists as women, easing Woman into the recently vacated God-spot that Barthes discerns as the guarantor of the Author. This would be to assume that a signifying space is already simply there, waiting to be filled with feminine/feminist enunciations. Such a signifying space has to be *produced* in the crossover between traditional boundaries and disciplines, in the exchange between critical theory, critical writing, critical practice that produce dissident knowledge in and beyond their productive critique of existing structures and sign systems.[10] As a writer, like the intellectuals historically associated with the first competitive avant-garde formation in the later nineteenth century, I share a political and theoretical context with feminists who are artists, a sense of common experiences in both personal and political histories. Collectively, we are producing a distinctive textuality through which to signify and enunciate a critical, historically self-reflexive, feminist subject.[11]

I am suggesting, therefore, that certain practices fulfill the kinds of textuality which Barthes defines as the distinctive character of modernism.[12] Perhaps those practices associated with the feminist avant-garde fulfill the project of modernism better than Modernist art criticism itself. To avoid misunderstanding here, let me be clear. Feminism has earned some currency by being positioned as either an instance of, or the exemplary moment of, post-modernism. True as this may be in some ways, it is also a stumbling block. While post-modernity undoubtedly defines our current horizons, we may be premature in abandoning the modernist project *tout court*. I am still very much a modernist, in some significant respects, though not in the obvious and very limited terms associated with the hegemony of a certain kind of American abstract painting delivered to us through the curatorial strategies of MOMA: what is usually taken on board by the shorthand term *Modernism*. Difficult and betrayed as the modernist project has been in its larger cultural frame, since its uneasy birth in the revolutions and betrayals of the late eighteenth century where rationality and slavery coincided with the abolition of the residual rights of women, I cannot see that feminists can abandon the hope of change that was modernity's corrupted legacy, nor the belief in the need to struggle for change, nor the need to offer a critique of power and to seek for an ethics of responsibility and a commitment to the dislocation or reallocation of power and knowledge.[13] The emergence onto the political and cultural stage of the twentieth century of many groups, peoples and minorities resisting their oppression within the still racist, sexist and homophobic terms of imperial modernity has condemned the universalist claims of modernism, and spiked its blind faith in rationality as the sole determinant of so-called progress. Yet these same constituencies have used the dreams of modernity and its forms to voice their demands for what else—freedom, equality and self-determination. Their critique is directed at the distributions of power based on the continuing social contradictions we call class, race and gender. The political analysis and critical theorization of class, race and gender are, however, themselves by-products of the contradictions within modernity. Contradictions are to be overcome; they are not superseded by invented terminologies. Terms such as "post" (post-Feminism, post-Modernism, post-Industrial) can easily lull us into a false sense of historical advance, when no change has fundamentally taken place, and the dominant systems have merely adapted faster than we have to the ever-shifting plays of power and resistance.

At the specific level of cultural practice, feminist interventions can be understood using Barthes's propositions about a new kind of readership, not because we wish absolutely to destroy all authority, but rather because we aim to locate it, critique it, disperse and as importantly to claim and qualify some aspects of its voice for the hitherto dispossessed and masquerading. This generates a distinct and emphatic textuality in which manufacture of certain kinds of objects functions as part of a larger strategic intervention, *the production of signifying space.* This Kristevan term can be taken in several ways. It corresponds to Barthes's notion of the text as the space for a reader to activate its semiotic and psychic traces into meaning. It also encompasses the social and ideological space of the sites of cultural practice—exhibition galleries and the pages of magazines and catalogues, books and articles. We have known for a long time that the museum and gallery are not merely the neutral housing for art objects. They too perform a kind of textual space, written with object-like signs that direct the viewer/reader in space as if through a narrative in a book. The kinds of art practices which interest me are those which use things, objects, forms and spaces to generate multiple textualities. They, nonetheless, accept the necessity to write the space of the reader by the way the things they put in the gallery define its spaces as something quite other than the typical capitalist spectacle of exhibition as consumption. Thus the formal presence of the aesthetically vivid works becomes the tokens of exchange between cooperating partners—producer and reader.[14] These two figures—structural positions—mediate the social production of meanings within explicit historical, biographical and psychological positionalities.

It is by stressing readership as part of production rather than its substitute, and readership as critical for a formerly excluded or occluded community of readers/viewers that an expanded sense of public is produced. We are all readers now, says Barthes. So why would we still need special advocacy for the producers and their productive texts? In fact, there is none, in the sense of promotion of marketable commodities. There is commitment on behalf of the readership to which I belong to create the possibilities of readings by those in it and beyond it through a reflexive production of a social image of the initiative and intervention the artists' work proposes or produces. Critical writing is thus but another operation co-producing the signifying space. I write to clear a space for feminist textualities to function—not because they lack a historical context, or a place in the trajectories of modern culture. Rather, those lineages have been violently and systematically disrupted or repressed. Instead of being able to note the historical position of feminism, taken for granted and inserted into common knowledge, each time we speak, we need to contest the continuing policing by the selective tradition which distorts feminist words by representing feminism as the tedious Voice of the Other to that history of Modernism, feminism as the monster from outside the city of culture.[15]

Thus my practice as a writer on contemporary artistic practices is concerned to refashion the historical knowledge of modern cultures. I want to comprehend in one dialectical movement the specificity of a range of different and singular women's participation in its production and the conditions of the repression of the knowledge of that involvement and refraction. This produces the leverage by which to set the modernist works that women have made against the Modernism selected and legitimated as the only course by "the privileged males of the white race." I have tried in more historical initiatives to fashion new theorizations of early modernist culture in terms of the deployment of looking within a promiscuous and enticing social space. Out of the matrix of the city was generated the apparent autonomy of the pictorial spaces—studio and canvas—where men were allowed, in Angela Carter's immortal phrase about Picasso, "to cut up women." We can then read the discourses of high Modernist painting and criticism, for instance Greenberg's ever-more disembodied opticality and support for studio based abstraction valorized through canonized *masters*, in terms of a sexual politics, never overtly stated but represented in a displacement onto the exclusive focus on artistic vision, visual truth and gestural mastery.

These provisional moves towards a feminist theorization of the field and practice might make it possible to offer some preliminary thoughts on what among the varieties of initiatives in culture enacted by women in the wave of the Women's Movement post-'68, effectively mount a feminist intervention, that is, calculated strategic practices that are both rooted in the cultural possibilities of modernist practices and that yet supersede it, critically, precisely by deploying against its ideologically overloaded and psychically predetermined visuality, complex and expanded textualities. The distinctions I would draw are not value judgments valid across the board. They represent a tactical maneuver defined by the desire to track the creation of feminism as a structurally altering signifying space where meaning, subjectivity and sexual difference collide and realign. Despite certain critical misrepresentations, this position is not a blanket endorsement of so-called text-image work, of scripto-visual art practices. Textualities, according to Barthes's theory of the text, means a "tissue of quotations drawn from innumerable centres of culture."[16] What Barthes means is yet again distinct from "appropriative strategies," the Baudrillardian play with the icons and sign systems of contemporary cultures. Textualities do refer to many sites, many systems, and draw upon diverse drives and pleasures, scopic as well as invocatory, spatial as well as tactile. At once cinematic, sculptural, graphic, visual, the point is the invitation to decipherment, the invocation to reading as a complex social subjectivity within yet always transgressing the limits of power.

I am not an art critic. Yet I am partisan. And I am not an art historian with a neutral scholarly overview legitimated by the passage of time. Writing historically about contemporary practice, I aim to concentrate on understanding a particular and limited, yet important range of what I call strategic practices. I want to avoid publicity and teleology in the name of a historically refracted understanding of new possibilities and critical necessities—a history in the making. That means delivering an understanding of the present configurations of power as they are enacted and challenged at the level of the text, cultural practice and semiotic innovation. I think artistic practices are as likely a place to find and produce a kind of social as well as self-knowledge when they function knowingly as strategic interventions and culturally as aesthetic realizations, in the full awareness of the predicament of attempting to generate critical knowledge in the midst of an administered, commodified culture. Writing in response to the intellectual and artistic interventions of contemporary artists, learning through reading is not, therefore, a matter of choice, but a choice itself to meet several compelling necessities.

notes

1 Roland Barthes, "The Death of the Author," in *Image, Music, Text*, ed., S. Heath, (London: Fontana, 1977), 143.

2 Julia Kristeva, "The System and the Speaking Subject," [1973] in *The Kristeva Reader*, ed., T. Moi, (Oxford: Basil Blackwell, 1986), 24–33.

3 Barthes, op. cit., 148.

4 Clement Greenberg, "Towards a Newer Laocoon," *Partisan Review*, 7: 4 (1940): 310.

5 For a feminist response to the death of Clement Greenberg, see my "Holes in the Fabric of Art Criticism," *Art Monthly*, July–August, (1994): 14–18.

6 I draw this formulation from Raymond Williams who writes: "We can recognise then ... that no mode of production, and therefore, no dominant society or order of society, and therefore no dominant culture, in reality exhausts the full range of human practice, human energy, human intention (this range is not the inventory of some original "human nature" but, on the contrary, is that extra-ordinary range of variations, both practised and imagined, of which human being are and have shown themselves to be capable." "Base and Superstructure in Marxist Cultural Theory," *Problems of Materialism*, (London: Verso Books, 1980), 43.

7 Karl Marx, "The Eighteenth Brumaire of Louis Bonaparte," [1852] in K. Marx and F. Engels, *Selected Works in One Volume*, (London: Lawrence and Wishart, 1970), 96.

8 Raymond Williams, *Marxism and Literature*, (Oxford: Oxford University Press, 1985), 115.

9 Gayatri Chakravorty Spivak, "Imperialism and Sexual Difference," *Oxford Literary Review*, 8, (1986): 225.

10 Spivak, op. cit., 116.

11 This phrase is a paraphrase of the term with which Nancy Miller concludes her "Changing the Subject: Authorship, Writing and the Reader," in *Feminist Studies/Critical Studies*, Teresa de Lauretis, (Bloomington: Indiana University Press, 1986).

12   John Mowitt, *Text: The Genealogy of an Antidisciplinary Object*, (Durham and London: Duke University Press, 1992).

13   Julia Kristeva, "Women's Time," in *The Kristeva Reader*, Toril Moi, (Oxford: Basil Blackwell, 1986), 210.

14   Walter Benjamin's concept of the Author as Producer predates Barthes's assassination of the classic bourgeois Author and offers an important figure for feminist aesthetics. See Walter Benjamin, "The Author as Producer," in *Understanding Brecht*, trans. Anna Bostock, (London: New Left Books, 1977), 85–104.

15   The reference here is to Laura Mulvey and Peter Wollen's film *Riddles of the Sphinx*, (Britain, BFI, 1976).

16   Barthes, op. cit., 146.

trouble in the archives

2

griselda pollock

griselda pollock

I WANT TO EXPLORE A PROBLEM—A paradox perhaps.

We talk of our field as that of the visual arts. Looking, seeing, these are the key activities of consuming art or studying the history of art. Kenneth Clark wrote guides called *Looking at Paintings* and John Berger confidently wrote that "seeing comes before words." The staunch defenders of the purity of art against social histories of art or theoretically informed criticism dread the contamination of the visual by the verbal, or the sociological. "Image" is set against "word." Conceptual art was an aberration; scripto-visual work a dangerous hybrid.

Where does feminism stand in relation to this debate? What is the state of the argument in feminist art history and criticism? Do we have a specifically feminist theory of the visual in relation to art? Do we want or need one? Isn't feminism itself a critique of the kinds of ideologies that imagine there is a pure realm of vision that exists before gender, race, class and all other social influences have their effects?

If the question referred to cinema, the answer would be more easily "yes, there is a feminist theory of the visual, at least of the politics of vision and spectatorship." Feminist film criticism is more or less definable by the specific terms of analysis it has developed around spectatorship and the sexual difference. Laura Mulvey's famous article of 1975, entitled significantly "Visual Pleasure and the Narrative Cinema" suggested that there is a gender hierarchy in film not just at the level of the kind of images of men and women, or even of masculine and feminine personae, or of the stories and characters. Rather, sexual difference operates through the imbalance between looking and being looked at which narratives orchestrate. Film conveys its messages through the way it organizes "the gaze." Seated, in the dark, in a state of suspended animation, the consumer of the cinematic message is a spectator *par excellence.*

Since the mid-1970s feminist theories of spectatorship in the cinema have drawn heavily, if never exclusively, on psychoanalysis. It allowed us to show how the field of vision, in the condensed and specific form cinema has manufactured for cultural consumption, is a major site not only of sexual ideology, but of the desires and fantasies associated with sexuality which shape and are shaped by the structure of sexual difference. This term specific to psychoanalysis and post-structuralist theories suggests that sex or gender are not innate, but are produced. Thus man and woman are not different, but we are *differentiated* by the different pathways cultures designate, for those cultures will name women and men. But as a result of this structural and not biological process of sexual differentiation, men and women may well experience themselves, their bodies, the world, differently, not just through different social experiences, but psychologically. The term feminine will then refer to a position, not an essence; yet it will also signify a possibility of different desires, fantasies, meanings, from what patriarchal or phallic culture defines as its norms. Femininity is, therefore, according to this theory, a complex issue, both a negative position in a male-norm culture, and a potential disturbance and revolutionary force because it is so—the more than what is normal, the different and the various, or in other words the heterogeneous. The dominant culture tries to define the feminine as what man is not; it therefore represses or excludes it, or uses it only as a cipher of "difference." Feminist uses of the theory of sexual difference suggest that the feminine is what transgresses what man defines as his norm, humanity, which, therefore, challenges all ideas of one standard, one concept of the human, singularity itself, for which the phallus is the prevailing metaphor. Femininity is not always, in this context, the imposed norm against which as feminists we are in revolt. It is a psychic space, a space of dreams and imagination, symbols and meanings which we have yet to explore, or which women authors and artists have been exploring, while we, under a rigid patriarchal policing, did not have the means to recognize it.

This, then poses another question: what of sexual difference in the field of the visual arts?

Certain kinds of feminist strategies in art practices during the 1970s and early 1980s were clearly influenced by film theory and its use of psychoanalysis. Writing of an exhibition in 1984 called *On Difference and Representation,* which showed the work of Barbara Kruger, Sylvia Kolbowski, Sherrie Levine, Marie Yates, Yve Lomax and Mary Kelly, Jacqueline Rose coined the phrase "sexuality in the field of vision." (Rose 1986) in order to argue that sexuality and sexual difference are involved in all acts of vision and thus of visual representation. She related her analysis to both modernist painting with its ideology of pure vision and its correlate visual perfection at the formal level, and to contemporary feminist work which interrupted that ideology for critical, feminist purposes. Admitting that feminist work interrogates the image for the way what is depicted reproduces social stereotypes and limited norms, Jacqueline Rose suggests that this kind of work goes "beyond the issue of content to take in the parameters of visual form (not just what we see but how we see—visual space as more than the domain of simple recognition)" (1986: 231). According to psychoanalysis, much of the drama of becoming a subject, i.e., a sexed person who uses language, involves the complex pleasures and displeasures associated with sight—which is not just about perception of the real world, that is, recognition. Looking is connected to infantile fantasies about mastery, to curiosity, to dread and to desire, which refers to an impossible longing for what is forever lost. Because sight is so much associated with psychic dramas, looking understood from a psychoanalytic perspective is more akin to the kind cinematic viewing, the world of dreams and fantasies about bodies in space, than it is like any ideas of direct perception of things as they are.

This conjunction of sexuality and the field of vision theorized through psychoanalysis focuses my problem—in terms of art history and art criticism. Do we subscribe to the idea of the visualness of the visual arts simply, or critically? What is the role of psychoanalysis in developing a specifically feminist work on art history and criticism as much as practice—today? Does it allow us to re-engage with issues of the image and vision which had to be distanced, in the first era of feminist work on the histories and practices of art, in order to get at issues of gender as a social and historical factor affecting the production and reception of art historically and in the present?

To answer these questions, I shall have to make a tour through our recent history.

Art history is both like and unlike cinema. Despite being concerned with the *visual* arts, the discipline of art history has never been exclusively defined by the visual object. The making of art, monuments, buildings, sculptures, paintings, prints and all the range of materials which are the topic of art's histories involve historical, institutional, sociological, economic as well as aesthetic factors. Feminists in this field have to deal as much with issues of training, patronage, access to exhibiting facilities, languages of art criticism, mechanisms of the market, the nature and effects of materials and specific making processes, as well as with the semiotic and ideological productivity of the "image" itself. As Linda Nochlin once famously said, "the fault lies not in our stars, our menstrual cycles, our empty internal spaces, but in our institutions and education."

But as importantly, when it first emerged as a critical voice, feminist art history and criticism had to challenge one of the fixed ideas which still dominated both contemporary art and art history—namely that art is purely a *visual* experience, that it is not shaped in any way by language and that it is independent of all social factors. Whether as formalism or aestheticism, these ideas made it impossible to raise the repressed question of gender. Art has no sex, it was said, and that claim depended on the idea of the purity of vision as non-social, or even as pre-social. Feminists in art history have, therefore, forged alliances with the emerging social histories of art which challenged the exclusive claims of the *visual* arts by studying the social structures which govern the production and exhibition of art and the social conventions by which meaning is produced through public rather than personal sign systems in which art works must participate in order to be *legible* to the communities for which they are produced.

Now, however, in the 1990s, because of the twenty years' work of deconstructing the normal ideas, the ideologies, about art's visual innocence, we are beginning to re-engage, but in ways that are critically, historically and theoretically informed, with what literary critic Terry Eagleton calls "the ideology of the aesthetic." To get at the political aspects of the arts, we don't need to separate the aesthetic and the sexual, the artistic and the political, as we tactically had to do in order to open up the field for debates about gender and art. It is clear now that no substantive feminist analysis of the visual arts could be developed which did not deal with questions of the visual—namely who is looking and who is looked at, why and how and with what effects. Feminist analysis has to have a way of discussing what is specific to the procedures and effects of the practices of making objects, images, for people to look at and through that initial gaze to understand, use and be affected by.

This has not meant reclaiming ideas about a pure vision. These are displaced by a different vocabulary which writes of texts, traces and graphic marks. This is not the invasion of the space of the visual arts by literary ideas any more than looking to social contexts means colonizing art by sociology. There is, I suggest, a new term which indicates the difference we have made: that is the body. To go back to the cinema, it makes us spectators by stressing seeing over bodily involvement. We suspend our own bodily existence and enter through visual identification with characters on screen into an imaginary space where we feel with or look at the immaterial, spectral bodies on screen. Something similar might be said to happen when we look at the great machines of history and religious paintings of the West or the massive murals and sculptural sequences of Indian or Buddhist cultures. But the key difference is that the arts of painting and sculpture (for example) have a materiality and a physicality. They are there as real objects in space. They have been made by someone. The physical thing which confronts us also bears traces of that making. The depicted bodies which narratively invite us to identify with them and enter their actions through imaginative association are traces of yet another body—or bodies, the body which labored to produce them and which is present as marks—painted gestures, sculpted signs and so forth.

The body in art replaces the ideologies of art as a matter of "the eye" alone. Bodies are not just physical machines. Our bodies are socially and psychically shaped, patterned and trained. If we bring in psychoanalysis here, and the theory of sexual difference, we might argue that the body is always a fantasy, in which the actual physical thing, muscles, bones, nerves, brains, heart, eyes and so forth, becomes a "body," an organized unity, only because at quite a late stage, between six and eighteen months, we slowly acquire an *image* of a body, an envelope, a boundaried space, into which we can put, or by which can be contained all the impulses, sensations, drives and other sundry physical and psychological experiences that the infant is subject to but which it does not yet own because it has as yet no image of what it is and what it is not. Through the images offered to the child by actual mirrors or by those around the child who provide for it a "reflection" of its potential self in the way they treat it and handle it, speak to and of it, the child acquires a body as a place, a house for its sensations which is never neutral—for the image of what it is to be a part of any culture is deeply expressed through the kind of body you are patterned into. The body images we internalize from the society into which we are born are gendered, classed and culturally specific. The body is never a given, an essence but a construct which emits signs of the social, cultural, gender position into which the infant is inducted not just through social conditioning, but also through this profound and early process of psychic formation which psychoanalysis has tried to explore and interpret. To be a subject is to acquire a meaning-ladened, sexed body.

The body which makes art—the artist—may make art about its body, which is never just my body, but always either a her or a his body, and in a world shaped by colonialism, a black or a white body. That means that in art, through images of bodies and those which appear to be images of nothing or something quite else, we may be able to trace the "figurations" of this embodied psyche. Because the psyche is indelibly marked by the culture which forms it, while also containing more than any culture will officially sanction, we can read art symptomatically for meanings shaped by the drama of the subject. Sexual difference may underpin the overt content or may only be discernible indirectly. In an early analysis of a range of artwork by women artists, Mary Kelly coined the phrase "feminine inscriptions"

(Kelly 1976; in Parker and Pollock 1987). The phrase has clear associations with writing and engraving, with the graphic marking of a surface. Kelly was trying to invent a way to read art works by women which involved the traces of both women as creators in their work and of specifically "feminine" desire and fantasy which spoke to feminine subjects. For instance, she suggested that the celebration and re-use of women's traditional craft skills could be linked to a desire for and homage to the mother, while the endless fascination with the female body and identity may indicate women's special and complex relations to narcissism. The word *feminine* used to have purely negative connotations as in Betty Friedan's *The Feminine Mystique* 1963, but it is used by Kelly in a descriptive sense derived from psychoanalysis to describe both women's predicament in a sexually divided culture ruled by the Father, and our special psychic resources in relation to the female and ultimately maternal body.

Here we can see that a feminist criticism involves a major shift from traditional art theory. The art work, especially in the form of painting, is not treated as "the window on the world" or the "mirror of the soul" where vision is pure and the artist is a kind of visionary. Instead art is perceived as something made, produced, by a social mind and psychically shaped body which "writes" upon its materials to produce a series of signs which have to be read like hieroglyphs or deciphered like complex codes. The real realm is not that of optics but graphics. The word "semiotics" defines this approach to the production of meaning through social signs which are produced and interpreted by social, therefore gendered, classed and culturally positioned subjects for whom meaning operates creatively at the point where how the subject is formed exceeds the roles, identities and positions which society tries to determine for us. Going well beyond social histories of art which tries to decipher and analyze the ideological, i.e., the socially determined and required meanings art may produce or work over, this kind of analysis reads for what else is being "said," for the unconscious discourse or the discourse of the unconscious which also patterns the art work. Again, because of sexual difference the unconscious may be a site of difference.

This kind of feminist analysis of art is the product of alliances between many areas of feminist practice and study and between different theories and methods from social history to semiotics. These alliances decisively changed feminist studies from formulations such as "women and…." in which each discipline filled in the gap with its own subject area (law, art, health care, art history, etc.). Instead larger themes emerged to provide common territories. These different areas of study revealed specific aspects of those general structures which defined and oppressed us "as women": sexuality, violence, language and what I want to focus us on here: sexual difference. There are dangers in this attempt by feminism to define what happens to us "as women" because it can easily degenerate into mistaking the experience of one group of women for the experience of all women. What "we", white woman? as Tonto might have said to the Lone Ranger had she, the Lone Ranger, been a white Western feminist and Tonto a working class woman of color. But feminism remains an important space where we can pose questions of why we are oppressed "as women", however differently, and in relation to whatever other structures of oppression under which women experience domination, exploitation and violation of their humanity.

This shift is typical of what has happened in cultural studies in general. In the early 1970s the emphasis was on sociologically based studies of culture as experienced meaning and socially defined relations; in the feminist case the key term of analysis was *gender*. This was displaced by a more philosophical and language-based set of theories in which culture is defined as structures which make meaning possible and produce the conditions of knowing and using these ultimately social meanings by making us subjects of them as well subject to them: the key terms here are *language* and *subjectivity*. The politics of identity—"as a woman"—were challenged by the analysis of how we become a feminine subject in a social system, speaking its languages but, more importantly, spoken, like the ventriloquist's dummy, by our culture's master voices which we imagine are our own. The term *subjectivity* is used to define this sense that we never achieve a fixed, completed identity, but are constantly caught up in a more unstable process of changing and often contradictory positions, some of which are obviously socially manufactured, while others are unconscious and based in fantasy.

What does all this mean for actual strategies in the study of art's histories? More than I can explain in this context for there are many directions being taken. Here I want to characterize just one area of feminist challenge to the histories of art. In addition to the study of neglected women artists, a lot of current research aims to to contest the canon—the received and authorized version of the stories of art. These are often just variations on a theme of heroic individual and masculine achievement. Reading this issue psychoanalytically, we could suggest that the canon inscribes a masculine fantasy in the archives of art's histories. These masculine inscriptions tell a tale of narcissistic fantasy of masculine omnipotence, freed from the real social and parental constraints which men have to submit to as the price of their privileged status in patriarchy. When feminism questions that canon and contests that fantasy it makes **trouble in the archives.**

The use of the term "archive" insists on the fact that what we study as history is not just the accumulated deposit of the past, being kept in libraries for us to study. What is preserved, conserved and classified as the material for historical study and the valued heritage of culture was put there according to selective social interests and the desires of selected classes, cultures and genders. The library and the museum are not innocent sites of storage; they are already texts shaped according to the interests and needs of certain groups. This canonized archive then actively shapes the present for us.

To define feminist interventions in art's histories as making "trouble in the archives" also represents a break with the natural forms of art historical writing. The monograph and catalogue uncritically elevate the individual author and assume that all the works of one author have a self-evident coherence. The individual is the core of the story and the art the illustration of that life of greatness unfolding through youth, maturity and revered old age. If we do not see the history of art in terms of the Olympic torch theory of a chain of great individuals, we can use the term archive to suggest a more ramshackle, heterogeneous record which can be examined using different lines of inquiry in which what would be studied would be relations between texts, images, events and individuals. A lot of feminist work concerns histories of sexuality which cut across individual artists' histories to make us look at conjunctions in which images of women and by women can be read as part of the larger discourse of power and ways of contesting it. Other kinds of work insist that colonialism and imperialism structured the cultural products of the West and art historians are asking how the representations of the colonizers, women as much as men, operated to disfigure what they named "the other" while also projecting utterly western fantasies onto the imaginary "other" their art invented.

The term "archive" has yet another implication. It makes us self-conscious as historians, demanding the necessary sense of self-scrutiny as we engage with materials which have several pasts: a historical moment of production, a historical moment of consumption, a historical moment of entry into art historical discourse, into the museum, the canon, the class-room, into our cultural "patrimonies", into a myriad of discursive frame-works and into our formations as subjects who make or study art, or just belong to certain cultures shaped by what is and what is not acknowledged by the archive.

The nature of the trouble we cause in dealing non-canonically with the narratives of and about art is created by posing the questions repressed by the archive: questions of class, race and gender. Recent feminist writing has, as I suggested above, moved from the question of gender to formulate the issues through the notions of sexual difference and sexuality. Psychoanalysis provides a different set of terms by means of which to theorize the visual field historically as an archive composed of graphically and manually pro-duced texts—drawn, printed, painted, sculpted, as well as written and enacted etc.,—in which "art" is treated not as the affirmation of the history of an individual's vision, but as the trace of embodied historical, gendered, classed, raced and sexed subjectivities.

The post-structuralist theory which informed this model of culture has been under attack from many quarters for being nihilistic, non-political and just plain difficult. Feminism was not merely a derivative follower of its theoretical acrobatics. Feminists have in fact played a major role in develop-ing many of its greatest insights because there were many significant corres-pondences between feminist challenges to notions of fixed or natural gender difference and post-structuralist critiques of Western philosophy and its humanist ideologies based on the universal norm MAN (white, middle class and heterosexual). So now, in the climate of radical reassessment in the 1990s, feminism must assess its own position vis-à-vis the theories on offer.

What is its specific project? Are we still in the business of pursuing the goals of nineteenth century feminists from both the right and left, who aimed for equality and social improvement of women's status vis-à-vis men's? This goal, however, can be shown to imply a norm, an ideal of sameness which does not take into account the many *differences* between women in relation to class, race, sexuality, able-bodiedness and so forth. Also it may lead us to reject the notion of *difference*, that women's experiences and desires may never be the same as those of men, whatever their class, race, sexuality or able-bodiedness.

Instead of wanting to be like men, or at least treated as if we were honorary members of a human race they defined only in their own image, we might have to admit that difference is irreducible and that it is valuable that it is so. This does not mean falling back into biological notions of sex and gender. Yet we are daring now to think about what the specific nature of women's experiences in and through their female bodies and feminine psyches might be and how they can be mobilized to project different images of the world, of subjectivity, of relations between strangers which are potentially important for all people.

So in all the work we do, as feminists with many varied allegiances in struggles around race, class and sexuality, we ask ourselves what kind of solidarity can be built to combat the negative value attached to "women" in our culture because women are defined as *different* from men (less reliable, should be looking after children, not so strong, can't paint, etc., etc.)? At the same time, we want to explore that *difference* politically and culturally, and to acknowledge the concrete, valuable but often antagonistic *differences* between women, who, for many reasons, may feel more solidarity with members of their own social or cultural groups who are not women. Residual universalism must be quashed with a political acknowledgement and a theoretical commitment to differences within the experience of gender, sexuality, class, race and cultural location.

Sexual difference has come to stand for an extended, overarching yet deep structure within which we can think the issues of gender, power, sexuality and culture. Yet, of course, if feminism is defined exclusively by its address to issues of sexual difference, it appears necessarily limited and exclusive. What of the issues of class, of race, of sexuality, of disability, of age, the injuries and oppressions of which weigh catastrophically upon the bodies and minds of women in utterly different and mutually alienating ways? Does a feminism which gives priority to the issues of sexual difference thereby reveal its true belonging to the dominant Eurocentric, white, bourgeois, heterosexual center? Does it thus parade as "Imperial feminism"?

Undoubtedly, the answer is yes. But also no. Yes, because mainstream feminism has often failed to acknowledge the antagonisms within the collectivity of women, and it has ignored the distinctive configurations of issues of class, gender, race and sexuality which make global statements about "women" impossible and when made, insultingly imperial. But there is a real difference between statements which assume that "we" all share "my" or "our" experience "as women" and the political project of using the varied but always significant ways in which some of us are positioned (if never exclusively) as "women" to mobilize us against all forms of sexual oppression. Oppression by sex may well be equally influenced by the divisions and alliances of race, class and sexuality, but it cannot, because of that, be denied that sex is a form of oppression. Despite justifiable critiques of 1960s–70s Western feminism from many communities of women, who felt excluded and negated by it, the project of late twentieth century feminism, however flawed by the very social conditions of its emergence in virulently racist and class societies, is neither irrelevant nor redundant. Even more as a result of the feminist exposure of the depths and extent of sexual oppression still operative today—indeed in Susan Faludi's word, of the backlash against women—a specifically feminist politics remains a necessity. However diverse our experiences as women, and complex our other allegiances, there is a politically created common ground in the naming and opposing of what forces oppress people "of the female persuasion" as *women* in every class, race and sexual configuration we can define.

But there is a historical reason for the no. Feminism's identification of the politics of sexual difference structuring the cultural stage is not merely about "women"—however limited that category may have been in practice. Gender may not be the only force which oppresses us, but it is one major force that feminism alone has struggled to make everyone acknowledge. No other political movement recognizes and deals with the specific ways in which we are used and abused by sex. Whatever other factors may also shape our lives, sexual difference, and the mechanisms which install it and regulate it, the meanings it has for us, must to be addressed.

"Feminist" must, therefore, refer to a critical perspective rather than an assumed collective voice. Indeed as we move from identity politics, from the speaking of experience, which often falsely generalizes the particular, and thus colludes with the dominant social groups, towards the critique of power systems in their specificity, the term feminist can be taken over and used to ensure that the organizing anger of the women's movements against oppression, violation and abuse is turned not against women, but against systematic oppression which is regularly enacted in forms of culture which enjoy the added bonus of being able to aestheticize their politics of power, calling it art, truth and beauty.

Sexual difference does not imply privileging the question of one's gender over other forms of social positioning. But it is about naming one specific structure which effectively shapes us in important ways. The term belongs to debates in psychoanalysis which introduced into the field of cultural studies and feminist theory the significance of the "psycho-symbolic". (Some more ugly post-structuralism coming!) That means not assuming that sexuality is natural and that gender is an effect of biologically different bodies—or even socially conditioned bodies. Instead sexuality and the differences between masculine and feminine are seen to be *constructed* at the level of the psyche (i.e., not the body) in each individual (according to their own pattern and personal history) as they pass through a series of stages which are the common structures for all humans on their way to becoming social subjects. These take the prematurely born human infant, a mass of incoherent sensations without any sense of its own body or personhood, to being a socially situated speaker, who can thus interact with other subjects, to having a sex (i.e., identifying as masculine or feminine) and a sexuality (i. e., oriented towards another person of the same or different sex who is neither the person's father nor mother): that is a subject available to work and to reproduce which is what the system is set up to ensure. The person becomes a subject—that is able to interact with other subjects in her society—because she learns to use language—that is, symbols. Thus the term psycho-symbolic refers to this passage through psychological formation into language, into communication. None of this is based on what is given by the body, but the body is then invested as it were with the culture's own meanings and laws. These "sexed" bodies function as the support for the psyche and for language and our bodies, thus colonized by our culture's meaning system, "emit the signs of that culture". This predicament is inevitable and ambivalent. For if we are not born a woman, but are made so through a precarious and unstable process, then we can change it, if we work the system differently once we understand its procedures and weak points. This is why psycho-analysis has been seen as both so hostile to women, and yet also so valuable as a description of the patriarchal ordering of sexual difference that fem-inists have taken it up as a way to study culture.

Psychoanalysis, moreover, serves a specific purpose for feminism in art history, precisely because it emerged in the late nineteenth century, and was itself a specific form of modern culture, contemporaneous with modernism in art. Although feminist art historians have ranged over the whole history of art, there is an unusual density of work taking place around the histories of modernism. In doing this work, we are often attempting to deal with our-selves as modern subjects, sexed subjectivities produced in modern Western culture's formations of race, gender, sexuality and class. As "art historians" or something else if we are no longer happy with that label, we feel the need to interrogate the legacy of official Western modernism, whose histories have often formed us academically or professionally.

Psychoanalysis is both a symptom of modern culture and a means for analyzing the kinds of subjectivity from which modern art was produced. Equally, despite itself, it ensures that we think of modern Western culture as fractured, conflicted and riven by *difference*—which allows us to interrogate it for its violence, ambivalence, for its desires and fantasies in terms of colo-nialism and capitalism, as much as in relation to the specificities of the mas-culinities and femininities unevenly formed and lived out in a rapidly changing world.

When I answered no to my own question about sexual difference, there was yet another dimension to the question. The dialogues made possible through a focus not on "women" but on sexual difference and the technolo-gies of sexuality bring us to other alliances. These cross-community con-versations and collaborations are especially important at the moment. In recent years the "oppressed" minorities have spoken out and slowly we find the institutions of culture and knowledge allowing us small spaces of our own—special exhibitions for black artists, women's shows, courses in women's studies or lesbian and gay studies programs. This is much more marked in the United States than in Britain. These special studies schemes appear to be a recognition of difference and differences. Yet I fear that the real gains contain a hidden setback. The special studies or special exhibitions which seem so tactically important to get some recognition of Hispanic-Americans, or lesbian and gay studies, really replicate the segregation of the society as a whole in these cultural or educational cells.

Through a focus on "sexual difference" we can equally address questions of homosexual oppression in art and art history. These questions cease to be considered only inside/aside "lesbian or gay studies" but can be aided by the critical feminist theories and methods which challenge the canons and archives of art and art history as a discourse framed in power relations around sex and sexuality. Equally sexual difference offers a model for understanding the ways racism operates through the cultural constructions of "difference," and post-colonial writers from Frantz Fanon to Hortense Spillers have argued that the struggle against racism must include a psychological-cum-cultural analysis.

Feminist interrogations of the repressed discourses of gender, sexuality and sexual positionality function in necessary alliance with those equally embattled by the effects of power in these areas. Interventions in discourses on culture and history from lesbian and gay perspectives enlarge the question of "sexual difference," showing how the formulation is not a synonym for gender, and not another fancy way of talking only about women. Sexual difference and its troubled origins in psychoanalytical theories are a necessary means to break down all naturalizations around masculinity and femininity, all attempts at heterosexist fixings. While feminists talk of contesting the canon in art history in terms of gender—the exclusion and marginalization of women—it soon becomes apparent that to confine the critique of the canon to women is once again both to refuse the differences between women in terms of class and sexuality as well as race, and to enact a heterosexist and Eurocentric assumption that issues of sexuality and sexual difference are exclusively part of the "woman question" that is, Man/Woman as the only form of the sexual question, the question of sexuality. The bourgeois fiction that woman is "the sex," that "woman is the sign of sex and sexuality," above which man rises in his transcendent universality, oppresses gays and lesbians in their struggles around issues of sexuality. At the same time it hides the fact that dominant discourses are discourses of a dominant, but complex and ambivalent, masculinity played out as much against male homosexuality as against those defined by the dominant culture as "women" within which category lesbians and women of non-European descent become invisible.

Finally, we can even return to the artist as well. Neither heroic individual nor seer, the artist is a creator and producer but also a specific kind of subject, the artistic subject—the signifying body, socially acculturated to that creative labor through the internalization of projected, mythic identities, the ideal ego of the artist. There are historically varying modes of artistic identity which both condition and are often doubled by the fantastic bodies produced in art. They were/are complexly structured in sexual difference, creating both possibilities and difficulties for would-be artists who were/are women of all classes, sexualities and cultures and for feminists attempting to write about the relations of women to the dominant identities of Western artistic culture in a pre-feminist or emergent feminist moment.

The issue of the image, liberated from the limited problematic of the visual as defined by traditional aesthetics, can now be theorized and usefully analyzed, but only if the frame of reference within which that analysis is made is no longer that of art history. Contesting the canonical discourse with art as pure and perfect object and artist as perfect imperial subject, feminists propose a different object—sexual difference—and a radically different concept of subjectivity whose processes are inscribed upon, traced in and fragmented by the cultural texts which compose the local but still hegemonic modern culture of the West/North. By means of the same formulations, we can also identify in creativity the dreams and fantasies, the desires which are ignored by that dominant culture, and which yet furnish the possibility of others: some already imagined for us and some painfully emerging out of a critical reading of the present and the predicament of our subjectivities, made by culture yet always threatening to exceed it.

references

Dawkins, Heather. (1991) *Sexuality, Degas and Women's History.* University of Leeds PhD.

Eagleton, Terry. (1990) *The Ideology of the Aesthetic.* Oxford: Basil Blackwell.

Fanon, Frantz. (1986) *Black Skins, White Masks [1952].* London: Pluto Press.

Foucault, Michel. (1972) *The Archaeology of Knowledge,* trans. A. M. Sheridan Smith. (London: Tavistock).

Kelly, Mary. "On Sexual Politics and Art" [1977] In *Framing Feminism: Art and the Women's Movement 1970–85,* ed. R. Parker and G. Pollock. London: Pandora Books, (1987), 303–312.

Linker, Kate. *On Difference: Sexuality and Representation,* (New York: Museum of Art and London: ICA, 1984–5).

Nochlin, Linda. "Why Have There Been No Great Women Artists?" In *Art & Sexual Politics.* ed. T. Hess and E. Baker (London: MacMillan, 1973).

Rose, Jacqueline. "Sexuality and the Field of Vision." In *Sexuality and the Field of Vision.* (London: Verso Books, 1987).

Spillers, Hortense. "Mama's Baby, Papa's Maybe: An American Grammar Book", *Diacritics,* 17:2, (1987). Discussed by Elizabeth Abel in "Race, Class and Psychoanalysis" in *Conflicts in Feminism,* ed. Marianne Hirsch and Evelyn Fox Keller (London and New York: Routledge, 1990).

femwatching in the 1990s[1]

griselda pollock

FIRST OF ALL, ARE THERE FEMINISTS THAT I can watch? Or rather, is it as a feminist that I watch?

I am interested in what women are placing in the world through art. It is a matter of indifference whether the artist says she is or is not a feminist. I think such labelling is a dated concept; it probably was always more or less irrelevant. But being a feminist is part of the baggage I carry from the Sixties. And there were several artists who shared this engagement with a feminist problematic, sustaining it in artistic practices.[2] Feminism as a force in our culture is still vibrant and important. But it has long been dispersed into forms other than that of identifiable groups or social campaigns. I take this title not to mean that *I* am reviewing *feminists*; rather I am watching with a feminist perspective, interest, heart and mind. For that purpose we need a dedicated art magazine alert to the possibilities of what I now call "inscriptions in, of and from the feminine."[3]

I constantly hear the refrain "I'm not a feminist, but...." It is clear that being a feminist is a not such a thing anymore, or that women don't feel that need to identify, or that being a feminist just means being white. But when you've been a feminist as long as I have (I know that's a dreadful thing to say, pulling the rank of age on younger women), you are stuck with the label. I embrace it.

One of the reasons I do is a historical debt. The more I know about the long struggle of women and the complex history of both the political and philosophical interventions by women, as well as the cultural campaigns, the more I think of identifying with feminism as a way of aligning myself with that history of revolting women. Yet feminism stands for something other than solidarity with a sequence of women's movements. It stands for traditions of thought, of rigorous intellectual and political questioning of how and why women got pushed out of the general category of humanity, and found themselves both people and chattels, both subjects and possessions, aspiring and horrifically abused.

In the last thirty years, under the banner of feminism there has been an intellectual revolution of the most astonishing kind. Although what has happened belongs in a history of "the woman question," the sheer extent of intellectual and creative work produced under the banner of feminism is unprecedented. When, in the early 1970s, I first found myself aware of the renewed women's movement, and joined or formed women's groups like the Women's Lobby or the *Women's Report* Collective, or the Women's Art History Collective we did not have much of a reading list. What we did have we fell upon, hungrily devouring any sustenance that we could cull from old Marx and Engels, Freud or Benjamin, and we were certainly thrilled to read Linda Nochlin or Cora Kaplan, to hear Buzz Goodbody or Juliet Mitchell. Now there is such a wealth of feminist theorizing that we need organised degree courses at all levels to get a grip on it. It is vital to acknowledge and appreciate this vast intellectual creativity that late twentieth-century feminism unleashed. Woman as intellectual has arrived. We have punched holes in almost every discipline and created several of our own. For those who want to know how women think about women and the world, there is no lack of brilliant role models. Women intellectuals tower over every field. Feminist theory is not just a minor irritant on patriarchy's tough hide offering a marginal, feminist perspective on art history or sociology, law or history: it is a force in itself that has questioned and transformed all the fields it has touched by forcing into the light of day the repressed question of gender, the troublesome issue of sexual difference, the problematic of power and violence.

Thus when I am advising students on a topic, I am always astonished and pleased to be able to indicate that there is a modern history of thought and practice in their area. Indeed I have recently had to reposition certain feminist practices at the end of the art history course and not in the contemporary art section. As women, these students are not having to invent the wheel each time they choose a topic. They are entering complex and much-worked-over fields, engaging with debates, and their own ideas can be nourished by a literature by women, addressed to women, concerning questions of women, a literature that is of the highest intellectual rigor and inventiveness. This literature is itself divided and differentiated, tackling the painful and agonistic divisions between women, issues of class, race, sexuality, physical ability, motherhood, survivorship and many other facets of women's wounded and wounding lives.

I have written of intellectuals, thought, literature. Perhaps the reader is thinking this is typical of the academic who privileges the word and forgets about art. But I have purposely used these terms. Art is part of this intellectual revolution. Art is a kind of thinking, in its own distinct ways. It is productive of new understanding, capable of generating meaning, bringing things into the field of intelligibility via its own singular pathways. These pathways track aspects of subjectivity that patriarchal thought has tried to eject from the house of philosophy, creating false dichotomies that feminists have systematically sought to tear down, seeing the dangers of *either/or* thinking with its dualities of mind/body, culture/nature, word/image, thought/feeling mapping so easily onto man/woman hierarchies.

But perhaps I think this because I work in the Fine Arts *and* Art History, and especially work with contemporary art and artists. So maybe it is a case that still needs to be made both to the world in general and to rest of the feminist world in particular. At the beginning of the women's movement, artists were seen as either decorative supplements, a bit of bourgeois self-indulgence at worst, or as useful when it came to making posters. Because of the strong sense of art as "expression," women artists were considered as both the authentic witnesses of true womanhood and the belated supporters of outdated bourgeois ideologies of individualism and expressionism. The chill winds of conceptual art blew uncomfortably through the studios and tagging along came a cartload of uncongenial theories about representation and signification, about ideology and the unconscious, about decentered subjects announcing the death of the author. The focus shifted towards analysis of cultural industries which manufactured representations of sexual difference, quarantining any talk of creativity and innovation, individual sensibilities and the formal possibilities of color or line. Who valued art or artists then but artists and their few supporters? Was it possible to be an artist and on the frontline of feminist enquiry? Did that mean making a certain kind of art in a certain kind of medium with a certain kind of career plan?

One of the remarkable things about living through three decades of feminism in the arts is to see more clearly what had to be done, what has been done and what is now possible because things have been changed by what was done. What had to be done was a ground-clearing exercise to free us from certain restricting assumptions embedded in high modernist art discourse and practice which was still haunted in Britain by residues of Ruskinian romanticism. Feminism mounted a critical assault on mystified ideas of the artist as a unique and autonomous creativity and on art history's celebratory narratives of aesthetically self-sufficient genius.

How was this to be done? This job involved several strange journeys through the arcane territories of structuralist and post-structuralist theories: semiotics, discourse theory, ideology and of course, psychoanalysis. Now transformed by feminist work in each of these areas, these theories became the instruments for "a return with a difference" to the tricky if suspended question of *art*—alias art production, visual culture, visual representation; anything but art. Whereas for years we had to talk about the production of art, I now happily talk about imagination and creativity, fantasy and poetic innovation. Things have changed, but this does not mean we have just gone backwards in a turn of the fashion wheel. Ground has been truly been cleared of mystifications and old ideologies and ideas have been clarified by passing through the prism of post-structuralist theories that have particular signi-ficance for feminism. So now these very terms art and artist are understood in different, demystified, and newly politically urgent ways.

Much of my thinking on this matter is encouraged by a careful and, I hope, appreciative reading of a major intellectual figure of our times, Julia Kristeva, whose thirty years of work was marked by a conference at the University of Leeds in June 1996, titled *Aesthetics, Politics, Ethics.*[4] Julia Kristeva's work combines an allegiance to the social and historical territory of concrete social relations, processes, power structures with a deep sense of the necessity to have some way to think about fantasy, affect, emotions, psyches. One of the points at which the political and symbolic ordering of social life and the unconscious forces at play in our own subjectivities encounter each other and possibly create some transformative work is what she calls poetic language, and what I extend to the visual arts. Julia Kristeva uses a historical argument to situate artistic or poetic practice at the cutting edge of post-modern culture. Instead of seeing art and literature as the cultural icing on the political feminist cake, "aesthetic practices" take on a special significance because of the theories about the interface between the social and psychological at the level of the sign: of the productivity of signs in creating both meanings and subjectivities. Kristeva manages to conjugate the Marxist analysis of the state and ideology with the Freudian discovery of the unconscious and archaic psychological fantasies so that we can at once see how societal forms register and shape not only issues of power around class, but those around difference, otherness, life, death, time and sexuality. Without the turn to religion and myth involved in some feminists' interest in the mother as the Great Mother, Kristeva reveals what fantasies underpin the equivocal, idealized and abused position of the mother in both individual histories and social ideologies. This is not to suggest that motherhood in fact or fantasy is elevated to an ideal by Kristeva. Rather she is seeking to analyze the workings of femininity within a culture that has only allowed it to be visible to us via the maternal image. Understanding how femininity has been contained by idealized or abject images of the mother allows us to begin to imagine the feminine beyond existing ideological fixations, including those typical of feminism itself.

Sexuality, fantasy, the unconscious, affect—these were hinted at in our founding slogan: the personal is political. But in the early Seventies, I had no idea how deep we would have to go in order to give the cryptic phrase profound theoretical underpinnings. Nor did I then sense how critical aesthetic practices might be in that journey of discovery. So I have found myself in the mid-1990s way out on a limb, having gone a considerable distance down this particular alley of the now vast and sprawling feminist enterprise. I find myself working at the far reaches of psychoanalytical theories, a place where I can explore the productive possibilities of sexuality, artistic practice and revolutionary change through analytical understanding of the feminine as a dissidence and a difference foreclosed within the current social and symbolic order.

I called this being out on a limb because I sense a wariness if not a hostility to the kind of feminist recasting of our theories of subjectivity and sexuality through art and thought that are associated with thinkers/artists like Julia Kristeva or Bracha Lichtenberg Ettinger.[5] I experienced this disjuncture this year when I attended a conference in the United States and chaired a panel connected with an exhibition that originated at the ICA in Boston and travelled to the National Museum of Women in the Arts in Washington, the Whitechapel in London and the Art Gallery of Western Australia in Perth. The exhibition was informed by Bracha Lichtenberg Ettinger's theories of the Matrix. Titled *Inside the Visible—an Elliptical Traverse of Twentieth Century Art: in, of and from the feminine,* the exhibition was curated by Cathérine de Zegher, from the Kanaal Art Foundation in Belgium. The show included thirty artists. All were women. But that did not make it "a women's show" in the old Seventies' sense of the word, a show just to prove that there are women artists. The artists come from many countries and span the century, thus breaking all the best curatorial rules which aim to keep things all neatly in their geographical and generational boxes in the imaginary museum's well-curated filing cabinets that are also demarcated by medium and style. Art from one period or medium should not bump up against that from another.

But what Cathérine de Zegher's exhibition revealed is that feminist theory can help us to create different genealogies which traverse our century linking practices across space and time that cumulatively reveal to us "inscriptions in/of/from the feminine." A different kind of legibility for work that hitherto languished unrecognized at dominant Modernism's margins is produced in a movement that allows us to use the retrospective vantage point of contemporary feminist awareness to recognize what is, in fact, our own pre-history and the precondition of current aesthetic moves. Not a carefully mapped series of influences going one way from great masters through to rebellious sons, and not lineages of canonically male or even female descent, Cathérine de Zegher's exhibition discerned a number of tendencies, thematics, concerns, which recur in practices by women engaging with issues of sexual difference and modernity. Her sections were Parts of/for; The Blank in the Page; The Weaving of Water and Words; Enjambement—"La Donna e mobile". Constantly interrupted in the attempt to revolutionise and modernise sexual difference, women artists have worked on the social and cultural margins of major art historical and sociopolitical maps to produce work that now seems richly resonant when allowed into conversation with art produced in other countries and at other times and with the product of over two decades of self-conscious feminist intervention. Breaking the mold of Western hegemony without in turn making a fetish of race and cultural difference as simply the other story, this exhibition, the first of its kind for almost ten years, exploded into the art spaces with no visible feminist flagwaving. It was, however, the product of a deep-rooted, distilled, considered engagement with certain trends in feminist thought and art that enabled the selection and the consequent dialogues between art works to be such a revelation.

One of the things the historical trajectory of the exhibition revealed was that women's struggle for change in the field of sexual difference has been interrupted and blocked at key moments by its historical opponent within modern society: fascism. Combining artists of the 1920/30s with those from the 1960s/70s and again from the 1990s produced a sense of the generations of feminism, each shaped in the politics of its own moment, each, nonetheless, part of an interrupted yet resilient engagement with women's struggle with modernity and against the politics that most directly reacts against women's claims: fascism, masquerading as tradition, nature or realism.

As we approach the end of the 1990s, this threat recurs. Neo-traditionalism haunts politics through fundamentalisms of every kind. Market-led economies may use us but as easily dispense with us when we make no more profit-led sense. I feel caught between the exhilaration of the feminist world I encounter through art and intellectual work and the chilling sense that the media and the economic interests it services are so fashion-led that they declare us redundant, passé and irrelevant.

The only resistance we can offer lies in continuous extension of historical knowledge of our current situation and its pre-histories and theorized understanding of the deep structures played out across our daily political and familial stages. Against the hegemonic cultural and economic axes of Berlin–Paris–London–New York–Los Angeles reflected in flash magazines and uptown galleries, we need to keep building other alliances, geographically extended and culturally diverse, generationally expanded and internationally defined by non-capitalist maps.

I have tried to make one little space for this kind of thinking through the Feminist Arts and Histories Network which I called into being in 1992 to create in the actual space of real meetings the imaginary community for which a chastened and self-critical feminism still stands. We have held three biennial conferences to create a regular space for us to meet and review both current concerns and long term strategies while ensuring that we know what women are thinking through art.

There is so much to say about contemporary art by women viewed from this perspective that I have to run a graduate course dedicated to Feminism and the Visual Arts to keep these different balls—theory, history and contemporary art practice—in the air. From this vantage point, *watching as a feminist*, things look extraordinary and exciting. Thirty years has made a huge difference and don't let anyone tell you that the show is over. We are really just beginning, and this time, we are really well-equipped. If this magazine is to play a role in that continuity, its decisions must be carefully informed by the necessity to intervene and be a major site for review and debate, information and criticism while guarding against a wholesale flight into the market. The radicalism of the seventies may no longer be appropriate simply because we have made an impact, but its ethics remain vital and I want to end with a quote from the perpetually important essay by Julia Kristeva, "Women's Time."

> At this level of interiorisation with its social as well as individual stakes, what I have called "aesthetic practices" are undoubtedly nothing other than the modern reply to the eternal question of morality.[6]

notes

1 Written for the re-issue of *Women's Art Journal,* London, as *MAKE—the Magazine of Women's Art,* 1996. The title was the given theme.

2 The argument against feminist art and for the idea of a feminist problematic engaged with through artistic practice was originally proposed by Mary Kelly in 1977 in her paper "Art & Sexual Politics" Winchester School of Art, 1977, reprinted in *Framing Feminism: Art & the Women's Movement,* London: Pandora Press, 1987.

3 See my "Inscriptions in the Feminine" in *Inside the Visible,* ed. Cathérine de Zegher (Boston: MIT Press, 1996).

4 The proceedings are published in *Parallax* no. 8 1998 (distributed by Francis and Taylor).

5 Bracha Lichtenberg Ettinger, *The Matrixial Gaze,* (1994), Feminist Arts and Histories Press, c/o Dept. of Fine Art at the University of Leeds. See also "Abandoned at the Mouth of Hell," in this volume.

6 Julia Kristeva, "Women's Time" in *The Kristeva Reader,* ed. Toril Moi (Oxford: Basil Blackwell, 1987), 210.

part II
feminism, history and contemporary practice in the visual arts

~~feminist~~ interventions in history: on the historical, the subjective, and the textual

4

griselda pollock

I had often thought of dedicating INTERIM *to Dora's mother—the woman who never made Freud's acquaintance. He assumed she had housewife's psychosis: too old for analysis? Too old to be noticed? In a sense, she underlines the dilemma for the older woman in representing her sexuality, her desire, when she is no longer desirable. She can neither look forward, as the young girl does, to being a woman, that is having the fantasized body of maturity; nor can she return to the ideal moment of maturity—ideal in that it allows her to occupy the position of the actively desiring subject without transgressing the socially acceptable definition of the woman as mother. She is looking back at something lost, acknowledging perhaps that "being a woman" was only a brief moment in her life.*

Mary Kelly, "Invisible Bodies: On INTERIM"

speaking as dora's mother

Dora's mother makes only a slight appearance in Sigmund Freud's case history, "Fragment of an Analysis of a

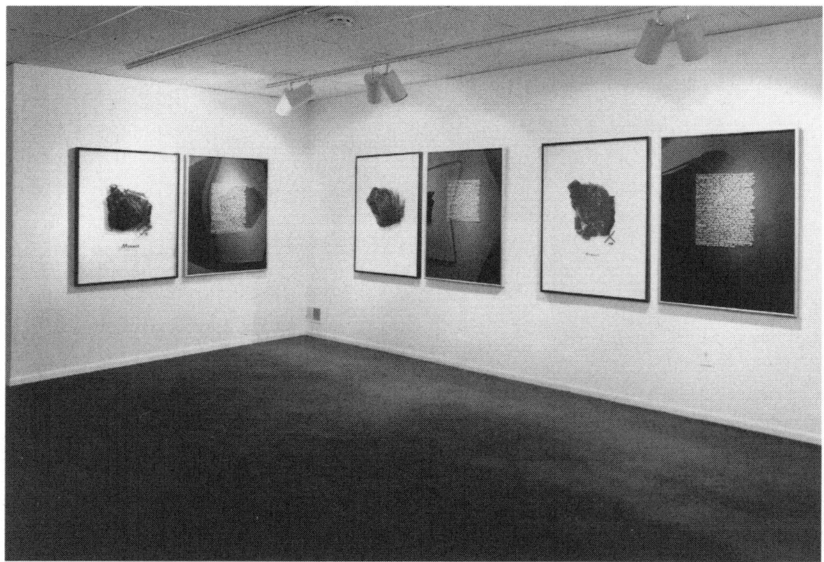

Figure 1.   Mary Kelly, *Interim Part I: Corpus 1984–5*. Installation view. Laminated photo positive, silkscreen, acrylic on plexiglass, 6 of 30 panels, 90 × 122.5 cm each. Henry McNeill Gallery, Philadelphia.

Case of Hysteria ['Dora']": "I never made the mother's acquaintance. From the accounts given me by the girl and her father I was led to imagine her as an uncultivated woman and above all as a foolish one, who concentrated all her interests on domestic affairs … . She presented a picture, in fact, of what might be called 'housewife's psychosis.'"[1]

In Mary Kelly's project, INTERIM, Dora's mother has a voice: she becomes a historical presence. For Freud, the older woman was an absence of desirability, hence of significance. To be written into history is to be desired, and history is now being written through women's desire to understand the historical moment of the Women's Movement begun in 1968.

The Women's Movement is undoubtedly one of the major political presences of the late twentieth century. INTERIM focuses on the memories and meanings of " '68" for a generation of feminists produced by that moment. Like the suffrage campaigns before it, the second wave of feminism revised the understanding of "femininity." By naming and contesting the social and economic forces which disempower women, feminists also opened an exam-

ination of the psycho-symbolic shaping of human subjects within sexual difference, asking not, "What is Woman?" but, "Is Woman at all?" Such a radical
critique of given notions of sexuality and gender raises important questions
for those of us, called women, who must live within the nomination, but
who struggle politically, personally, and culturally to overwhelm its limits,
while recognizing, at the same time, its specific pleasures.

Like Mary Kelly's earlier project, POST-PARTUM DOCUMENT, which generated a signifying space for the mother as the subject of desire, INTERIM disperses into our culture another repressed presence, the sexual woman
broaching what is called "middle age," a woman whose desire exceeds our
culture's limited imageries of the feminine. INTERIM breaks a taboo by speaking a femininity where it is symbolically negated, but not in order to affirm
some other, primordial femininity or radical difference. Here Kelly follows
Michéle Montrelay: "The adult woman is one who reconstructs her sexuality
in the field that goes beyond sex." By creating imageries and discourses to
utter the position of the older woman, INTERIM causes femininity and its sexualities to pass into discourse, and, as importantly, it precipitates their entry
into new relations to the woman-as-subject, rather than object, of the look.
The silence and iconic passivity encoded as femininity (so strikingly
signified by Dora's mother, who is both silenced by, and "pictured" in
Freud's text) is disrupted by women's discourse, their pleasure in the
signifier, and "their theoretical as well as creative work, especially on sexuality itself."[2] Creative work is thus no second-order discourse, recirculating
knowledge formed elsewhere. It is productive of definitions and meanings
for the subjects of femininity—that is, those who are subjected to, and who
also realize their subjectivity through, the positions of femininity.[3]

In assembling the materials for INTERIM, Kelly logged scores of conversations with women entering a stage in their lives marked negatively by our
culture's *figurations of femininity*, or the alignment, typically, of femininity
with an image of the woman as the object of man's desire, or the mother.
Like a Freudian case study, INTERIM puts its subjects under analysis. By listening to personal and political histories for symptoms, it excavates the psychic
investments sedimented in memory and traced across both women's and
culture's fantasies about the body, power, history, and money. Like Freud's
"dream work," "art work" aims to produce new knowledge by restructuring

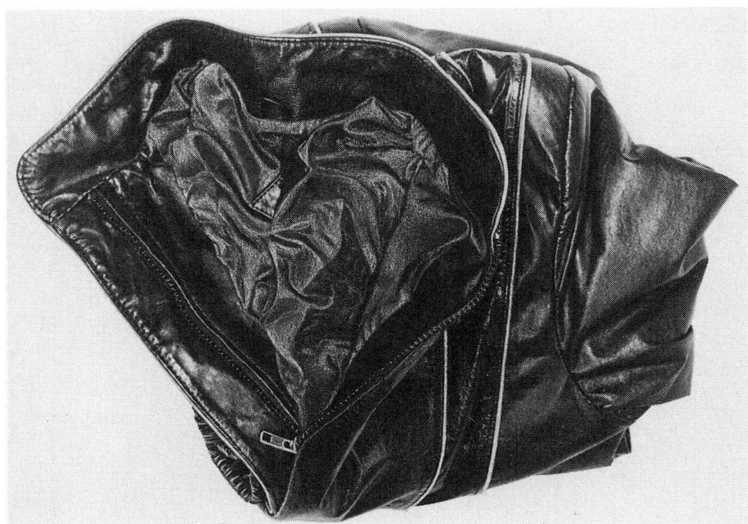

Figure 2.   Mary Kelly, *Interim Part I: Corpus: Menacé 1984–5.*

the relation between the forms of representation and the material struggling for—or against—it. In INTERIM, the point of view of the woman we symbolically call "Dora's mother," combined with a review of the historical period since 1968, produces a new and useful understanding of what structures femininity and its moments, historically and individually, and what might yield other orderings.

What are the strategies of representation adequate for the double articulation of such a historical project—at once, case history and transforming analysis? As a first step, INTERIM specifies the discourses and institutions in relation to which feminine identities are defined and regulated: money, body, power, and the socio-political. It then "plays" over them in its humorous delight at the instability of any subjectivity. At the same time, it voices the fantasies and desires that make femininity excessive—that is, always exceed its culturally coded definitions—but which are registered in its representations as being both "more than" (excess) and "not quite" (lack). INTERIM, therefore, enunciates femininity as transgressing the norms in order to produce new feminist possibilities. It displaces women's subordination to these figurations by activating a signifying space where voices and presences resonate in multi-layered textualities which press on the very limits of sexual definition—of that which defines "women's place in the processes of reproduction and its representations."[4]

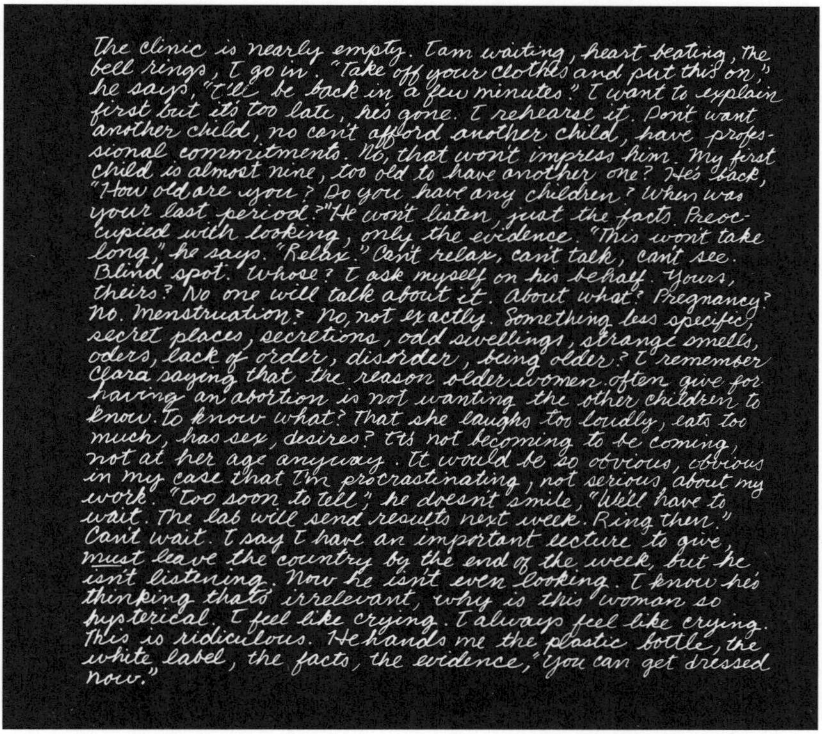

The clinic is nearly empty. I am waiting, heart beating, the bell rings, I go in. "Take off your clothes and put this on," he says, "I'll be back in a few minutes." I want to explain first but it's too late, he's gone. I rehearse it. Don't want another child, no can't afford another child, have professional commitments. No, that won't impress him. My first child is almost nine, too old to have another one? He's back, "How old are you? Do you have any children? When was your last period?" He won't listen, just the facts. Preoccupied with looking, only the evidence. "This won't take long," he says. "Relax." Can't relax, can't talk, can't see. Blind spot. Whose? I ask myself on his behalf. Yours, theirs? No one will talk about it. About what? Pregnancy? No. Menstruation? No, not exactly. Something less specific, secret places, secretions, odd swellings, strange smells, oders, lack of order, disorder, being older? I remember Clara saying that the reason older women often give for having an abortion is not wanting the other children to know. To know what? That she laughs too loudly, eats too much, has sex, desires? It's not becoming to be coming, not at her age anyway. It would be so obvious, obvious in my case that I'm procrastinating, not serious about my work. "Too soon to tell," he doesn't smile, "We'll have to wait. The lab will send results next week. Ring then." Can't wait. I say I have an important lecture to give, must leave the country by the end of the week, but he isn't listening. Now he isn't even looking. I know he's thinking that's irrelevant, why is this woman so hysterical. I feel like crying. I always feel like crying. This is ridiculous. He hands me the plastic bottle, the white label, the facts, the evidence, "you can get dressed now."

Figure 3.   Mary Kelly, *Interim, Part I: Menacé 1984–5.*

The phrase is Julia Kristeva's. It speaks to the necessity for feminists to grasp hold of the idea of sexual difference as operating both as a *political economy of sex* (or the determinate socio-economic arrangements for the regulation of sexuality and the perpetuation of the species, which enjoin a legalized, appropriative heterosexuality) and, in Freudian terms, an *economy of desire* (that is, the organization of subjectivity around separation, division, and lack, an organization which simultaneously supports identity and threatens to disrupt its always fictitious stabilities).

INTERIM is an intervention in the spaces of representation in the domain of contemporary art. Its significance can only be fully apprehended by recognizing its filiation with three moments in the cultural field, in which it is: a work of the scale and ambition of the grandest history paintings; a work whose formal strategies and signifying possibilities are radicalized in the manner of the high modernist project it recapitulates and supersedes; and, finally, a work which articulates the complexities of subjectivity in historical and social formations, a major theme in the critical culture of which Mary Kelly's work over the last twenty years has been a major initiator and representative.

In the 1970s, the idea of a critical practice, socialist or feminist, being realized in a single, definitive work was canvased and rebutted. Mary Kelly's INTERIM clearly refutes the possibility in its form as a multi-faceted discourse as much on, as within, the practices of art. Its four sections include diverse materials, formats, and connotational registers: silk-screened perspex panels of posed garments and hand-written stories; glitzy galvanized steel greetings cards mounted at eye level, with printed inscriptions and a running gag forming a visual rebus; steel books bearing a designer's layout of text and photographic image; and three-dimensional steel forms quoting United Nations statistics. A viewer is presented with few icons, but many images, no single text, but many textualities. A visually startling and spatially dominating work, INTERIM seduces with quite specific material and aesthetic pleasures.

Yet it demands more than a specular form of consumption. Like painting, it provides striking emblematic images and the invitation to identify with postures, gestures, and states of mind. Like classic cinema, its meanings build up by repetition and stylistic rhymes, by plots and subplots, characters and stories, dialogue and catchphrase, expressive mise-en-scéne and dramatic moment. Like the modern social landscapes of a Godardian film, it gives us snatches of lives, fantasies, and social spaces. Like sculpture, with its glinting surfaces and material presence, it alternates between strict, almost minimalist, formalities and playful, rebus-like asymmetries. Finally, like Brechtian theatre, it both engages us with its witty and entertaining vision of current issues, and offers to transform us into creative partners through its use of identification, analysis, and, most radically, humor. Thus, to comprehend the multiple purposes and layered meanings produced by interaction with the work of Mary Kelly, we have to recognize the many strategies—visual, textual, material, dramatic, formal, metaphoric, and metonymic—in play.

By politically reconceptualizing the rhetorics of both high modernism and postmodernist spectacle, Kelly formulates a distinctively feminist intervention in the spaces of representation. Femininity has, traditionally, been

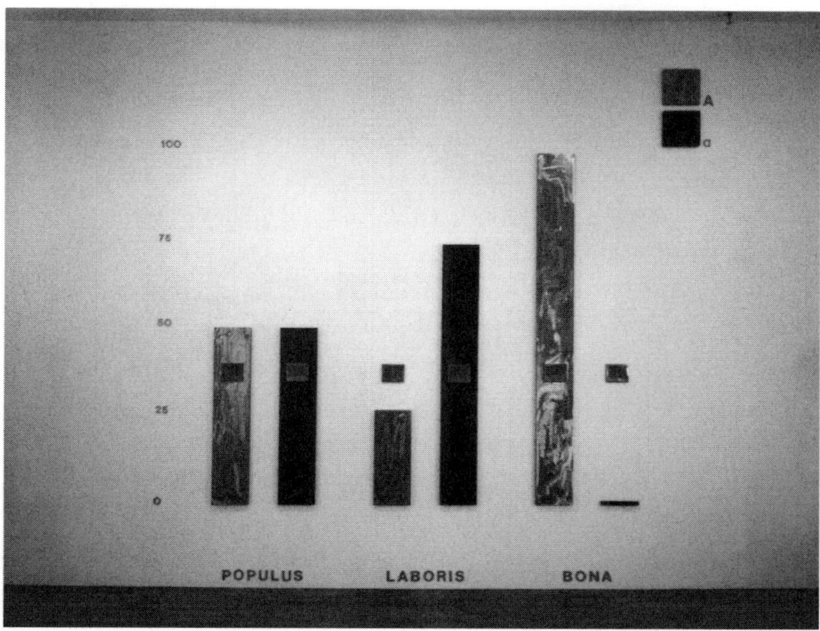

Figure 4.   Mary Kelly, *Interim Part IV: Potestas, 1989*. Etching, brass and mild steel, 14 units, 250 × 285 × 5, Collection Helsinki City Art Museum.

positioned as the antithesis of, and threat to, the rigors and disciplines by which Great Art only can be made. This has entailed the exclusion of women from recognition within the privileged domains of high culture, and femininity's discursive construction as the essence of triviality, decorativeness, sentimentality, easy pleasure, and romance. In a word, kitsch. As Andreas Huyssen has argued, the structural division between avant-garde and kitsch is gendered.[5] Postmodernists have questioned modernism's negative evaluation of its "other" by making "appropriations" of mass cultural forms as the signifying material for high art practices. Mary Kelly, however, does not rely on quotation and recycling. She originates forms to produce objects, which she arranges according to a logic that invokes both modernist traditions and mass cultural forms. She thus creates a new space within which both sides of the great divide—high art and popular culture—meet. It is a revealing confrontation. On one side, the work speaks repressed femininities by evoking reviled cultural forms, such as the woman's magazine, the romance, the fashion world, and the supermarket (which are also represented as critical sites of contemporary femininity, invested with power and pleasure as well as anxiety, and in need of political readings). And on the other, these forms (of/as femininity) are installed in the gallery with an absolute "mastery" of the discourses and formalisms of high modernism. So, Kelly's work suspends the false dichotomy between the masculinized discipline of high art and the pejoratively feminized popular culture at the specific point at which the regime of sexual difference shapes both the discourses of modernism and its, often, harmlessly "revolting" postmodern offspring. Dominating its gallery space as a series of material forms, INTERIM, moreover, refutes empty, post-modernist gesturing at reference: it is all about the production of presence. Its objects support traces of subjectivities which are offered to the visitor for reconstituting. What might have been a modernist space only, displaying discrete objects, is converted into another, far more radical one. The event staged by INTERIM creates a signifying space in which the change wrought through feminism can be perceived, and still more radical change becomes possible to imagine.

The phrase "signifying space" is also Kristeva's. In her essay "Women's Time," she too defines feminism as being positioned on a historical thresh-old, as reviewing the history of the Women's Movement, up to and since 1968, in an effort to imagine a way forward. She writes of three generations in Western feminism, two historically current, and the third, a space in the future beyond the politics of equality or integration, and the culture of sep-aratism. The first of these aims to use political campaigning to introduce women into, what Kristeva calls, linear, historical time. Rejecting political solutions, the second involves a programmatic insistence on the radical specificity of women. Art and literature, it says, are to be used to explore the cyclical rhythms and monumental temporalities of the life cycle of women, in an effort to make a language for "the intrasubjective and corporeal experi-ences left mute by culture in the past."[6]

Having examined the traps of reverse sexism, in which she sympatheti-cally deciphers the violence which women experience in this culture, Kristeva tells us that she can now imagine a new signifying space, wherein feminism would be able to question the very sacrificial system by which every subject, every identity, every sex is formed. Such new significations will not emerge from the repressed culture of women, or somewhere radically outside the system; they must be made by a specific kind of transgression within the system itself. In Kristevan theory, meaning is the effect of a signifying process. This involves the constant play between unity, which attempts to fix meaning and normalize its performance, and process, which both precedes and exceeds any systematization. At one and the same time, it makes any meaning possible and provides for the possibility of transformation. Signifying practice, such as a new textuality or artwork, "means the acceptance of symbolic law together with the transgression of that law for the purpose of renovating it."[7] Kristeva sees modernism as a challenge to arrangements of power embodied in both social institutions and symbolic forms—the signifying system—a challenge mounted by transgressions in signifying practices, which are the sites of exchange between the system and the subject. What Kristeva did not say was that the heroic revolutions of modernism have been effected in the name of men, who are unable (and unwilling) to dispute seriously the system and its symbolic order.

The Women's Movement, with its interventions in signification, is the historic and necessary realization of the Kristevan conception of modernism.[8] The claim that feminism only can supersede modernism is not made by all in the Women's Movement, nor all feminisms. It is a possibility only now being created—at the intersection of a feminist intervention in the textual, the subjective, and the historical.

Mary Kelly's work has always attended acutely to the mapping of sexual difference within both the registers of the socio-economic and the politico-psychic: "In her field of vision femininity is not seen as a pre-given entity, but as the mapping out of sexual difference within a definite terrain, a moment of discourse, a fragment of history."[9] Her work, moreover, has consistently used the material provided by what our culture might dismiss as women's gossip. Consciousness raising turned conversation into a political resource. Those of us who were part of consciousness raising groups found the terrain of sexual difference, and found history, marked upon our bodies and minds, and written in the discourses which form us, and press as the limits of our fantasies. INTERIM claims the importance of that feminist procedure while, at the same time, interweaving it with theorizations developed in the exchanges between feminism, marxism, political theory, semiotics and linguistics, psychoanalysis, and film and cultural studies, over the past twenty years.

Since 1968, women have been living in both historical time and monumental time. We have been having children and growing older. These "historical" processes we have experienced with a modified consciousness, or, in psychoanalytical terms, an altered subjectivity which our involvement with the Women's Movement has produced. INTERIM hints at how such a subjectivity can be signified, and, in addition, how the very question might be posed within the symbolic system of culture. It is at the intersection of the historical movement of women and the dialectics of feminist theory that INTERIM creates its signifying space.

> *It's not that our identity is to be dissipated into airy indeterminacy, extinction; instead it is to be referred to the more substantial realms of discursive historical formation.*
>
> Denise Riley, "Does Sex have a History?"

working with dora's mother

Feminists have not only questioned the ideological category *woman*, they have begun to doubt the stability of the collectivity *women*. Denise Riley has even suggested that it is a historical formation, embedded in relations of power. Such arguments—which go so far as to anticipate the disappearance of the category—may seem perplexing in the context of a political movement based on the solidarity of women as women. This paradox is at the heart of contemporary feminist theory. Women, as female people marked by gender and sexuality, will not disappear. It's the notion of women as the negative and "other" of a masculine norm, founded on the privilege of the phallus, that is to be displaced.

Mary Kelly's project over the last twenty years has been an intervention in the debates and theorizations of woman, women, and femininity, which have characterized the Women's Movement since the end of the 1960s. One of her early projects, *Women and Work* (1974–5, with Margaret Harrison and Kay Hunt of the Women's Workshop of the Artist's Union), emerged from British feminists' alliance with the struggle of working women for unionization. She also participated in the making of a film about the unioniz-

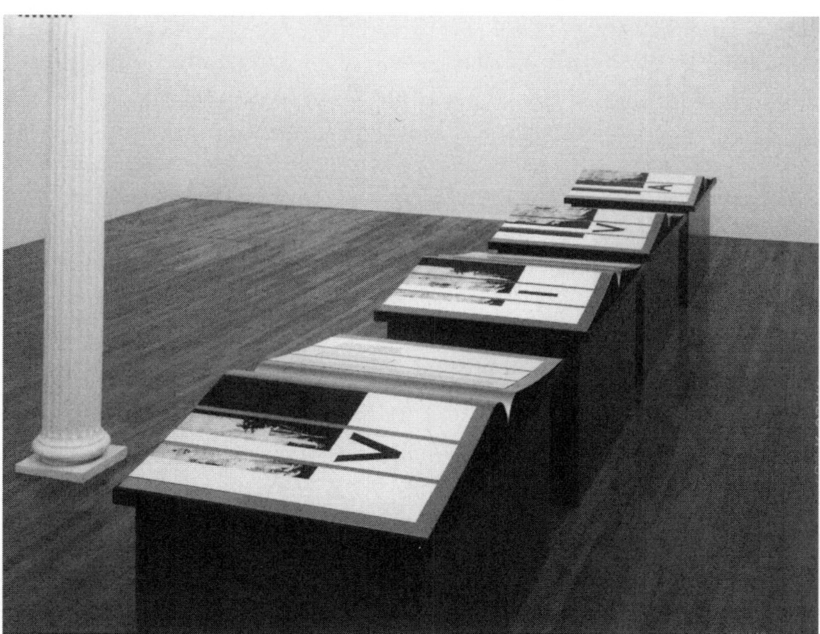

Figure 5.   Mary Kelly, *Interim Part III: Historia*, 1989. Silkscreen, oxidized steel, stainless steel on a wood base, 152.5 × 90 × 72.5. Collection MacKenzie Art Gallery, Regina, Canada.

ation of women contract office cleaners, *The Nightcleaners* (Berwick Street Film Collective, 1975). *Women and Work* was an installation which examined the sexual division of labor in a London factory following the passage of the Equal Pay Act. It used many forms of representation and documentation, including film, photography, life stories, official documents, tapes, and statistics. In its conceptualization of the cultural as a site for the interrogation of the socio-economic, the project should be compared with the work of an artist like Hans Haacke. And, unlike an exposé which uses already theorized notions of social power, the installation produced unforeseen knowledge.

While it clearly revealed the ways employers were installing an even more rigid division of labor to avoid paying women equally, the texts in the exhibition also unexpectedly showed that work and home meant different things to male and female employees. This difference could be read as evidence of emotional or psychic meanings invested in everyday life which make visible what a psychoanalytical vocabulary would call *desire*. Diaries were displayed which recorded the daily schedules of the men and women. These indicated that while work was a time of activity and meaning for men, it was dead-time for women, who focused instead on itemizing their chores in the home and their time with their children. Kelly began to recognize women's investments in areas typically defined by feminist theory as being confined to the unpaid sector of the capitalist economy. The social division of labor and women's predominance in childcare could be read as sites for the psychically-construed pleasures and re-enacted losses which constitute the subjectivity of motherhood. At the time, feminist theory tended to define motherhood as a sociologically conditioned role, in opposition to the conservative claim that it was an expression of biological femininity. The evidence in *Women and Work* pointed to still another way of understanding what it could mean for women: it might be the complex activation of a woman's desire, and its reconfiguration within a patriarchal symbolic order.

Debates such as these were radically reoriented by the publication, in English, of the ideas of the French feminist group, *Psychoanalyse-Politique*, and its politicized readings of psychoanalysis, which foregrounded the psycho-symbolic axis over the politico-economic.[10] Mary Kelly had also become a mother by this time. In the crucible of a historic change at the personal level and at the level of political theory, and an intellectual change fostered by her own artistic practice, Mary Kelly began POST-PARTUM DOCUMENT (1973–9; 135 units in six parts). A work constructed over six years, documenting the reciprocal relations of a mother and child within the gender division and its symbolic representation in language, the DOCUMENT created a significant intersection for debates in the Women's Movement and theoretically grounded arguments then current in art practice.

Its decisive formal feature was that it was a multi-part installation which arranged objects carrying the actual traces of the social process of child-care—diaper liners, a child's drawings, comforter, gifts, and writing slate—within representational schemas which pictured the dominant analytical frameworks of patriarchal culture: science, medicine, education, and art. Conceived within the frame of conceptual practice, but developing a specific discursive relation between its objects and narratives, the DOCUMENT clearly signified its purpose as art. Here was no anti-modernist polemic, suggesting that women's voices could only be articulated by oppositional cultural forms, circulating in alternative cultural spaces. Kelly's strategies formally signified the polemical presence of feminist discourse in contemporary cultural practice—part of an oppositional cultural formation whose significance depended on the relations it implied, by dialectical negation, with hegemonic high modernism.[11]

The cultural community in which POST-PARTUM DOCUMENT was formally and theoretically generated was an expanded one, and included British independent film-makers, the cultural theorists around *Screen* Magazine, and the photographers and theorists, such as Victor Burgin, whose critical interventions were known as Third Area work. The fine artists in this community produced a political critique of The Museum of Modern Art's selective version of modernism, and excavated projects of the twentieth century which articulated the necessary relations between the political and the cultural in ambitiously modernist, but, rarely, purely visual or painterly forms.[12] Important resources for this work were the writings and practices of Brecht, Althusser and Lacan:[13] "The problem, the political problem, for artistic practice in its ideological intervention, could be precisely the transformation of relations of subjectivity in ideology."[14]

POST-PARTUM DOCUMENT was also marked by specific reorientations in the cultural and theoretical debates within the British Women's Movement. When Lacanian theory was first taken up, it often posed women's negative entry into the symbolic order. Feminist readings of psychoanalysis subsequently produced innovative theorizations, in particular with regard to the significance of the maternal body as a repressed, but necessary, support for language and subjectivity.[15] Mary Kelly's DOCUMENT was an attempt to create a reading of femininity through a woman's relation to the maternal body as the site of fantasized plenitude and, also, of symbolically defined loss. A conceptual formal strategy with narrative spaces, relays of signs across materials on which the social relations of the mother-and-child were inscribed and traced, was the means she used to create a signifying space for a maternal discourse. But, by its documentation of the loss of the child as it grew, developed speech, went to school, and learned to write its paternal name, the work could have confirmed woman's negation in the patriarchal system.

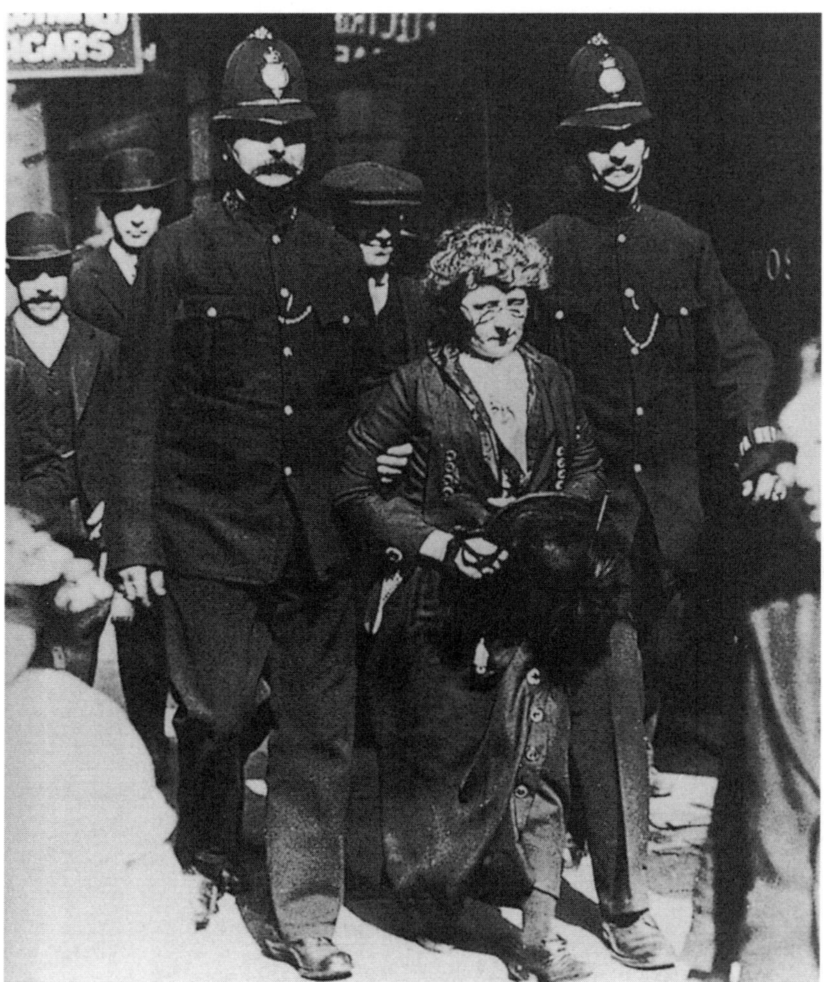

Figure 6.   *Arrest of a Suffragette*, 1905. Artist's archive material for *Historia*. Collection Mary Kelly.

Instead, Kelly's project concluded with a social reading of the child's accession to language at school, a social institution through which the mother experiences not only the loss of the child to society, but anxieties about inadequate educational provisions. She argued that while the place that the mother occupies as an effect of the signifying chain seems inevitably to make her a failure, or, at best, a victim of circumstance, the position she takes up in representing this place to herself is not one of resignation only. It is not the mother's hopes, aspirations, and ambitions for her child which ultimately are lacking, but the possibility of their realization because of economic constraints, social practices, and the political effects of separation from the means of production, possession, and "advantage."[16]

The journey from *Women and Work*, which attended specifically to the economic moment of production and class, to the maternal body and the psychic instance of femininity, was never a move away from questions of social power and economic relations. As the DOCUMENT showed, power and money impinge on the maternal subject through her personal, historical formation in the social practices of childcare. Shaped by the moment of feminism in which it was produced, the DOCUMENT is a representation of a specific time in women's historical subjectivity. By working through personal, theoretical, and cultural materials in the work, Kelly articulated a space for change where none had been imagined—in the notion of woman biologically defined as mother. In other words, her signifying practice became the site for effecting necessary changes in our knowledge of ourselves, of our psycho-social formations of the "subjectivity in ideology."[17]

This formulation itself betrays a historicity. By the late 1970s, questions of power were being theorized less in terms of ideology than of sexuality. The work of Michel Foucault had become important. As with Freud, women played major roles in his histories. In *The History of Sexuality*, Foucault defined sexuality as a historical construct which is an "especially dense transfer point for relations of power."[18] One of the four mechanisms of knowledge and power centering on sexuality Foucault explored was "the hystericization of women's bodies," and he cites J. M. Charcot and his student, Freud, as contributing, in radically opposed ways, to the figurations of femininity. (Freud made his decisive "discoveries" in his early case studies of hysteria, "Anna O" and, of course, "Dora.")

INTERIM itself is shaped by and reshapes our understanding of this historical conjoin of femininity and its body. *Corpus*, for example, is Mary Kelly's discourse across, from, and through our culture's hystericization of the feminine body. It reworks Charcot's photographic iconography of hysterical postures, in which women's mute bodies were made to expose themselves to his clinical gaze. Further, the regime of power Foucault anatomizes both saturates the feminine body with sexuality, and regulates it in a familial order it is constrained to embody as wife, mother, daughter, and sister. These positions are simultaneously sites for the deployment of power over women, and occasions for resistance. *Pecunia* draws on this schema of power and its

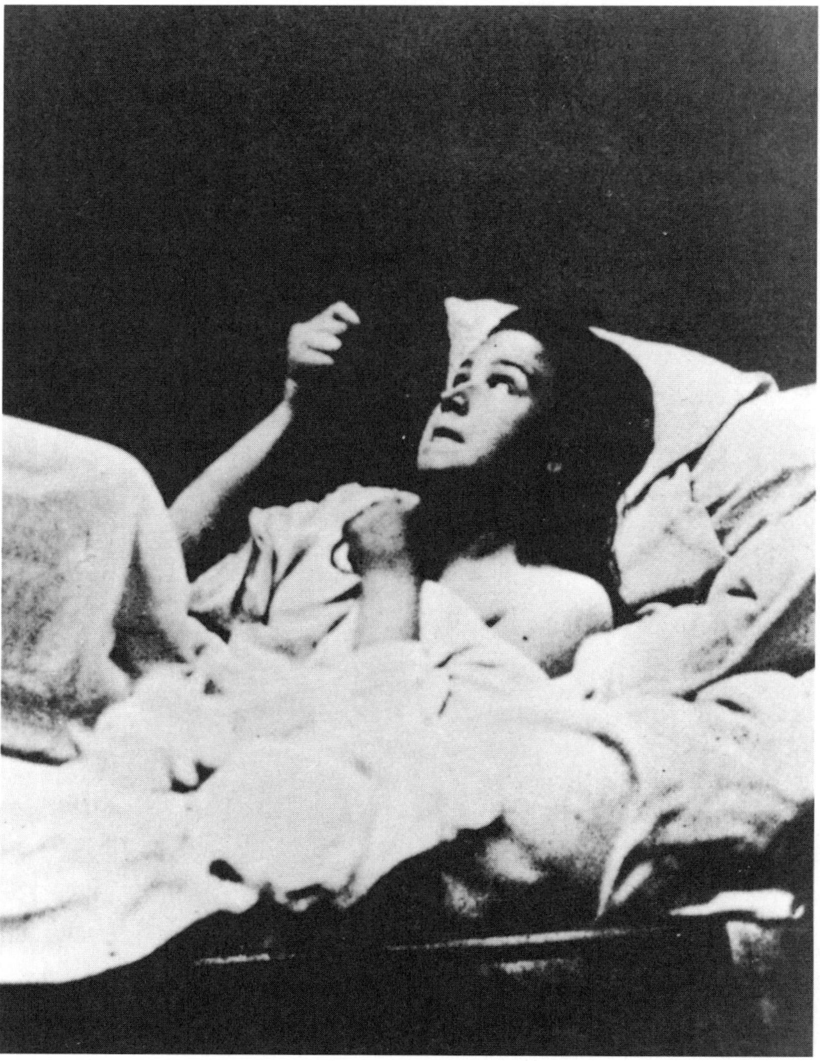

Figure 7. Jean-Marie Charcot, *Attitudes Passionelles: Menacé* from Nouvelle Iconographie de la Saltpetriére, Paris, 1878.

conventional pathologies. But, using a Freudian model, Kelly also suggests the force of desire pressing on these positions, which are both places in a regulative system of alliance (a socially defined kin system) producing gender identity, and sites of psychic formations of sexuality (with all the potential disruption to the Law which institutes it that this implies).[19]

Both *Pecunia* and *Corpus* address the sexualization of the feminine body, but they posit a gap between it and its subject. This rupture becomes possible for the woman that these positionalities strategically target as surplus—Dora's mother. Kelly's play of images, stories, and references to the many systems of representation which form subjectivity and sexuality, produces a signifying space for this repressed but powerful subject. INTERIM re-poses Freud's (and Lacan's) famous question, "What does woman want?" by representing the desire of the woman he would not notice. Therefore, through its own case histories and fragments of analysis, INTERIM summons a historical presence never theorized by Freud or Foucault—the feminist subject. This subject does not, however, spontaneously know herself. Through INTERIM's layered archeology, bricolage and mise-en-scène, the conditions for the production of knowledge of her historical presence as that subject finally

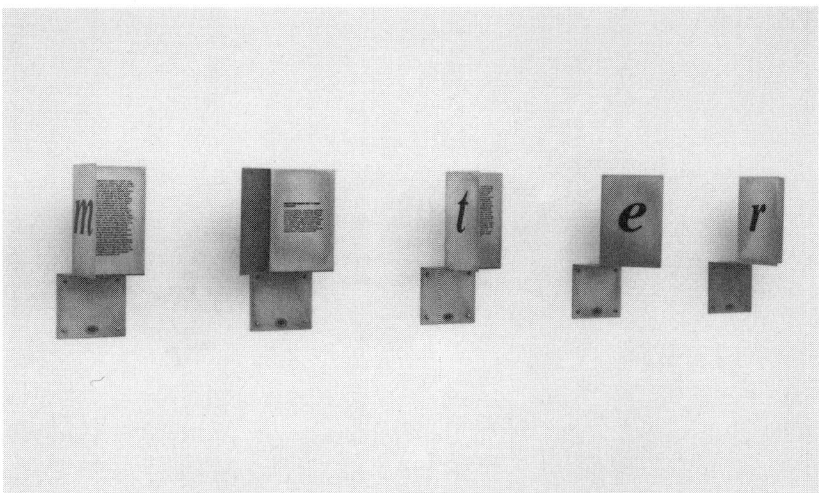

Figure 8.　Mary Kelly, *Interim Part II: Pecunia*, 1989. 20 units, 40 × 16 × 29, silkscreen on galvanized steel, Collection Vancouver Art Gallery.

become available. The work's objects and texts function as a screen onto which Mary Kelly projects the traces of the historical, personal, and theoretical processes that turned the feminine subject into an object of feminist analysis, and thus produced the possibility of the feminist subject.

Filmic in its complex uses both of invocatory as well as visual drives, INTERIM produces a new kind of textuality. The presence of words and writing is a taboo in modernist art, though it is a characteristic presence in postmodernist work. Mary Kelly uses a variety of signifying formats strategically to challenge modernism's fetishization of the visual as the site of truth, and to suggest that other registers are equally part of both social and psychic meaning. Her work incorporates knowledge of post-structuralist theorizations of the "text" which critique fixed meaning in favor of an insistence on the precariousness of all meanings, which are held to be but an effect of a signifying process. "Text" also refers to social relations in which any signifying activity occurs.

Any artwork ambitious to be read as a historical text cannot try to revive the contained and delimited meaning of traditional history painting. It cannot, moreover, be satisfied with the harmless, modernist play of the signifier in its endless evasion of meaningfulness. Rehearsal and quotation from the overloaded sign systems of contemporary mass culture, similarly, are insufficient. Julia Kristeva writes of aesthetic practices as needing to take ethical responsibility for the production of political knowledge. One conceivable site for such an ethico-political supersession of history painting, modernist art, and postmodernist spectacle is the calculated and playful textuality of projects like INTERIM. They summon and redefine all our presences in the signifying spaces they create by their interventions in the historical, the textual, and the subjective. These are initiated as feminist, but inevitably exceed that originating moment to affect all subjects, all identities, all sexes.

notes

1 Sigmund Freud, *Case Studies I*, Pelican Freud Library, vol. 8 (London: Penguin Books, 1977), p. 49.
2 Mary Kelly, "Invisible Bodies," *New Formations*, no. 2 (1987): 12.

3 Elizabeth Cowie, "Woman as Sign," *M/F*, no. 1 (1978), argues that signifying practices do not merely reflect or represent definitions of women (which are produced in socio-economic or political practices perceived to be more primary or
   foundational), but they construct and circulate meanings for the term *woman*,
   which are never independent of, but equally are not reducible to, definitions produced in other social practices.

4 Julia Kristeva, "Women's Time," *The Kristeva Reader*, Toril Moi ed. (Oxford: Basil
   Blackwell, 1987), p. 190.

5 Andreas Huyssen, "Mass Culture as Woman: Modernism's Other," in *After The
   Great Divide* (London: Macmillan, 1986), pp. 44–65.

6 Julia Kristeva, "Women's Time," p. 94. In the global and post-colonial struggle of
   women, this dialectic around sameness and difference poses even more acute
   dilemmas. Do the differences between women outweigh the potency of the sexual
   difference, which inflects any experience of exploitation, be it of race or class,
   just as much as these social formations themselves inflect any structure of sexuality or gender?

7 Julia Kristeva, "The System and the Speaking Subject," *The Kristeva Reader*,
   pp. 22–9.

8 It is not femininity that is itself the negative end point of rupture, as Kristeva
   once argued. It is the politics of the psycho-symbolic, as conceived by certain
   tendencies in contemporary feminism, which can activate that point.

9 Mary Kelly, "Desiring Images/Imaging Desire," *Wedge*, no. 6 (1984): 7.

10 It was Juliet Mitchell's *Psychoanalysis and Feminism* (London: Allen Lane, 1974)
    which had such an impact. Her arguments appeared in her earlier *Women's Estate*
    (London: Penguin Books, 1971). The spread of interest gave rise in 1976 to The
    Patriarchy Conference, at London University, the same year that a significant
    debate in the women's press was generated by the exhibition of the first parts of
    Mary Kelly's POST-PARTUM DOCUMENT at the Institute of Contemporary Art,
    London. Excerpts are reprinted in Rozsika Parker and Griselda Pollock, *Framing
    Feminism: Art and the Women's Movement 1970–85* (London: Pandora Press,
    1987), section III. 9–11, pp. 203–5.

11 The term *oppositional* functions in relation to Raymond Williams' work. He
    specifies that, in any cultural formation, there will be dominant, emergent, and
    residual practices. In addition, the emergent may be merely alternative, that is,
    waiting its turn to be dominant, or it may be truly oppositional, and articulate
    meaning excluded and repressed by the combination of interests and powers
    which form the dominant hegemony. Raymond Williams, *Marxism and
    Literature* (Oxford: Oxford University Press, 1977).

12 Current arguments about the possibility of reviving history painting, which
    claim to be overcoming modernism's refusal of social or political reference, seem

a little belated in the context of the much more sophisticated and historically grounded set of strategies being articulated by Burgin, Kelly, Mulvey, and Wollen, among others.

13 Griselda Pollock, "Screening the Seventies: Sexuality and Representation in Feminist Practice—a Brechtian Perspective," in *Vision and Difference: Femininity, Feminism and Histories of Art* (London: Routledge, 1988).

14 Stephen Heath, "From Brecht to Film: Theses, Problems," *Screen* 16, no. 4 (1975/76): 39. See also: "Ideology is not to be replaced by some area of pure knowledge; rather from within ideology, art, as realism in the Brechtian sense, attempts to displace those formations of ideology by posing the specific relations of those formations on the mode of production." Stephen Heath, "Lessons from Brecht," *Screen* 15, no. 2 (1974): 108–9.

15 The issues raised by feminism's initial engagement with psychoanalysis in Britain are covered in the collected papers given at The Patriarchy Conference, London University, 1976. See also the debate generated by the exhibition of POST-PARTUM DOCUMENT in 1976 at the ICA, reprinted in Rozsika Parker and Griselda Pollock. *Framing Feminism: Art and the Women's Movement 1970–85* (London: Pandora Press, 1987), section III. 9–11, pp. 203–5.

16 Mary Kelly, *Post-Partum Document* (London: Routledge, 1983), p. 168.

17 See note #15.

18 Michel Foucault, *The History of Sexuality, Volume One: An Introduction*, (London: Allen Lane, 1979), p. 103.

19 For an excellent discussion of this point, see Jacqueline Rose, "Feminism and the Psychic" in *Sexuality in the Field of Vision* (London: Verso Books, 1986).

painting, feminism, history 5

griselda pollock

IN THE PAINTING "THE PAINTER AND HIS Model" (1917), Henri Matisse represents an artist at work in the privileged space of modern art, the studio. Not a documentary image of Matisse's actual working space on the Quai St Michel in Paris, it symbolically represents the ideological conditions in which modern art was created—by *the* painter in *the* studio. The painter, Matisse, is a man, as is *the painter* he symbolizes. More often the man/artist is clothed, while the model, prototypically a woman, is naked, and often supine in some gracelessly uncomfortable posture. Matisse's reversal juxtaposes a caucasian flesh-coloured and possibly nude artist to the crumpled mess of faceless costume in the armchair in the corner, his female model. Masculine nudity, associated with Apollonian intelligence and creativity, signifies a mastering and active body, and strips the artist of any specific social or historical signs other than the white masculinity with which he is clothed because he is the artist. The body is not anatomically sexed; cultural connotations provide its gender through the assimilation of the term artist to man.

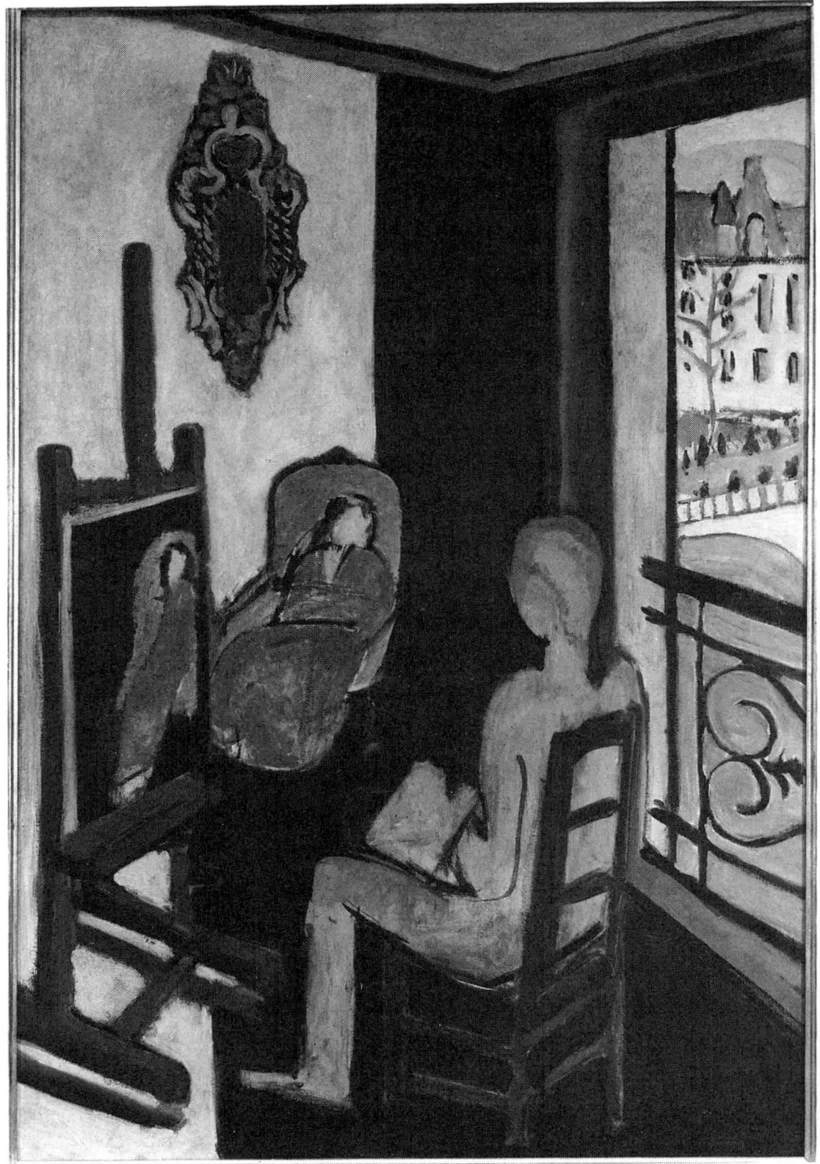

Figure 1. Henri Matisse, *The Painter and His Model*, 1917, Musée Nationale d'Art Moderne, Paris. © Succession Matisse/DACS 1992.

The painting is a palimpsest of three orders of space which define modern western art-making. It is a social space shaped in the concrete social and economic relations in one particular studio in Paris in 1917 in which a white bourgeois man paid a probably working-class woman to work for him. Then it is a representation of the symbolic space of art, the studio, and it makes a statement about the basic components of art-making—the artist, the model and the site of their one-way transaction, the canvas. Finally it presents to us the space of representation, that canvas, upon which is painted a fictive body which has been invented by the combination of the painter's look and gesture. A social and a sexual hierarchy are pictured: the artist is canonically male (signalling the fusion of Culture with masculinity); *his* material is female (the assimilation of nature, matter and femininity). By its formal disposition of man/artist: woman/model, the painting articulates the symbolic value and symbolic gender in western modernism's discourse of the "body of the painter."

This essay examines the problematic for women created by this regime, and I shall argue that the complex relations between painting (art), feminism and history can be rhetorically tracked in the contradictory placements and significations of two bodies: the "body of the painter" and the "feminine body." Women want to make art, they want specifically to paint, a desire which is as much about wanting the right to enjoy being the body of the painter in the studio—the creative self in a private domain—as it is about wanting to express individualistically the none of the less collective experiences of women. These are potently connected with and represented by aspects of our bodies, life-cycles and sexualities. There are different theories about how much and what of this "body of woman" women can represent against the grain of the dominant culture's trope of the active male creative body and the supine female object body, narratively figured in Matisse's reflexive modernist painting. The field is thus triangulated—the painter's body, the feminine body and the contestation of both through feminist discourse and practice of "the woman's body."

But in that formulation some "women's bodies" are effaced in a false universalism. If the white woman's body has been objectified and prized as the material of fantasy and art, the black woman's body, brutalized and violated under slavery and racism, has not been figured so extensively in this privileged exchange.[1] However negatively present, indeed over-present, the white body of woman has been part of the spectacle.[2] The politics of white feminist resistance may thus involve a set of strategies of calculated invisibility and its corollary insistence of *presence* signified "an-iconically." For black women, however, the outrage against their absence in hegemonic cultures, and the insistence upon other traditions in the representation of women, dictate the necessity for a creative production of *presence*. This involves strategies for insisting on visibility through figuration and the production of icons.[3]

> I am a Blackwoman and my work is concerned with making images of Blackwomen. Sounds simple enough—but I'm not interested in portraiture or its tradition. I'm interested in giving space to Blackwomen presence. A presence which has been distorted, hidden and denied. I'm interested in our humanity, our feelings and our politics; somethings which have been neglected … I have a sense of urgency about our "apparent" absence in a space we've inhabited for several centuries.[4]

There is no doubt that the body is a critical site of our oppressions and exploitations, the locus of social disciplines and violations, the field of pleasure and desire as all are traversed and differentially lived across the wounds of class, race, gender and sexuality. Diverse political campaigns and opposing theoretical programmes converge—in distinctively post–modernist fashion—upon this social, psychic, political, physical and metaphorical image of ourselves—the body, which is not inert matter or irreducible physicality, but figure, sign, space, name. The questions I want to pose are preliminary and strategic in character, mapping some of the contradictory pressures since the early 1970s which have shaped western feminist thought and cultural practice by reading a series of images of bodies in the studio.

the artist in the studio

A photograph by Hans Namuth of Jackson Pollock (d. 1956), perhaps as a result of these very photographs the most famous "body of the painter," frames the producing body and the arena of his activity, the canvas itself, supine on the floor receiving from his flurry of gestures the marks and traces of his presence and action. The sexual hierarchy pictured in Matisse is not visualized directly in Namuth's photographs of Pollock at work. But the legacy is there in the potency and activity of the masculine body now directly mastering the supine feminine space of the canvas, patterning that surface, that imaginary body, with his inscriptions.

Abstract Expressionism (the artistic movement epitomized by Pollock's manner of painting) reduced reference to a world, however stylized or oblique, and substituted these vivid, metonymic traces of the "body of the painter," epitomized by "the gesture." Pollock's practice was critically valorized in different ways, all of which celebrate, however subtextually, a colonizing masculine mastery. Harold Rosenberg, who coined the phrase "Action Painting," redefined this new art process as a kind of existential drama acted out in the theatre of the canvas's fictive space. Clement Greenberg defined Pollock in relation to his theory that the destiny of each modern art was its sacrifice of all ambitions for painting save those dictated by the material character of its medium. Painting, quintessentially defined by its flat, two-dimensional surface covered with coloured liquids which induce optical effects, achieves its modernist purity when it has banished literary subject matter, narrative and social content. Greenberg defined the law of modernism as the purification of each art: that "the conventions not essential to the viability of a medium be discarded as soon as they are recognized."[5] This process, however, did not in fact result in abstract art as such. The purity of the visual signifier, seemingly emptied of all reference to a social or natural world, is still loaded with significance through its function as affirmation of its artistic subject.[6] Abstract Expressionism is a celebration of the "expressivity" of a self which is not to be constrained by expressing anything in particular except the engagement of that artistic self with the processes and procedures of painting. Thus "painting" is privileged in modernist discourse as *the* most ambitious and significant art form because of its combination of gesture and trace, which secure by metonymy the presence of the artist. These inscribe a subjectivity whose value is, by visual inference and cultural naming, masculinity.[7]

The subject encountered through traces of his action upon the canvas is a self, imagined to be capable of total self-expression, free from division and articulation, producing meaning directly without the mediation of symbol or sign.[8] At a psychic level this must be read as a regressive fantasy to a moment when the proto-subject first imagines itself unified. It invents an imagined memory of being able to communicate spontaneously and fully by means of the infant's primitive but physically freighted tools, the look and the gesture. For this reason the fantasy exerts a powerful appeal to all artists irrespective of their sex, for it evokes the imaginary phase, a moment in the process of being made a human subject which is common to us all, despite the fact that the inflections of culturally ordained sexual difference are already shaping different trajectories which will match our forming sub-jectivities to the positions of masculinity and femininity. But for all that this ideology of art services bourgeois mythologies of the self-possessing and self-realizing individual in this imaginary form, we must recognize that its function is also decisively on the side of the Symbolic; that is, the cultural-social-political order. The imaginary individual, as all the images so starkly insist in their iconography, is a man, empowered by his privileged place on the symbolic side of the division theorized as "sexual difference."[9]

"where are the women?"

In our book *Old Mistresses* (1981),[10] Roszika Parker and I juxtaposed a pho-tograph by Ernst Haas of Helen Frankenthaler, a second-generation abstract expressionist, to Namuth's Pollock. The pairing iconically suggested what we dared not write. Is there a visible difference between men and women artists? Do Pollock's slashing and throwing of paint, his gyrations around a supine canvas, enact a macho assault upon an imaginary, feminine body? Are the traces of paint on canvas the residues of a psychic performance? Is this "*écriture/peinture masculine*" at its most vivid? How could we then read Frankenthaler's pouring, pushing, smoothing gestures as she knelt on or near the canvas as a surface continuous with her space and movements? Is this a feminine modality inviting us to invent metaphors uniting femininity and fluidity for these luscious effects? Do these gestures of the labouring, painting bodies register some profoundly different way of being in the body and being in artistic space which the viewer might then read in terms of the signs of gender and sexuality? Are the procedural and hence the resulting formal differences within a modernist discipline symptoms of sexual differ-ence? Are sexual politics there in the formal and technical processes of high modernist art?

At that moment we had no language in which to raise these questions, let alone answer them. The problem then, as now, is to find terms in which to analyse the *specificity* of women as subjects in a social and historical world without confirming that particularity as nothing more than difference; that is, that women are just women. It would be easy now to mobilize Irigaray and Kristeva to create a feminine poetics of painting through which to commend the specific qualities of Frankenthaler's practice of abstract painting. (See the section on "Post-modernist Feminist Modernisms" below.) But affirmative action, however theoretically inspired, cannot spring us out of the still powerful model of modernism which is a historically specific enunciation of sexual difference.

Of course women share the fantasy of the creative self, desire that privileged space of imaginary freedom called the studio. Feminism and the discourses of art are, however, locked in a profound contradiction at the site of the expression of the creative self. Feminist theory problematizes notions of the self, of woman, of the subject, arguing that these are not essences, the pre-social sources of meaning, but intricate constructions in social and psychic space. Furthermore, feminist cultural theory refuted absolutely the idea that art was a kind of blank space upon which to deposit meanings through the singular look and self-affirming gesture. A historical and materialist thesis challenged affirmative and expressive theories of art by insisting that the materials for art are social, part of socially and historically determined signifying systems.[11] Art is not the privatized space of self-generated significance; it is a form of textual politics.

Textual practice is, furthermore, institutionally constituted. Modernist art theory, as the images discussed above suggest, privileges the studio as *the* discreet space where art is made, relegating gallery or exhibition, journal or art lecture to a subsidiary role of circulation and consumption, an act of interpretation or use coming after the singular creative event. Feminist materialist theory suggests that the studio, the gallery, the exhibition catalogue are not separate, but form interdependent moments in the cultural circuit of capitalist production and consumption. They are also overlapping sets within the signifying system which collectively constitutes the discourse of art. While the spaces of art have specific and local determinants and forms, they are, furthermore, part of a continuum with other economic, social, ideological practices which constitute the social formation as a whole. The interconnection between art as text and art as institution no longer permits the galleries alone to be blamed for sexism. It is necessary to interrogate the political effects of images of art as symbolic presence, as figuration of the artistic self, no longer present in person as "he" was when, as "master" of "his" world, he made "his" art-work. The sociality of art is "the question of institutions, of the conditions which determine the reading of artistic texts and the strategies which would be appropriate for interventions (rather than 'alternatives') in that context."[12] Feminism, therefore, provides a theory of interventions within a field of signification, rather than an alibi for female expressivity; that is, for seeking to secure women's equal right to the "body of the painter." A critical debate hinges on this distinction and it is the purpose of this chapter to examine the politics of it.

sexuality in the field of vision

Feminism and politics have been common-sensically associated with the content of art, not with formal issues. But this is a misapprehension. Judy Chicago, for instance, wanted to create not merely a feminist iconography but a visual language, a semi-abstract imagery based on the metaphor of female sexuality. Refusing the repression of its physical form in the visual arts (all those nudes without pubic hair or any indication of genitals), she portrayed the history of women through ceramic evocations of female genitalia. "The Dinner Party" (1978) opposed the silencing of women; women could speak through their labia, as it were. Powerful as a statement, the implications have troubled feminists, for the equation of woman with body, of sexuality with the genitals, seemed too limiting and indeed dangerous.

In contrast, feminist theory derived from psychoanalysis and film studies worked on what Jacqueline Rose defined as "sexuality in the field of vision."[13] Sexuality is understood not to be tied to genitals and gendered bodies. Sexuality is a representation. The "sexual component of the image" goes beyond merely recognizing that figurative images play a part in the production of norms and stereotypes of gender. There is a cultural politics of sexuality in visual form and space itself, as well as in the practices of looking: "the aesthetics of pure form are implicated in the less pure pleasures of looking."[14]

Psychoanalysis has provided an account of a politics of sexual difference secured in that relation between looking/seeing/form, especially in its analyses of fetishism, voyeurism, narcissism and exhibitionism. The "body of woman" is perpetually figured in multifarious spaces of representation as both a threat of lack (bodily mutilation standing as metaphor for psychic disintegration) and an aesthetically super-perfect body whose beauty or harmony displaces the threat of lack. Matisse's painting narrates the threat, in the punishing dehumanization of the model, while it is disavowed and compensated for in the formal, almost abstract harmonies, the aesthetic beauties reworked by his artistry in the painting-within-the-painting of that model.

Rose states: "We know that women are meant to *look* perfect, presenting a seamless image to the world so that man, in that confrontation with difference, can avoid any comprehension of lack. The position of woman in fantasy therefore depends upon a particular economy of vision."[15] Much art can be seen to submit to that economy of vision—a fixed difference in which man is empowered with the look, rendering his fantasy of perfection, art formally beautifying the threatening otherness of woman. This is the sexual economy circulated through paintings and photographs of the man artist in his studio with his woman model. Indeed, part of the political force of critical, feminist art practices has been a purposeful strategy of fracture, of disruption of aesthetic perfection and the ease and fullness of familiar cultural pleasures. What has characterized a diversity of feminist modes is a refusal of an exclusive "visuality," with its fantasies of looking, and a concurrent exploitation of a wider range of semiotic forms which call upon other drives, such as the invocatory, and other sign systems, including writing/inscription, incantation, rhythm, memory, echo.

Yet modernist painting at its height, Pollock's for instance, put that drive for aesthetic perfection at risk. The studio became the site of a terrifying and heroic struggle in which the artist abandoned every support, instrument, convention and tradition—even the body of the woman.[16] Reducing his means to himself and the paint, he set out to see if he could still make a picture work, conquer lack and recreate aesthetic unity. This battle was re-presented publicly in the language of avant-gardism—a great new endeavour, shedding the habits of the past, adventuring to create a future, pushing culture onwards into uncharted spaces: heroic, progressive, individualistic, it celebrated modernity's promise of freedom, which, read from other perspectives, signalled conquest, colonization and violence. Spurious and partial, freedom was enjoyed in imaginary, aesthetic spaces figured by the western, avant-garde, masculine artist; but that freedom was a powerful attraction, as sometimes the only freedom on offer.

modernism's appeal for women

The tradition of modernist painting is still significant and alive, and there are plenty of important women practicing there. But it is interesting that there has been little serious feminist work on it. Few feminists have thought of putting on an exhibition of these modern "mistresses," while Victorian or baroque art by women has been fertile ground for exhibitions and publications. But in 1988–9 The Arts Council of Great Britain circulated an exhibition, "The Experience of Painting: Eight Modern Artists," of which, significantly, half the artists were women: Gillian Ayres, Jennifer Durrant, Edwina Leapman and Bridget Riley.

The very title already declares the liberal humanist character of its project. "Before we speak of the experience of painting let us consider our experience of the world," writes Mel Gooding in the exhibition catalogue. That "our" is inclusive, suggesting a condition in which we all share experience of the world: "Memories, dreams, desires, our imaginings of history, our projections of futurity, our sense of what is true and what is false, all converge upon this moment, as we stand, say, upon a beach, and looking seawards, smell the salt upon the air and feel the wind cold upon our cheek."[17] History and time evaporate before the timeless moment of being in nature—a highly romantic concept which typically enlivens the technical procedures of painting to give them metaphysical resonance: "Art may reflect something of this evanescence but its purposes are deeper than a mirroring of the actual. It is an imaginative and metaphorical interaction with the world and its objects, answering to the deepest human impulse."[18] This apologia is far from Greenberg's rigorous, disciplined, modernist project for abstract painting. Indeed it echoes the romanticism by which women's work is often "feminized" and dehistoricized in one lyrical movement towards the monumental time of nature.[19]

The catalogue is prototypical in other ways, presenting each artist as an individual in his or her aesthetic cell, prefaced by a photograph of each person at work in her or his studio. The image is accompanied by the familiar artist's statement, couched in individualistic terms, projecting this liberal humanist vision through the aesthetic vocabulary of pure formalism. The major presence is Gillian Ayres, featured on the cover—not active as is Pollock in Hans Namuth's evocation of the painting body in the studio—but seated like Matisse's model, compressed against the overwhelming colour and activity of paintings and paint-pots which seem not to be the product of this contemplative figure. She states her lifelong commitment to abstract painting:

> Abstract art has been the vital force in visual art in this century. This is nothing to do with myself, with my own commitment to abstraction. Modernism meant a lot of different things, and some of those things one may not like or agree with. But what it meant above all was hope in a brave new world. And what did go on under modernism was a *questioning and thinking* … And under modernism that questioning was almost the condition of being creative.[20]

What I am trying to discern here is the contradictory formation in which a woman like Gillian Ayres has worked for thirty years, empowered by the possibilities of modernism which allowed her to be an artist while not prescribing what she should paint as a woman. She is also sharing in the project of modernity, a belief in progress, a critical sense of how that progress is created by "questioning and thinking." Artistic practice is posited as a privileged site of such open experiment: "You could simply say that imagination is *anti-cliché*, against known experience. You're always trying to find something you haven't seen before, an experience that is true to oneself."[21]

What interests me is the way in which imagination and the critical faculty are captured within an exclusively aesthetic domain. Jürgen Habermas has characterized modernity precisely by such divisions of social life into specialist compartments—science, morality, aesthetics.[22] Mainstream twentieth-century modernism, the extreme bourgeois realization of the autonomy of art, offered to women a means, but a vicarious one, to experience freedom. That is why they embraced it and, despite all, dedicated their lives to "painting." In that studio, with the canvas on floor or wall, women imagined themselves free; if not from being women, free from being seen and defined exclusively in those terms. Once outside the door, they would once again have to be women, forgotten or ignored, condescendingly acknowledged until such time as the particular practice lost its place as culturally dominant. British abstract art in the 1990s is not where culture is at, and so the women who gave it vitality achieve belated recognition for their work in the house of culture, when everyone else has moved to another room.[23]

When Charles Harrison reviewed this show, he suggested that postmodernism might represent a shift as significant as that which ushered in modernism itself (which happened in the late nineteenth century for painting) and left many nineteenth-century academic painters desiring to continue to explore the still rich resources of their tradition, yet, as a result of the substantial reorientation signified by modernism, "deprived of cultural and historical authenticity."[24] Harrison's argument seems particularly pertinent to the feminist debate about painting. History, not feminism itself, has

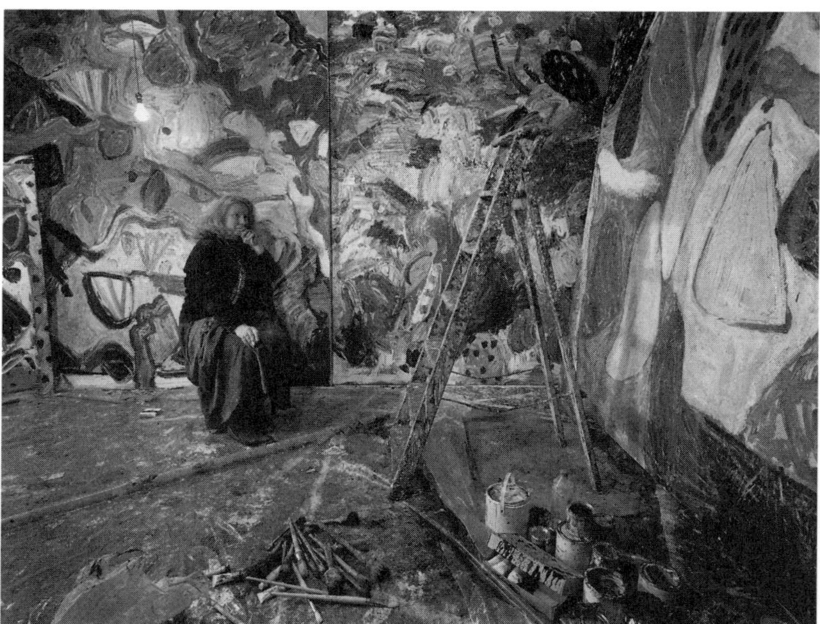

Figure 2.   Marten Charles, *Gillian Ayres in her Studio*, 1988.

altered the terms and conditions of cultural practice. Yet feminist politics insists that within the community, we take seriously women's demands and do not judge their viability according to any given orthodoxy. Painting is not only very much on the agenda in art education, but it answers to many women's powerful desire for a way to represent women's experience as whole, human and thus equally important. Indeed that is what I think the call for feminist painting is about. It registers a demand for a permitted space in which the women who wish to be artists can experience, in the creative freedom of the studio and canvas, those expanding and personally challenging adventures symbolized through an encounter with the blank canvas, aided only by one's brushes and paints and fired by ambition and a sense of limitless possibility. In the name of what can feminists argue against such claims for women's right to participate in the modernist project, especially now that the formalism of Greenberg's modernism has been suspended and post-modernist painting allows the painter to enjoy the grand gesture, expressive figuration and, most importantly, historical and personal reference?

The answer is whatever we mean by post-modernity. But that is too trite, for we have only just begun to analyse post-modernity from a feminist perspective.[25] Modernism offered to women a delusive freedom from being defined as "the sex," as woman. Yet in its institutions and critical discourses modernism patrolled the boundaries of masculine hegemony not so much by an overtly gendered discourse, but obliquely. In an article entitled "Mass Culture as Woman: Modernism's Other," Andreas Huyssen identifies the force of gender politics in the rigidly policed divide between mass culture—defined as engulfing, dangerous, trivial, easy, feminine—and authentic, high culture, which is represented in masculine terms as a project requiring steely determination and single-minded dedication to preserve true art against the diluting threat posed by popular art.[26] The gendering of mass culture bespeaks a sexual politics, but it is also the form of a division created by capitalism of which both high modernism and popular culture are fragmented pieces. Huyssen writes: "I know of no better aphorism about the imaginary adversaries, modernism and mass culture, than that which Adorno articulated in a letter to Walter Benjamin: 'Both [modernist and mass culture] bear the scars of capitalism, both contain elements of change. Both are torn halves of freedom to which, however, they do not add up.'"[27]

Huyssen's suggestion of a "masculine mystique," secured across the division of high and popular culture, has direct repercussions for feminist theory and practice in the post-modern moment. Huyssen, for instance, questions the fashionable idea of the "femininity" of avant-garde writing proposed by Kristeva, who argues that femininity signifies the repressed and the transgressive (a point taken up later as a possible route to a feminist theory of abstract painting). Huyssen reminds us of the pervasive fantasy of a "male femininity," in the work of Flaubert for example, a fantasy induced perhaps as a necessary reaction against the excessive masculinity demanded by the discipline of high art with its relentless abstention from pleasure—"the suppression of everything that might be threatening to the rigorous demands of being modern and at the edge of time."[28] Kristeva, celebrating the femininity of Mallarmé's and Joyce's negative aesthetics, was dealing in imaginary sexualities and disregarded a tradition of writing by women and their complex social, ideological and semiotic inscriptions within modernism, produced under the sign of woman. Huyssen points out that "the universalizing ascription of femininity to mass culture always depended on the real exclusion of women from high culture and its institutions."[29] Now that women are visible as practitioners in high art, the gendering device becomes obsolete but only because "both mass culture and women's (feminist) art are emphatically implicated in any attempt to map the specificity of contemporary culture and thus to gauge this culture's distance from high modernism."[30]

Huyssen falters just where we must not—is there not some significant distinction between "women's art" and "art" qualified by feminism? The practices which constitute the most visible *feminist* interventions in culture are not to be defined according to the gender of their expressive subject, and not through residual modernist terminology as scripto-visual, photographic, video, or whatever other medium. By the same token we cannot be debating women's right to use oil or acrylic paint on canvas. To do so would be to renege on such political distance as we have achieved through the last two decades of feminist theory and practice in the cultural sphere.

In mass culture the manifest body, however, is the body of the woman, which becomes the very antithesis of individuality celebrated in high culture's body of the artist. The feminine body in mass culture is the symbol of saturation by the commodity, the field of play for money, power, capital and sexuality. As the body of woman lost its necessity and supremacy within modernist formalism, it continued to be ceaselessly circulated by its corollary, mass culture, which further devalued this body because it was produced without the authorizing signature of the artist.[31] Thus two bodies—the body of the painter and the body of woman—the signs of difference—stand opposed in modernist culture, caught up in the series of binary oppositions which figure sexual difference to us across these inter-related domains.

Feminist practices cannot simply abandon either of these bodies, but whatever constitutes the feminism of the practice results from the necessity to *signify* a relation to this complex.[32] That is not the same as desiring somehow to have a share in the painter's body while producing new meanings for the feminine body. They exist as a relation, fabricated interdependently across the disparate spaces which make up culture. Thus feminist interventions in the spaces of representation have begun to qualify and differentiate the feminine bodies fabricated in culture's inter-facing hierarchies of race, class, gender, sexuality and age. But such practices are rarely single works, or merely series. They form complex installations, documentations and events, which aim to create a signifying space in which the historical changes wrought by feminism can be perceived and represented while others still more radical can be imagined. The freedom here is not imaginary self-realization within the confines of the canvas, but the register of concrete struggles on and beyond the battlefield of representation.

after modernism, feminism?

Political feminist culture of the sixties and seventies was a part of a critique of modernism which in turn was symptomatic of a skepticism about *modernity*. Its legacy of belief in human progress and the humanist, rationalist ideals of freedom have been savaged by the revolt of those it had enslaved, violated, and repressed. But feminism itself, taken in a long historical perspective, is also a product of the Enlightenment project and of modernity.[33] Originally named the Women's *Liberation* Movement, its project was conceived of by the second wave in terms of emancipation from social structures of inequality. What the narratives of modern art paradigmatically represent finds echoes in the project of feminism—the self-realization of women/subjects/selves liberated from the constraints of external pressures and socially induced limits. Just as the materialist thesis on culture suggests an interdependence of text, institution and the production of sexual differ-ence, materialist feminist theory has moved from this inside/outside dichotomy of individual caught in a web of social oppression to a structural mode of analysis of our condition as systematically social, political, linguis-tic, cultural and psychic. In place of utopian dreams of the new society of post-liberation times, there is a stress on enacted resistances, oppositions, negotiations and the accumulation of local and particular strategies of inter-vention and redefinition.

I do not, however, think it is sufficient to suggest that we have witnessed a shift in feminist theory over two decades which has, as it were, propelled feminism across a frontier, from its modernist liberation theology into some post-modernist relativism. Indeed, it is the predicament and paradox of women's struggles which constantly disrupts both neat historical narratives and theoretical constructs.

Since they seem to have much in common, feminism has been cited as a prototypical form of post-modernism. Indeed, much recent feminist art has been assimilated to post-modernism, especially those self-consciously "strategic practices" conceived by Barbara Kruger, Mary Kelly, Cindy Sherman, Lubaina Himid, Susan Hiller, Jenny Holzer, Marie Yates, Yve Lomax, Martha Rosler, Sutapa Biswas, Mitra Tabrizian, Jo Spence, Zarina Bhimji, Mona Hatoum and so forth.[34] Their work is a site for a sustained analysis of the meanings of sexual difference authored by culture, across which "cultural body" they inscribe feminist readings.[35] Each artist has a "project," a defined set of concerns and resources, but they cannot be assim-ilated to the paradigm of the expressive, self-affirming artist signified by "the painter." Wherever their work is made, the point at which its meanings are produced is a public space where viewers read its signs in relation to a wider field of representations and histories, collective as much as individual. While being exhibited, even in an art gallery, such work implies the social spaces and semiotic systems of both culture as a whole, and specific, often repressed or silenced constituencies to which the work so calculatedly refers, and which it reworks to produce as critical *presence* in culture as a whole. It is this radical reconceptualization of the function of artistic activity—its procedures, personnel and institutional sites—which is the major legacy of feminist interventions in culture since the late sixties. What distinguishes such practices from the generality of post-modernism is the refusal to abandon a sense of history and political effect.

post-modernist feminist modernisms

Nothing reveals more clearly the perverse trajectory of the last two decades than the fact that this legacy is now seriously contested within some sections of the feminist art community. What was but a decade ago hailed as the feminist gesture of liberation in art is now felt to be oppressive, elitist and avant-gardist. There is an explicit call to reunite feminism and painting. Such debate between feminist definitions of appropriate cultural forms and practices takes place, however, against a shifting cultural landscape which includes a major *post*-modern reinvestment (economically as much as curatorially and critically) in painting and the privileged identities the term *embodies*. Neo-expressionism, new figuration, gesture painting: a diverse array of practices restored to the markets and the galleries their prize commodity—the body of the artist through look and gesture now marketed as style.[36]

The new appraisals of women's painting represent it as radically "different" from post-modern painting by men. Gender is thus positioned as outside the process of representation but expressed through its evocation of the gendered author. Sarah Kent writes:

> Postmodern painting is often referred to as post-political. One might equally
> name it post-moral, post-idealist or retro-visionary. It is a form of mourning
> for lost power, lost belief and lost confidence, in which actual significance is
> replaced by overblown self-importance, inflated scale and hysterical bombast. It
> is a masculine art form, a witness to the crumbling of certainty and centrality.
> Women do not share this sense of dislocation and despair.[37]

On the contrary, Sarah Kent writes that women painters feel strong, optimistic and rooted, and quotes Alexis Hunter, who claims that women are working from a "position of integrity". While gender is the basis for a "difference" within post-modernist culture, it is so through a modernist conception of the wholeness of the artistic subject, which is now only possible for a woman artist. The power comes from the celebratory revelation of the feminine, usually negatively connoted and othered.

Sarah Kent's introduction to a recent exhibition of the work of the painter Rosa Lee opens with a reference to Luce Irigaray's critique of western rationalism as founded on identity, stability and binary opposition. Femaleness is typically placed on the side of the unbounded, irregular, disorderly. Painting becomes a means to express this other, feminine imaginary: "Rosa Lee's paintings can be seen as an attempt to give form to those areas of experience and knowledge suppressed by the constraints of rationalism ... Cradled within the geometry of Lee's paintings are flashes of the unruly, dark, wanton or barbarous aspects or the irrational that are associated with the feminine."[38] In 1987 *Feminist Review* published a paper by Rosa Lee which conjoined feminism, painting and post-modernism in its title. Her question was this: "Is it possible to produce a radical art form without recourse to the strategies of deconstruction adopted by feminists such as, for example, Mary Kelly, Rose Garrard, Susan Hiller or Nancy Spero?"[39] Rosa Lee devoted much of her article to the work of Therese Oulton, a celebrated British painter who is not so much abstract as non-figurative. Her vast canvases are represented as critical attempts to renew artistic language by a subversion of the grand tradition of painting from Titian to Pollock. These claims are based upon structuralist theory about the radicalness of insisting that art is nothing but its means; structuralism is often a merely theoretical formulation of what we know as modernism. Oulton's work is also appraised via French feminist theory, which associates femininity with negativity and transgression of patriarchal languages. "In these paintings the quest for renewal rests upon a series of 'refusals' which result from a critique of painting's traditions ... the paintings refuse any one fixed interpretation ... It is through the subversive juxtaposition of paradoxes that the possibility of creating a new, non-representational artistic language emerges."[40]

Painting by such women is characterized as feminine precisely because it resists representation, a claim that draws upon Kristeva's thesis that femininity is unrepresentable within a phallocentric symbolic. But for Kristeva, femininity is not synonymous with women or their bodies. It is a specificity complexly produced in the psychic and social semiotics of culture, lived out, experienced by those designated thereby as women. This is a profound distinction between notions of gender as rooted in essential properties named being a man or being a woman (which can be defined biologically, psychically or sociologically) and notions of sexual difference as an effect of a process always already written upon us, but which can be theoretically grasped as a projection only fixed at a relatively late stage of our formation as human subjects. It is the gap between the making of sexual difference, the signifying of sexual difference and identities construed across the process and the naming that gives us hope—for there it is that transformation and revolution are possible.

Indexed only to art, annexed to a still modernist art theory, the subtle misreadings of French feminism provide an updated alibi for the model of the artist in the studio producing a singular, individual practice, whose traces define the painting, and give spectators access back to the artistic subject. Lee, Oulton or Newman: these names, like those of Matisse and Pollock, are moments of a gender category, in the former case, women. The fact of the gender of the artist invites a reading of the work as an expression of femininity. Negatively positioned in patriarchal culture, it is celebrated for its negativity in this critical discourse. At the level of experiential and aesthetic effect these readings are seductive and enriching. But the use of French feminism's reworking of the term "feminine" within the paradigm of "the artist in the studio" tends to confirm, because it so confidently affirms, a fundamental difference of the feminine, or femininity only as fundamental difference. The binary opposition remains in place and the feminine, however much it is locally valorized by women painters and viewers, continues its prescribed role as cipher against which masculinity erects its domination. While we may try to insert the woman's body into the space of the studio—both practically and symbolically in discourse—the project easily succumbs to merely replaying the deep structures of that system: woman as difference, inchoate, unspeakable, enigmatic, metaphor for all that is outside representation and meaning except as lack. The formal achievements of these undoubtedly marvellous painters paradoxically confirm it. Now it is women's painting, not their body alone, that must be beautiful, formally satisfying, managing the risk of chaos to secure pictorial unity.

The implicit binarism also has effects in relations to other distinctions, differences between women with regard to race, class, sexuality, age, disability. Black women artists assert the need for definition as a priority. The difference their bodies have been forced to signify allows little of the pleasures of inchoateness and abandon. Oversensualized and underdefined in relation to the term woman—both sexually brutalized and enslaved as the anonymous laboring body—other representational strategies are demanded to negotiate spaces for their occupation and redefinition of the term femininity to accommodate their history and desire.[41] Each community inscribes its values and meanings upon the terms woman and femininity, which circulate promiscuously, seeming to refer to shared meanings when, in fact, as signifiers, they are often indeterminate, chronically historical and variable. Yet Denise Riley cogently argues: "These difficulties can't be assuaged by appeals to the myriad types and conditions of women on this earth. They are not a matter of there being different *sorts of* women, but the effects of the designation, 'women.'"[42] Any strategy that relies on the givenness of meaning, woman, women, femininity, must find itself potentially confirming the dominant, preferred meanings, once more conjuring up a false universality, itself a touchstone of modernism's liberal lie.

Of Lubaina Himid's *Freedom and Change* (1984), Gilane Tawadros writes:

> Himid's women displace what Stuart Hall has called the "centred discourses of the West," but this does not simply imply that the grand narratives of the West are simply to be replaced by an alternative, totalizing narrative. Rather this process of displacement "entails putting in question (Western culture's) universalist character and its transcendental claims to speak for everyone, while being everywhere and nowhere" ... In opposition to the universalizing tendencies of modernism, *Freedom and Change* assigns central importance to the position of difference.[43]

To make a difference is to work to create the means to signify difference, and that cannot mean merely changing sides or perspectives. It means taking on the systems which themselves make sexual difference and hinge that formation to so many other social differentiations. This involves recognizing the specificity of the level and effect of sexual difference, however differently various social communities live it. There are neither hierarchies of oppression nor synchronous listings—race, gender, class and so forth. There are specific configurations, each of which formations—gender, class, race—occurs through particular processes requiring appropriately forged methods of analysis and strategies of opposition.

Gilane Tawadros argues that Lubaina Himid articulates "a positive conception of the ethnicity of the margins, or the periphery … a recognition that we all speak from a particular place, out of particular history, out of a particular experience, a particular culture, *without being contained by that position.*"[44] Particularity is a strategy of resistance to modernism, which, with western feminism, shares the western discourse of centrality. Yet western feminism, in pursuit of the means to analyse the particularity of some women (which it oft-times imagined were all women, admittedly), has identified a formation—sexual difference—which, however configured through the prism of many particularities, is a determinant on all of us. Denise Riley writes:

> The now familiar device for challenging essentialism from a feminist perspective attacks its false universalism in representing the experiences of, usually, middle-class, white western women as if they embraced all womankind. But this move to replace the tacit universal with the qualified "some women's experience" is both necessary and yet in the end inadequate. Below the newly pluralized surfaces, the old problems still linger.[45]

post-modernist feminist post-modernisms

In 1987 Katy Deepwell also wrote an article "In Defense of the Indefensible: Feminism, Painting and Post-Modernism." She polemically intervened against what she took to be a theoretically inspired prescription of feminist art practice—an orthodoxy of scripto-visual work—and she initiated a reconsideration of the admittedly problematic relation between feminism and figurative painting. "What is at issue here is the potential of painting as a medium through which feminists can mount a challenge to notions of art prevalent today: a challenge in images, methods, and readings, different to the existing order."[46] "Painting as a medium" evokes shades of Greenberg's modernist definition of art by its materials. But "painting" is much more than an artistic technique, a medium. Since the late eighteenth century, and certainly since the beginning of this, the term has referred to the hegemonic cultural form which is constituted by the combination of a subject (the artist), an activity (the practice in the studio) and a web of symbolic meaning woven through that figure in that space by means of the economic investment in the commodity it produced.[47] It is a historical naivety to imagine that the debate about feminism and cultural practice is reducible to whether it is OK to use acrylic on canvas as well as video or photographic montage.

But Katy Deepwell focuses on questions of the means of signifying women's particularity—not theorized as negativity, but as materials of lived experience and specific interests. The space of art is one which narrates and in doing so legitimizes that which is made visible in its recurring stories. The script of figurative painting in the west has been massively masculine, servicing its fantasies and representing its white dominance. Women desire to write new stories, their stories, into this narrative. In the Victorian period, as in the moment of surrealism with its echoes of that earlier bourgeois age, narrative, figurative painting offered space for women's inscriptions, as often supportive of dominant ideological formations as against the grain.[48] Under a post-modernist cultural dispensation, strict Greenbergian formalism has been displaced. Reference and figuration are permitted. As Sarah Kent suggests, women are placed differently from men in this moment. Feminist liberation politics, affirmative, experiential and revelatory, comfortably cohabits with a positive adoption of the new possibilities of figurative painting. But again, it seems that while recolonizing painting with specific meanings for and of women, both the notion of woman and the notion of art as self-expression—however collective a self; that is, women—are unexamined. As a result the positivity of what is expressed (women's experience and viewpoint) will continue to be determined negatively as a subcultural expression (only women's, only black women's, only lesbians, only mothers' experience and viewpoint) by the structural sexism of the institution within which the work, like all art as text, will signify.

where histories converge

To take the issue beyond the troubling and impossible relation between "feminism" and "painting" we need a third term, "history."[49] The women's movement is predicated upon a seemingly self-evident collectivity, women. We have not, however, always been and are never only "women." Indeed feminism in the western form is a historical product of the fact that sex has a history.[50] The historian Denise Riley has argued for the necessity of a historical understanding of the formations and alterations of the collectivity "women" in European history. From the seventeenth century and reaching a culmination in the nineteenth century, female people in the west undergo a historical process of increasing sexualization, whose effects are uneven according to hierarchies of power called class, race and gender. Riley's phrase "the long march of the empires of gender over the entirety of the person" points to the redefinition of women as "the sex," as only their sex—or rather "the sex he uses." Ruled by reproductive biology, white bourgeois women were subjected through a range of new disciplines and social practices which resulted in what we could name "overfeminization." Women—the name already encoding class- and race-specific references—became extensions of Woman, weighted with a sexuality that excluded from the definition of "woman" most forms of political or economic power. In the formation of this highly sexualized division in western bourgeois society between masculine and feminine spheres, cultural forms, institutions and practices played a significant part at the level of representation. The femininity of "women" was negotiated both by their inclusion in cultural narratives and imageries, though in a restricted range of types and settings, and by their exclusion from culture's most prestigious practices and institutions, such as the Royal Academy or History painting. None the less, women did practise professionally as artists, but in ways which as often reinforced as much as they criticized the sexualized, gendered vocabulary of bourgeois society. But, paradoxically, if femininity was on the cultural agenda, it meant there were cultural opportunities in which to examine the question of sexual difference and to speak out both from, and of, the specific psychic spaces and social bodies bourgeois culture *engendered*.[51]

Feminism emerged as a protest from within this overfeminization of bourgeois sexual order. An immediate if not simultaneous historical effect, it disputed the enunciations of femininity, but from within the boundaries of this sexually divided universe. But by the beginning of this century, to claim space in modernity, it became necessary for women to distance and denounce both bourgeois and nineteenth-century feminist enunciations of femininity. For women artists, for example, wishing to escape the possible but always limiting sphere of feminine art, the spaces and practices of cultural modernism permitted an apparent liberation from the culture's traditional overfeminization of women.[52] Women artists aligned themselves with the modernist project, which seemed to offer them access to freedom, equality, the chance to be just an artist—to be the body in the studio, free like Matisse's from time, place and, however momentarily, gender. In contrast to the highly gendered modes of the nineteenth-century bourgeois culture, the emergent modernist community appeared to embody the liberal ideal of humanity blissfully indifferent to gender.

Indifferent it was—to women, and any other community. Without any serious deconstruction of the masculine power it had sustained, this liberal ideal reinscribed that gender's privilege. What it offered women and the white bourgeoisie's colonial others was participation in modernism, on condition that they effaced their gender/cultural particularity. Well known in the study of racism, the discourse of tolerance has also functioned within the modern politics of gender.[53] Women had to choose between being human and being a woman.[54] As artists this was a paradoxical experience. In her probing interviews with women artists of the modernist generations, Cindy Nemser repeatedly recorded the pressures these women experienced to "become one of the boys" in order to have access to the profession they desired.[55] Throughout the twentieth century, with honourable exceptions, women artists forged artistic identities under this modernist arrangement, signing their initials or defeminizing their names, like Lee Krasner, the painter who was married to Jackson Pollock.[56] The process of becoming an artist did not tolerate public avowal that being a woman made any difference. But being a woman made all the difference to the size of the studio you got to work in, to whether you got exhibitions, or to the terms in which your work was written about.

Helen Frankenthaler, for instance, was an up and coming post-graduate painter when she attracted the attention of leading modern art critic Clement Greenberg. He sent her to visit Jackson Pollock in his studio at East Hampton and she was duly astounded by his novel painting methods and the solutions his work was suggesting to the impasse of post-cubist art. It is generally agreed that Frankenthaler learnt that lesson well and in her immediate exploitation of techniques of staining and soaking unprimed canvas, in paintings such as *Mountains and Sea* (1952, Washington National Gallery), effectively created the next move in the game of avant-garde painting, a move which was taken up in the later 1950s by Kenneth Nolan and Morris Louis. In 1960 Clement Greenberg hailed Louis and Nolan as the leading American painters, the only ones who moved the art game on. His article is shadowed by a presence—Frankenthaler's. She is not acknowledged in his history of modernism, except obliquely in this passage securing Louis's pedigree: "His first sight of middle period Pollocks, and of a large, extraordinary painting done in 1952 by Helen Frankenthaler called *Mountains and Sea,* led Louis to change his direction abruptly."[57] That is the sum of her historical presence in a kind of art writing that is all about a league table of goals and innovations. In other works, she is removed from the linear, historical time of Greenberg's modernism. Her work is lyrically associated with landscape and nature—projecting Frankenthaler out of art historical time into a monumental temporality of eternal femininity.[58] Greenberg at least did not subject Frankenthaler to that fate, but his virtual silence eradicated her as effectively from history. While this may well be a product of his sexism, it is also an effect of modernism itself—how can gender be said to inflect facture, strategic painterly moves on late cubist space, relations between geometry and colour on a flat surface? It obviously can, as I have argued above, but it has required the perspective of feminist critique to found a vocabulary with which to deconstruct the in*different* of modernist discourse.[59]

Late twentieth-century western feminism can be named a reaction against modernist liberalism's "underfeminization." Bourgeois society made sex a central categorization, an extremity which framed the resistance—a desire to escape being a woman. Art, like money and power, offered a respite for the lucky few. But the categorization remained, if not at the political level then economically, legally, in employment and social welfare, etc. Being a woman made a difference, and feminism, has, since the late sixties, worked to repoliticize femininity.[60] The problem is how to develop enunciations of femininity that can cut across the twin poles of femininity as absolute difference (the nineteenth-century model) and femininity as a social disadvantage to be overcome in the ambition for equality with men (the twentieth-century liberal position). As Toril Moi has argued, western feminism is an impossible undertaking, a political struggle in the name of women, aiming either to render such a nomination a matter of indifference or to valorize difference within a system of binary oppositions which systematically values one term, man, over its negative other, woman.

> Given this logic, a feminist cannot settle for either equality or difference. Both struggles must be *aporetically* fought out. But we also know that both approaches are caught in the end in a constraining logic of *sameness* and *difference*. Julia Kristeva therefore suggests that feminism must operate in a third space: that which deconstructs all identity, all binary oppositions, all phallologocentric positions.[61]

This third space, projected in Julia Kristeva's essay "Women's Time" (1979), is the theoretical space associated with the feminist analysis of sexual difference—that is, of a system by which human subjectivity is constituted and which no one can escape. This is perhaps also the space in which to think the issues of difference which feminism in its late twentieth-century form has not.

Femininity has also to be thought beyond its imperial bourgeois origins.[62] If women are not a stable or given unity but a historical category, a designation, we must think that for each aspect of social existence the same applies: class, race, sexuality. Each one person is captured by a plurality of categorizations, each of which works over, to reconfigure, the other categorizations. At the same time the dominant categorizations encounter and negotiate with historical residues, as well as emergent formations, which may be simply alternative or actively oppositional. Thus identities are not just plural (an idea typical of post-modern indifference). They are historical complexes of textured difference. The confrontations between imperial feminism and black feminists hinge on the misrecognition of the historical conditions of both attitudes. Feminism, a politics privileging gender, is the troubled effect of western bourgeois sexualization with its phony universals. The phrase "black women" can be read to emphasize women as the category and black as the qualifier, as a composite noun; or to put the stress on black as the category and woman as the minor term, qualified by belonging to a larger community of the diaspora. These are the registers of historical and political affiliations and experiences which speak of the necessity to grasp persons as living, specific configurations of historical placement around deeply and mutually interactive categorizations—race, class, gender—which are never discrete totalities, but complex formations operative as much at the level of psychic as of socio-economic construction.

body, signs and history

In 1986 Lubaina Himid produced a major installation work, *A Fashionable Marriage*. Her strategy for signifying her presence as an artist, and that of the political community she represents, is based not on essentialist notions of expression, but on historically and semiotically strategic plays with signs. She names this "gathering and re-using": "Gathering and re-using is an essential part of Black creativity, it does not mimic and it is inextricably linked to economic circumstance. Each piece within the piece has its own history, its own past and its own contribution to the new whole, the new function."[63] In the installation Himid uses large cut-outs, objects and paintings to rewrite creatively the scene of the Countess's Levée from the British eighteenth-century artist William Hogarth's series *Marriage á la Mode* (1745). That painting included an African man serving hot chocolate and a small African child unpacking various trophies of colonial theft. Recostuming each figure in contemporary identities, Himid's complex piece produced a discourse on history, politics and art, shifting these black presences from being traces of colonial violation to being the protagonists of contemporary historical consciousness. On the left side is the white British art establishment of critics, journalists and funding bodies, and attentively listening to them, a white feminist artist—a body compositely constructed through references to the work of Helen Chadwick, Susan Hiller and Mary Kelly. On the right side, Mrs Thatcher entertains her lover, Ronald Reagan, who offers an invitation to the Third World War as they recline beneath Picassoid replicas—themselves evidence of cultural appropriations definitive of modernism. The two key figures who stand as commentators and points of identification are the small child, unpacking now nuclear weapons, who represents a black consciousness of what is really going on, and the black feminist artist, positioned where the man serving chocolate had been; but now, instead of servicing the white feminist, the black feminist artist is standing resolutely apart, refusing to lend her energies to the careers of white art, because of the pressures of a real history.

This is a history piece, a work about and generically of that ambition the term "history painting" in the west signified. But is also has a connection with orature, an African discourse on history as a community's necessary and collective memory in the present. It speaks the urgency of the historical, at a moment when post-modernism is characterized as a loss of historicity, and of difficulty in mapping ourselves within a global capitalist order.[64] Indeed this insistence on the historical is claimed as a defining characteristic of contemporary black art practices by Gilane Tawadros. She puts post-modernism at a distance from black artists, following Habermas, who sees post-modernism's break with modernism as a mere feint, which leaves a continuity in western thought and power systems in place. Tawadros also argues that modernism banished history for a sense of timeless novelty and of modernity as the achievement and end of history. Importantly she sees the strategies of the artists she analyses as creating what she calls the "'populist modernism' of black cultural practice, which signals a critical appropriation of modernity which stems from the assertion of history and historical process."[65] Insisting on the ambivalence of identities and the impossibility of fixed boundaries, the artists she discusses—Lubaina Himid, Sutapa Biswas and Sonia Boyce—operate in a "zone of indiscernibility," "which does not attest to the primacy of difference and dispersion over and above historical and political exigencies."[66]

Himid's "Fashionable Marriage" makes the installation itself the site of work. It is an event in history as well as a critical representation of it. It is a multi-layered text there to be deciphered and read by the spectator, who must recognize and rework her identifications in the encounter with these large-scale figures. There is no sense of the privatized studio where meaning is traced on to inert matter by the creative subject. But there are representations of artists in this public space, embodiments of conflicted and antagonistic positions, placed in social, cultural and his-torical relations, not separated into discrete apartments of identity and expressivity.

The composite white feminist artist, located by this text inside the world of art, looking only to it and not to the wider historical emergency, is defined by traces of works by white feminist artists which deal above all with femininity and the configurations of the feminine body. This implies that strategic practices on signifying systems are somehow less historical and removed from political effect, are ultimately only modernist in their concern with intervening in a specific domain. But it has been one of the major effects of feminist theory and practice both to expand what is understood as political, and to grasp the realm and institutions of representation as decisive in social and historical formations of all constructions of difference.

One of the feminist practices critiqued in Lubaina Himid's "body of the feminist artist" is Mary Kelly's installation on the temporality of femininity, *Interim*, a work which examines the question of ageing. Including both these pieces here is not a move to create false continuities by finding common artistic tendencies. Both Himid and Kelly are obliged to generate signifying systems and signifying spaces by strategic intervention in the field of modernism, post-modernism and popular cultural forms. Lubaina Himid's popular is of course more extensive than western mass media, though African culture has been part of western modernism, and western mass media have colonized African culture. What the distinct practices of Mary Kelly and Lubaina Himid share is the necessity to locate their practice as an intervention in this historically constituted semiotic territory and its institutional sites.

Interim is a historical project which continues Mary Kelly's investigations of culture's *figurations* of femininity. In this piece she asks if being a woman is only one moment in our lives. She is examining "women's" relation to the ageing body, women entering a stage in their lives marked negatively by the culture's alignment of femininity with an image of either nubile sexuality or maternal bliss. What is our identity when our relation to the enunciations of femininity falter, and how has this been transformed by the lived histories of women since 1968? That is, what difference has feminism made?

Interim identifies four key themes which constitute enunciations of femininity: the body, money, power and history itself. The multi-part installations comprises perspex panels with silk-screened photographs of women's clothing arranged in styles which evoke the dominant discourses on the feminine body, fashion, medicine, romance; with galvanized steel greeting cards ironically and humorously reworking the sentimentality which mystifies women's life-cycles in their positions as mother, wife, daughter and sister; with steel books opened as in a newspaper library telling the stories of women who were aged 30, 20, 10 and 3 respectively in 1968; with monumental forms which schematically present UN statistics on gender and wealth, labour and population. At once spectacle and presence, the signifying space it generates refutes the pure visuality of modernist art. Like painting it provides striking and emblematic imageries. Like classic cinema its meanings build up by repetition and stylistic rhyme, plot and sub-plot, character and narrative, expressive *mise-en-scéne* and dramatic moment. Like sculpture with glinting surfaces and tactile forms, it plays with minimalist formalities and rebus-like assymmetries. Like Godard's social cinema it gives us snatches of lives and fragments of fantasies generated across familiar social spaces.

Interim provides no icons but many images, no single text but many textualities. In its totality, the project politically reconceptualizes the rhetorics of the highest of high modernisms as well as the spectacles of postmodern sign systems, and it is here that the decisively feminist intervention is made. Extruded from modernism, femininity was allied with popular culture, sharing its triviality, decorativeness and easy pleasure. Postmodernism has challenged the negative evaluation of popular culture by appropriating its forms as the signifying materials of a high art practice. Mary Kelly does not merely quote or recycle. She originates new forms, which defy the great divide and force both sides into politically explicit confrontation on the territory defined by feminism's insistent but critical enunciation of femininity. The work speaks of repressed femininities by evoking in the art gallery the reviled cultural forms of the woman's magazine or the supermarket, the doctor's waiting room or the pages of romantic fiction. The point is neither to celebrate nor to validate, a reversal of negative evaluations. The effect is to question both the anxieties and the pleasures of femininity as it is lived and as it has been politically reconstrued through political transformation of the category of "women" since 1968. Suspending the dichotomy between the masculine mystique of high culture and the pejoratively effeminate lures of popular culture, Mary Kelly maps the specific points at which the regime of sexual difference shapes both modernism and its post-modern offspring alike. This involves a specific theoretical input, linked, in the "History" section, to the growing interest in psychoanalysis within sections of the feminist community. "Sexual difference" is not a synonym for gender; it signals a conceptualization of human subjectivity which (1) helps understand the sexing of the subject—that is, that masculinity and femininity are psychic constructions—and (2) defines the human subject as split between conscious and unconscious. The latter makes it clear that the former, sexing, is incomplete and that all subjectivity is a construction fissured and unstable, shaped by the unconscious and desire. Feminist interest in psychoanalysis does not privilege sex over other forms of social oppression, but insists that we consider the level at which subjectivity is formed, and therefore the level and the mechanisms of identity which social formations operate across.[67]

The events staged by *Interim* and *A Fashionable Marriage* create "signifying spaces" for specific and distinct enunciations of both the political and the aesthetic. The phrase is Julia Kristeva's. In her essay "Woman's Time,"[68] she defines western feminism as being made up of three generations, two historically current, a third in the process of being imagined. The first generation campaigns for equal rights and legislative redress against discrimination in the name of women's human rights. A second, concurrent generation rejects political solutions and insists on the radical specificity of woman's difference, using art and literature to found a language for the "intrasubjective and corporeal experiences left mute in culture in the past." Either effacing the issue of difference or extravagantly insisting upon it in a kind of reverse sexism, this paradox can also be seen to shape debates on race and ethnicity. Kristeva wanted then to imagine a moment of feminism which will effect a radical questioning of the system by which all subjectivity, all identity, every sex is necessarily formed. That is to say that the division (the saga of separation and loss which produces the split unconscious/conscious condition we call subjectivity) is to be prised away from its self-presentation as a product of given sexual division, so that we can articulate the inevitable fact of difference not as binary opposition but as specificity and heterogeneity.

What this means is that such new significations will not emerge either from a repressed culture of those always-already women, nor from a position of radical alterity, outside the system. They can only be the effect of a calculated strategy of transgression of the system's own divisions and orders. For Kristeva, meaning is the product of a perpetual play between unity (those forces like the state, family, religion, which try to fix meanings to a particular arrangement of power) and process (the drives and semiotic potential of sound and form, which unity tries to harness to its systematization). Thus in any system there is both order and the possibility of disruption and transformation. Signifying practices such as a new kind of text or art-work mean "the acceptance of the symbolic law together with the transgression of that law for the purpose of renovating it."[69] This theory of meaning and change allows for little of either the affirmative or expressive theses of various feminist cultural practices.

Kristeva hailed certain avant-garde writing strategies as transgressive and made them synonymous with femininity as a patriarchal order's obvious negative. She failed to acknowledge that the heroic revolutions of modernism against the state, family and religion were executed in a concretely powerful system of sexual and racial power, so that the revolutions were effected only in the name of men, unable and unwilling seriously to dispute the basis of their own privilege. As neither modernism nor post-modernism, the women's movement, with its complex relations to both moments and cultures, intervenes in signifying practice as the historically necessary realization of Kristeva's reconceptualization of modernism. This is a possibility only now being generated or recognized in the practices of those women who mount a feminist intervention at the level of the textual, the subjective and the historical.

Kristeva attributes a particular significance to aesthetic practices—and not as a minor field colonized by feminism for women's edification. In the historical project of the resistance movements, we can counter the scars of imperial capitalism in culture, where modernism's utopian ambitions for renewal, change, unforeseen possibilities were stunted by their confinement to an imaginary realm of subjective freedom (the studio). Semiotic understanding of the place of signification in the process of power attributes a strategic function to aesthetic practices, which remain a necessary realm for individual enunciation and creation.

> It seems to me that the role of what is usually called "aesthetic practices" must increase not only to counterbalance the storage and uniformity of information by present day mass media, data-bank systems, and, in particular, modern communications technology, but also to demystify the identity of the symbolic bond itself, to demystify, therefore, the *community* of language as a universal and unifying tool, one which totalizes and equalizes. In order to bring out—along with the singularity of each person, and, even more, along with the multiplicity of every person's possible identifications … —the *relativity of his/her symbolic as well as biological existence,* according to the variation in her/his specific symbolic capacities.[70]

The ideological individualism of modernist culture gives way to an acknowledgement of a concrete historical singularity, itself both social and psychic, both symbolic and particular to a kind of existence of and in the body. Thus we achieve a sense of sexual particularity in lieu of being tied to bodies that are only allowed to speak of a monolithic difference. For Kristeva the socially produced and semiotically signified singularity of the subject is set up as an active agent against the galloping forces of modernization, the information society in which individuation is a means of administration of power. Overcoming the specializations through which modern society has oppressed its populations, aesthetic practices are necessarily allied to politics, not secreted in the studio escaping from contamination as the condition of defending the purity and purpose of art.[71]

The burden of Kristeva's piece, like the complex forms of feminist art practices, is to represent the stakes for feminism in terms of ambition clearly indebted to the project of modernity.[72] We cannot fail to sense the gravity of the undertaking nor the pleasures it promises. The debate for feminists involved in "aesthetic practices" cannot be reduced to a question of "painting" or scripto-visual forms. It is a historical project, an intervention in history, informed by historical knowledges, which means not forgetting, in the act of necessary critique, the history of western feminism.

notes

1 There is of course some representation of black women in western art, and a substantial iconography associated with sexual services and fantasized erotic scenarios. But it is indicative that in orientalist painting, for instance, where a

European and an African woman are represented in a harem or bathhouse, the two bodies are very differently treated to locate the white body as the object of desire. This point needs much more careful analysis and documentation than is possible here.

2 See R. Dyer, "White," *Screen*, 29 (1988), pp. 44–65, and *Heavenly Bodies* (Macmillan, London, 1986) for further analysis of the relations between femininity, whiteness and representation.

3 In the work of Sutapa Biswas for instance, "Housewives with Steakknives," the Hindu goddess Kali is represented to oppose western definitions of femininity as passive and powerless. On the notion of icons see Frederica Brooks, "Ancestral Links: The Art of Claudette Johnson," in Maud Sulter (ed.), *Passion: Discourse on Blackwomen's Creativity* (Urban Fox Press, Hebden Bridge, 1990), pp. 183–90; also quoted in Lubaina Himid (ed.), *Claudette Johnson: Pushing Back the Boundaries* (Rochdale Art Gallery, Rochdale, 1990), p. 5. See also Maud Sulter, "Zabat: Poetics of a Family Tree," in Sulter, *Passion*, pp. 91–105.

4 Claudette Johnson, quoted in Himid, *Claudette Johnson*, p. 2.

5 Clement Greenberg, "American-type Painting," *Art and Culture* (Beacon Press, Boston, Mass., 1961), p. 208.

6 On the notion of the artistic subject as the subject of art see Griselda Pollock, "Artists, Mythologies and Media," *Screen*, 21 (1980), pp. 57–96, reprinted in Philip Hayward (ed.), *Picture This: Media Representations of Visual Art and Artists* (John Libbey, London, 1988), pp. 75–114.

7 That this operation was Eurocentric is specified by Rasheed Areen in *The Other Story* (Hayward Gallery, London, 1989); that his challenge to a white hegemony in modernism remains masculinist underscores the sexual politics of this formation. See Rita Keegan, "The Story So Far," *Spare Rib*, February 1990; Sutapa Biswas, "The Wrong Story," *New Statesman*, 15 December 1990, pp. 41–2.

8 For an extensive analysis of this typical art school ideology, see Terry Atkinson, "Phantoms of the Studio," *Oxford Art Journal*, 13 (1990), pp. 49–62.

9 Michéle Barrett, "The Concept of Difference," *Feminist Review*, 26 (1987), pp. 29–42.

10 R. Parker and G. Pollock, *Old Mistresses: Women, Art and Ideology* (Pandora, London, 1981), p. 147.

11 This can be understood in one of two ways. Taken in terms of communication, it suggests that social practice and use invest things or sounds or images with the capacity to function as tokens of exchange between members of a group or system. These tokens are bearers of value and significance; meaning is produced by them in a transaction that involves the receiver as much as the sender. Taken in stricter semiotic terms, the idea of signification excludes the sender and receiver as agents of making meaning and throws meaning on to the effect of the chains of signifiers, which produce positions for us to occupy as speakers (I, you, he, she, it). Thus man,

woman, artist, are not meaningful because of a relation to, a reference from sound or word to, something already there, with its innate meaning, but only in their relations as signifiers within a system. That system then defines us as we occupy the places, the terms, that it sets. The signifying systems are not abstract or a historical, but the place where the culture, the social system is, as it were, written and thus writes itself upon us as both its users and its effects. See Christine Weedon, *Feminist Practice and Post-structuralist Theory* (Basil Blackwell, Oxford, 1987).

12   Mary Kelly, "Reviewing Modernist Criticism," *Screen*, 22: 3 (1981), pp. 41–62; p. 57.

13   Jacqueline Rose, "Sexuality in the Field of Vision," in Rose, *Sexuality in the Field of Vision* (Verso Books, London, 1986), pp. 225–34.

14   Ibid., p. 231.

15   Ibid., p. 232.

16   The female nude had become in early modernist art the image for the ambitious artist to dominate and excel with. Modernists continue to perform this initiation ritual: Manet's *Olympia*, Picasso's *Demoiselles d'Avignon*, Matisse's *The Blue Nude*, De Konning's *Woman* series, F. N. Souza's *Black Nude* and so forth.

17   Mel Gooding, *The Experience of Painting* (Arts Council, London, 1988), p. 2.

18   Ibid.

19   See J. Kristeva, "Women's Time" (1979), in T. Moi (ed.), *The Kristeva Reader* (Basil Blackwell, Oxford, 1986), pp. 186–213.

20   Gillian Ayres, statement, in Gooding, *The Experience of Painting*, p. 13.

21   Ibid.

22   Jürgen Habermas, "Modernity—An Incomplete Project," in Hal Foster (ed.), *The Anti-Aesthetic: Essays in Postmodern Culture* (Bay Press, Townsend, Wash., 1983), pp. 3–15; p. 9.

23   This brilliant insight into women's perpetual fate in art was first developed by the late Buzz Goodbody in a lecture at Bedford College, London, in 1973.

24   Charles Harrison, "The Experience of Painting," *Artscribe International*, 75 (1989), pp. 75–7; p. 76.

25   I define post-modernity as the socio-economic and ideological processes which currently define our horizons. Post-modernity refers to an epochal shift, whereas post-modernism refers to the cultural forms generated in this larger social transformation, which are the site for both affirmative and critical cultural responses to post-modernity. The distinctions are drawn from Clive Dilnot, "What is the Post-modern?" *Art History*, 9: 2 (1986), pp. 245–63, and Hal Foster, "Postmodernism: A Preface," in Foster, *The Anti-Aesthetic*, pp. ix–xvi.

26   In 1939 Clement Greenberg wrote a mighty defence of the avant-garde culture threatened by fascism, in terms which implicitly feminize the masses and the ersatz culture, kitsch, which capitalism served up to them: "Avant-garde and Kitsch," in Greenberg, *Art and Culture*, pp. 3–21.

27 Andreas Huyssen, "Mass Culture as Woman: Modernism's Other," in Huyssen, *After the Great Divide: Modernism, Mass Culture and Postmodernism* (Macmillan, London, 1986), pp. 44–64; p. 58.

28 Ibid., p. 55.

29 Ibid., p. 62.

30 Ibid., p. 59.

31 Of course it was never really lost to high culture and makes a major reappearance in surrealist discourse, and again after Greenbergian modernism by means of pop art's deceitful appropriations of comics and movie stars. Post-modernism represents yet another way high art has tried to get back to the feminine body— but only by confirming that mass culture is now almost synonymous with it.

32 I use the term here to mean the production of meaning by the production of new means to produce meaning. Most theories of art are referential, using terms like reflect or express, or even represent. These imply that there is something, a person, a thing, a world, with its already formed meaning, which art, as a secondary system, reflects, expresses or re-presents. Signification is a theory that argues that meanings are produced by the relation of signifiers, sounds or letters, in systems. Meaning is produced for the world, not derived from it. Feminism does not merely express already known meanings that real women know. As a movement we are making new meanings, enunciating, from a specific place and historical condition in the world, a femininity that has to be signified.

33 Alice Jardine, "At the Threshold: Feminists and Modernity," *Wedge*, 6 (1984), pp. 10–17; Gayatri Chakravorty Spivak, "Imperialism and Sexual Difference," *Oxford Literary Review*, 8 (1986), pp. 225–39.

34 Craig Owens, "The Discourse of Others: Feminists and Postmodernism," in Foster, *The Anti-Aesthetic*, pp. 57–82.

35 Many of these artists are specifically concerned with issues of identity, race, class, imperialism. I do not mean to subsume these within feminism, but hopefully to suggest that feminism is a variable term, not the property of those who privilege gender over everything. The meanings of feminism are constantly being expanded by women as they politically reconceive that identity in relation to other formations of power and consciousness.

36 See Kelly, "Reviewing Modernist Criticism," p. 45.

37 Sarah Kent, "Feminism and Decadence," *Artscribe*, 47 (1984), pp. 54–61; p. 61.

38 Sarah Kent, "An Introduction," *Rosa Lee* (Todd Gallery, London, 1990), n. p.

39 Rosa Lee, "Resisting Amnesia: Feminism, Painting and Postmodernism," *Feminist Review*, 26 (1987), pp. 5–27; p. 25.

40 Ibid., p. 24.

41 The issue of black women and visibility in relation to modernist and oppositional cultures was proposed by Michelle Wallis in her response at the panel "Firing the Canon," College Art Association, New York, 18 February, 1990.

42 Denise Riley, *Am I that Name? Feminism and the Category of "Women" in History* (Macmillan, London, 1988), p. 111.

43 Gilane Tawadros, "Beyond the Boundary: The Work of Three Black Women Artists in Britain," *Third Text*, 8/9 (1989), pp. 121–50; pp. 122–3.

44 Stuart Hall, "New Ethnicities," in *ICA Documents 7: Black Film/British Cinema* (Institute of Contemporary Arts, London, 1988), p. 29, cited Tawadros, "Beyond the Boundary," p. 123.

45 Denise Riley, *Am I that Name?*, p. 99.

46 Katy Deepwell, "In Defence of the Indefensible: Feminism, Painting and Post-Modernism," *Feminist Art News*, 2 (1987), pp. 9–12; p. 9.

47 Painting is thus simultaneously a medium, an expressive resource, an institutional practice, a critical category, a form of economic investment, a curatorial term and a symbolic system. Any analysis which selects only one of the inter-related facets, such as medium or resource of expression, is smuggling back a covert form of modernism.

48 Deborah Cherry, *Painting Women: Victorian Women Artists* (Rochdale Art Gallery, Rochdale, 1987); soon to be published in an expanded, book-length study.

49 History means more than an authoritative narrative of events. History stands for three things: first, an archive, what a culture remembers. It matters what is in the archive and how it is recorded. History refers to remembering what has been happening. History refers to a context, a way of understanding where we are, because there has been a process creating the present conditions, forces and problems. This makes for historical consciousness. But this is not a consciousness of change as progress and development, some alibi for the present. History also means understanding discontinuity and fracture; it also implies recognizing continuities where we seem to see change. Post-modernism itself may be one such delusion. Feminism is a historical event, but it has historical conditions, knowledge of which we need to inform current practices and decisions. History then is strategic understanding of location and the stakes.

50 The statement is taken from Denise Riley's paper, "Does Sex have a History?" reprinted in her *Am I that Name?*, pp. 1–17.

51 See Tamar Garb, "L'Art Féminin: The Creation of a Cultural Category in Late Nineteenth Century France," *Art History*, 12 (1989), pp. 39–65.

52 It is significant that so many women of the early twentieth century emigrated to Paris, the city of modernism, where through some aspects of its precocious metropolitanism they could have access to a serious art education, exhibition and a literary culture. Gwen John is only one of the better-known artists who joined the phenomenon Shari Benstock called *The Women of the Left Bank* (Virago Press, London, 1987). Modern Paris also hosted a protest against the heterosexuality of the overfeminized bourgeois societies that women artists and writers fled.

There were many Afro-American women who were drawn to its modernist spaces.

53   Bill Williams, "The Anti-semitism of Tolerance: Middle Class Manchester and the Jews 1870–1900," in A. J. Kidd and K. W. Roberts (eds), *City, Class and Culture* (Manchester University Press, Manchester, 1985), pp. 74–102.

54   This argument has resurfaced in the challenge recently made by the exhibition *The Other Story*, curated and introduced by Rasheed Areen, Hayward Gallery, London, 1989. Critics found themselves unable to negotiate the worlds of art and the worlds fissured by racism: to be taken seriously as artists, critics advised artists to forget their skin colour—the key term. No idea of the arguments about hegemonies, ethnicities, cultural imperialism, "coloured" (a term advisedly used) the mainstream critics discourse. There was art without colour, there was colour without art. The point Rasheed Areen intended to make was that they interfaced historically in the production of art by Asian and Afro-Caribbean artists and politically in negative appraisal by white critics.

55   Cindy Nemser, *Art Talk: Conversations with Twelve Women Artists* (Charles Scribner, New York, 1975).

56   Anne Wagner, "Lee Krasner as L. K.," *Representations*, 25 (1989), pp. 42–57, is an excellent study of the contradictions of women and modernism through the case of Leonore Krasner, alias Mrs Jackson Pollock and latterly a celebrated figure in the feminist canon.

57   Clement Greenberg, "Louis and Nolan," *Art International*, IV (1960), pp. 27–30; p. 28.

58   See Parker and Pollock, *Old Mistresses: Women, Art and Ideology*, pp. 145–51.

59   I have elsewhere argued precisely that modernism is to be read as a sexual politics at all levels including the technical and aesthetic devices and use of space and facture. But the increasing pre-eminence given to such apparently neutral facets of an artistic process serve to efface the sexual order they represent, and the only visible evidence is the persistent celebration of artistic "mastery." See my "Modernity and the Spaces of Femininity" in Griselda Pollock, *Vision and Difference* (Routledge, London, 1988), pp. 50–90. This problem is reflected in the unevenness of feminist art history as a whole. Certain periods have solicited thorough-going analyses of women's practice in art and their relation to institutions as much as their use of imagery, composition and relation therefore to ideology and meaning. Sexuality and gender can be complexly discussed for the art of the Victorian period, but what does a feminist say when confronted with a woman's practice in mainstream modernist abstract painting, such as that of Gillian Ayres, Britain's leading exponent?

60   In 1963 Betty Friedan wrote of "the problem that has no name" in her famous, silence-breaking book, *The Feminine Mystique* (Bantam Books, New York, 1963).

61 Toril Moi, "Feminism, Postmodernism and Style: Recent Feminist Criticism in the United States," *Cultural Critique*, 9 (1988), pp. 3–22; p. 6.

62 Valerie Amos and Pratibha Parmar, "Challenging Imperial Feminism," *Feminist Review*, 17 (1984), pp. 3–20; pp. 9–12.

63 Lubaina Himid, "Fragments," *Feminist Art News*, 2 (1988), pp. 8–9; p. 8.

64 F. Jameson, "Postmodernism, or the Cultural Logic of Late Capitalism," *New Left Review*, 146 (1984), pp. 53–93.

65 Tawadros, *Beyond the Boundary*, p. 150.

66 Ibid.

67 For instance, see Homi K. Bhabha's use of the psychoanalytical category of fetishism in relation to the power and effects of the colonial stereotype, "The Other Question—the Stereotype and Colonial Discourse," *Screen*, 24: 6 (1983), pp. 18–36.

68 Kristeva, "Women's Time," pp. 186–213.

69 Julia Kristeva, "The System and the Speaking Subject" (1973), in Moi, *The Kristeva Reader*, pp. 24–33; p. 29.

70 Kristeva, "Women's Time," p. 210.

71 "At this level of interiorization with its social as well as individual stakes, what I have called 'aesthetic practices' are undoubtedly nothing other than the modern reply to the eternal question of morality" (ibid.).

72 The phrase indicates the thesis of Jürgen Habermas, "Modernity—An Incomplete Project" in H. Foster (1987), pp. 3–15.

abandoned at the mouth of hell or a second look that does not kill: the uncanny coming to matrixial memory 6

griselda pollock

Our civilisation is going through a depression … We intellectuals must seek out the causes of this discontent, this is not the time for advice. It is the moment for diagnosis … I believe the moment of militancy is over and we are living in a therapeutic age in which we must face up to our problems.

Julia Kristeva[1]

I have told of the desert through the indestructible memory of the void whose every grain is a tiny mirror.

Edmond Jabès[2]

After Auschwitz there is only ash, desert, effacement, ruin, and nothingness, but each of these catastrophes, each of these voids, has its own way of being reflected, being spoken, and of being remembered, in the always open and forever unfinished book.

Richard Stamelman[3]

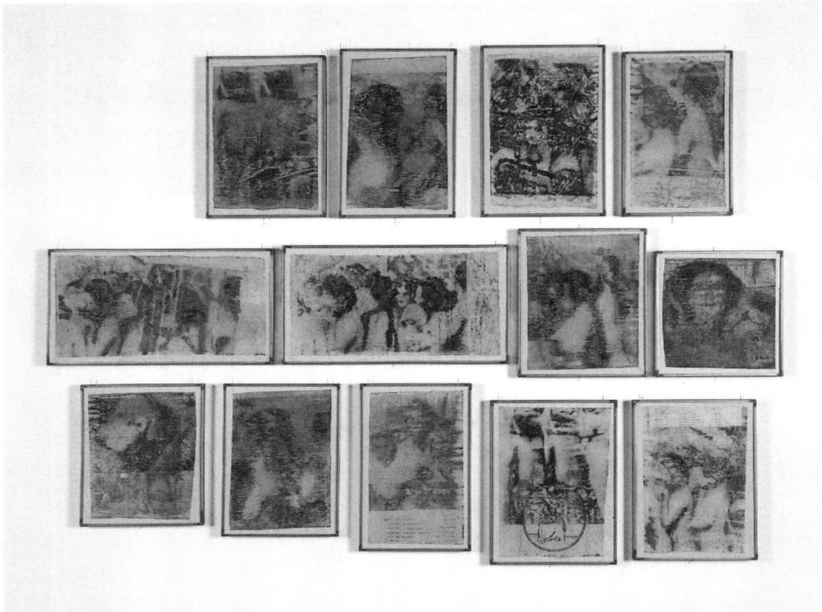

Figure 1.   Bracha Lichtenberg Ettinger, *Eurydice*, 1992–6. Installation *Face á L'Histoire*, Paris, Centre Pompidou 1996–7.

a desert in theory: amnesia, foreclosure and the matrixial gaze

I have long been fascinated by Izak Dinesen's short story, "The Blank Page" which tells of a curious museum of "women's art," a convent in which are hung the framed squares of pure linen sheets from the nuptial beds of royalty and aristocracy that bear virginity-proving blood beneath armorial bearings and plates declaring great dynastic names. But one canvas stands apart and merits special notice. It attracts more gazes, and incites the most profound contemplation. "The frame is as fine as any, and as proudly carries the golden plate with the royal crown. But on this plate no name is inscribed and the linen within the frame is snow-white from corner to corner—a blank page."[4] As the feminist critic Susan Gubar argues, within such a gallery of "women's art," what does not enter signification "in blood" via the circuits of woman as object, appears blank.[5]

Yet it is by the unswerving loyalty to that paradox that the women who visit the gallery are moved to the most profound contemplation of other stories that might be traced upon an only *apparently* uninscribed surface, that might be projected upon the always open screen of the blank page in the book of women and memory. It is through that which offers no representation to vision—no object to the mastery of sight—that another kind of psychically affecting gaze peeps through, to touch, move and surprise rather than capture the viewer, in an exchange with the unknown and unknowable, unnamed other, whose non-presence is not absence, although, through the still unmarked bed sheet, this other "she" will never belong to the unitary, phallic order of meaning production that can only make sense through absolute oppositions such as either/or, present/absent, used/virginal, self/other, mark/no mark. Perceived *inside the visible* emptiness, "it"—a non-phallic field of meaning and affect—impinges across the threshold of the subjectivities, the viewers of the blank page, who are called into co-emergence and changed at that borderline with this other, unknown feminine.

> In that open space of conjunction of presence and absence, where transgressions of visuality, where "a rhythm, beat or pulse … acts against the stability of visual space in a way that is destructive and devolutionary (where) the beat has the power to compose and dissolve the very coherence of form on which visuality may be thought to depend" [Krauss], where inside/outside pulsational scansion leads to absence and repetition as primary meaning-engendering instances, the matrixial gaze creates ontogenetic interconnectivity as a sub-symbolic meaning of borderlinks and shareability, … leading to the enigma of the meaning of *shareability of trauma and phantasy*, and the *co-response-ability* with the unknown Other.[6]

The metaphor of the "blank page" brilliantly creates a multiple image, hinged both to the blankness that veils female dissidence in the phallocentric text and to the possibility of meanings otherwise that press from behind upon its heterogeneous, pulsational surface, to reach out and lure another kind of awed, shocked, wondering, uncanny looking and response that we might hypothesize contacts the nonvisible, nonphallic strata of subjectivity.[7] Solacing in the annulment of a mastering gaze, this non-image displaces the politics of the optical and the visible that are the foundations of a phallic order and touches another kind of place "inside the visible."

The "blank page" reconnects art to the materiality of its practice as a nonvisual trace of a sexed bodily referent. Thus might we imagine it as an allegory of the invisible specificity of a feminine body that moves from materiality (canvas/touch) to Symbolic (word/thought) without the disfiguring fantasy of the imaginary/image—"of Woman," or of the bloodied sign of her wounded, castrated condition under patriarchal logic. It stains the spot where women's marks and meanings appear unreadable according to the dominant narratives of art, art history, modernity and Modernism, while, to a differently tuned "eroticised psychic aerials" (the phrase is Bracha Lichtenberg Ettinger's) that seek "inside the visible" for the index to dissident meanings, lives and traces of other configurations of the subject and the body, the surface is rich in possibilities for anyone desiring to decipher there "inscriptions of the feminine" as dissidence, difference and heterogeneity.

In the short story, the "blank page" survives not only in the convent's museum of women's art, but in the storyteller's art: "Where the story-teller is loyal, eternally and unswervingly loyal to the story, there, in the end, silence will speak. Where the story has been betrayed, silence is but emptiness."[8] Bracha Lichtenberg Ettinger's work touches the question of speaking of silence and producing "images of absence"[9]: that which blanks out the feminine at a structural level in Western culture, and that which has muffled the anguish and the horror of the Holocaust. But none of this is emptiness; it is not-yet signified, or rather, it hovers at the limits of signification awaiting some filter for its affects to traverse that threshold without ever being able to be contained with existing signs. In the later twentieth century questions of the oblivion of the feminine and of the Jewish experience in Western culture converge at the unexpected crossing point of feminist theory and painting.

Luce Irigaray and Hélène Cixous have written eloquently of women's need to imagine new signifiers that would allow a feminine Imaginary and a feminine Symbolic to be effective parts of the culture that, at present, leaves women in exile, in dereliction, in the wilderness of a blanked out page.[10] Writing the body (Cixous's *écriture féminine*), or drawing images from the morphology of the female form (Irigaray) cannot be collapsed into empirical anatomy—visible fact. Both theorists/poets accept that the body provides some irreducible materiality for psychic experience. But that bodilyness is always semiotically mediated, unconsciously imagined, lived, experienced through the defiles of a range of significations from the most archaic pictograms up through fantasy to fully Symbolic, linguistically communicable thought.[11] These ranges are in constant interplay.

The question is, as Bracha Lichtenberg Ettinger argues, whether we have the filters necessary to allow transfer between these strata of subjectivity, from the archaic, almost in contact with the Real, through to the levels of phantasy (the Imaginary) and thought (the Symbolic). Under a phallic Symbolic, we lack signifiers for feminine otherness within a system of meanings exclusively organized around a single, sovereign signifier, the Phallus. Thus, as Lacan confusingly, but correctly, stated: in such a system, there can be no sexual relation because phallic thought allows no other sex except the One and that which is not the One, its Other.

The feminist problematic—and where else but painting might it be explored?—is the process of inventing such semiotic resources that enable us to read through the screen of "the blank page." Thus feminine corporeal specificity and the fantasies through which it is traced within our psyches might become signifiable for us, to us, and to our cultures that will be radically altered by this realignment through this as yet unthought feminine difference.

Such a project can be linked to the larger feminist encounter between theory and creativity. It puts in place, however, another feminist possibility that is both less positivist and celebratory than the Cixousian call to women to write their "sexts."[12] It is, moreover, better able to theorize, and thus access, the possible resources for a recognition of the feminine that we do not yet know as a vital and necessary condition for radical change to our world, riven by forms of intolerance of the Other: the hatreds of class antagonism, racism, antisemitisim, sexual violence and homophobia.

The political languages of protest against exploitation, domination and discrimination are well developed. The means of imagining and articulating other models of enounter between subjects, between social groups, between forms of difference hardly exist. This is because most political languages are, at their fundamental and structural level, phallic: they think about the world only in terms such as Either/Or, With us/Against Us, One of us/One of them. Fascism is an extreme realization of this model. So is modernity, as Zygmunt Bauman has argued in his revealing study of modernity's terror at ambivalence.[13] This is not to reduce the social and political to the psychic. The formations of subjectivity, however, shape our means of understanding the world and its fantasies infiltrate our political imaginations. To speak of the phallic does not refer to men; it signifies a way of thinking that is structured by paradigms of assimilation or exclusion, love or hate, incorporation or rejection, like or unlike, presence or absence, on/off, either/or. For Lacan, the phallic is "neutral" in so far as this signifier organizes all subjectivity under the law of castration which retrospectively redefines all gaps, separations, differences, foreclosing the feminine from the realm of meaning and rendering it as inaccessible to women as it is to men. In her major theoretical revolution that leans upon but radically challenges the phallocentrism of Lacan, Bracha Lichtenberg Ettinger goes beyond all existing feminist critiques of phallocentrism's repression of an already imagined feminine Other to propose a an expanded and shifted Symbolic, the *matrixial,* based on a symbol for the unsignified feminine difference, the **Matrix**.

the matrix

The Matrix is a symbol, just as the Phallus is in the theory of Jacques Lacan. Here a symbol is never a symbol **of** something; it has no intrinsic meaning; it is a signifier. As signifier, a symbol like Matrix or Phallus is a term in a system by which meaning is produced through the play of difference among signifiers. As a symbol, Matrix allows into discourse a stratum of human subjectivization framed by the invisible specificity of the feminine body, a subjectivity based on encounter, not castration/splitting. It is, therefore, not a symbol of the feminine body as the very idea of the body imago is already phallic. The Matrix permits the structural effects and fantasy-generating possibilities of the invisible specificity of the feminine body as encountered by its then unknown other to be signified for a subject, since a signifier is a subject for another signifier and we are subjects only through the work of the signifiers.

A symbol is a form; its content or referents derive from archaic and later imaginary affects governed by what analysts call pictograms: like on/off; absent/present; love/hate, and, later by phantasy, and finally by thought.[14] None of these strata is related to perceptual reality. All human subjects, men as much as women, carry traces of their encounter with the invisible specificity of the feminine body from the most archaic moments when they

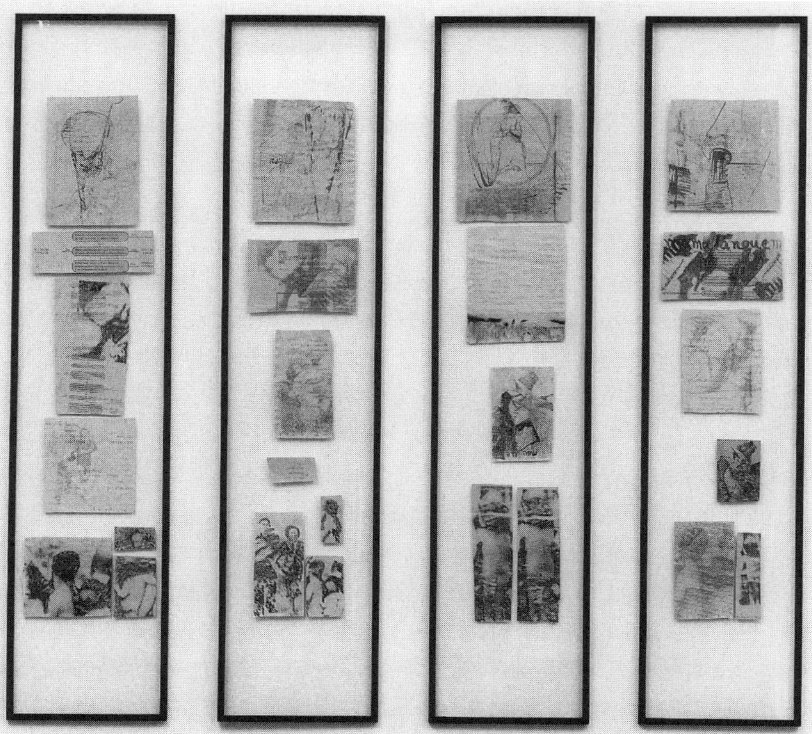

Figure 2.   Bracha Lichtenberg Ettinger, *Matrixial Borderline*, 1990–91. Polyptych, 4 panels of ensembles composed with 25 elements, (4×) 160 × 35 cm, India ink, pencil, pastel and photocopy on paper, plexiglass.

were but protosubjects. The Matrix serves to hypothesize affects persisting from this stratum that concern a relational borderline between mutually unknown and unknowable entities, which Bracha Lichtenberg Ettinger names "I" and "non-I."

The Matrix is not a sign of women, but a means to signify the plurality and severality which constitutes the specificity of the feminine that monistic, either/or phallic culture has excluded, allowing no pathway except into psychosis or hallucination for the sensations or pictograms that might yield a paradigm "in the feminine" for this mutually affecting and jointly subjectizing encounter between several (part) subjects, for subjectivity as an encounter that does not have to choose between I and non-I.

Bracha Lichtenberg Ettinger is a major feminist theorist in the field of psychoanalysis. But she is an artist and and it was in her daily contemplation of her own painting that the initial sights that were later transposed to and reframed as psychonalytical theory first emerged. She has written:

> The work of art does not illustrate or establish theory; theory can only partly cover—uncover—the work of art. Sometimes the work of art produces seeds of theory from which, upon elaboration, art slips away. These seeds should be sown elsewhere. The most graceful moments in the covenant between art and theory occur when theoretical elements, only indirectly or partly intended for particular works of art, and visual elements which refuse theory, collide. In doing so they may transform the borderline between the two domains so that art is momentarily touched by theory while theory takes on new meaning.[15]

Thus art and theory enter a matrixial covenant which sometimes requires each to follow its own path but in the understanding of a fundamental joint-ness. What is lost to the one, painting, when it is spoken of, may be refound in another revelation in the space of theory; while what is not possible to imagine theoretically may be lured into understanding in the borderspace of mutual transformation at the encounter with painting, which is never just the image, just the visible. Theory is not the doctor of art, the latter being the patient in need of diagnosis and explanation. Neither is art the cure for our overindulgence in theory.

In painting and its poetic reflection in her *Carnets*, Bracha Lichtenberg Ettinger witnessed this dimension of joint recordings across time and place, beyond memory, in the probing of private and social amnesia for those lost in the catastrophe named *Shoah*—the near destruction of European Jewish civilisation between 1933 and 1945. Before I address the distinctive role of painting created by the artist for this encounter with what the artist has named "une mémoire de l'oubli," we must travel a little further into her theoretical elaboration of the Matrix for art.[16]

the matrixial gaze

The Matrixial Gaze takes a radical step beyond the impasse of current feminist theories of the gaze, the image, and the feminine by working through late Lacanian theories of the Real and phantasy, and by shifting a feminist

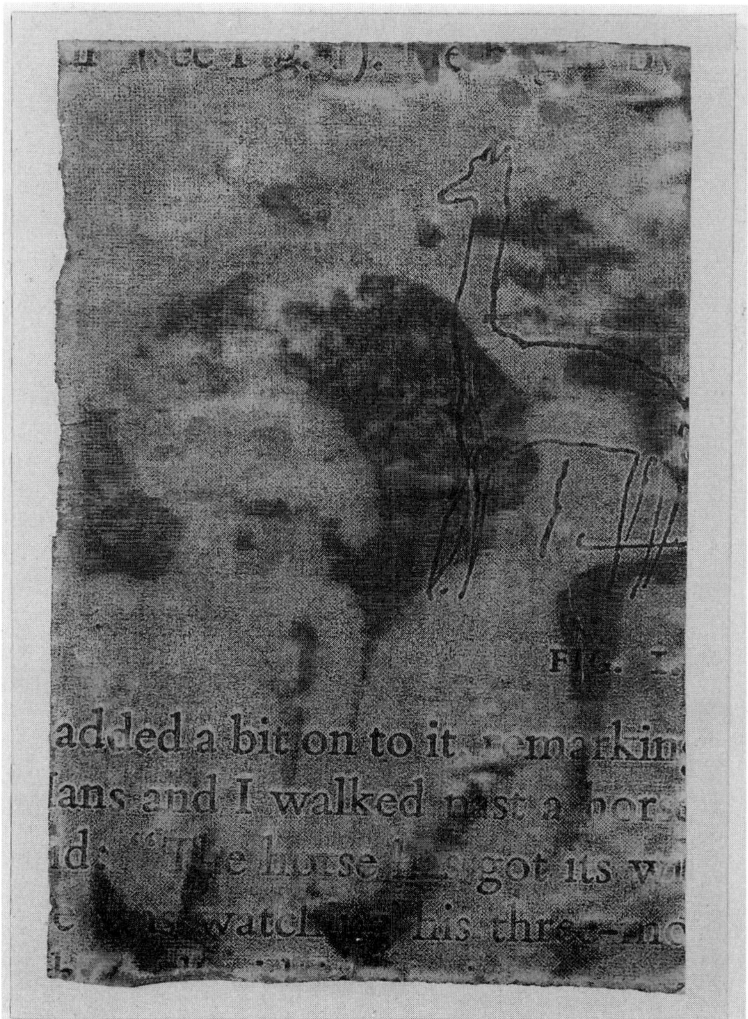

Figure 3.   Bracha Lichtenberg Ettinger, *Eurydice*, no. 1. 1992–94. 39 × 25.5 cm. (mounted on chassis: 41.8 × 28.8 cm), oil and xerox on paper mounted on canvas.

perspective from the cinematic apparatus that seems to illustrate so perfectly the post-Oedipal, post-castration, "armed" gaze of mastery towards another kind of visual tactility specific to post-modern painting and relevant to a feminist intervention in painting's traditions.

Bracha Lichtenberg Ettinger distinguishes several possibilities of the gaze: the Oedipal, the phallic and the matrixial. What feminist theory has identified—and got stuck with—as the "male gaze" is this: *Oedipal castration* focuses sight and turns vision into an ordering, selecting, separating or unifying function. "Being in focus, the 'armed eye' can now 'take aim at the target' and 'claim omnipotent and ominscient Knowledge.' The gaze which has thus been civilised by the means of the Oedipus complex is a conscious, alienating, cultural tool of power, in the service of the Ego."[17]

Behind the *Oedipal* gaze, Lacan identified another, what can be named the phallic gaze, which means the gaze as a phallic *objet a*. This odd formulation, *objet a*, refers to lost part-objects and the archaic m/other [mother/other] that are forever unattainable, but once hovered on the borderlines of corporeal, sensory and perceptive zones. The *objet a* puts into play the lacks that generate the subject in desire before an Oedipal ordering of sexual difference organized around the idea of castration that then sets up sexual difference in its own, phallic have/have-not image. Translate the yearning for the gaze as *objet a* into everyday speech. What is it that we look for, try to see, long to feel rather than see, or momentarily feel we might have glimpsed that gives us intense pain and pleasure, perhaps when we look at painting, or search another's face in love? Before the Oedipal gaze that masters, positions, possesses, dominates, there is the phallic gaze as a lost *objet a*. It is, in part, a fantasy of the mother's gaze. Yet if we found it, the experience would be profoundly shocking, unsettling, uncanny. The maternal gaze, disappeared into the phallic gaze as *objet a*, functions as a lost part of the intimated self, and hence the site of desire, that gives rise to **unconscious** fantasies of comfort/solace in relation to the visual, which are not focused. They are not about what we see, thus about representaton of objects. Neither are they about being seen, exhibitionism. They play over the gap between active seeing and the passive receiving of a look. We might then imagine the gaze being like an almost tactile envelope, an embrace, a sensorial, corporeal environment that, being lost as we separate from the mother, is fantasied, in retrospect, as if it had been once possessed as an object. (It never was and only acquires this almost objectified status after the event, which is, in part, what makes it, by definition, unrepresentable, beyond representation, its limit, and yet structural to the subject's formation because that experience of a gap, a loss is what presses us through the defiles of the signifier to become a speaking subject.)

Bracha Lichtenberg writes:

> If exposure to the gaze by which painting attracts us also "touches" us and soothes something in us, if painting as a manifestation of the gaze satisfies something in us as spectators, then a specific appetite unique and fatal to the eye as a zone separated from its part-object unconsciously tapers the gaze as its point of support. There is a scopic appetite whose tantalizing prey is the gaze … . The imaginary "evil eye" as a revelation of the phallic *objet a* of the gaze is on the borderline of appearance. Appearance is a screen that hides the gaze, and the enigmatic powers of art are not competing with that screen, but with what is beyond it.[18]

Bracha Lichtenberg argues, however, that even with this modification we are still unable to imagine an ordering of meaning, fantasy and desire outside the phallic paradigm which retroactively names all desire, all loss, all separation in its own model: on/off, either/or: castration. She wants to track a matrixial *objet a* connected to yet another kind of gaze.

> The matrixial (*objet a* of the) gaze is between shared *thing* and lost object, belonging to plural-partial subjectivity … in the matrixial stratum of subjectivisation modelled upon feminine/prenatal relations we cannot speak of alternation between absence/presence, but, instead, of continual attuning and readjustments of distance-in-proximity. This creates primary meanings as borderlinks, as becoming-with, as shareability and differentiation-in-co-emergence, and not as absence related to an invisible figure of difference, not even as an in/out nor as an on/off scansion that is always linked to the subjects as One versus the Other, and transformation as castration. Through the matrixial gaze that approaches me in painting, I am transformed by *it* only in so far as it is transformed by me.[19]

Our current concepts of sexual difference are phallic—so Woman is the *off* term: not-man, castrated, lacking, or just unnameably beyond, *jouissance*, Other, *Thing*, *objet a* for a man: the sublime blankness of the blank page perhaps. Structurally, therefore, the feminine is positioned only as the opposite or negative of the phallic. This means *nothing*. But Bracha Lichtenberg Ettinger wants to suggest that this *nothing* is not just any *nothing*. Like the so-called Blank Page, this *nothing* is all that we can currently imagine as the specificity of the feminine. By "feminine" I do not invoke some biological or psychological, essential nature of women. Neither do I mean the abstract linguistic positionality conceived by post-structuralist thought. What Bracha Lichtenberg wants to suggest by taking on the *nothing* that phallic thought barely acknowledges is that the feminine might signify a possible system of meaning and subjectivity that runs along beneath, subjacent to the phallic, yet foreclosed—i.e., closed out without a means of being known—by a Symbolic that is ruled by the single and sovereign signifier, the Phallus.

The phallic paradigm models the subject on the opposition of One and the Other. The legend of being a subject is the story of those cuts which separate out the symbiotic or autistic infant into singularity: weaning from the breast, from the image, and accessing it to language via castration anxiety. Phallocentricism produces identification fantasies and repulsion fantasies that later inform the political relations to difference: sexism, racism, homophobia. What is like me, I incorporate or identify with. What is not like me, cannot be like me and is other. It must be rejected as threatening to my own integrity as subject. Any encounter or change caused by the other registers as potential "castration" i.e., damage to this narcissistic fantasy of the unified subject.

The *model* of later pregnancy, however, provides an *image*, and I stress model and image over any delusion of simple fact (even though the corporeal trace of the Real is belatedly effective within the psyche that will later reclaim it), of a moment when part-subjects—mother and mature baby *in utero* do not confront each other as whole objects or as differentiated subjects—coexisted unknown to each other, but without either rejection or assimilation, in relations that can only be called non-phallic. This stratum of the several who are constantly and creatively changed by their co-existence comes before the conflictual model of subject as One versus Other, which is not only phallic but Oedipal. The matrixial addresses a moment of difference that is not pre-Oedipal, but frankly non-Oedipal for it is not based on absence versus presence, but suggests a sensationally and imaginatively co-determining subjectivity. In later prenatal moments, there is a minimum of difference for the two part-subjects are other, unknown to each other, so this is not a phallic image of cozy symbiosis. Yet they share a space across whose thresholds mutually subjectivizing effects are passing. These may be active for the mother-to-be, and implied for the infant-to-be. The becoming-mother fantasizes; the becoming-infant registers and garners in the last period of uterine life an array of sensations that, post-partum, may function as the resource for the drives and later inscription as fantasies and thought "*in/of the feminine*". But in a phallic system there are no signifiers or images retroactively to capture this dimension of archaic sensation and drag it across the signifying threshold into memory, fantasy and understanding that could radically realign the way we imagine social as well as sexual difference. It remains only as a threat of psychosis, a hallucination or it may be what touches us uncannily in the encounter with art.

Puzzling over the lures and pleasures associated with art works where the paradox of a visibile tactility that touches the internal organization of the drive through materiality and structure (a post-modern, post-abstract painting for instance) rather than through representation (i.e., content or image) might allow us to recognize what Lichtenberg Ettinger has named, using the Latin term for womb, **Matrix.** The matrixial is not a place—a container image like Julia Kristeva's or Plato's *chora*. It conjures up a *borderspace* where we must primarily imagine subjectivity even in its most minimal and primordial possibilities as an *encounter* between several (part/partner) subjects. It deals with possible, even if designified, meanings that arise in slight movements in-between closeness and remoteness, or proximity and distance—and not, as in the phallic model, between absence or presence.

the uncanny

Bracha Lichtenberg Ettinger derives support for this hypothesis from a careful scrutiny of Freud's key essay on "The Uncanny." "The subject of the 'uncanny' is ... undoubtedly related to what is frightening—to what arouses dread or horror."[20] The original German word is *unheimlich* which Freud shows to be not so much the opposite but the ambivalent subspecies of the term *heimlich*, meaning homely, homelike, or belonging to the house, familiar, comforting, well known. Carefully tracking the uncanny through Hoffman's tale of doubles and mechanical dolls in *The Sand Man,* Freud reveals the sensation of the Uncanny to be a reanimation of infantile complexes which have been repressed, or primitive beliefs that have been

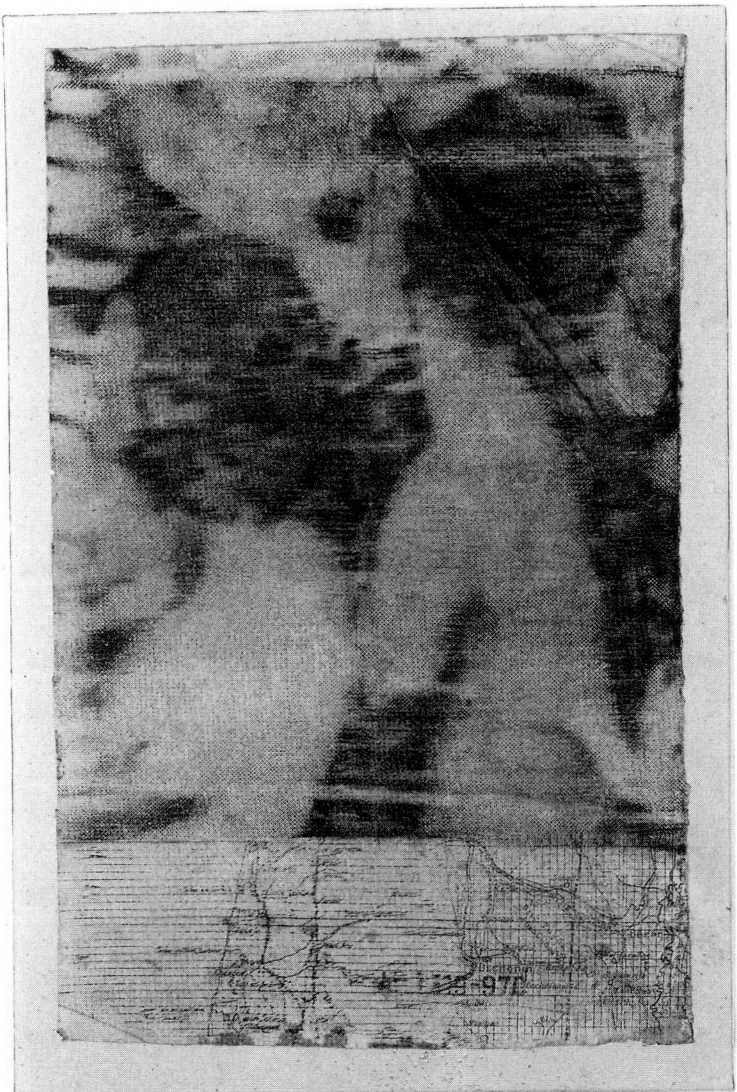

Figure 4. Bracha Lichtenberg Ettinger, *Eurydice*, no. 2. 1992–6. 38.3 × 23.1 cm. (mounted on chassis: 41.4 × 26.5 cm), oil and xerox on paper mounted on canvas.

surmounted by adult thinking—like dolls having life, or natural forces dictating our destiny. Freud's main analysis of the Uncanny focuses on castration anxiety. In passing, however, he expands these infantile complexes beyond just "the castration complex" to include "womb fantasies, etc."[21] Bracha Lichtenberg Ettinger seizes upon this reference to some other organization than the phallic that fuels the castration paradigm. She calls it a "different web of meaning donation/revelation" which has been consistently ignored while the castration model has received such majestic treatment as to expand to fill the whole horizon of theories of subjectivity and sexuality.

As she suggests, Freud did not deny the womb as the structure for a feminine dimension of subjective formation; but he did insist upon the significance of the prevailing *denial* of the womb in the masculinist psyche (and its theorizations of the psyche in general)—indicating the problematic for the masculine subject forced into recognition that it does not possess all the valuable organs, potentialities, powers concerning life. Such a narcissistic blow leads to the individual and, within the resulting phallocentric order, collective repression of the womb-experience as any sort of support for fantasy, identity, sexuality. Given the womb's inevitable significance as the primary matrix of human sensory experience, and if only external visibility through pregnancy and fantasies about childbearing, it becomes even more surprising to grasp how deeply excised the womb is from theories of subjectivity that happily ask us to imagine the psychic apparatus leaning upon fantasies of male body parts and their presence or absence. Our culture shudders, as I suspect my readers are doing, at any suggestion that the womb might be talked about seriously, in public, as the basis for a major theorization of the subject, when Lacanianism has trained us never to blanch as we publically lecture about penises, castration and the terror of the supposed genital lack of woman.

I must stress here that we are not dealing with the womb as the baby-hatching container. This is itself an image that negates femininity in the name of the phallus: woman as vessel, as emptiness filled with baby as phallus.[22] Reclaiming Freud's passing acknowledgment of womb-fantasies concerns the primordial intimations of several part subjectivities in an encounter, issues of borderspace, proximity in distance, relations without relating—all terms invented by Bracha Lichtenberg Ettinger to name this matrixial stratum as a result of puzzling over experiences in and of painting from the point of view of an adult subject negotiating trauma and memory. Matrix is a way of imagining severality, and the negotiation of otherness and difference in a paradigm radically different, in radically creative ways, from that we are offered through the Phallus as the signifier of subjectivity formed in separation, aggression and ultimately monist thought. Translating the word womb into the Latin form, *Matrix,* which has given us the mathematical idea of a primary structure, reminds us of the *structural* dimension, the signifying dimension that we are seeking to locate for that which might be called the feminine. The Matrix refers to the womb experience, not the organ, and thereby signifies, in a completely new sense, the feminine as a structuring of subjectivities and relations that can negotiate difference without either assimilation to the same or antagonism to the other.[23] The feminine as a "web of meaning donation/revelation" has massive implications for all that we think and fantasize about: subjectivity, sexuality, vision, art, society, death, memory.

Freud suggests the uncanny is an eruption of repressed memories and complexes within which infantile ways of making sense of a threatening world produce ambivalent understandings of living and dead, real and imaginary, known and remembered. Corpses, automatons, ghosts, doubles are the key triggers of the uncanny in literature and art. (This will be important for later discussions of Eurydice.) In the psychoanalytical terms later developed by Lacan, the uncanny re-opens a passageway between the Imaginary and the Real; and from that archaic and unsignifiable realm, the Real, intimated by us only through the gaps, holes, in the means we have of imagining—fantasy/images—and thinking—thought/words. The psychic apparatus works in retrospect, tailoring archaic impressions and affects into forms dictated by later structures such as fantasy and thought, that is, semiotically. Without signifiers either of an imaginary or symbolic kind, nothing is accessible to us. Repression locates certain materials at a distance from our consciousness by submitting them to the unconscious that is formed simultaneously within our entry into language. The unconscious is a system of meaning donation and revelation that is the underside of language, rather than the repository of what precedes our delivery into linguistic signification. So there is a beyond both language and the unconscious, of which the *objet a* is an index. But even then we are already very advanced, psychologically speaking, because an object is almost already part of the dialectic of the subject-object relations. Lacan tortures the limits of our strained understanding by positing beyond the object, a *Thing* as a sign of something more archaic than an object—as the limit case of imaginability that is in fact beyond our imagining and yet it structures us. The *objet a* lies between Thing and object and is that impossible referent to the losses which constitute us, in the *après coup*, as subjects. For us to be, *objet a* must vanish, and where it bursts forth, we uncannily experience our own disappearance. In a phallic organization, that is.

In the early Lacanian scheme, Woman stands with *objet a*, Thing, and with *jouissance* as this unsignifiable excess, this formative *nothing*. Bracha Lichtenberg Ettinger has for many years made a series of paintings using this title *Woman Other Thing*. But perhaps, as Freud almost laconically admitted, there are other pathways for these materials to impress themselves upon our receptive registers, what Bracha Lichtenberg Ettinger calls our psychic aerials, to which a new kind of painting might attune us. Bracha Lichtenberg Ettinger writes:

> It is the emergence of the *objet a* to the surface, which causes that vague anxiety of the "uncanny"—that oppressive feeling of distortion inciting unease, that strangeness, that veiled champerone of the return of the repressed. Instances of the "uncanny" arise, says Freud, when "something which ought to have remained hidden comes to light"…" "when the distinction between imagination and reality is effaced, as when something we have hitherto regarded as imaginary *appears before us in reality,* or when a symbol takes over the full functions of the *thing* it symbolises."[24] Yet a psychoanalytical *thing* is not an object; it is even more archaic than an object. The phallic and the matrixial *objet a* are *not yet* or *not-any-more* objects, but between things and objects.[25]

The uncanny is one site for exploring a recurrence of some archaic sensation/affect, which having undergone repression, becomes surrounded by anxiety when it recurs. Thus, as Freud insisted, the unheimlich is closely related to the heimlich; what was once familiar becomes disturbing through something that prompts it to surface or burst forth, whatever the affects it originally carried. Thus the idea of being buried alive, writes Freud, is felt by some to be the most uncanny thing of all. Yet, he argues, it is a transformation of another fantasy that was not at all terrifying, but might have even been pleasurable, "the phantasy, I mean, of intra-uterine existence."[26]

I want to use these thoughts about a "matrixial" Uncanny as a way to think about memory. Memory is already a sophisticated level of representation. Memory only comes when some distance has been achieved from trauma. Trauma remains unsignified, too close, a pressure, experienced as anxiety or insensate oblivion. Memory is trauma delivered into representation, given a distance by the signifier in which we can then recognize ourselves as the subjects of the memory rather than the locus of a continuing trauma.[27] But in order to become memory, trauma of a specific kind might require its own filters, pathways and signifiers to relieve it. If one thinks of trauma as a kind of raw psychic event that, as it were, possesses the subject desubjectivized by trauma's occupation of psychic space, allowing no distance necessary for signifying it, then memory is that relief of the signifier that allows us to live beside the affect. The trauma of the Holocaust for its survivors and those who "inherit" it untransformed and unmourned as the children of survivors, or as those who come after it, has for the last fifty years tested the very possibilities of representation and memory. This may be, as so many historians and writers have argued, because "that which happened" (Celan) breaches the limits of representation, exceeds the very possibility of commemoration.[28] One reason for this is that we continue to think in terms of history as a past from which we in the present are removed. But trauma, as psychic life in general, knows no tenses. Survivors live through time, but not necessarily in time. As Freud revealed, the psychic apparatus functions in a continual besidedness, a sedimented concurrence of infantile and everyday which are in a constant relay and mutual confusion. Never forgotten, because it could never be reduced to memory, the Holocaust is continuously lived by its survivors—who, in some crucial senses, did not survive it. They live it, as do those other generations it continues to touch.[29] The unforgotten has been, however unremembered by the rest of Europe. In the last decade we have witnessed a slow awakening of awareness of "that which happened" at Europe's industrial, cultural and historical heart in the middle of the twentieth century. Culminating in films, archives, museums and the public commemorations of the "liberation" of the death camps in 1995, "the Holocaust" has taken fifty years to begin to enter the circuits of public notice. How will we remember? Will it need a new kind of memory not to kill again with a second look?

The Uncanny is not a memory of some event. The Uncanny is a traumatic psychic phenomenon that suggests that buried within us may be the affects—trauma being such affect neither good nor bad but powerful—garnered from moments of sensate being, that have been not only repressed into the typically unconscious form of amnesia that can uncannily jump out at us when prompted by an untoward coincidence, but have been foreclosed.

foreclosure

Forclusion—the French term—is a technical term developed in Lacanian psychoanalysis to denote the mechanism at the basis of psychosis when the subject expels the signifier necessary to connect the subject's psychic material with the social collectivity of language and sexual identity. Foreclosure is different from repression, because the foreclosed signifiers are not even part of the unconscious. They do not return, like the repressed. They re-emerge "in the Real," particularly through hallucination.[30] The feminine, as a specificity able to order a particular array of meanings and fantasies as much for the masculine as for the feminine subject, is forecluded within phallocentric culture. It haunts that culture, beyond even its most archaic signifiers and pictograms, beyond its objects in close affiliation to the *Thing*. That is, its signifiers are expelled from the semiotic and hence psychic universe structured alone by the sovereign signifier, the Phallus. That is why it is so vital to entertain the possibility of a signifier for the feminine: not a signifier **of** the feminine which would again be an image of what phallocentric culture projects onto the "blank page," the nothing it calls Woman but to which it gives an obsessive figurative form as Eve, Madonna, Venus, Medusa, Eurydice and so forth. The signifier for the feminine would allow to filter through from archaic sensation, trauma, to memory and representation, that which could realign our experiences/arrangements of sexual difference, and by extension all forms of social difference and alterity.

This expulsion of the signifier of the matrixial feminine—not from Eden, but from sense, meaning, culture—turns the feminine subject into a "crazy woman"—another of the key figures in Bracha Lichtenberg Ettinger's visual world (fig. 2). Woman has been has been imaged and designated for all

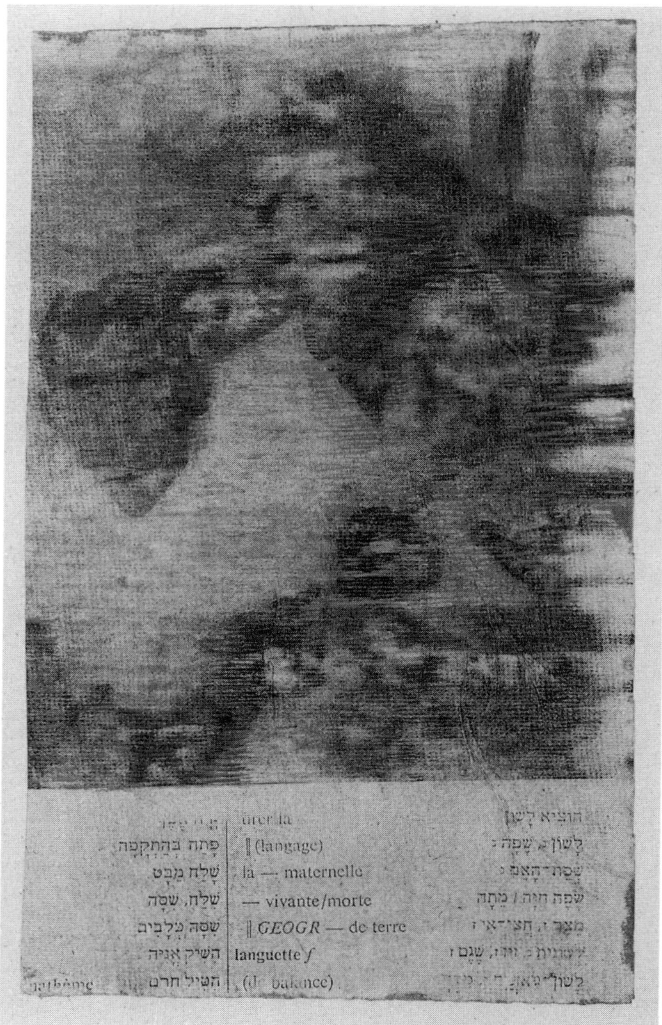

Figure 5.   Bracha Lichtenberg-Ettinger, *Eurydice,* no. 3. 1992–4. 38.7 × 23.4 cm. (mounted on chassis: 42.2 × 27 cm), oil and xerox on paper mounted on canvas.

patriarchal time as the crazy woman, bacchante, maenad, hysteric.[31] What is the recurrent name of her craziness but *hysteria,* derived, of course, from the Greek word *hustera,* meaning womb? Hysteria and the new theory of the Matrix stand in historic and mythical confrontation.

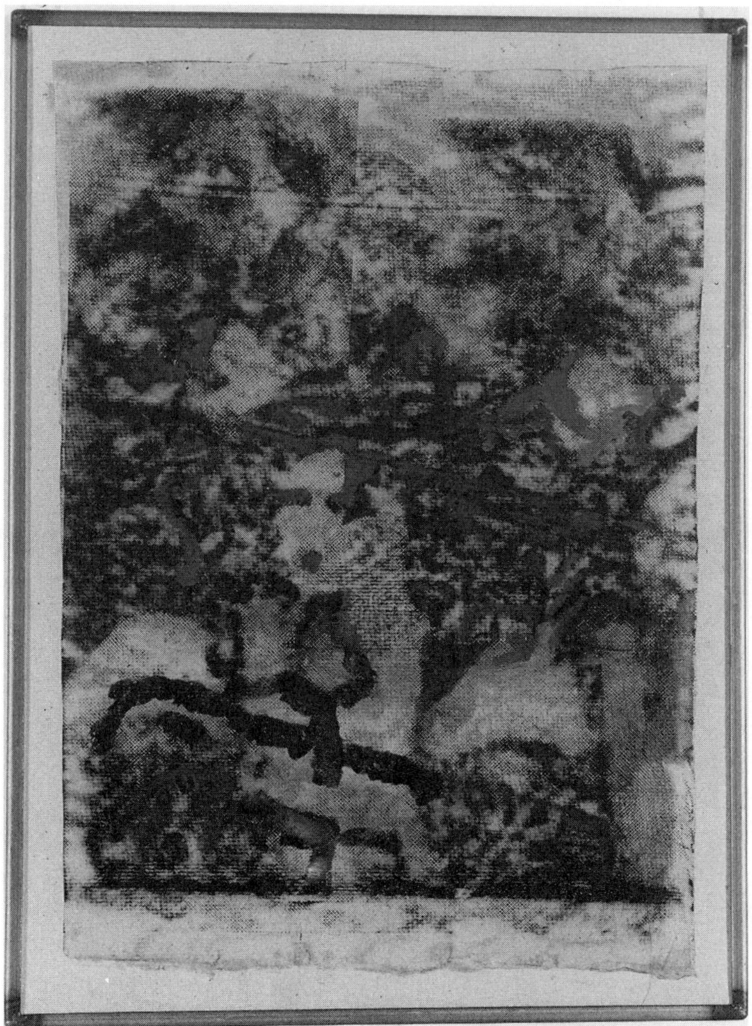

Figure 6.   Bracha Lichtenberg Ettinger, *Eurydice*, no. 6. 1992–5. 39.3 × 26.8 cm. (mounted on chassis: 43.2 × 30.5 cm), oil and xerox on paper mounted on canvas.

hysteria

In Western culture since the Greeks, the womb has been the very sign of women's irrationality if not insanity. The womb is the metaphor that encloses woman within her sexed body. Yet, beyond the image of that

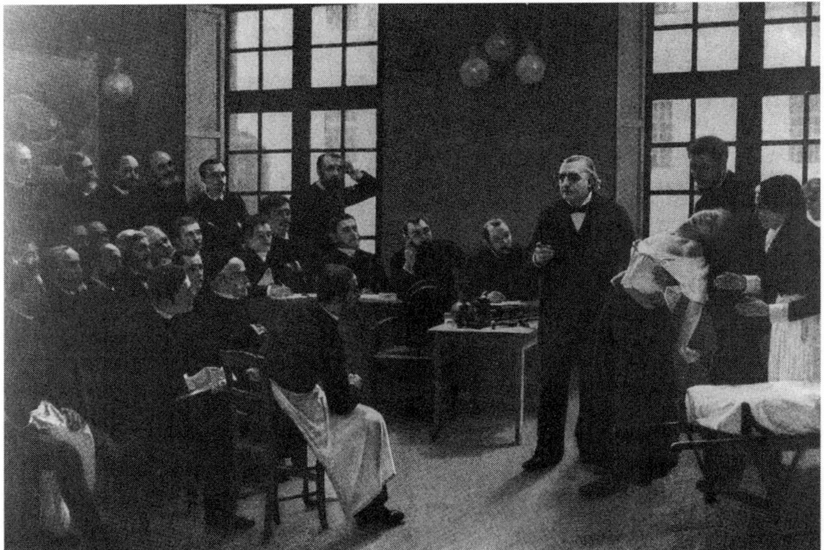

Figure 7.   André Brouillet, *Charcot Lecturing at La Salpetrière*, 1887. Engraving after the painting.

enceinte the specificity of the feminine associated with the encounter of the several signified also by the womb could be the sign of the feminine that might offer us a future. Greek misogyny underlies the Western thought through its profound incorporation into Christianity: in Western Europe, we live in a Greco-Christian universe. From the Greeks through to Jean-Martin Charcot (1825–1893), hysteria represented woman as the disorderly site of lack whose subjection to her wandering or empty womb needed to be policed by the judicious application of the masculine phallus, the medical gaze, or even the ovarian prod (used by Charcot to stimulate the hysteric seizure) (fig. 7). It was with the ever-enlarging group of young women, the daughters of the bourgeoisie and working class, diagnosed as hysterics, that psychoanalysis itself began—but with a difference. In his weekly open sessions at the hospital of Saltpetrière, Charcot displayed the female hysterical body not only within his medical framing, but to a photographic gaze (figs. 8 and 9). In the mid 1880s, Sigmund Freud studied with Charcot and later translated his work on hysteria into German. Then, learning, via Joseph Breuer's case notes about Berthe Pappenheim, alias Anna "O" of "the talking

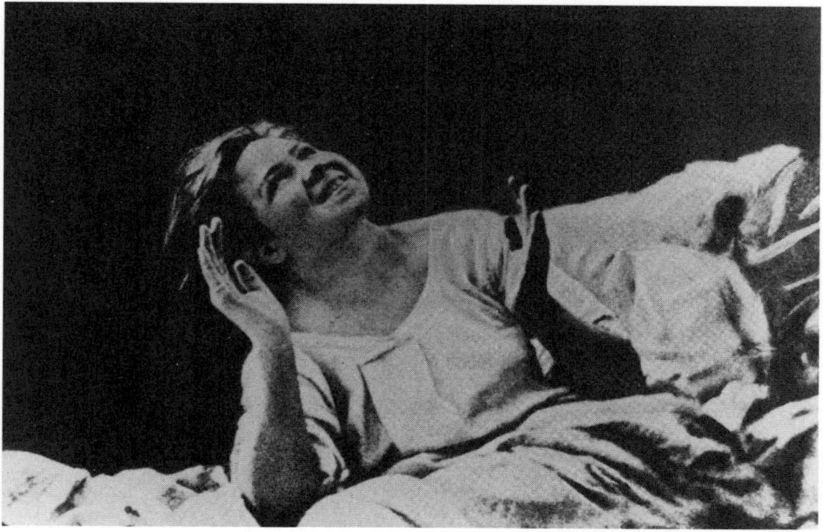

Figure 8.   Jean-Marie Charcot, *Attitudes Passionelles: Extase,* from Nouvelle Iconographie Photographique de la Salpetrière, 1878.

cure," Freud realized the necessity to transpose the visual study of the symptomology of the bodily sign into the relief of speech delivered to a listening partner: and he co-created analytic discourse.[32] Instead of the Oedipal gaze of mastery enacted by Charcot, whose iconography of the hysterical body has played directly into modern art from Degas through Picasso to contemporary advertising, analysis imagined a space of encounter and transference, acoustic rather than optical in its therapy, and, as Julia Kristeva has argued, the scene of love.[33]

Analytic discourse forms one of four discursive apparatuses identified by Lacan in which the subject becomes, or fails to find itself, within language and desire. In all forms of discourse there is a form of social relation between the signifying partners, knowledge and truth, which gives rise to four fundamental patterns: the discourses of mastery, of bureaucracy (also known as the university), of hysteria and of analysis. To explain this fully would take us many pages to elaborate in detail, but its significance here derives from the move I am wanting to make from the classic image of the relation of knowledge, interpretation and cure, represented by the etching

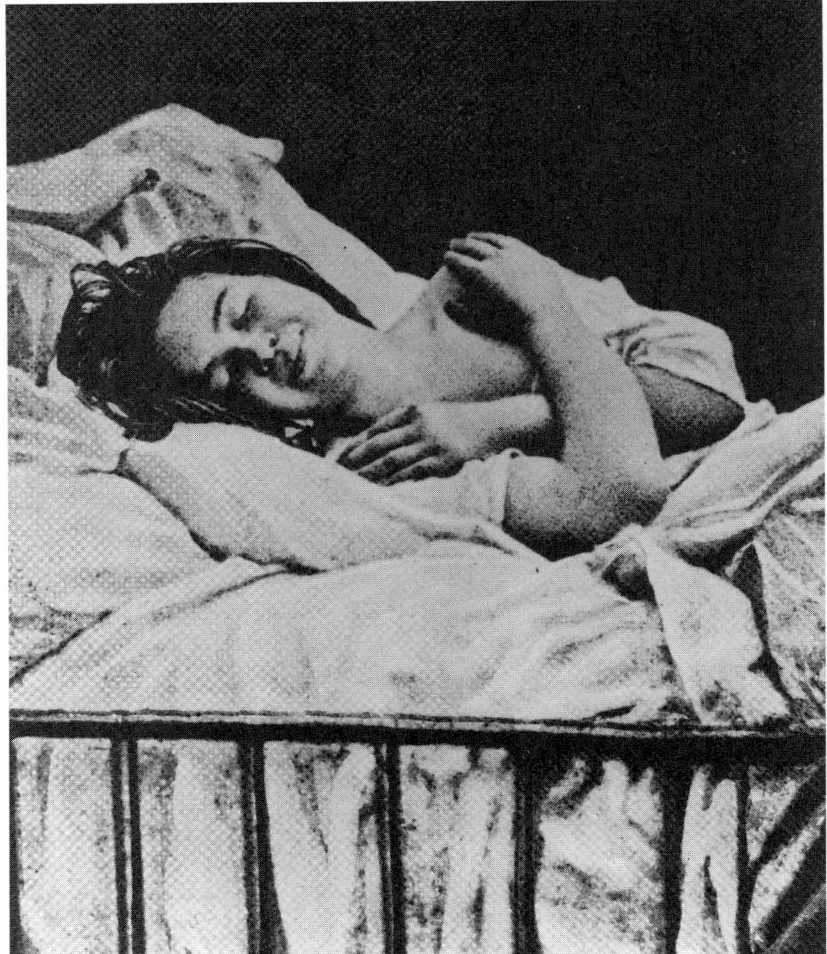

Figure 9. Jean-Marie Charcot, *Attitudes Passionelles: Erotisme*, from Nouvelle Iconographie Photographique de la Saltpetrière, 1878.

of Charcot lecturing at Salpetrière (fig. 7), to the experience of the paintings of Bracha Lichtenberg Ettinger via the alternating figures of the hysteric and the analyst.

The discourses of mastery and bureacracy claim a privileged relation to knowledge which is presented as truth, unsuspecting that, as revealed by Freud through his theories of the unconscious, we cannot access truth for it

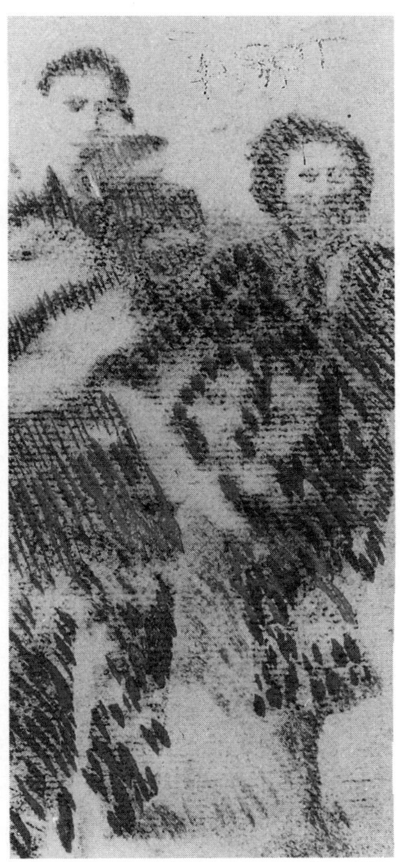

Figure 10.   Bracha Lichtenberg Ettinger,
detail of *Matrixial Borderlines*. (fig. 2)

is always hidden from the barred Subject who is split between conscious and
unconscious. The hysteric typically poses to the doctor/analyst questions
from the barred place of the feminine within patriarchy: Who am I? Man or
Woman? Alive or Dead? Sane/Insane? But the question is put in such a way
as to render it unanswerable by the one supposed to know: the doctor, who
is "umanned" by the hysteric's radical confusion/dissolution of identity and
by her displacement of signs onto the body. Analytic discourse, ideally,
allows of some movement in these otherwise closed exchanges by opening
up a passage for the *desire* of the analysand through the discovery of the
lack in the analyst—that he/she is not the master and neither is he/she
"unmanned" by the questions. In Lacan's technical diagrams outlining this

complicated scheme, our friend *objet a*: the leftover of *jouissance,* the hole in the signifying network, plays a significant role. The *objet a* is revealed in the analytical discourse by the silence of the analyst which reduces the analyst from master/bureaucrat because "the analyst doesn't have it." In that encounter with the *objet a,* with lack, the analysand is dehystericized. What is this silence and does it have anything to do with the doubly "Blank Page" of the feminine and the Jewish in the twentieth century?

> Certainly not conventional silence, for it is indeed necessary to be silent in order to hear the other who speaks, but the refusal to respond there where the analyst would have something to say, but the leaden silence which comes to redouble that of the analysand, but against the mute question, anguished echo of the limits of the Other's knowledge. The being of the analyst is silent, through which he makes himself a massive and enigmatic presence.[34]

The silence of the analyst (taking the place of the Doctor in post-modern culture as suggested by Julia Kristeva's proposition that we live in a therapeutic age) is what allows the analysand to be released from being locked into the desire of the Other or spinning unattached in doubt. Thus the analysand gains some space for the possibility of desire and re-entry into the relays of intersubjectivity. Parveen Adams—from whom I just quoted— has used Lacan's model of the four discourses in her analysis of a major feminist project: Mary Kelly's 1990 installation *Interim* (first shown at the New Museum of Contemporary Art, New York) in order to place this within and beyond a certain feminist culture.

Faced with distortions and misrepresentation, in the 1970s feminism looked to its artists and image-makers to produce "positive" images, new identities, affirming ego-ideals. To deliver such would be to place the artists in the position of the master or the bureaucrat. In the 1980s, a critical interrogation of the very category of image, identity and representation gave rise to practices that might make the art thus produced *hysterical,* as indeed Elizabeth Bronfen has argued about one of the artists currently questioning all identities of the feminine: Cindy Sherman.[35] But Parveen Adams writes:

> Certainly the analyst talks, and this artist makes images. And at the limit of the analyst's speech, there is silence, while at the limit of this artist's images, there is emptiness. They both function to refuse the imaginary capture by a positive

world in which identity is *pret à porter*. They both seek to undo the confusion between the object and the ego ideal … . Well there are pictures that give us images as objects of desire, and there are pictures that work at the limit of the images. *Interim* gives us the places of *objet a* at the limit of the image.[36]

Once again we are at the limits of visibility, and Parveen Adams can only see the uncanny, castrating apparition at its edge, however signficant a move it is to reject feminist dreams of an imaginary wholeness of female identity. Mary Kelly's work represents a sustained tradition of feminist engagement with psychoanalytical theory, issues of the gaze, representation and process of artistic practice as the site of an interdisciplinary investigation staged in an aesthetic theatre. But within the still early Lacanian paradigm that such feminism has absorbed there are still only questions. Take for instance Emily Apter writing also on *Interim*.

> In focussing our attention on the status of Lacanianism in the work of art, Mary Kelly's *Interim* raises larger issues pertaining to the merging of psychoanalysis, feminism and art practice. How do women as artists and spectators provide a critique of the historical gender bias of psychoanalytical theory without resorting to the essentialising frames of femininity or "women's art"? How does one dislodge the scopic domination of women in the clinic or on the couch through an archive of images placed "under the gaze"? How does one perform gender or "send up" masculine and femininity so as to unfix, ironically, the reified codes of sexual identity while preserving the pathos and sorrow of a "different" female body growing older? How does one seduce visually without fetishizing the female body?[37]

Apter mentions dislodging the scopic domination of the clinic (Charcot and his photographic iconography, used and displaced by Mary Kelly's work *Corpus* Part I of *Interim:* Ch. 4) or on the couch (Freud, who had the Charcot engraving over his couch when he was forced to flee to London in June 1938). Feminism's emergence into the cultural field as a distinct force though never a style or movement, has, nonetheless, been associated with the break from painting. Escaping from the narrowed confines of high modernist painting, women artists in the 1970s–80s embraced the possibilities of photography, video, film and a hybrid interweaving of verbal and visual sign systems as amenable to the feminist critique of the very scopic regime which imprisoned us in "images of women."[38] In the 1990s, painting once again

> My parents are proud of their silence. It was
> their way of sparing others and their children
> from suffering. But in this silence all was
> transmitted except the narrative. In silence
> nothing can be changed in the narrative
> which hides itself. If being haunted is the
> direct testimony of repression, the ceremony
> is a testimony of testimony.
>
> *Matrix. Hala(a)—Lapsus* 1991:85[40]

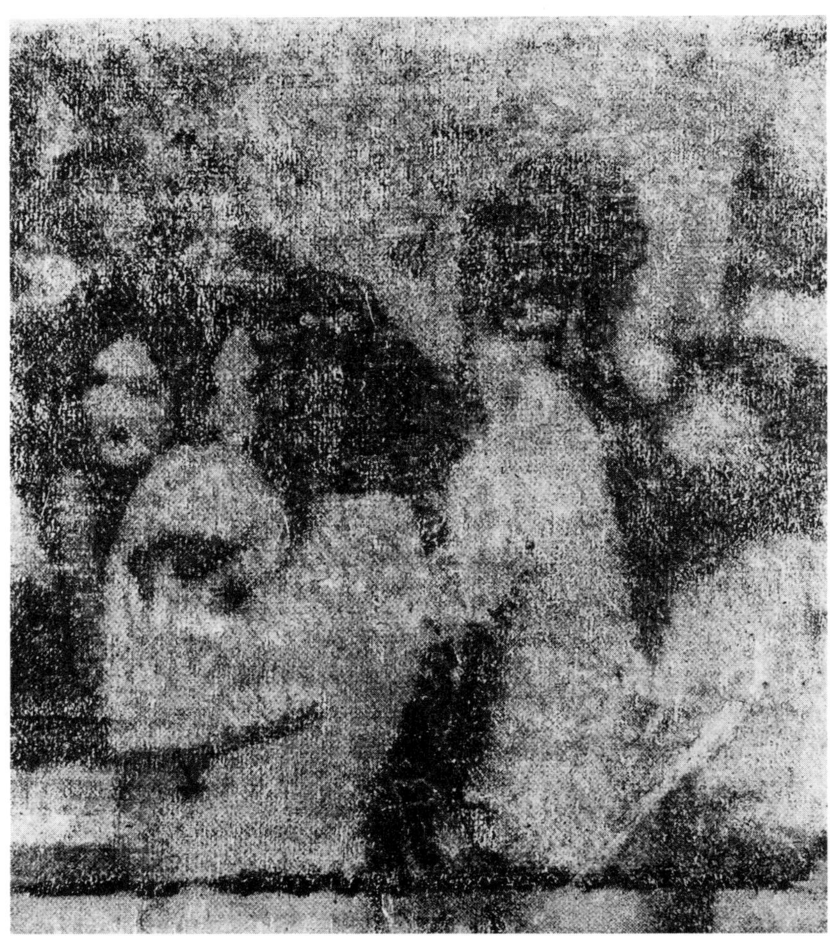

Figure 11.   Bracha Lichtenberg-Ettinger, *Autistwork*, no. 1. 1993. 32.5 × 28 cm (43.5 ×
37.5 cm framed), oil and photocopy on paper mounted on canvas.

perhaps signals a move that is, as I have argued elsewhere, "after painting" (its Western history from the Renaissance to Abstraction) and "after history" (the defining moment of *Shoah*).[39] This painting tips into the visible that which is, like the Blank Page, beyond a phallic screen. The painting I am thinking of is by Bracha Lichtenberg Ettinger, which can thus be placed in a genealogy with the feminist project, while opening a radically new chapter of possibility through its negotiation and transformation of painting.

Bracha Lichtenberg Ettinger's paintings are not blank, but because of a traumatizing history, they do deal with the silence of the Other.

grief colors

I am amazed at the emotion that can be produced by the introduction of an image in some analytical cures when, at a particular moment, the subject is paralysed either by feeling (he finds language inadequate to his truth), or by the rigid character of logical development (the superintellectual discourse). The arrival on the scene of the image, sometimes sugggested by the analyst, is what I call an "image implant"…

Julia Kristeva[41]

I have mentioned a therapeutic age and considered the analytic scene. What of painting? Is there a way that an image takes us to the limits of the visible, "folding into the visible" that which is by definition outside representation, yet presses upon it? If we could be moved by this encounter, rather than scared to death as with the uncanny, could it be the borderline visibility of a matrixial *objet a*? Freud's reflections on those traumatized by shell shock in the First World War prompted his theories of the compulsion to repeat and the death drive.[42] What might be the relations within Bracha Lichtenberg Ettinger's painting of recurrent images and her repeated revisiting of their sites/sights? Is she and are we the viewers, Orpheus, returning always to the mouth of hell only to lose again and to kill again? Are the Jewish women glimpsed in her paintings Eurydice perpetually abandoned, even by our backward glance into history?

Julia Kristeva explains her use of image-implants in analysis: "The analyst can introduce a narration in images … The type of narration, presented in visual form can provide the necessary link with frozen feelings and cold worlds."[43] Kristeva values what she calls the "transverbal dimension in communication" and "the plastic aspect of the icon as signifier."[44] A particular kind of frozen feeling and cold world enclosed the trauma of both the loss and survival of the Holocaust. Can the plastic aspect of the icon as signifier, retuned through a matrixial aerial that escapes even this either/or, word/ image, be the source of relief, a consolation, despite the horror of what the image as icon shows us? What is this the power of color, reds, violets, blues, piercing the gray of a melancholically diminished monochrome? How does it work when we cannot detach the color from its visual rhythm, its pulse, produced by the process of the paintings' fabrication—the size of touch, the kind of brush, the weave that produces the veil of color that is never description nor abstraction, but holds our gaze to an impossible encounter?

Luce Irigaray has drawn issues of color and painting into the analytic scene in her paper "Flesh Colors." While contemplating the senses in general in relation to psychoanalysis, hearing, balance and voice, Irigaray reminds us of the privilege Freud bestowed on the dream-image; and she recalls depression where the world seems to become colorless. Color is more than perceptual; indeed it has a profoud intimacy with psychic processes. She then proposes that analysts should encourage patients, metaphorically, to *paint*, quoting Paul Klee: "The point about painting is to *spatialise perception* and make *time simultaneous*." [45] Is Klee's a matrixial insight?

Bracha Lichtenberg Ettinger does not choose her documents (fig. 11). They come to her, co-habiting her studio space as the almost-presences of what cannot be lost to the child of survivors, working in and with the "transgenerational memory" that has been so repeatedly identified as a feature of the children of Holocaust survivors. She has discerned a specific aesthetic procedure relating to the Matrix. The defining tropes of figurative meaning in the phallic system are the tropes of metaphor and metonymy. As tropes of substitution, they have been related to the axes of meaning in the dream: condensation and displacement. The matrix has its own aesthetic trope: metramorphosis.

> Metramorphosis is the process of change at the borderlines and thresholds between being and absence, between memory and oblivion, *I* and *non-I*, a process of transgression and fading away. The metramorphic consciousness has no centre, cannot hold a fixed gaxe—or if it has a centre, it constantly

slides to the borderline, to the margins. Its gaze escapes the margins and returns to the margins. Through this process the limits, the borderlines, and thresholds conceived are continually transgressed, or dissolved, thus allowing the creation of new ones.[46]

In the *Eurydice* series of 1992–99, Bracha Lichtenberg Ettinger returns repeatedly to—"a tiny document of *Shoah*" (fig. 12). The Hebrew word means destruction. Edmond Jabés:

> We can't approach the Whole except by way of the detail. We can only approach by little bits a certain totality which isn't even one.... The grain of sand makes us aware of the sand; this handful makes us ever so slightly aware of the desert. But the desert—you can't embrace the desert in its entirety all at once. You can only enter it through the grain of sand.[47]

So a catastrophe as unimaginable and unmournable as *Shoah* is approached through a fragment, one grain in the modern desert of Judea. "The tiny document of *Shoah*" is a photograph. But as a photograph it is the property of the murderers of the women it depicts. It makes its viewers Orphic witnesses to a certain death which might be re-enacted everytime the photograph falls under a gaze. To look at its contents is to be forced to identify with the genocidal gaze that literally and metaphorically killed humanity. So how do we encounter this "tiny document of *Shoah*" outside of the visual parameters where photography, always loaded with a deathly freight, came too close to a non-metaphorical, and therefore, hideous, *real* -ization. One device is to align ourselves otherwise with the look of the Other, the woman captured in its ghastly frame, Eurydice.

> This woman has more to look at than the watchers of the painting ... but what she looks at is inhuman.
> *Matrix. Halal(a)—Lapsus 1992: 84–5*

The look of Eurydice, unlike that of Orpheus—always filled with his own desire and its projection onto the image of the woman such looking always kills—is a look into the face of death, of trauma, of disappearance. The *Eurydice* paintings are, necessarily, not a reworking of the photograph, not its replication, not its reproduction, not its appropriation in the

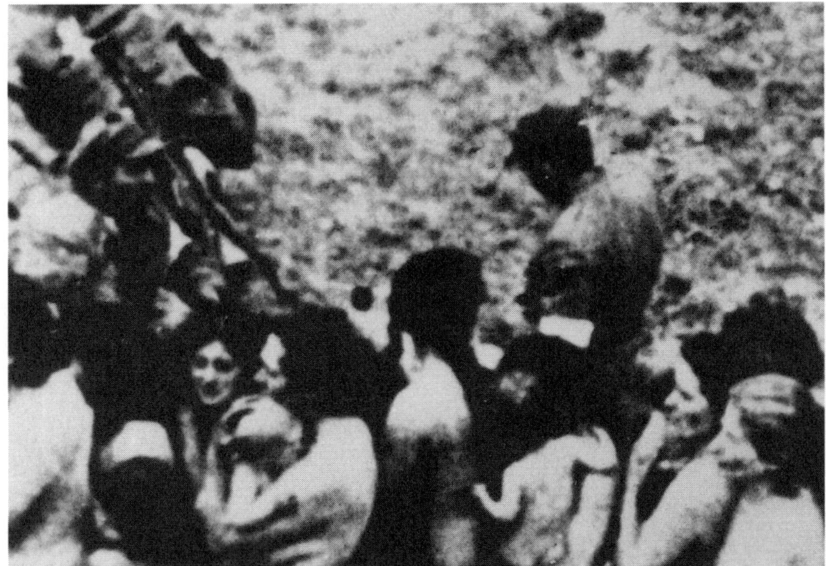

Figure 12.   Anon. Detail of a photograph. Mizrok, Ukraine, 1941.

post-modern tradition of "appropriated[48] imagery" (fig. 12). It is something from radically revised Duchampian tradition: a ready-made. Found in the archive of modernity, it is the ready-made of that history, that cannot but carry the ruins of its post-Benjaminian history to us, bringing us face to face with both the human and the inhuman, with the point between two deaths. At this point the opposition between bourgeois myths of artistic originality, that post-modern appropriation merely parodied and never displaced, and the culturally given, simulacrum, found object, takes a dramatic turn through a historical and psychic entanglement.

> From the matrixial angle, both the *ready-made* borrowing of the other's myths and inanimate objects, and the *originals* stemming from the self are not on opposite aesthetic poles but in the same basket; both suckle on the mythical pre-discursive zone in which—from the Phallic angle—the Other and the inanimate object appear as *my* strangers, and *self* and *not-self* are either the same or opposite. The matrix has not only aesthetic but ethical implications. In the phallus, there is the impossibility of sharing trauma and phantasy; in

the matrix, up to a certain extent, there is *an impossibility of not sharing them.* From here, in our *post-Duchampian era,* we may dissolve oppositions between ready-made … and materials [that are] mine. Art may lead us to discover our part of the shared responsibility in the events that are not "inside" the Other-self.[49]

As paintings, Bracha Lichtenberg Ettinger's work with these traumatizing ready-mades, the documents of *Shoah,* offer *material* resistance to the Oedipal, mastering, bureaucratic gaze enacted fascistically by the photograph (figs. 13, 14, 15). As I have argued, such a gaze is the product of the Oedipal structuring of subjectivity and sexuality and it has been institutionalized within major modern cultural apparatuses such as the cinema and photographic reproduction in its many forms. It has been named the masculine gaze (Mulvey) and the eye of power (Foucault). Can the power enmeshed with Oedipal visuality be sidestepped even while painting still plays in the field of the (just) visible? Is this perhaps a new definition of the possibility of matrixial painting in our historically altered present that they call the post-modern, when we mean post-Auschwitz?

Zygmunt Bauman has argued that the Holocaust is the exemplary project of modernity: bureacuratic rationalism applied as a technique for correcting a perceived social disequilibrium, for clearing the social garden of its hybrids and weeds.[50] He has exposed a hitherto unacknowledged intimacy between the defining projects of modernity—bureaucratic rationalism, industrial technology and the dream of social gardening—and the National Socialist program for the so-called Final Solution, which has placed the Holocaust beyond its marginality as a "local" Jewish question, while equally raising the Jewish experience in and of modernity to its place within the general theory and history of that modernity. Living in the period of post-modernity must, by this logic, be conditioned by either the memory of, or the amnesiac repression of that telling and terrifying face of modernity that the Germanized name of a Polish place burns into western consciousness: Auschwitz. It is probably significant that we do not even use the Polish name, Oswieçim, further erasing from Western knowledge the soil and one of the languages of the Jewish culture of Eastern Europe that, having struggled and flourished in all its diversity since the fourteenth century, was completely destroyed in the middle of the twentieth.

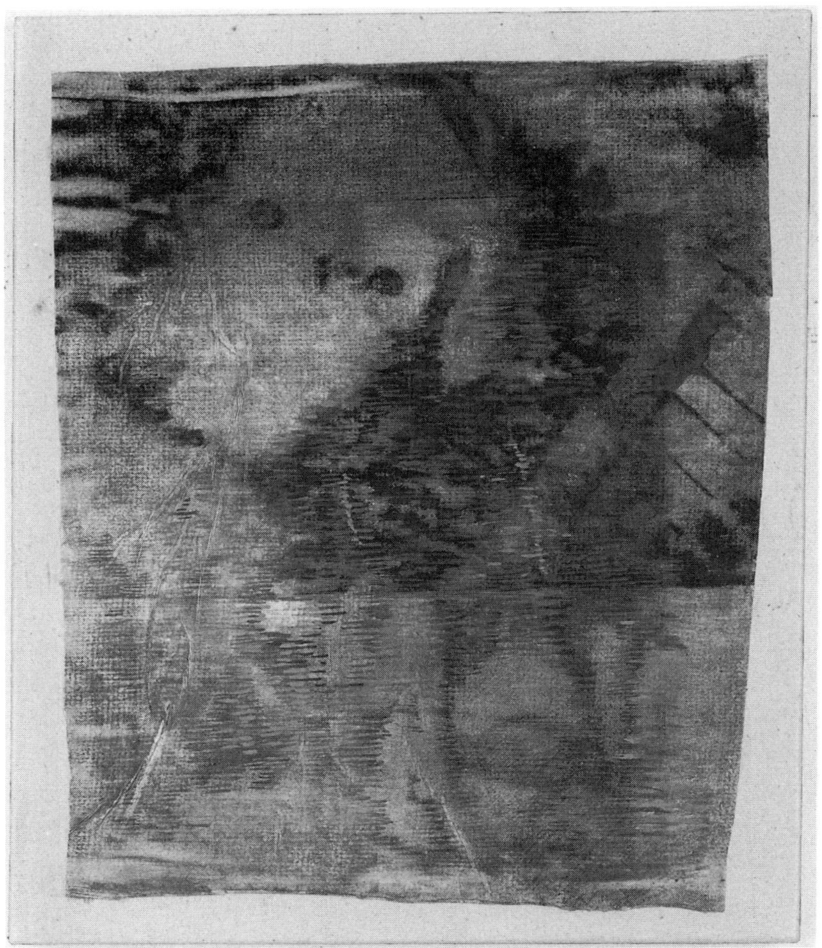

Figure 13. Bracha Lichtenberg-Ettinger, *Eurydice*, no. 9. 1994–6. 32 × 26 cm. (mounted on chassis: 35.7 × 29.3 cm), oil and xerox on paper mounted on canvas.

I said "material resistance." I am referring to the kind of transformation of "the tiny document of *Shoah*" through color, touch and the kind of pulsational intensities that the paradox of opaque densities of color applied with a repeated stroke, touch by touch, layer by layer produces. Put through the paradigmatic anti-auratic machine, a photocopier, whose process is interrupted before the photographic image can be fixed, the document's new

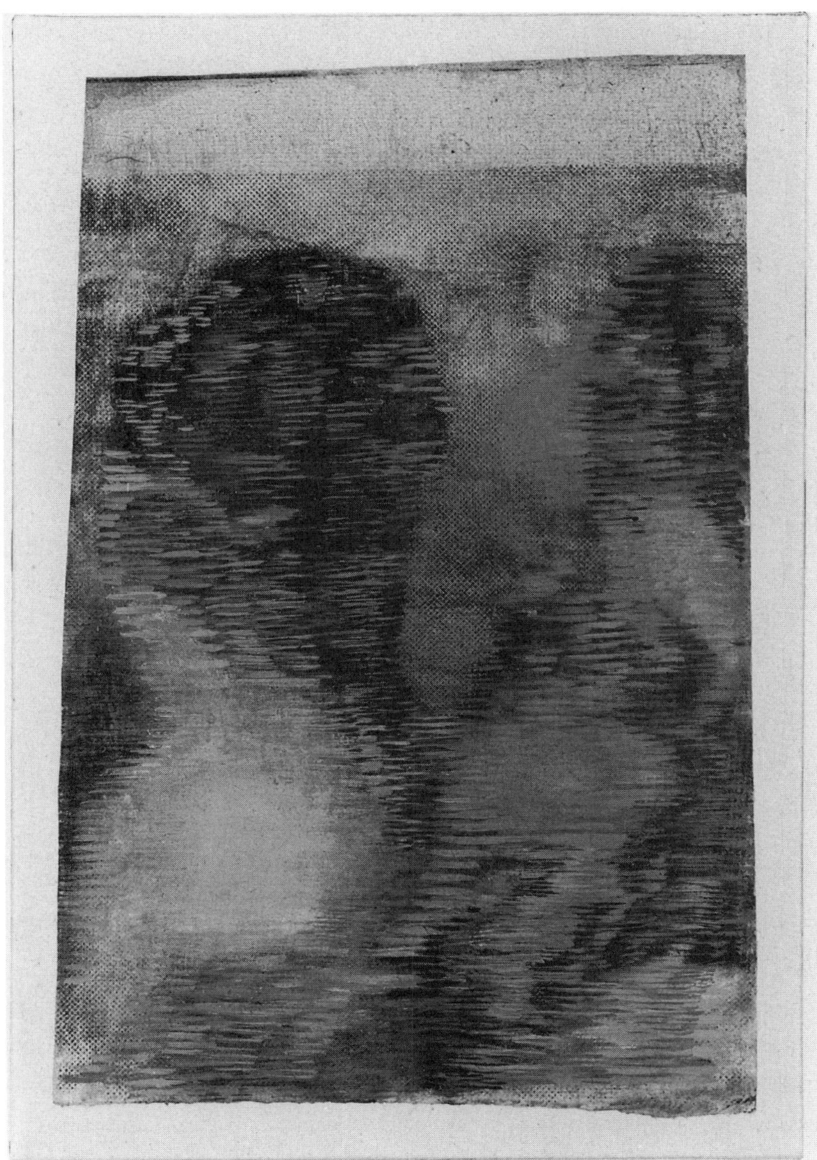

Figure 14. Bracha Lichtenberg-Ettinger, *Eurydice*, no. 12. 1994–6. 38.5 × 24.5 cm. (mounted on chassis: 42.5 × 28.5 cm), oil and xerox on paper mounted on canvas.

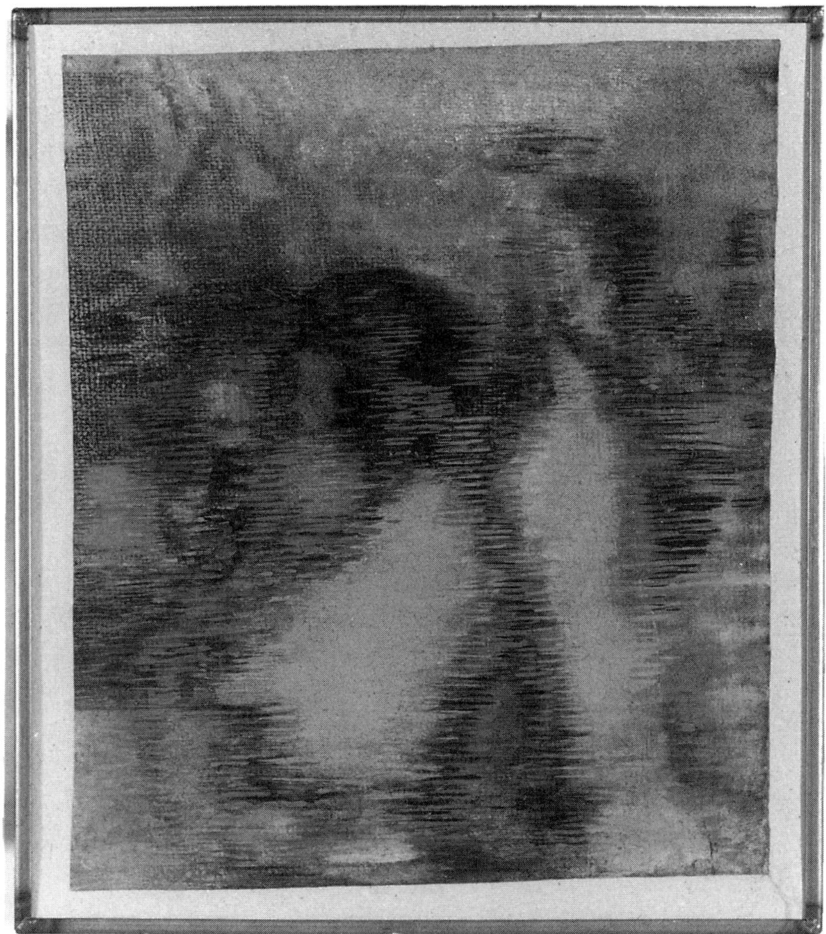

Figure 15.   Bracha Lichtenberg-Ettinger, *Eurydice*, no. 13. 1994–6. 34 × 27.3 cm. (mounted on chassis: 37.3 × 31.2 cm), oil and xerox on paper mounted on canvas.

apparition in the *Eurydice* series makes us see the grains of photoscopic dust, black dust, a dust that can double for the ashes, what Elaine Marks names *les cendres juives.* She comments on French Jewish writers "after Auschwitz":

> In their texts, the French word *cendre(s)* may function as a figure for both or either death and rebirth, for mourning and celebration, for Jews who were exterminated in the gas chambers and in ovens, and for the philosophical problem of the trace. *Cendre(s)* points not only to the product of incineration

and its dispersion, but to anonymity and also to the figure of the Phoenix, reborn from its own ashes."[51]

> Each black grain has its freedom. And its freedom is also mine. I am lost before each black grain—Black sorrow—this loss is in me and in painting.

These grains, these strings and tunnels, could be vision and the gaze, or it could not be that at all, even if it's a matter of perception. The grains are conceived in the matrix.

> Like a matrix I am at the service of black grains in my service; I am lost before the black grains lost before me and lost for me. Loss can be a hole by which we approach, each time other. Metramorphic thought that aims at the interior invisible, made visible by painting.
>
> *Matrix. Halal(a)—Lapsus* 1989: 57–58[52]

We can thus begin to approach what is happening—to her, to us, to them, in Bracha Lichtenberg Ettinger's work with "memory traces" rather than images. In part the artist works in ash because of mourning, because history and family were incinerated and because the debris of that history is cinders. In part the artist revisits the dusty traces with color, her mark allowing all that we learn from the abstract modernist painters about the being-for-itself of the medium to offer its uncanny solace. However hard we look, here will be no computer-aided image enhancement that will produce identification of the people in this scene. Color-freighted paint produces only affect-enhancement, moving us both closer to the trauma traced within the undone photographic image, and to the grace of color that touches that impossible void signified by the turn to Eurydice's perspective.

Photographs remain a key device for historical record and personal recall. Looking back through family albums, or working through historical archives, the photograph provides what Roland Barthes described as the "here and then" experience. It traverses time, interrupting the clean break between now and then, here and there.

> The type of consciousness the photograph involves is truly unprecedented, since it establishes not a consciousness of being-there of the thing (which any copy could provoke) but an awareness of its *having-been-there*. What we have is a new space-time category; spatial immediacy and temporal anteriority, the photograph being the illogical conjunction between the *here-now* and the *there-then*.[53]

For Barthes, the photograph produces a spectatorial consciousness, distinct from the fictional and identificatory gaze of the cinema. Given this structure, in relation to an image that takes us to a poignant proximity with a horrific historical there and then, the photograph makes us mere spectators of people not *having been there*, but *being there at the point of their erasure*—the photographs hold us for a moment to the site where in their forms the psychic freight of the *objet à* bursts upon the screen. For these events were, as Dori Laub has named the Holocaust, events without witness.[54] In order not to be voyeurs of the suffering of the other, Bracha Lichtenberg Ettinger's "painting" makes us gleaners of its *cendres juives*. Like the poet Elaine Feinstein's Eurydice, we limp through this century on "a path of cinders" and suck in "volcanic ash."[55] But the artist restores to these events a witness-painter and asks us to be *witness*-viewers.

Images encode the relations of their production: the relations between the possessing gaze and those possessed by the gaze. Independent of the actual participants in any photographic act, these relations replicate a structure that, marked by the Oedipal formations still dominant in Western culture, produces a hierarchy, and a hierarchy that is both gendered and engendering. The gaze becomes the point of production for meanings that are projected onto and hence carried by the object of the gaze. Thus we arrive at Laura Mulvey's now notorious formulation:

Woman then stands in patriarchal culture as signifier for the male other, bound by a symbolic order in which man can live out his phantasies and obsessions through linguistic command by imposing them on the silent image of woman still tied to her places as bearer of meaning, not maker of meaning.[56]

The photographic and cinematic apparatuses disperse this structural tendency across a range of imagery and narrative forms, but they are metaphorically revealed most insistently in the representation of woman as spectacle. In this art historians have then traced back a pre-history in the historical representation of the female body in painting, in that strangely exnominated genre called "the nude." Supplied by mythology with narrative cover for this stark exposure of masculine fantasy, the fable of the Three Graces has offered painters a device for elaborating this viewing pleasure by representing a trio of women from different angles and viewpoints gracefully dancing in an idealized landscape of desire. This vision of Woman is intimately connected with the Orphic fantasy that culminated with the beginning of European opera at the opening of the seventeenth century. Analyzing the first operas, one titled *Euridice* (1607) and the other, by Monteverdi, *Orfeo* (1607) Klaus Theweleit asks: Why does the new medium of opera emerge around 1600 in Italy? and Why is it ignited by the constellation Orpheus/Eurydice?[57] In his subtle analysis of the new ideology and politics of love encoded by these operas, Theweleit discerns two significant developments around the central drama of Orpheus's backward look as he leads his beloved Eurydice out of Hades: the displacement of the traditional idea of blind love with a love incited and thus dependent upon vision; and the concomitant effect of the "murder" of the woman by love, for she is absorbed into the art and suffering of her lover, who in her absence, forms a couple with his music. Orpheus takes over her heart and her soul. Thus Theweleit concludes:

> Just as Renaissance painters encode the gaze upon countrysides that are intended to be seen as "beautiful" or "harmonic" with a calculated female body, the musicians here encode the site of appropriate hearing/precise reproduction of their music with the ear/soul of the "most beautiful" woman.[58]

Through Orpheus, Theweleit argues, opera produced the modern couple of the artist and his art, in which the woman is torn apart, into ear, soul, heart and eyes, and becomes, in anticipation, the recording remembrance:

> They manufacture (in the work of art) the dead woman they need for this, simultaneously lamenting her irreplaceable loss (a social tribute) and resorting to inherited "mythological" recording and representational apparatuses. In the

course of its performance, the expiring art work draws its notoriety for a certain sacredness not least (indeed, perhaps first) of all from its ritual sacrifice of the most beautiful woman before the eyes (and ears) of all. But amid the sacrifice it is primarily the *reconstruction* of recording devices and perceptual occurrences that is staged with the help of the dead body.[59]

Nothing so starkly illustrates the radical rupture sliced into these enfolded traditions in Western culture by the event of *Shoah* than the juxtaposition of Raphael's *Three Graces* (fig. 16) which stands at the beginning of the new chapter in Western painting in the Renaissance, when painting elaborated this sexual structure of viewing pleasure, beauty and death, with the "tiny document of *Shoah* "transformed into *Eurydice.*

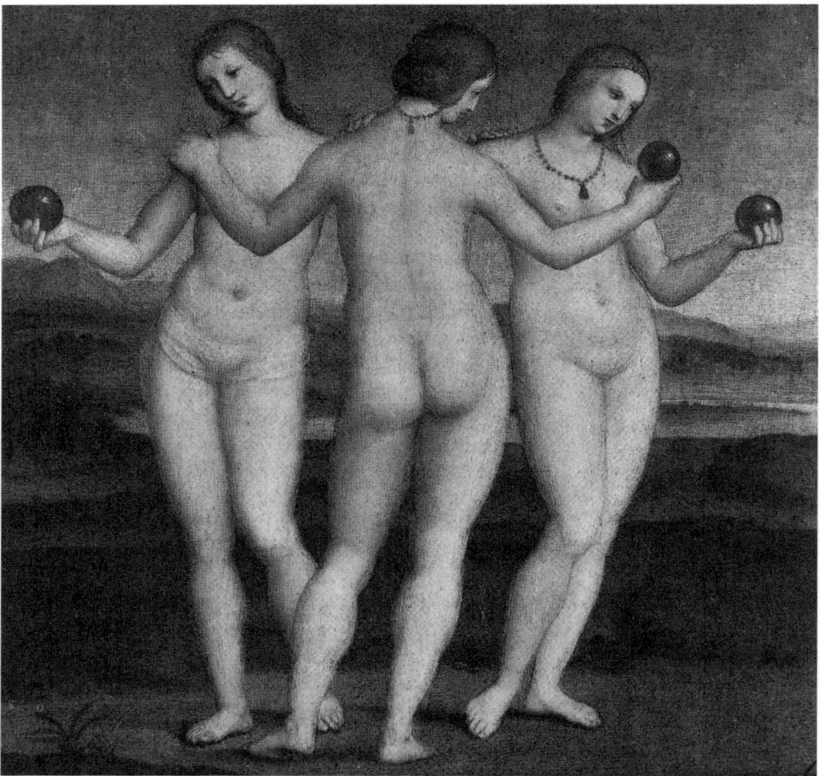

Figure 16.   Raphael, *Three Graces*, 1504. 17 × 17 cm, oil on panel, Chantilly, Musée Condé.

In Raphael's little piece of classicism all of woman appears before us, rhythmically swaying to the needs of compositional balance, each gently inclined head gracefully contemplating a sphere held within its line of sight. These graces "look," but at nothing, except that which ostensibly reflects what is allowed to them to be: perfect, beautiful, empty. Woman is a sign, a signifier but not for the meaning of the feminine. In patriarchal logic, Woman, as nothing, lends her form to signify the masculine as presence, as the possessor, the place and producer of meaning that hinges upon disappearance. Threatening absence, the female form must be aestheticized to erase even the threat of the apparently visible absence. Thus Woman, her veiling nudity, and Art allegorize each other in a fetishing move of psychic defense and aggression by phallocentric culture. Contemplation of three almost identical repeating variations on the sign woman/beauty/art, offers the viewer access to a sense of beauty that is created by the conflation of formal aesthetically contrived harmonies and the empty form that is called the female nude—a fetish of the death necessary to this art. The containment of the dissonant female body within the finely drawn contours of the classic shape, all sexuality erased and closed up, makes woman surface and disguise, keeping all abjection and threat of difference at bay by the willing performance of the masquerade of her vacuous otherness.[60] Any attempt to inscribe "that which happened" (thus the poet Celan referred to the Holocaust) will have to undo the history of Western painting and its specular use of the nude body, to paint, as I have argued, "after painting" as well as "after history."

In some of the *Eurydice* series (Figs. 14 and 15), the ghostly shapes of three women appear before us. In the paintings, they are not fixed by the photography that once pinned them under a deadly gaze. They come back to us from a twentieth century hell, never a return, but an apparation, a memory traced in black grains. This "readymade" of history undoes Raphael's Western paradigm of art/woman/beauty. In *Eurydice,* three women appear on the very threshold of a visibility that is borderline of what we can bear to watch: one almost seen from the back with her head averted from us, one seen in profile carrying her baby, a third turned towards us. They are not nude; and the body can never again signify as it did for Raphael, before history, before Auschwitz. Here/there, the body has been stripped naked for an imminent and chaotic encounter with a cruel death that itself was transformed from the defining event within an individual's biography to an administered effacement of a number within a "species."[61] Where there was fluent ease between three postures in Raphael, the apogee of the Western artist's facility in making the female body signify grace, there is now dissonant anxiety that we can hardly bear to contemplate and the dreadful disorder of mortal fear as the abyss opens before them. There is no harmonious balance in their huddled desperations, their appeal, no relief in the fetishism of aesthetic perfection from the vulnerability of the embodied subject's encounter with death, or its continuing, uncommemorated terror.

In correspondence over this new work, the artist referred me to another Raphael painting that had been on her mind as she worked. This was *The Fire in the Borgo* (figs. 17 and 18). Painted in 1516–17, the fresco shows Pope Leo III (795–810) taking the oath in St. Peter's Basilica and crowning Charlemagne. It also shows another Pope, Leo IV (847–55) celebrating a victory over the Saracens and extinguishing a fire which had burned down

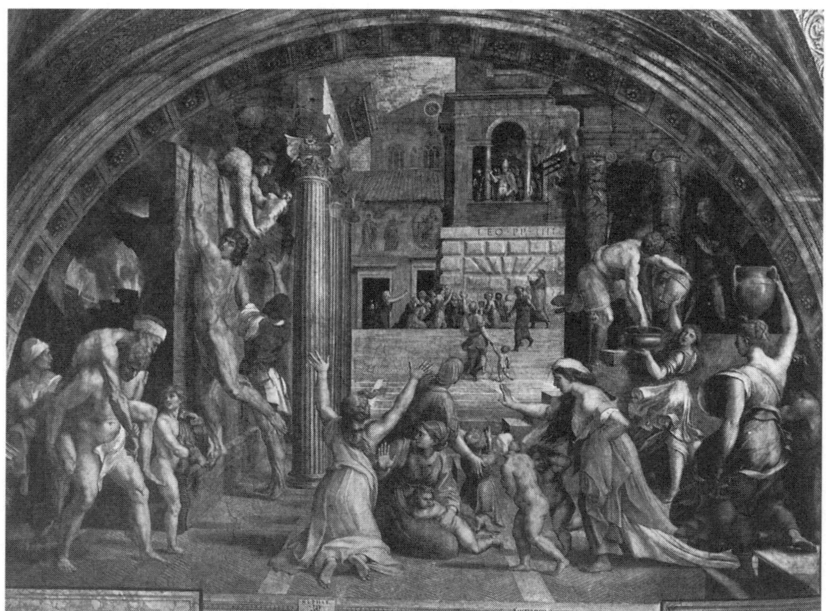

Figure 17.   Raphael, *The Fire in the Borgo*, 1516–17, fresco, Rome: Vatican.

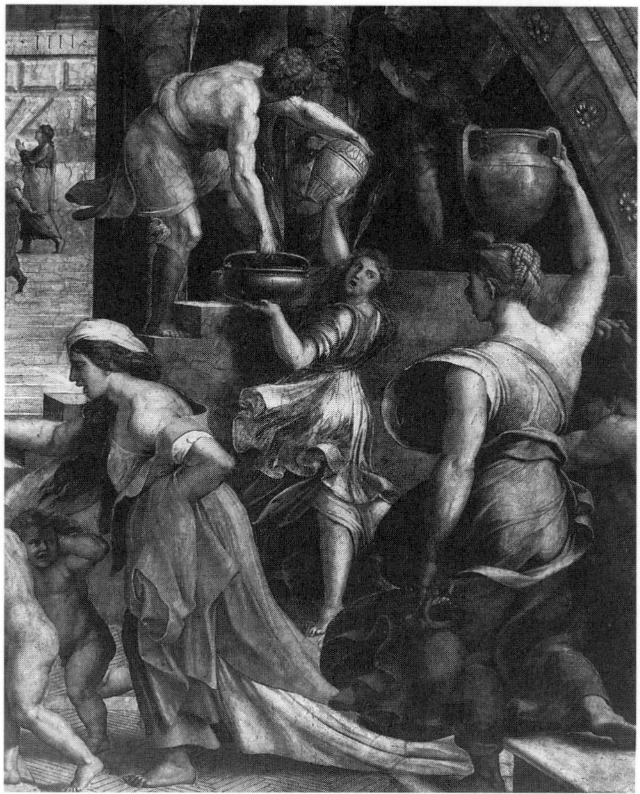

Figure 18.   Detail.

the Saracen quarter near St. Peter's in the papal city. In Raphael's dramatic
and action-packed fresco, we witness a dangerous situation. A mother and
her swaddled child seek desperately to escape the fire. The mother hands her
swaddled babe down to the reaching arms of a strong young man. Young
and old, strong and infirm, other mothers and children are rescued or take
up poses of anxiety and fear. One althletic male nude looks back at us—an
escapee? a rescuer? This gaze invokes the spectator to mark both the menace
of the fire and the energy of the rescue, while in the background Pope Leo
IV blesses the crowd. Contemplating Raphael's mastery of the muscular and
the pathetic to tell the story of danger, deliverance and celebration, we can
well imagine the terrible sadness that must filter through to the artist as she

meditates on, and with, her "tiny document of *Shoah*"—the Jewish disaster the Catholic Church did not condemn. The artist writes: "In our big fire no brave men came to the rescue." (figs. 19 and 20) The gender relations, then, within the *Eurydice* paintings, are not the replication of the formula "men look: women are looked at." The presence of women in the frame of death marks an unalleviable absence and makes the paintings signify the abandonment not present in the original photographs that were themselves the bureaucratic record of the fascist state's machinery of murder.

For many years Bracha Lichtenberg Ettinger has found herself involved with the woman of the averted look that is a part of this document. Equally the woman with her child in her arms haunts her (figs. 11 and 4):

> I want her to look at me! That woman, her back turned to me. This image haunts me. It's my aunt, I say, no my aunt's the other one, with the baby. The baby! it could be mine. What are they looking at? I want them to turn toward me. Once, just once. I want to see their faces.
>
> The hidden face and the veiled face are two moments calling to each other: moments of catastrophe.
>
> *Matrix. Halal(a)—Lapsus, 1990: 67*

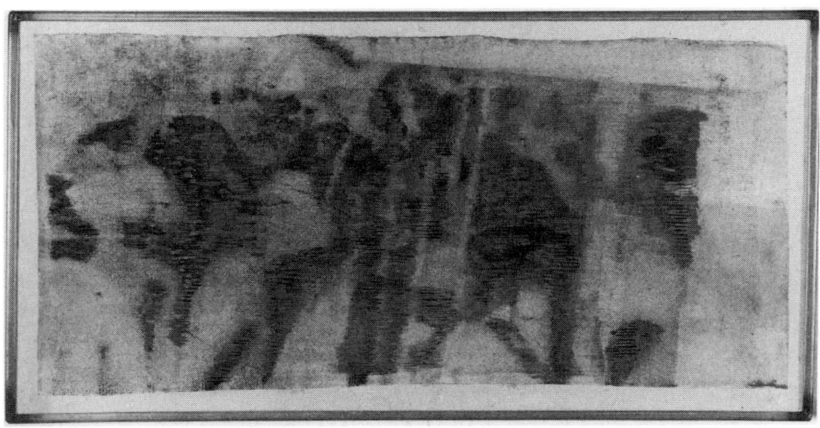

Figure 19.   Bracha Lichtenberg-Ettinger, *Eurydice*, no. 15. 1994–6. 25.2 × 52 cm. (mounted on chassis: 29 × 55.5 cm), oil and xerox on paper mounted on canvas.

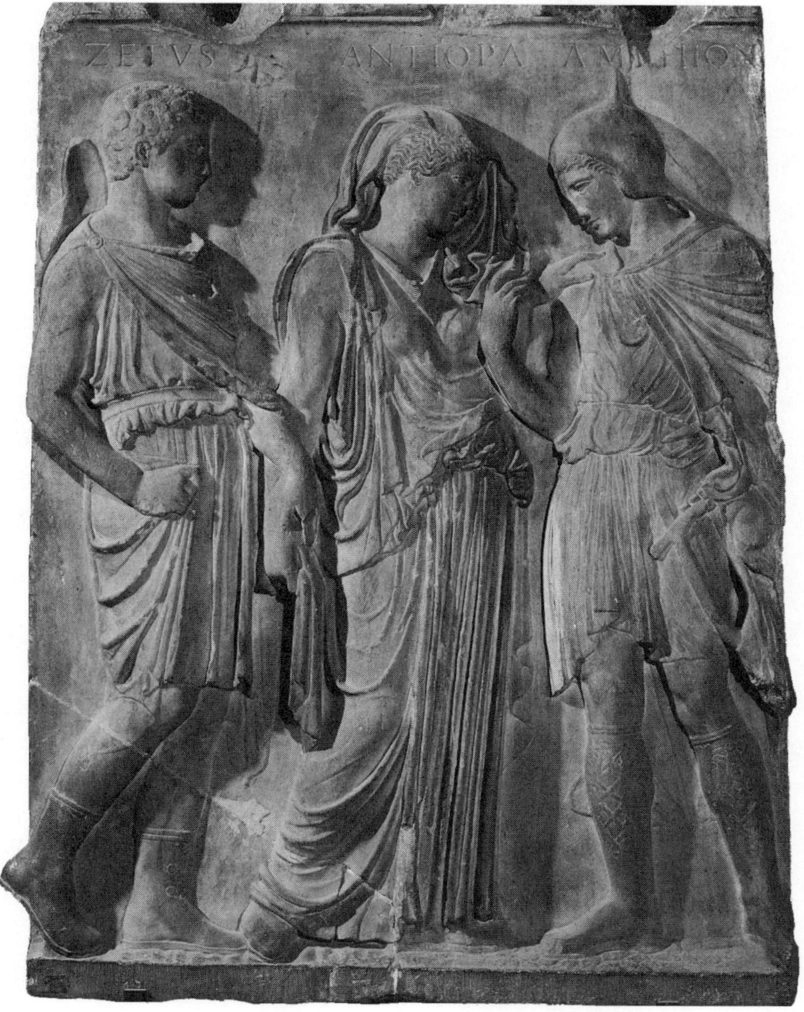

Figure 20.   *Orpheus, Eurydice, Hermes*, marble, 5th century BCE. Paris: Louvre.

In these paintings, the artist is drawn also to the woman who looks back with an almost lost appeal, at which her wandering around the image is arrested. Each of her "Three Graces"—Eurydice looking at death and looking back at us from the moment in the history of Europe's abandonment of the Jewish people—represents a different possibility, not at the level of the imagined real of their actual situation, for they had no options, but in terms of our relation to the trace-image that serves as a point of encounter—forever an almost-encounter between a past and a future. The averted head leaves us in a position of being forever *behind*, a position in space, but in Hebrew, the language in which this art is imagined and thought, the word also means *after*, a moment in time. We see only the back of the head and after, we know and yet cannot bear to know where she went.

Bracha Lichtenberg Ettinger records in her *Carnets* her bonds with that figure through the story of Ruth. Ruth was a Gleaner. Ruth, the stranger, the foreigner, the inverted exile, followed after/behind the reapers. Ruth may be a figure of the artist and Ruth signifies a place of encounter between time and space that is all of us, at this moment. The Biblical narrative can be reread in our times as the story of a loss. Naomi is the survivor, bereaved of husband and both sons, who comes back from the foreign place of her trauma. The story of survival, the Book of Ruth, also tells of a covenant between the survivor and the gleaner and between a past of trauma and a future in the feminine through Ruth, the stranger and the other. Through the poetics of the story of Ruth the Gleaner, the artist explores a matrixial covenant in the feminine that promises some aspect of futurity in the feminine to a world that, like Ruth the Gleaner, comes "after the reapers."

> Again and again, Ruth comes from behind or after …. Ruth's exile is the inverse of mine but it's also an inverse exile. She leaves the space of No (non-site) to seek truth, meaning, lover, God, a promised land with an open future; origin is revealed as linked to the future.
> Is what hurts in front of her or behind her? Before or after?
> *Matrix. Halal(a)—Lapsus 1990:74*

In the series *Eurydice,* Bracha Lichtenberg Ettinger delves ever deeper into this fragment of Jewish history which is the history of modernity, learning from it the possible significance of other key images that constitute the compelling universe of absence with which the artist is compelled ever to touch: her archive has long included a doll with its unblinking, non-human gaze fixed on us, unseeing yet representing the child's universe and the terror of seeing, (fig. 13) a link back to the uncanny *Olympia* from Hoffman's *The Sand Man;* an image of a "crazy woman" from a nineteenth century treatise on madness (fig. 2, *Matrixial Borderlines*), a link to the history of hysteria and psychoanalysis; and a photograph of her parents walking down a street in Lodz in 1938 from whose forward movement the impossible gulf of disaster forever separates us, them, the artist, Europe (fig. 10)—a link to the traumatized family album that was destroyed by the Nazi ghettoes and transports. Eurydice is another cultural narrative that can be reworked as an allegory for the Jewish/feminine postmodern which is post-Oswieçim.

As Emmanuel Levinas has written, Western Europe lives in a "Christian atmosphere"; it shapes the calendar and provides the implicit images of both high and popular culture from Redeemers to Passions. What narratives of history can reclaim for memory the forgotten and the lost without subjecting Jewish grief to an alien, Christian or Greek imaginary? Elaine Marks writes that it is possible to read in Emmanuel Levinas' critique of Christianocentrism a parallel to the feminist critique of phallocentrism. In the unconscious and non-conscious of images and texts that constitute our cultural horizons, the feminine and the Jewish occupy a comparable and related position of an included but unrelieved alterity. Thus is revealed a significant affinity between the thought of Emmanuel Levinas and his ideas for a Jewish Renaissance, and the work of his friend Bracha Licthenberg Ettinger, working in her painting towards a *symbologenesis*—a creation of signs—that would allow the foreclosed of both Jewish history and the feminine the relief of signification and the chance to realign our culture "after history." Elaine Marks writes:

> In *Difficult Freedoms* Lévinas is less concerned with writing about Auschwitz than with coming to terms with what made Auschwitz possible. He does this by raising the "Christian Question" and displacing the meaning of *cendres* from death, through violence towards Others, to rebirth, through Talmudic texts that emphasize the ethical relationship to the Other.[62]

all about eurydice[63]

BLE: I'd like to ask you a question about the alterity of the feminine. At one point you spoke of the feminine as a flight before the light.

EL: In other words: not to show oneself. A flight before demonstration.

BLE: I took it as a metaphor for a kind of movement of disappearance. Not to be fixated by the look. For me, in the Matrix, a kind of withdrawing/ contracting (*rétirance*) before the light of consciousness leads to meeting with an unknown other. Is there an interiority that is not the passage of the infinitely exterior? What would Eurydice say? Can the subject-woman have a privileged access to the feminine?

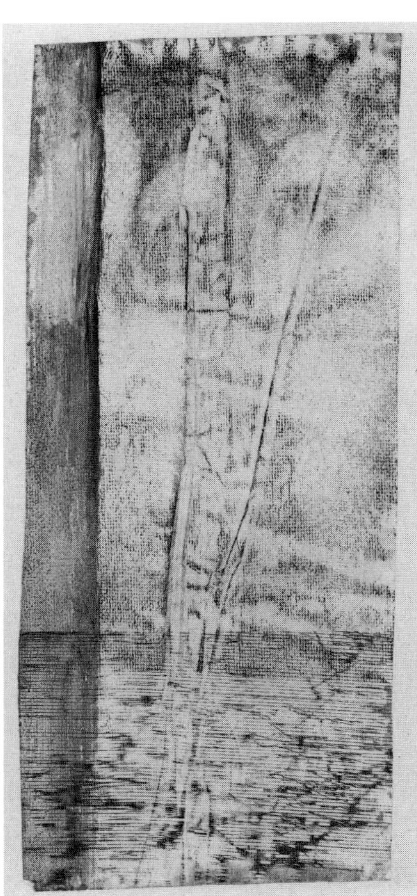

Figure 21.   Bracha Lichtenberg Ettinger, *Eurydice*, no. 16. 1994–6. 51.7 × 22 cm. (mounted on chassis: 55.3 × 25.5 cm), oil and xerox on paper mounted on canvas.

EL: I think that the heart of the heart, the deepest of the feminine is dying in giving life, in bringing life into the world. I am not emphasizing *dying*, but, on the contrary, *future.*

Emmanuel Levinas in conversation with Bracha Lichtenberg Ettinger[64]

About 1510 the Venetian artist Titian painted *Orpheus and Eurydice* (fig. 22). It is an almost medieval conjunction of several episodes of the Ovidian narrative within one canvas. On the left, and in the foreground, the poet-musician's young wife, Eurydice, is bitten by a monstrous serpent on her heel as she languishes in an ideal landscape that is already Christian— witness the steeple that presides over the distant town. That ecclesiastical presence tips the Greek wood nymph Eurydice into a Christian imaginary where she doubles with the Christian vision of Eve: woman as the source of the trouble, condemned at her expulsion from the Garden of Eden to bruise the head of the serpent and suffer the pains of childbirth. Divided by a massive rocky outcrop, the righthand side of the painting illustrates the subsequent episode when, offered the chance to save Eurydice and bring her back to life from the mouth of hell, if only he does not look at her, Orpheus

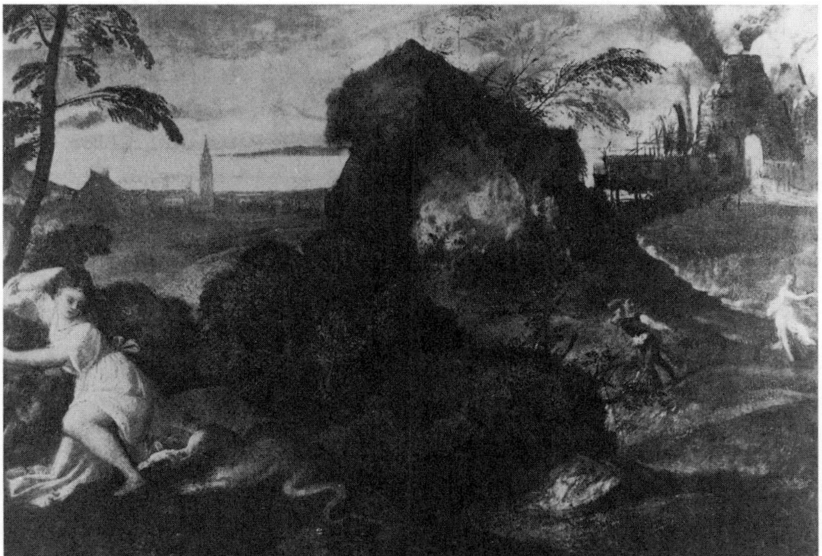

Figure 22.   Titian, *Orpheus and Eurydice*, Bergamo, Accademia Carraro, oil on panel, 39 × 53 cm, ca. 1510.

looks back and Eurydice is halted on her journey back to the earth, light and life. Behind her is the Venetian artist's semi-industrial image of hell—like a giant furnace, belching chimneys, and fiery furnaces within.

Titian's painting confirms the nesting of Greek thought within Christianity. For Eurydice conflates with Eve via the serpent. The scene of the poet and his almost-revived wife iconographically doubles with an expulsion from the Garden. In this case, however, Orpheus escapes (from hell) and remains among the flowers. Titian makes the couple sway apart as the power of Orpheus's look drives Eurydice back into hell. Titian's vision of Tartarus cannot be read without a shock in our time. Uncannily it offers an image for that hell realized under the Third Reich near a little Polish town, Oswieçim. In his First Diaporist Manifesto for a Jewish painting in the late twentieth century, R.B. Kitaj tells us how he "fell upon the chimney as an analogue to the crucifix in European art and used it nervously in several paintings."[65]

What was the power of the sixth-century Greek myth for the Christian imagination of the sixteenth and seventeenth centuries—from Titian to Monteverdi? Why is that almost a century after this painting, the official commencement of the operatic art form as we know it was itself inspired by this same tale, following a range of orphic laments? Beginning with Peri's opera *L'Eurydice* of 1600, this late Greek legend has spawned over 65 known operas from Monteverdi's *La Favola d'Orfeo* (1607) through to the perennially popular *Orphée et Eurydice* by Gluck, first sung in 1762 and revived in a revised French version by Hector Berlioz in 1860, and considered to be the birth of modern opera. At its heart is the dream of a mortal being brought back from the dead, which also finds its double in Christian theology.[66] But its appeal must also lie in the fact of its hero figure being a musician and poet. Orpheus has for centuries embodied the poetic mastery of the male writer/musician. His journey into the underworld illustrates the origins of creative mastery in masculine knowledge of "the dark continent: death and sexuality which is also Woman."

Most opera composers could not bear the mournful ending of the mythic legend, in which, separated from his wife, Orpheus is subsequently torn to pieces by Circonian (Virgil) or Thracian (Ovid) women at the behest of Dionysius. In a very Christian move, Monteverdi had already taken Orpheus to heaven for an eternal reunion with Eurydice (son-God reunited with his

Mother), while in the eighteenth-century beginnings of bourgeois modern sentiment, Gluck has Amor come on stage to commend Orpheus for his constancy and fidelity, and then Amor brings Eurydice back to life singing: "Do not doubt my power! I come to rescue you from this dreadful place; henceforth enjoy the pleasures of love!" (Act III). Thus the opera allows death to be triumphed over and Amor functions as a redeemer in which love and marriage, as at the end of all good bourgeois plots, stand in for all resolutions of conflict and loss.

Eurydice, the wife of the poet, is both his muse and the lost object of Orpheus's desire. Dead, she furnishes both his arcane knowledge and the sources of his poetry in a loss that he both needed and, in some senses, desired. His backward look killed her, a second time. Eurydice is the absence filled by the poet's words and traced in his music. In Gluck's opera, the most famous aria:

> "J'ai perdu mon Eurydice,
> Rien n'égale mon malheur.
> Sort cruel! Quelle rigeur!
> Je succombe à ma douleur."

is sung towards the end of Act III after the anguished exchange between Eurydice, who cannot understand her husband's apparent coldness, and Orpheus, hurt by her doubt looks back. The stunning beauty of this music shockingly dispels the agitated mood of recitative misunderstanding. After the grating crescendo of despair, this exquisite aria lifts the listener on its wave of sweet violins to the disconcerting fullness of Orpheus's singing the word *douleur*. This poem in song tells us of his loss while it comforts us with its "haunting" beauty. The aestheticization of feminine death and its necessity to the male poet could not be more striking.[67] He resurrects not the woman but his desire, necessarily created in the absence of the primary object of desire, remade as a trace, an "image of woman" in his art.

The legend allegorizes woman in phallocentric culture: the primary object of desire is the Maternal body, which, in this logic, must be abjected, lost to language but refound as a memory, and a symbol. Sublimated in the "*image* of woman," this, in turn, has also to be refashioned according to the aesthetic exigencies of the castration complex to produce art. The function of woman as lost object is the paradox of signifying the loss necessary to masculine subjectivity and desire, while being reformed, on the other side of language, as the aetheticized mask, as a fetishized masquerade that both commemorates her "death" and veils it with the sign of beauty that has nothing to do with her femininity.

In developing this argument we could follow Julia Kristeva's arguments about the relations between abjection, feminine melancholy and the necessity, for the cause of love, for the imaginary father.[68] Kristeva sees abjection as the necessary and only means of separation from the maternal, semiotic *body*, filled with drives and pre-objects.[69] Via the screen of what she names the imaginary father—a figure who represents the desire of the mother veering away from the child—the child can separate imaginatively from the mother's corporality, and eventually symbolically connect with the mother's love.

Julia Kristeva appears not to be repeating the classic psychoanalytical move which casts the mother only as the prelanguage Other to be displaced by the Oedipal Father as the condition of language and subjectivity. Kristeva is suggesting that the child must find a way to separate from the haven of the maternal body and its fantasies of maternal interiority. The mother's body has to be lost in the Real but the mother is to be found as a symbol, as a memory, through the signified intersubjectivity of love. The imaginary father is the screen for, and thus the means of contact with, the mother's desire. Her desire—for that which is more than or other than the child, indicating the mother's lack and the break with the symbiotic bond with the child—enables the child to imagine both the mother and itself as separated subjects. Desire, predicated on lack, breaks the archaic identification with, and horror of remaining inside, the maternal body.

Julia Kristeva puts abjection in a critical place in her history of the subject because it represents the dangerous borderline signified by the maternal body, between life and death, inside and outside, being the corruption of all divisions. The abject, writes Kristeva,

> might then appear as the most *fragile* (from a synchronic point of view), the most *archaic* (from a diachronic one) sublimation of an "object" still inseparable from the drives. The abject is the pseudo-object that made up *before* but which appears only *within* the gaps of secondary repression.[70]

Kelly Oliver glosses this: "the abject appears in the structure/logic of the subject as its most fragile relation to the object: and it appears in the history/chronology of the subject as the earliest relation to the object."[71]

With this theory and its insights Kristeva takes us to the very limits of phallocentric psychoanalysis. Yet her theorization still remains inside its paradigm of castrative separation, trying to negotiate some space for the archaic mother and yet still making her abjection the condition of subjectivity. This remains a phallic model. There can only be subjectivity when there is some subject/object relation, some imminent **I** and **not-I,** Self and Other.

Bracha Lichtenberg Ettinger's revolutionary theory of a matrixial stratum of co-emergence of an **I** and a **non-I**—a significant distinction—dares to suggest that borderlines do not have to be phobically defended, considered perverse and transgressive. Separation does not have to involve abjection. Why? Because Bracha Lichtenberg Ettinger proposes to shift the phallic paradigm so that we might glimpse partial subject–partial subject relations across this threshold of minimal difference that is presumed even within the maternal/infant encounter. In her theory, the mother is never just a body, but a fantasizing, subjectivizing subject, always and already, even if, at a later, postnatal stage, another retrospective infant fantasy engulfs that relation and objectifies/abjectifies the maternal body as a *place*/Thing from which the infant subject must be severed. The Phallus is the signifier of this later predicament; the Matrix allows the former possibility to surface alongside and propose realignments of moments or levels of subjectivity.

This distinction between Kristevan theory and that of Lichtenberg Ettinger is critical for the way we approach the legacies of Nazi genocidal representation—the archive of photographs that appear to be the historical record, the fascist shape of memory. These house the unmourned losses of the Jewish people and those exterminated in the camps for their sexuality, ethnicity or politics. It is often felt that the mere reproduction of the images of those on their way to the death chambers or starved to death, or executed and buried in mass graves revisits a second death, a second Orphic look that kills again. Faced with the horror, the people in these images too easily become abject. As dying, dead, and as people subjected to systematic Nazi torture of dehumanization, they may appear to contemporary viewers abjectly as too other, on the other side of the threshold where the viewer phobically defines a subjectivity by banishing the abject. From the viewer's repulsed refusal of contact with that threatening dissolution of the subject menaced by abjection, the viewer tries to reconstruct some sense of being alive and being at least human. We, the viewers, are **not-them**. Yet not to identify with them is to be positioned with the Nazis, with those who criminally ordained the division between the human, with the right to life, and the untermensch condemned to extermination. The uncanny, the ghost, the corpse, these "returns of the repressed" threaten to tip the viewer into touch with the Real of the Thing that the object tries to sublimate. And so we recoil from the image where, through the pressure of unprecedented human horror, sublimation fails. But these images are for many of us not 'them.' They are us. They could be us. They may be our beloved ones. Each person captured in these images represents a world, a lover, parent, child, relative, school friend, that was lost for someone.

There is, through matrixial theory, another possible—and a necessary—structure. This allows us to experience the encounter not in the phallic mold as subject/abject, but as a matrixial movement between subjects not quite secure or fixed in the logic of subject/object, and not deferred in time, but brought into affective immediacy by luring a matrixial, almost tactile gaze across the borderlines of the visible. Fragile, yes, borderline, yes; and creative of another stratum of subjective affect in which we have to share responsibility for trauma and phantasy. Bracha Lichtenberg Ettinger has called this matrixial complex *Eurydice* (fig. 23) to connect her project also with a woman artist's identification with the silenced, abandoned, forgotten other of Greek and Western myth. Eurydice can, nonetheless, be moved onto a Jewish historical terrain. In this the artist shares in the larger feminist project to rewrite, in the feminine, the myths that are Western culture's deeply and stubbornly gendered unconscious.

Several women poets have given Eurydice a voice in this century. I earlier quoted the Jewish poet Elaine Feinstein's *Feast of Eurydice*. In H. D.'s (Hilda Doolittle's) *Eurydice*, a long lament, the poet imagines Eurydice not silent, but speaking to Orpheus:

> So you have swept me back,
> I who could have walked the earth with the live souls
> above the earth,

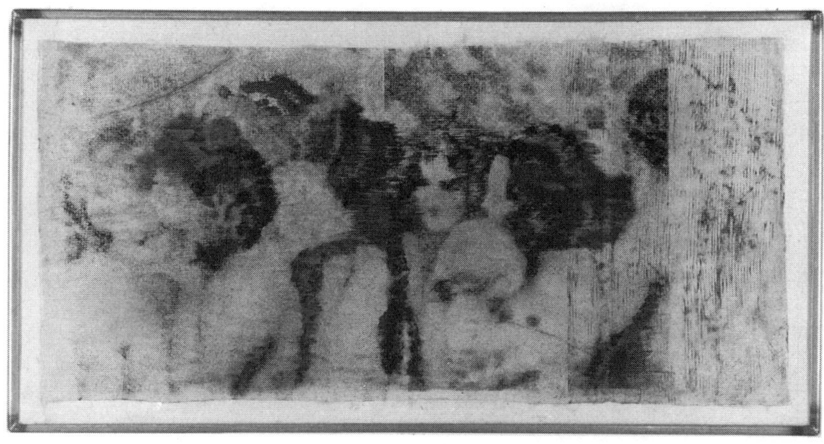

Figure 23.   Bracha Lichtenberg-Ettinger, *Eurydice*, no. 14. 1994–6. 25.4 × 52 cm. (mounted on chassis: 30 × 55.4 cm), oil and xerox on paper mounted on canvas.

> I who could have slept among the live flowers
> at last;

Orpheus is accused:

> so for your arrogance
> and your ruthlessness
> I am swept back
> where dead lichens drip
> dead cinders upon moss of ash;
>
> so for your arrogance
> I am broken at last,
> I who had lived unconscious
> who was almost forgot;
>
> If you had let me wait
> I had grown from listlessness
> into peace,
> if you had let me rest with the dead, I had forgot you
> and the past.

And then Eurydice asks bitterly:

> what was it that crossed my face
> with the light from yours

> and your glance?
>
> . . .
>
> What had my face to offer
> but the reflex of earth …

She concludes, however, by asserting her own subjectivity against his erasure of her in his own image, which he projected back at her. It was the glance of the poet who never saw her, the woman, at all.

> At least I have the flowers of myself,
> and my thoughts, no god can take that;
> I have the fervour of myself for a presence
> and my own spirit for light;
>
> and my spirit with its loss
> knows this;
> and though small against the black,
> small against the formless rocks,
> hell must break before I am lost;
>
> before I am lost,
> hell must open like a red rose
> for the dead to pass.[72]

This Eurydice condemns the male narcissism at the basis of the masculine poetic tradition. She resists her own sacrifice for the sake of his art, where she must be silenced and only be sung. Eurydice becomes the figure of the woman as poet who must refuse to be her husband's mirror. At the end she claims a selfhood separate from the deadly duet, but at a price of her own suffering, her own psychological journey. [73]

Bracha Lichtenberg Ettinger is not offering the Eurydice complex as a simple means of feminist reversal. Nothing allows us to identify with the Eurydice of the Shoah, those abandoned at the mouth of hell, in an eternally designated moment where horror too great for us to imagine leaves but the ash of a terrible incineration of humanity. Yet she works with a Eurydice complex that alerts us to the Orphic structure embedded in, while undone by, this defining moment of Western modernity. As a painter, manipulating the absence bearing grains and the yearning touch of painted color, Bracha Lichtenberg works with images that make us witnesses for the event at which there were no witnesses to reflect the destruction of humanity. Avoiding the phallic logic of abjection, she returns again and again in her work to reconnect with the traces of the once living as they were before death. Thus she also escapes the Christian topos of resurrection which haunts the bourgeois retelling of Eurydice in its operatic forms. Her Eurydice is released from being the trope of masculine creativity: death sublimated through aestheticization. She must look at us and yet there will never be an encounter—only its endless missing (fig. 23). What does this Eurydicean look/non-look open up? this abandoned "she" of the Jewish people for whom no one came to hell to rescue her before six million had died, this "feminine" that phallocentric culture casts into oblivion? What is the gaze of loss/disappearance—Eurydice—that haunts us, and in its painted encounter even solaces us, across the borderlines of history and death, that stretches from the dead, from hell, to our time? What will happen to us when we engage with the color of her grief in a painterly, matrixial moment created by paintings that draw us through uncanny tracings and veils of color into an intensity of affect dissolving the borderlines, and opening at the threshold of visibility, "another web of meaning donation/revelation" about memory, oblivion and histories "in the feminine"?

> There are no memories.
> There is no memory.
> There is not even an unknown.
> There is no oblivion.
> Metramorphosis fails and delivers the anonymous.
> Testimony of nothingness.
> Requiem for the future.
> Beyond
> before
> after
> in front of
> behind. To excess.
> Painting is not the image itself even it if is deliverance from the image. Deliverance from an excess—space that defies the masculine symbolic of the idea of God. Excess of before, of beforehand, links the internal and the

> face. The excess of behind and of after
> links feminine and other.
> *Matrix. Hala(a)—Lapsus* 1989: 71.

notes

1 Jonathan Ree, "Interview with Julia Kristeva," in *Talking Liberties* (London: Channel Four Television, 1992), 20.

2 Edmond Jabès, *The Book of Questions*, trans. Rosemarie Waldrop (Middletown: Wesleyan University, 1991), 400.

3 Richard Stamelman, "The Writing of Catastrophe: Jewish Memory and the Poetics of the Book in Edmond Jabès," *Auschwitz and After: Race, Culture and "the Jewish Question" in France*, ed. Lawrence D. Kritzman (London: Routledge, 1995), 276.

4 Isak Dinesen [Karen Blixen], "The Blank Page" in *Last Tales*, [1957] (London: Penguin Books, 1986), 104.

5 Susan Gubar, "'The Blank Page' and Issues of Female Creativity," in *New Feminist Criticism*, ed. Elaine Showalter (London: Virago Press, 1986), 292–313.

6 Bracha Lichtenberg Ettinger, *The Matrixial Gaze* (Leeds: The Feminist Arts and Histories Network at the University of Leeds, 1995), 50.

7 Here lies an early prefiguration of both John Cage's music of silence and Robert Rauschenberg's white paintings.

8 Isak Dinesen [Karen Blixen], op. cit., 100.

9 Christine Buci-Glucksman, "Images of Absence," in *Matrixial Borderline*, Bracha Lichtenberg Ettinger (Paris: Les Cahiers des Regards, 1993), 12–17.

10 Hélène Cixous, "The Laugh of the Medusa" in *New French Feminisms*, ed. Elaine Marks and Isabelle de Courtivron (Brighton: Harvester Press, 1981); Margaret Whitford, *Luce Irigaray: Philiosphy in the Feminine* (London and New York: Routledge, 1991).

11 This reading of Cixous and Irigaray is enriched by the theorizations of Bracha Lichtenberg Ettinger, painter and major feminist theorist. I am indebted here to her "Metramorphic Borderlinks and Matrixial Borderspace" [1993] in *Rethinking Borders*, ed. John Welchman (New York: MacMillan, 1996), 125–159.

12 The phrase is from Hélène Cixous, "The Laugh of the Medusa," in *New French Feminisms*, Isabelle de Courtivron and Elaine Marks (Brighton: Harvester Press, 1980), 255. It compounds sex and text.

13 Zygmunt Bauman, *Modernity and Ambivalence* (Cambridge: Polity Press, 1991).

14 A pictogram is the representation of the *originary* psychic space (considered to be closest to the body) as theorized by Piera Aulagnier, *La Violence de l'Interprétation* (Paris: Presses Universitaires de France, 1975).

15 Bracha Licthenberg Ettinger, "Woman-Other-Thing: A Matrixial Touch," in *Matrix-Borderlines* (Oxford: Oxford Museum of Modern Art, 1993), 11.

16 J. F. Lyotard, "L'Anamnèse," talk presented at the Israel Museum and Van Leer Institute, Jerusalem, 1995.

17 Bracha Lichtenberg Ettinger, op. cit., 11.

18 Ibid, 13.

19 *Matrixial Gaze*, op. cit., 47.

20 Sigmund Freud, "The Uncanny" [1919] in *Art and Literature*, Penguin Freud Library, Vol. 14 (Harmondsworth: Penguin Books), 1990, 339.

21 Ibid, 371.

22 I must stress that the matrix does not replace the phallus; it co-resides with it. Thus for a mother the baby may well become in fantasy a phallus. The Matrix is not an idealization of motherhood but deals only with those fantasies and affects mutually occurring in pregnancy as a subjectivizing experience of several subjects. Once we have mother and baby we have a phallic dyad superbly accounted for by existing psychoanalytical accounts. The possible co-existence of moments of a matrixial stratum is supported far more in thinking about aesthetic experience than in entering the labor ward.

23 Psychologically, if we accept such a possibility, there can therefore be matrixial disturbances. Analysts may be able to discern forms of trauma and neurosis whose basis lies in disorders of this stratum. Such a theory neither idealizes motherhood nor pregnancy nor blames women for upsetting their children at an even earlier age. It does imply that there is a subject of pregnancy—and already a severality—an assertion that enhances women's right to determine their own bodies in opposition to the phallic theories that reduce the pregnant woman to a carrier without the rights of a subject.

24 Ibid, 345, 367.

25 The author helps her reader here by a definition offered by Pierre Fédida: "The object contemporaneous with perception and judgement corresponds to a functional organisation of the 'exterior world', which rests upon conceptual units … objectively defined by consciously attributable limits and diachronic separation. The *thing* is distinguished from the object in that it participates in elementary communication between feeling and being moved … the thing is an ante-predicative and pre-conceptual *aesthetic reality*." Bracha Lichtenberg Ettinger, *The Matrixial Gaze* (University of Leeds: Feminist Arts and Histories Network Press, 1995), 15.

26 Freud, "The Uncanny," 363.

27 I derive this distinction from the work of Dori Laub with survivors of the Holocaust. See Dori Laub, "An event without a Witness," in *Testimony: Crises of Witnessing in Literature, Psychoanalysis and History*, Dori Laub and Shoshana Felman, eds. (London and New York: Routledge, 1992), 75–92.

28 Saul Friedlander, *Probing the Limits of Representation: Nazism and the "Final Solution,"* (Cambridge, MA: Harvard University Press, 1992).

29 There is a growing literature on this "transgenerational transmission." See Helen Epstein, *Children of the Holocaust* (New York: G.N. Putnam's, 1979): Martin S. Bergmann and Milton E. Jucovy, *Generations of the Holocaust* (New York: Columbia University Press, 1982); and most recently, Anne Karpf, *The War After; Living with the Holocaust* (London: Heinemann, 1996).

30 J. Laplanche and J. B. Pontalis, *The Language of Psychoanalysis*, trans. Donald Nicholson-Smith (London: Karnac Books, 1988), 166.

31 Elaine Showalter, *The Female Malady: Women, Madness and English Culture, 1830–1980*, (London: Virago Press, 1987).

32 Sigmund Freud and Joseph Breuer, *Studies on Hysteria*, Penguin Freud Library, Vol. 3 (Harmondsworth: Penguin Books, 1991), 95.

33 Julia Kristeva, *Tales of Love,* trans. Leon S. Roudiez (New York: Columbia University Press, 1987).

34 Michele Silvestre, "Le Transfert" in *Demain de la Psychanalyse* (Paris: Navarin, 1987), 76. Cited in Parveen Adams, "The Art of Analysis: Mary Kelly's *Interim* and the Discourse of the Analyst," *October*, Fall 1991, No. 58, 89. I am indebted to this article and to Patricia Elliott, *From Analysis to Mastery: Theories of Gender in Psychoanalytic Feminism* (Ithaca and London: Cornell University Press, 1991), for these ideas about analytic discourse.

35 Elizabeth Bronfen, "The Knotted Subject" in *Generations and Geographies in the Visual Arts: Feminist Readings*, ed. Griselda Pollock (London: Routledge, 1996).

36 Parveen Adams, op. cit., 93.

37 Emily Apter, "Fetishism and Visual Seduction in Mary Kelly's *Interim*," *October*, Fall 1991, No. 58, 107.

38 Griselda Pollock, "Missing Women: Rethinking Early Thoughts on Images of Women," in *The Critical Image*, ed. by Carol Squires (Seattle: Bay Press, 1990), 202–19.

39 Griselda Pollock, "Gleaning in History: or coming after/behind the reapers: The feminine, the stranger and the matrix in the work and theory of Bracha Lichtenberg Ettinger," in *Generations and Geographies*, op. cit.

40 This is a quotation from the artist's *Carnets: Matrix. Halal(a)—Lapsus* published under this title by the Museum of Modern Art, Oxford, 1993.

41 Catherine Francblin, "Interview with Julia Kristeva," *Flash Art*, March 1986, No. 126, 45.

42 Sigmund Freud, *Beyond the Pleasure Principle*, Pelican Freud Library, Vol. 11 (Harmondsworth: Penguin Books, 1984).

43 Francblin, op. cit., 45.

44 Ibid.

45 Luce Irigaray, "Flesh Colors," in *Sexes and Genealogies* [1987], trans. Gillian G. Gill (New York: Columbia University Press, 1993), 155.

46 Bracha Lichtenberg Ettinger, "Matrix and Metramorphosis," *Differences*, 4:3 1992, 201.

47 *A Threshold Where We Are Afraid: Edmond Jabès in conversation with Bracha Lichtenberg Ettinger* (Oxford: Museum of Modern Art, 1993), 9.

48 See Griselda Pollock, "Screening the Seventies: Sexuality and Representation in Feminist Practice" in *Vision and Difference* (London: Routledge, 1988), 155–199; and Paula Marincola, *Image Scavengers: Photography* (Philadelphia Institute of Contemporary Art, 1982), and Abigail Solomon-Godeau, *The Stolen Image and Its Uses,* (Syracuse, New York: 1983).

49 *Matrixial Gaze,* 51.

50 His two major books on this subject are *Modernity and the Holocaust* (Cambridge: Polity Press, 1989), and *Modernity and Ambivalence* (Cambridge: Polity Press, 1991).

51 Elaine Marks, "*Cendres Juives:* Jews Writing in French 'after Auschwitz'" in *Marrano as Metaphor: The Jewish Presence in French Writing* (New York: Columbia University Press, 1996), 115.

52 These quotations are from the artists *Carnets (Notes on Painting)* published under this title by the Museum of Modern Art, Oxford, 1993.

53 Roland Barthes, "Rhetoric of the Image," *Image-Music-Text*, S. Heath, ed. (London: Fontana Books, 1977), 44.

54 Laub in Laub and Felman, op. cit. Witnessing is critical to maintaining the humanity of those on whom these horrors were inflicted. Part of the Nazi crime was to deny the victims witnesses so that they became tied into the criminal duet with their torturers: see especially pp. 81–2.

55 Elaine Feinstein, *The Feast of Eurydice* (London: Faber and Faber, 1980), n.p.

56 Laura Mulvey, "Visual Pleasure and Narrative Cinema," *Screen*, 1975, vol. 16, no. 3, 7; also reprinted in *Visual and Other Pleasures*, London: MacMillan, 1989.

57 Klaus Theweleit, "Monteverdi's *Orfeo*: The Technology of Reconstruction," in *Opera Through Other Eyes*, David J. Levin, ed. (Stanford, CA: Stanford University Press, 1994), 148.

58 Ibid, 172.

59 Ibid.

60 Lynda Nead, *The Female Nude: Art, Obscenity and Sexuality* (London: Routledge, 1994).

61 Theodor Adorno, "After Auschwtiz," [1949] in *Negative Dialectics*, trans. E. B. Ashton (New York: Continuum, 1973), 362.

62 Elaine Marks, "Cendres Juives," op. cit., 120.

63 I hope the intended reference to the famous film *All About Eve* is noted.

64 *Time is the Breath of the Spirit: Emmanuel Levinas in conversation with Bracha Lichtenberg Ettinger* (Oxford: Museum of Modern Art, 1993).

65 This quotation is actually from R. B. Kitaj, "Varschreibt!" in *Holocaust Remembrance: The Shapes of Memory*, Geoffrey H. Hartman, ed. (Oxford: Basil Blackwell 1994), 117. R. B. Kitaj, *The First Diasporist Manifesto* (London: Thames & Hudson), 1989.

66 The dream of a mortal being brought back from the dead has become inscribed in Western culture through the Christian religion where it has been argued that Orphic elements were rehoused. Freud argued that the doctrine of original sin was of Orphic origin and within the Christian sacrament some trace of ancient mysteries were to be detected. Christianity solemnizes the necessary atonement for the original sin through the sacrifice of the young son-god who then rises and lives forever. Sigmund Freud, *Totem and Taboo* [1919] (Harmondsworth: Pelican Books, 1938), 235–6.

67 Elizabeth Bronfen, *Over Her Dead Body: Death, Femininity and the Aesthetic* (Manchester: Manchester University Press, 1992), raises these conjunctions but does not discuss Eurydice as its trope.

68 I am indebted to Kelly Oliver, *Reading Kristeva: Unravelling the Double Bind* (Bloomington: Indiana University Press, 1993), for this clarification of Kristeva's important theories.

69 Ibid, 64.

70 Ibid, 59.

71 Ibid, 59.

72 H. D. [Hilda Doolittle] *Collected Poems 1912–1944*, Louis L. Martz, ed. (Manchester: Carcanet Press, 1984), 51–5. I am grateful for Diane Purkiss, "Women's Rewriting of Myths" in *The Feminist Companion to Mythology*, Carolyne Larrington, ed. (London: Pandora Books, 1992), 441–458, for alerting me to to H. D.'s poem.

73 Elaine Feinstein also inverts the poetic trope of Orpheus in her long poem, *The Feast of Eurydice* (London: Faber & Faber, 1980). She too traces the intimate links between creativity, femininity, renunciation and death but her Eurydice finds comfort in the final reunion in death of the poetic couple.

part iii
historical
re-visions

griselda pollock

proximity and the color of desire: the laboring body and its sex

7

IN 1886, IN AN ANONYMOUS LETTER to the *Wigan and District Advertiser* (30 January, 1886: 2), Arthur Joseph Munby (1828–1910) wrote, "for my own reasons, I have for more than thirty years, studied the subject of female labor, not merely in books and at second hand, but *with my own eyes and on the spot*" (my emphasis).[1] Having thus looked, Arthur Munby then rehearsed this proximity in writing detailed accounts in diary notebooks, complete with verbatim conversations recorded in a transcription of Lancashire dialects. (There are nine notebooks devoted to his sixteen visits to the mining district around Wigan between 1853 and 1887.) He also recaptured his visual encounters in photographs of women miners he bought locally or arranged to have taken in one of the many photographic studios operating in Wigan.[2] In one such image, taken on 11 September 1873 at Little's studio in Clarence Yard, Wigan, Munby is also photographed (fig. 1). It is a rare occurrence, unique as far as I know. The photograph, therefore, represents a moment of proximity. The woman in the photograph is the

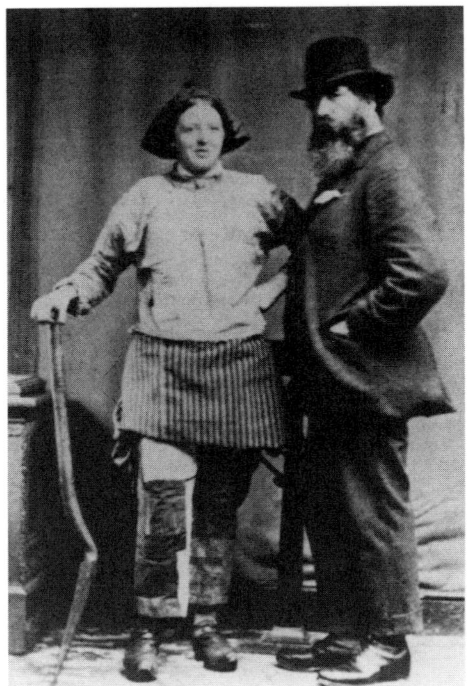

Figure 1.   Robert Little, *Ellen Grounds, aged 22 a broo wench at Pearson and Knowles Pits, Wigan, taken 11 September 1873. (Arthur Munby)* 1873, Munby Collection (113-1-c), Trinity College, Cambridge. Reproduced by kind permission of the Master and Fellows of Trinity College, Cambridge.

Wigan miner Ellen Grounds who appears in several photographs and is described in the diaries which Munby kept (fig. 21). In his diary entry about the studio session with Ellen Grounds, Munby writes that he stood beside her "to show how nearly she approached me in size" (11 Sept., 1873). While the photographic collection and the diaries of Munby have become quite well known since the opening of his archive at Trinity College, Cambridge in 1950, the fact that Munby also made sketches and watercolors is less publicized. This article sets out to explain why.

I seem to have been working on this archive forever. It is paradigmatic in my research project on "working women and bourgeois men in visual representation in the nineteenth century." The archive solicits different readings. None exhausts the possibilities and complexities of its word-image relations, its class-gender hierarchies or race-sexuality axes. So far I have published on the theoretical issues it raises around class and gender in feminist analysis and on the nature of "the secret" it contained that required its being sealed for forty years.[3]

Attempts to explain Munby's "secret" as his personally perverse sexual fantasies about large, working class women have fallen before the theoretical revisions to histories of sexuality offered by Foucault, who argues that Victorian sexuality was endemically "perverse,"[4] and by the deployment of psychoanalysis in contemporary feminist theories of subjectivity and culture. Yet again, photographs of women miners, acrobats, milkmaids, servants are regularly used now as merely useful documentary images of Victorian "female labor" and are not read as sites of private pornography. Finally Lee Davidoff has shown how Munby's interest in and relationships with working women can be read in relation to the symbolic meaning of bodies in bourgeois ideologies of class and gender, that were shaped in childhood through the specificities of childcare in the bourgeois household.[5]

I want, however, to argue against this "normalizing" trend. The "secret" that is part of this archive is indeed a shocking one. But it can only be discerned if we track the relations, or rather the relays, between the three instances of representation which compose the archive—writing, photographs and drawings. As an art historian, I am drawn specifically to the unpublished album of sketches from which a few examples have been extracted and reproduced. But there has been a polite and thus a political oversight of many of them. It is not that they contain a "truth" disguised in diary and photographic collection or that they "express" Munby's feeling or views on working class women more directly. I want rather to develop the argument around drawing and visualization, drawing and both the represented and the representing body. This allows us to see both the "dangers of proximity" and the defense mechanisms incited against that moment of *"with my own eyes"*. It was conflict that necessitated the compulsive writing and the tedium of the repetitious photographs. It is necessary to reconstitute the economy—social, symbolic and psychosexual—within which the various acts of representation interact.

One of the sketches represents Munby's encounter with Eliza Hayes, age 25, on Rose Bridge (fig. 2). It is, like the diaries, a recollection of a meeting. It

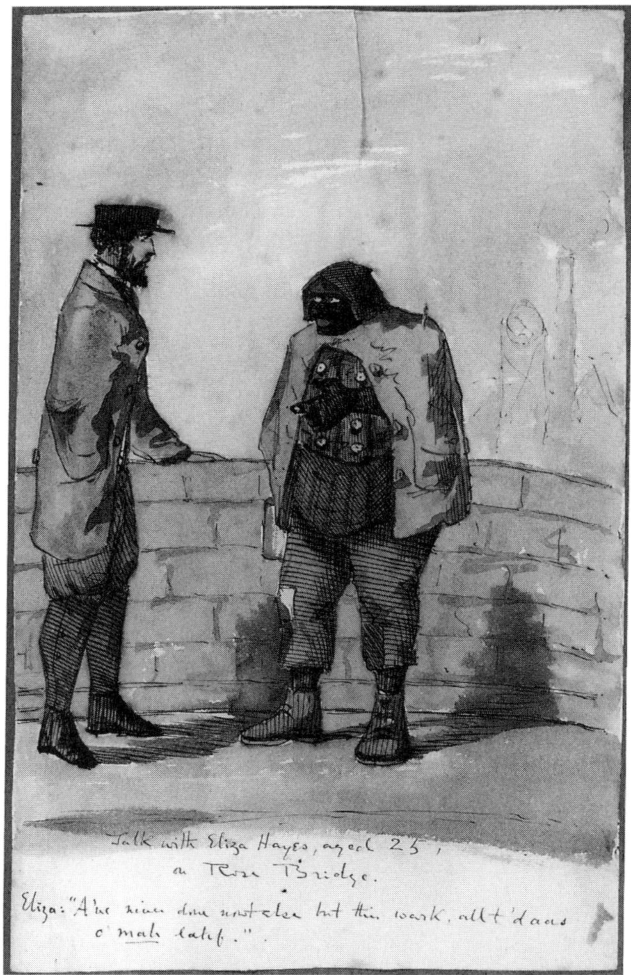

Figure 2.   Arthur Munby, *Eliza Hayes, aged 25, Rose Bridge (and Arthur Munby)* Munby Album, Munby Collection, Trinity College, Cambridge. Reproduced by kind permission of the Master and Fellows of Trinity College, Cambridge.

is, however, a drawn "reconstruction" made by an amateur draftsman. This is what makes it interesting and revealing when read in the way I propose as opposed to an art historical analysis which might merely be embarrassed by its obviously untutored awkwardness as composition and delineation. What we see in the sketch is an aesthetically unmanaged exposure of the significance of that encounter for the person who wanted to commemorate it by a drawing *with his own hand.* It is a shocking image. What has been attended to here and made *visible* could hardly be even implied in the photograph showing Munby and Ellen Grounds together in one space (fig. 1). It is the radical disjunction between two images with similar components that alerts us to the different meaning, purpose and effect of various media in this economy of representation.

The sketch does not aim to create the potential similarity between Munby and the miner the photograph could stage for him to contemplate later. Instead the use of ink and added color demarcate a radical difference between the two figures which is not reducible to any simple statement of conventions of gender. The key measure of difference between the two figures is in fact color. "She" is black–ened. We could also note that he is tall and lean and she is large and square, that his features are sharp, his hands delicate and his feet petite while her hand is almost bigger than her almost featureless face. In that crucial phrase, all we can see are the whites of her eyes—his terror projected on her terrorizingly illegible face—and her full lips. Taken together these distinctions cast what is at once an encounter between a man and a woman, a bourgeois and a working class person within a racializing and racist stereotypology. The strangeness of the confrontation with an example of "female labor," her sex anchored by the linguistic message giving her a name, Eliza Hayes, is being represented as both a disordering of gender difference and the construction of racial difference at the point where gender difference breaks down. Yes, this "Eliza Hayes" dresses, stands and is as big as a "man." This disturbance of the order of sexual difference experienced simultaneously as the site of class is visualized through the [European bourgeois] semiotics of racial difference produced within the cruelties of colonial discourse.[6]

The developed state of the figures in the foreground means that the encounter and the detailing of this seesawing of sameness and exaggerated difference are the chief attractions for the producer of the drawing. Yet nothing in a drawing should be ignored. Its being there demands at least cursory consideration. So what of the faintly indicated mining buildings in the background, which cannot escape being described as crudely phallic? They occur on "her" side of the drawing narrating the place she has worked "all the days of her life" (see hand written inscription under the drawing). Balancing the "male" figure on the left, they also frame the "female" miner within a doubling of masculine signs. As their minimal form invites us to read the image formally, we note the correspondence between the shadow "he" casts and the phallicized shape of the lift shaft with its rounded top— the wheel for the cage in fact, in contrast to the the way the shadow of the "woman" miner—the part that is cast on the wall—can be read as a woman in profile in conventional female garb. Note too that the shadows reverse their respective sizes. This secondary version of the manifest drawing stages an encounter between a mature woman and a large phallus.

As a semiotician inspired by Mieke Bal's notions of "reading," I should handle all of this evidence.[7] But what I am interested in is what is happening in this drawing notionally *before* the restitution of a phallic masculinity indicated so crudely by the industrial towers and his phallic shadow. I want to concentrate on the fantastic scenario in the foreground—where difference is both suspended and aggressively inflicted, where white men's race becomes a critical term in the interplay of "class and gender."

There is of course a commonsense explanation. Work around coal mines begrimes the workers. There were probably miners of African descent in an area so close to Liverpool where there was a considerable black community.[8] But blackness, however derived, acquires symbolic function in these texts. Munby does comment repeatedly on the miners' "blackness" in his diaries. But the sign, *black,* stands not only for dirt, and dirt for sexuality, but for difference at the point where both dirt and sexuality—signified as a matter of color—are caught in up in the troubled field of subjectivity, sexuality and vision in a bourgeois imaginary that is white, colonial and masculine by virtue of the way these terms coincide and mutually inflect each other.[9]

In this article I shall focus—eventually—on photographs and writings which result from Munby's encounters with Ellen Grounds and on the album of sketches from which the Eliza Hayes drawing is taken.[10] The main point I shall argue is this. The Munby archive has been selectively studied at a cost. Examining the relations *between* diaries, a photographic collection and an album of sketches will suggest that different media, forming the basis for different practices of representation, service different psychic needs which determine for each element, writing, photograph, drawing, a specific place and role in *an economy of representation* which is both an economy of desire and an economy of power. We cannot read the several kinds of textuality as the unified and unifying expression of their coherent author, Arthur Munby. They are an index of the fractures within a historically positioned subject whose discontinuous psychic interests, desires, narcissistic and sadistic impulses will be spread across an interrelating but fissured field of representations. These furthermore belong to a discursive formation in whose spaces we can find the work of canonical artists and writers, travel literature, governmental inquiry and working-class militancy.

Thus to escape from a kind of fetishising of Munby as an individual or a quirk I want to establish a broad field in which these images from the Munby archive may be seen to operate—a field that I would define by the terms sexuality and surveillance. Sexuality and surveillance stake out the problem of doing feminist historical analysis of nineteenth century visual culture in direct opposition to the dominant modes of art history—monograph, movement, style, descent, work of art. Sexuality and surveillance propose a project informed by, but not contained within, the major formulations about the social and psychic construction of subjectivity and of sexual and cultural difference provided by the theoretical writings of Michel Foucault and Sigmund Freud. Their theories address common themes—the gaze, sexuality, the subject, discourse/representation—but in incompatible ways as a result of which, despite what they share in terms of topics, they produce distinct theoretical objects. The gaze of mastery is not at all the same as the gaze of desire, for instance. The social subject produced in discourse is not the split subject created psychosymbolically by language and the unconscious. But as analytical discourses shaped by the historically specific material which they propose to investigate and theorize, "Freud" and "Foucault" converge upon the question raised by my larger project: Under what conditions and with what effects did working class women enter the spaces of bourgeois representation in the nineteenth century?[11] Labor and the laboring body fall into Foucault's analysis of the bourgeois technologies of discipline, surveillance, knowledge and hence power which colonized the social as well as individual body in the nineteenth century. He further argued that in the specifically bourgeois construct of "sexuality," sex became the cornerstone of identity, saturating, with perverse sexualities, the bodies of those the system aimed to discipline and those they feared as transgressors of its regime. Foucault's theories are, however, indifferent to the questions of gender and hence of the ways class and gender interface in this bourgeois regime of sexuality. Sexual difference figures only momentarily, in its absence, in his study of discourses surrounding the loss of fixed sex such as his case study on the hermaphrodite Herculine Barbin.[12] Yet his theories of bourgeois sexuality do note its implicit racism.[13]

But what happens if the laboring body is sexed and implicitly raced as in the case of Ellen Grounds or Eliza Hayes? Within regimes of bourgeois representation, can that body be sexed? Is racialization the sign of the conflict? Does it not produce levels of contradiction that then provide spaces for masculine fantasy or feminine pleasures? While it is important to acknowledge the latter, they are not available for study through this archive. The reference should function to mark the possibility of a different class and gender meaning for the bodies which are the topic of Munby's fascination and curiosity.[14] My purpose is to reverse both the gazes of mastery and of desire which motivated the formation of the Munby archive, making its subject, the white bourgeois man, the object of a feminist reading. This repositioning implies a solidarity with the women represented and refigured in the images, in the knowledge that there existed a chasm between what Munby *saw* and what the women he scrutinized, photographed, drew and wrote about "imagined" about themselves.[15]

The marking of the body as a site of sexual difference, however, invokes a different theoretical corpus, psychoanalysis, which theorizes the body as a representation, a figuration invested with conflicting meanings and potentialities because it both provides the materials—the drives—for the figuration of psychic subjectivity and is, in the same process, organized by psychic representations of its materiality.[16] Questions of the sexed laboring body in representation might then be framed as follows: What were the pleasures for bourgeois men in looking at representations of laboring bodies which were also female bodies? Did these bodies fall simultaneously, or contradictorily, under the incommensurate gazes of surveillance and of desire? The laboring woman's body appears to escape, or at least, to deviate from the bourgeois semiotics of the visibly gendered and fixed different bodies of Man and Woman, as the very sign and confirmation of the naturalness of difference, hierarchy and masculinity with its privileged status. Did images of laboring women's bodies circulate from Parliamentary report to popular journalism to the walls of official galleries and pages of private albums (fig. 2) as elements of the bourgeois deployment of the technologies of sexual regulation of the body of the proletariat? Were they not also exciting in their defiance of intended discipline, in their total disordering of the the visibility of difference, inching across the field of law to that of desire so as to offer for a moment, erotic, if not pornographic, pleasures in that most unlikely terrain, knowledge? Finally what light could we throw on bourgeois racism by noting the conjunctions in these spaces of gender and color, of sexuality and blackness?

other times, other places, the same thing?

The singularity of the Arthur Munby archive has directed undue attention to his psychosexual peculiarity. I want to point out simply that Munby was not unique in his fascination with the complex of dirt, bodies, sex and female labor. Indeed there are a range of texts from literature to painting, from illustrated journalism to political discourse in the nineteenth century which inhabit this tropic territory. At the intersection of surveillance and sexuality, mining and its communities solicited a range of representations which both throw light upon the Munby archive and create a continuity that allows us to think historically about sexuality and desire in classed, gendered and racializing formations. The mining industry provided the bourgeois tourist with sights/sites that were at once socially peripheral yet fascinating, that were imagined as dark and nether regions, that were the places the bourgeois encountered abjection *and* arousal, where black and white were freighted with overdetermined symbolic and psychic loads. In Zola's novel *Germinal*, published in 1884, these materials are offered in a highly developed literary code. Character allows him to distinguish the femininities and sexualities played out in bourgeois stories of mining communities. There is the adolescent girl, Catherine, dressed as a boy, who is the focus of masculine desire:

> Catherine was ready first. She stepped into her miner's trousers, put on her
> coarse linen jacket and fastened her blue cap over her knot of hair. In these

> clean, Monday-morning clothes she looked like a little man, and the only trace
> of her sex was a slight swing of her hips. [31]

She is contrasted with the overblown and sexually saturated young woman, Mouquette: "whilst she, shaking with giggles, strutted about among them in her indecent attire. The bulges of flesh, exaggerated to the point of deformity, were both comical and exciting"[42].

Finally there is the mother, Maheude—"the shapeless body of female worn out with bearing young, all flabby under her cotton coat and trousers" [494].[17] Zola's story is set in a mining community in Northern France in the 1860s when women still worked underground. (They were excluded in 1874.) Early in the novel, he writes of his outsider hero, Etienne Lantier's disturbing realization of this fact.

> As he turned round, Etienne once more found himself pressing against
> Catherine. But this time he became aware of the curve of her young breast,
> and suddenly understood. "So, you are a girl?" he murmured in amazement.
> She replied in her gay, straightforward way: "Yes, of course! What a time it has
> taken you to find out."[49]

In 1880 Vincent van Gogh, a later reader of *Germinal,* chose to begin his proposed drawing career with a scene drawn from what he had seen *on the spot and with [his] own eyes* in the mining district of the Borinage in Belgium (fig. 3). For all its beginner's awkwardness, the drawing comprises the key components of a clichéd visual *phrase,* and it is hence typical of what I have elsewhere defined as Van Gogh's copybook apprenticeship.[18] Dating from August–September 1880, Van Gogh's drawing mimics the illustrated journalism of English magazines like *The Graphic,* to which he hoped to sell his work. This straggle of miners going to work in the early dawn, in a wintry landscape made cold by snow, and painful through the sharply pointed branches of bare thorn bushes, quotes Jean François Millet's *Going to Work* (1851–53 Cincinnati Art Museum), and through that image, the medieval scenes of seasonal peasant labor and the theme of the expulsion from the Garden of Eden (Masaccio's famous fresco would make the point here). The selection of the tramp to and from work as a setting for pictures of working people is more mundane. These were the only occasions when workers were visible to the artistic tourist or travel journalist as can be glimpsed in two

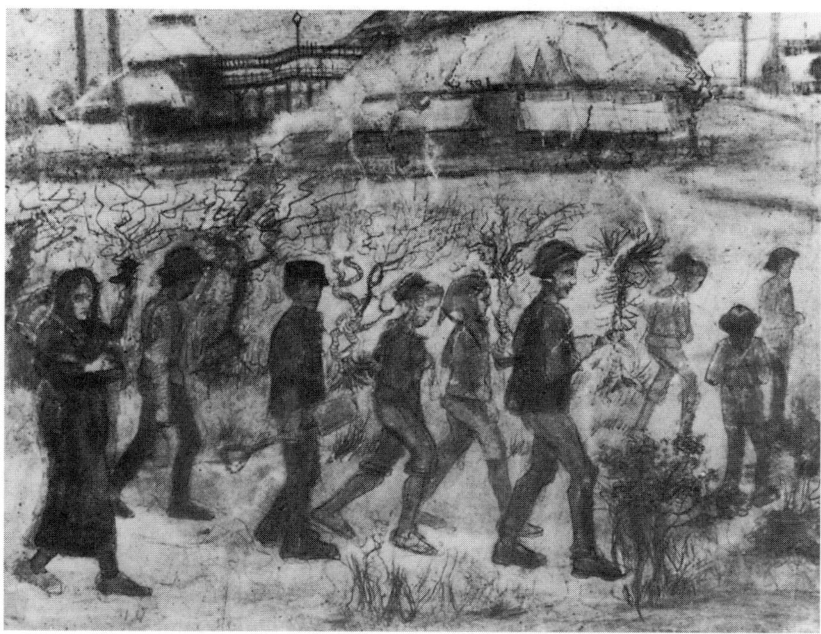

Figure 3.   Vincent van Gogh, *Miners Going to Work*, 1880. Amsterdam: Vincent van Gogh Museum.

related images, one a much later photograph by Gustave Marissiaux (1872–1929), *Return from the Mine Horlog Mine Tilleur*, 1904, and the other a painting by Van Gogh's Belgian contemporary Constantin Meunier (1831–1905), *Return from Work*, 1881 (fig. 4). Zola also used this sight.

> And all along the road from the silent village to the panting Le Voreux a line of shadows tramped slowly through the blast. The colliers were off to work with shambling gait and folded arms, for they did not know what else to do with them. Each one had his *briquet* on his back. Though they were shivering in their thin clothes, they did not quicken step, but plodded on, strung out along the road like a trampling herd ... . The miners squared their shoulders, folded their arms, and set off in a straggling line, with a rolling gait which made their big bones stand out through their thin clothes. As they went along in broad daylight, they looked like a band of Negroes who had fallen in the mud.[19]

Meunier's painting alerts us to what is only tentatively present in Van Gogh's drawing—the *women* miners. Belgium was one of the last European

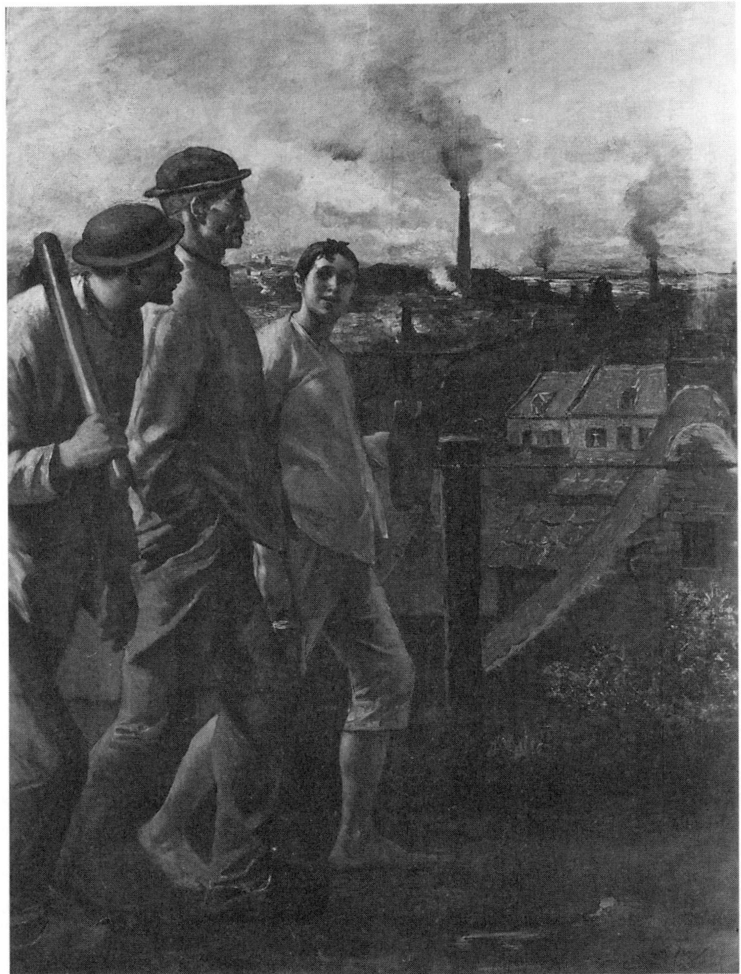

Figure 4. Constantin Meunier, *The Return from Work*, 1881. Brussels: Musée Constantin Meunier.

countries to forbid women's labor underground. Van Gogh's drawing includes both the conventionally dressed women surface workers, in skirts with shawl and bonnet, and the women who went down into the pits like Catherine—"dressed like lads." Their costume included short knee-length breeches and jackets which attracted a variety of kinds of attention and interpretation as the quote from Zola above indicates and paintings and drawings by Meunier and Cécile Douard further demonstrate. Douard (1866–1941), a French artist who worked in Belgium, made these women the subject of major paintings and drawings which alternated between deviance and sexualization. In some works she stressed the size and strength of women doing heavy labor underground pushing and hauling the coal-ladened trucks from the cutting face to the collection depots (fig. 5), while

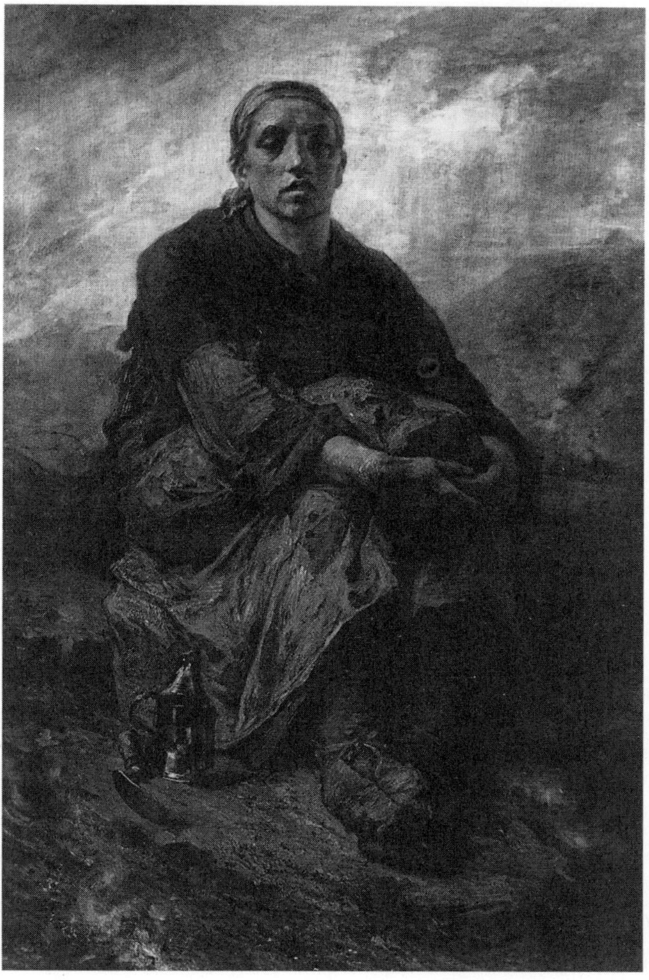

Figure 5.   Cécile Meuard, *Haulier, Seated Resting,* Charleroi: Université du Travail Paul Pastur.

other scenes of women waiting to descend make the costume expose a more conventionally feminine body which in pose and viewpoint becomes almost coy.

However feebly realized, Van Gogh's drawing includes the key components of a dispersed discourse on the mining communities as exemplars of the radical alienness of industrial labor while not locating that alienation as a social effect in and of capitalism. The inclusion of the betrousered women miners, however, is the least developed element of this work. These trousered women in the drawing are unemphatic in direct disproportion to the anxiety they aroused. In Meunier's painting, by contrast, attention is drawn to the young woman miner by narrativizing the scene. She turns "in her gay and straightforward way" toward her companions and thus towards the viewer. She holds her clogs in her hand which in turn makes the viewer notice the nakedness and size of her bare feet and calves. Nonetheless, the uncertain inclusion of the underground women workers in Van Gogh's beginner's attempt underlines the critical point of fascination which motivated the repeated gaze of the bourgeois tourist at this industrial site—the laboring body and the problem of its sex—or shall we say the problem that a laboring woman posed to a regime of sex whose privileged sign and ideological foundation was a body, believed to secure that regime by the natural and given character of its difference.

Now let me introduce a written text, *The Belgians at Home,* published in 1911 (the date of the exclusion of women from Belgian pits) by an Edwardian novelist and travel writer of no great distinction, Clive Holland. Holland's is a mundane text, balancing the factual with the picturesque, the exotic with the frankly horrific. It shares with many other texts, both painted and written, a way of constituting an object for investigation and consumption, a system for establishing "truth" about labor, the body and sexuality.

The text is a tapestry of several orders of discourse which collectively produce social knowledge for an authoritative, bourgeois gaze. The passage that interests me narrates the journey to Mons, part of the industrial South of the country. It begins with a **socioeconomic** discourse which supplies a way of knowing strangeness through official facts and figures. The region has been transformed by the rapid impact of industrialization which now conditions its character and appearance. Unfettered and sudden industrialization of a region crudely exploited the work force and its natural resources. This is, according to Holland, a now-historical fact which it is safe to know in 1911 because the text can reassure the readers that this harsh face of capitalism has been transcended. Conditions are now much improved and better managed. The acknowledged evils of the system in "the bad old days" have been transferred, however, to the gene pool of the local workers. Their bodies have internalized the past; their physical appearance bears traces of those "hard times." Social and economic relations are thus distanced through an **anthropological** discourse. This transition is the site of a bourgeois process of *racialization* of its social others. The workers in the mining industry form a physiognomic type. They have become a "race":

> … The effect of this almost unremitting, arduous and unhealthy toil has been the production of a race dwarf-like in stature … This strange weird type, which chiefly comes of the third and fourth generation of miner is particularly noticeable.[20]

The body is thus a key sign for the displacement of social relations and its effects, in Lenin's phrase overwork and underconsumption, and for the emergence of the strategy of racialization of the working class. History and society evaporate before the concrete physicality of appearance and its apparently genetic foundations. Upon this basis, a **sociological** discourse can once again operate because the workers have been othered so radically, racially, that they no longer can implicate the bourgeois readers despite their incomes supplied by shares in the great mining companies. The text can then discuss the social customs and habits of this "race" apart. They are, we are then told, illiterate and irregular, their marital and sexual arrangements frankly deviant. Local cultures cannot be imagined as specific customs within the diversity of human populations. The implicit judgment according to an unspoken norm introduces a **moral** discourse through which the culture of this race is roundly condemned: "It is the habits and customs to which we have referred which make Hainault a dark blot upon the map of Belgium, a district notorious for its immorality, crime and brutalized population" (Holland, 125).

Kinship systems specific to a particular community, which were determined by economic factors related to methods of payment and employment current in the mining industry, are represented as deviations which indicate the corrupted and criminalized character of the people. An unspoken norm generates both a national and a transnational class identity for its non-mining and non-Belgian readers. For the mining communities, marriage meant the removal of a son's or daughter's wage from the parental household, and was often delayed until younger children could replace their older siblings' earning capacities. Miners were often paid for team work, and family labor ensured that scanty wages remained in the household rather than being shared out with subcontracted labor. The specific cultural and social forms of the mining communities were negotiated responses to specific economic conditions. Poor wages caused hardship and suffering, but the typical kinship arrangements could not be said to brutalize, demoralize or criminalize a population. As Angela Davis has argued about the specific strategies of resistance in slave households, the management of interpersonal relationships and sexual mores was at least one space in which the dehumanization of enslavement and exploitation of the worker could be resisted.[21] That the miners can be imagined as "brutalized" reveals the presence of the laws of sexuality governing the bourgeois social and subjective constitution. The text reveals unconscious motivations precisely at the point at which the sociological and economic discourses give way to a moralizing yet fascinated exploration of sex in the life of the mining community. The implicit assumptions of Holland's text, its baseline for nature and truth, articulate the ideological formations of bourgeois society fixated on female chastity as a necessary corollary of the maintenance of private property which can only be secured through legally contracted heterosexual relations and legitimated reproduction. It is only the absence of the bourgeois law as the regulatory condition for "sexuality" (used here in Foucault's sense of a specifically bourgeois construct) which renders the practices of other populations illicit or transgressive. This text, like Munby's, perpetually summons up the opposing but normative term of the binary opposition in order to position the reader in relation to the fascinating but ultimately abnormal social other.

The fictive landscape of work and degradation which the text has been sketching is finally populated with its most lucid and overdetermined sign—the body of laboring women.

> As one cycles along the road on the way to Mons ... one meets at sundown the stunted generation of miners flowing in their hundreds and thousands out of the colliery gates, dull with fatigue and often bemused with the effects of the *schnick* they have been drinking all day. Nor are the women and girls more pleasant figures: perhaps even less so. One passes hundreds of them low of stature, with bare arms grimed with the dust of the coal they have been hauling and tipping out of huge wicker baskets upon railways sidings into the awaiting trucks, *faces hard with the degradation of unfitting toil,* arms and figures like those of prize fighters—masses of muscle, almost denuded of any curve or softness. At first one may mistake them for gangs of boys or lads ... Often their muscular legs are bare, and their feet merely thrust into wooden sabots. Often their feet are shoeless. Beings which those gifted with the kindliest charity can scarcely look on save with disgust (Holland, p. 126).

We seem at first to be in Van Gogh's landscape, but at twilight not dawn, when stunted miners flow out, exhausted and drunk. But as the gaze distinguishes the women and girls, we are precipitated into Douard's frank confrontation with a woman haulier (fig. 5). Despite their low stature, the effect of this labor is not to stunt woman but turn them into prizefighters. (Recall Munby's interest in Ellen Ground's stature.) Size then becomes the sign of their deviance, which proliferates all over their bodies—grimy arms, bared legs, roughly shod feet. A fictive body is aggressively assembled from these overcharged parts. We cannot sufficiently stress both the familiar (in the sense it is still with us) and the alien nature of the nineteenth century bourgeois man's obsession with women's exposed legs. Apart from the regulated trope of the nude, women's legs were never represented unclothed. Abigail Solomon-Godeau's important study of a French archive, in which a countess aberrantly presented her naked legs to the photographer, significantly titled "The Legs of the Countess," argues that even in pornography the exposed was always related to the stockinged in the act of dressing or undressing.[22] While dancers and other performers may not have worn skirts, their revealed legs were sheathed in tights to ensure what she calls "the transformation of carnal flesh into the sublimated sculptural form of aesthetic, albeit eroticized, delectation."[23] It may be that the obsessional interest in the mining women had something to do with a costume which covered the groin but "revealed" the legs, an inversion of the the bourgeois lady, who wore no underclothes but hid her legs. We can fairly certainly surmise that the issue of blunt nakedness of the leg worked *metonymically* in regard to the masculine erotic gaze moving from leg to genitals, but that it equally functioned fetishistically as defense and disavowal in relation to men's fantasies and fears about the sight of women's sex.

To return to the passage quoted from Holland's text, the imaginary traversal of the body is concluded with the equally troubling disorder of the face: "hard with the degradation of unfitting toil." Face and body signify paradigmatically in relation to a chain whose other pole contains idle and curvaceous bodies, softened faces and elevated or fitting occupations. The structuring absence of the text is the bourgeois/feminine body, maintaining through its absolute difference from the masculine body, a gender division which is at the same time a hierarchy of the sexes. The bodies of the laboring women throw into confusion this femininity and unravel the signifying chain which secures bourgeois masculine identity and authority.

These bodies disorder a world of visible knowledge and transparent difference: at first sight, they can be mistaken for boys. In the art form of the female nude, the feminine body was configured as if a soft, pink bonelessness and undulating curvaceousness were not so much natural, as nature only as culture could reveal it, simply coincident with the form and skin of woman, as in Cabanel's *Birth of Venus* (1863, Paris, Musée d'Orsay). Holland's text uses the word "denuded," which means to be made naked, for bodies which are in fact fully and often coarsely dressed. The paradox indicates a loss of the confidence which the aesthetically constructed nude normally secured when sexuality entered the field of vision. The erotic charge of the female nude, the obverse of its function as the truth of woman, is displaced here by the anxiety about a costume which is a state of undress, which covers and exposes in equal proportions. In bourgeois culture, we find the ironic pairing of the artificially fashioned form of the female nude and over-costumed lady, hatted, gloved, corsetted, and so swathed in meters of heavy cloth that scarcely a trace of the body was visible. The female body in both seemingly opposite instances is rewritten through fetishism, of art form or of costume, both of which signify the masquerade, that is femininity as artifice appearing as merely acculturated nature. The sight of working women wearing trousers, which so insists upon the fact of bipedalism, thus signifying women's similarity as humans to men, and yet, simultaneously inviting the viewer/reader to imagine the specificity of what happens between their legs, exposes the bourgeois fiction and fetishization of woman through what I have to dare to call an insistent and unmediated exposure to physical nature. Nature here does not signify an essence, but an undifferentiated territory, which like Kristeva's semiotic, is the recalcitrant materialism of which signs are made. There are their legs, muscled, dirty, walking, unavoidably visible, factual. Like the little boy in Freud's legend of sexual difference, when encountering the genitally specific female body as what seems an uninscribed nature, the male does not know what he has seen. Later the semiotic frame of phallocentric culture names what was seen as absence and makes it the very sign of lack. But in the case of these evidently powerful, unswathed, unveiled, uncorsetted bodies, the fascination lies precisely in the suspension of that law of difference with its expulsion of the masculine subject from its pre-Oedipal fantasy of oneness or likeness to the grand, powerful and mercifully as yet undifferentiated maternal body.

Seesawing across this unregulated body of the laboring woman, the text represents the women miners of Belgium as a transgression of femininity, and this is as much a question of class as of gender. They have too much, and are too visible. The idle feminine lady has to be summoned by the text to define the deviance of women workers and as the consolation for the dreadful sight of what labor has done to them. Here a sketch from the Munby album might serve as illustration of the unfixing of "femininity" which this text struggles to contain by invoking the culturally invented "natural" woman as opposed to these deviants (fig. 6). These coincidences between Zola, Van Gogh, Meunier, Douard, Holland and Munby, serve *not* to trace a descent, or a set of influences, but to produce a Foucauldian genealogy for the bourgeois fantasy of the laboring body and its problematic sex. Rigidly encased in a costume which physically inhibits her movements and renders her the mannequin of a femininity she is required to perform in person and daily ritual, the lady is excluded from labor and money, from mobility in the public realm, from locations of power. There on the roads of Mons, Holland shows his readers the blatant lawlessness of women who walk like sailors along public roads, bodies half-exposed, on their way to and from the work which earns them precious little, but money all the same. In this context, the evocation of this tiny, white, delicate, rarefied femininity is

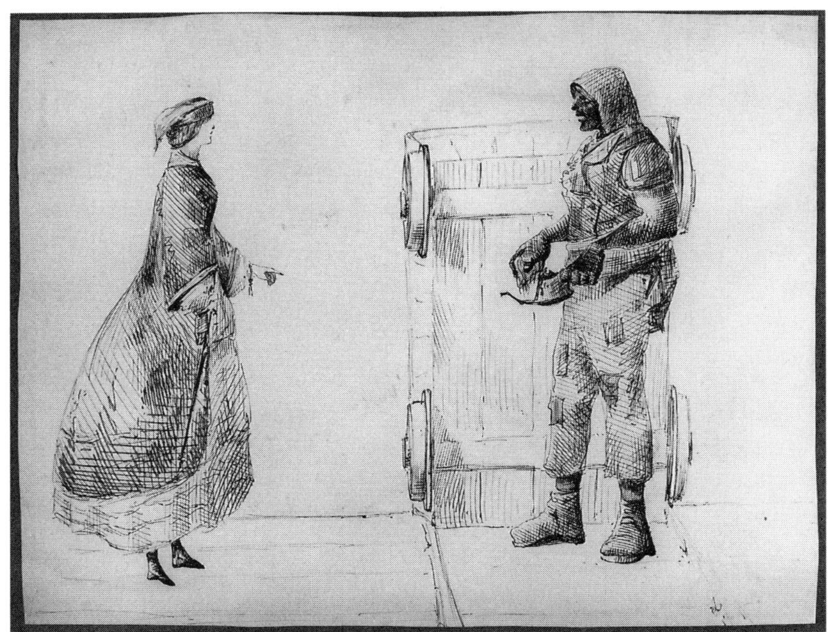

Figure 6.   Arthur Munby, *Miner and Lady*, Munby Album, Collection, Trinity College, Cambridge. Reproduced by kind permission of the Master and Fellows of Trinity College, Cambridge.

part of the signification of bourgeois masculine power, racially as well as in terms of class and gender. Proletarian women such as these miners defied this order, neither confirming the visual axis of sexual difference, nor exhibiting through their bodies and gestures a powerless deference. In baring and bearing the signs of work and exploitation upon a body which should signify female gender precisely through the absence of both, these working women confused the field of vision by configuring class yet defying bourgeois codes of gender by their physical size. This conjunction of labor and sexuality disturbs the regime of truth upon which the touristic vision was premised. Yet it exercised sufficient fascination to solicit both extended scrutiny and the most energetic and compelling prose, even if the desire to see and traverse every deviant element must finally be disavowed as too disgusting to contemplate. The text assumes its distance from the deviant configurations dirt and moral corruption only after it is has truly rubbed its readers' noses in it. Here we can see the laboring woman's body, particularly that of the miner, as the point at which the forces of surveillance (regulation, mastery and discipline) and sexuality (fascination, mystery and desire) converge to overdetermine the presence of these troubling bodies in bourgeois representation.

masquerade and fetish: the semiotics of appearance and difference

There are photographs of the Belgian women miners in the Munby archive. But the majority of his photographs are of a group of about 1,300 British women miners, living in an ten-kilometer radius of the town of Wigan, Lancashire. They were surface workers—known as pit-brow lasses.

Women had been banned from underground employment in British pits by an Act of Parliament of 1842. During a British parliamentary commission on The Employment of Children in the Mines, men from elite social groups in government visited the coal mining districts of the country and "discovered" that women as well as children were laboring underground in this industry. The wealth of first-hand evidence from the women themselves recorded by the commissioners insists upon the hardship of the labor in terms of conditions, hours and pay. The conclusions drawn by those advancing a bill for the sudden and absolute abolition of this labor with all its attendant hardships on working people in single industry communities, were couched in terms of shame, terror and moral panic at this "evil." All the argumentation against the vested interests of capital were couched in highly gendered terms and required a constant assertion of the unnatural character of this labor for women and of the moral dangers which threatened further to denature woman as they worked long hours in mixed company, unsupervised, deep in the darkness of the earth. Bodies were crucial signifiers in this struggle. Commissioners described the dress or rather undress of the mining women. They crawled along tunnels dragging heavy wagons of coal dressed only in a pair of breeches, with a leather belt around the waist to which was attached a chain, which, passing between their legs, attached them like horses to their loads. One commissioner noted, "the chain, passing high up between the legs of the girls, had worn through large holes in their trousers, and any sight more disgusting or inde-cent or revolting can scarcely be imagined as these two girls at work—no brothel can beat it."[24] The 1842 report contains one of the first instances of graphic illustration as opposed to technical diagrams accompanying a par-liamentary document. Despite its gauche simplicity, or rather, because of its evident lack of artistic skill, it provided convincing visual evidence to cor-roborate the horrors imagined in the verbal report. Because it could not be accused of using artistry to fabricate the scene, the drawing appeared to offer vicarious yet vivid access to both the site and the sight of the immoral-ities hitherto shielded in darkness and distance. This illustration was also independently circulated in London salons, and its currency as proof of the "pornography" daily enacted in the mines, contributed to the buildup of pressure which assisted the rapid passing of Lord Shaftesbury's bill for the removal of women from the mines.

Women continued to work in British mines out of economic necessity since there was often no other employment in their region. But they did so in disguise, dressed in clothes borrowed from brothers and fathers while others accepted work thus dressed on the pitbanks. In 1863 the House of Commons received a petition from the National Association of Coal, Lime and Ironstone Miners of Great Britain, in which, among other demands for protection against the unfair practices of the coal-owners, the Union stated: "That the practice of employing females on or about the pitbanks of mines and collieries is degrading to the sex and leads to gross immorality, and stands as a foul blot on the civilization and humanity of the kingdom."[25]

During the hearings of the Select Committee of the House of Commons set up to examine the miners' complaints, evidence was taken about women's labor at the pits. The costume of the women regularly featured as a symptom of the evil female labor caused to the femininity (read domesticity) of the women as potential wives and mothers: It was called "a man's dress" and one witness added, "I believe in some cases it drowns all sense of decency betwixt men and women, they resemble each other so much."[26] Thus the erosion of visible difference is held responsible for a deviation from a desired mode of behavior which here found the labor aristocracy attempting to enlist the gov-erning bourgeoisie in disciplining working women into a cultural and social ideal of feminine domesticity.[27]

Evidence for the "peculiarity of dress" and hence the moral danger was supplied by photographs—the first time that photographs were submitted as evidence to a parliamentary enquiry. Given the date of this photograph of Ellen Grounds, age 17, made by Robert Little in 1866 (fig. 7), it is possible

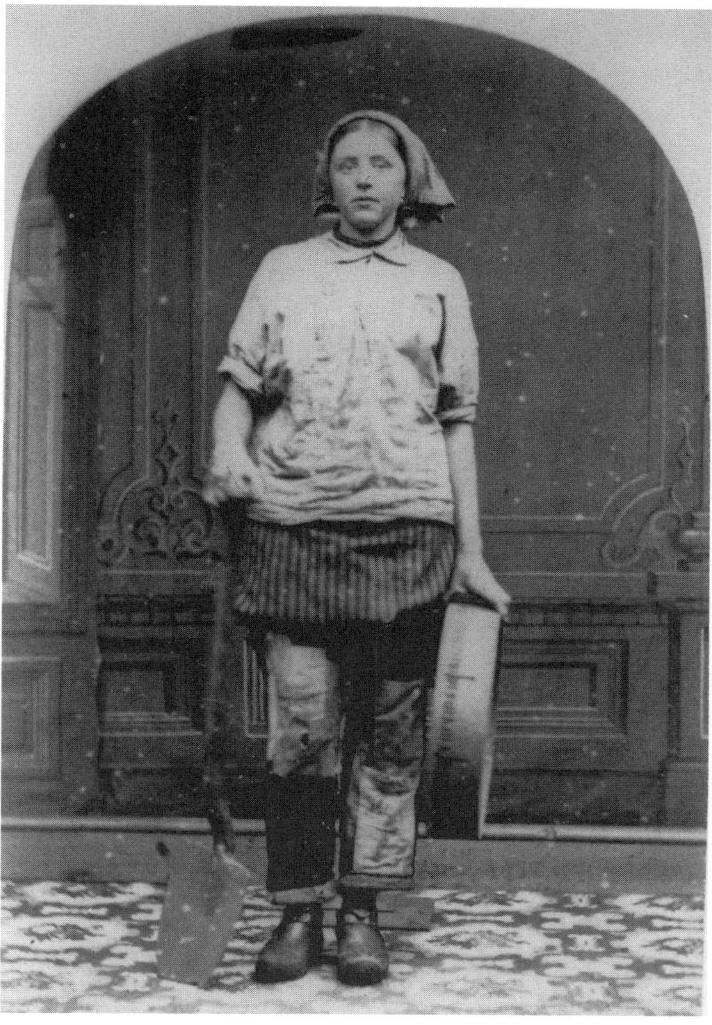

Figure 7.   Robert Little, *Ellen Grounds, Filler, Rose Bridge Pits, aged 17,* 1866. carte-de-visite, Munby Collection, III-6-b. Reproduced by kind permission of the Master and Fellows of Trinity College, Cambridge.

that her image was placed before the Committee as typical of the working costume of the Wigan pitbrow workers. While indicating the development of discourses linking vision and truth with which photography was becoming implicated in the new disciplinary technologies, their appearance indicates the belief that degradation and immorality would be visible in the physical appearance of the body—a moral and spiritual lack would be there for all to see. What is there, in the photographs, to be seen is, however, only clothes and studio props—presenting a striking incongruity between the pastiche of country house grandeur serving as the cheap studio backdrop with the crudely patterned carpet and the roughly dressed and booted woman, leaning against a just-visible wooden body prop, awkwardly handling an-out-of date riddle and spade. The costume of deviance, however, is supplemented by the rhetorical devices of posture, gesture and position of the body in relation to the photographer's and hence the viewer's gaze. This involves frontality, feet spread apart, and often hands on hips or otherwise firmly placed. Photography does not record a body in representation but produces a symbolic body for and through representation.

Representatives of the mine owners opposed to any further curtailment of their access to cheap female labor arranged for the Committee to see another set of photographs of the same women. Mr. Gilroy, manager of one of the major mining concerns in Wigan, had his "girls" photographed in their Sunday dresses, which were meant to signify not costume, but the outward and visible signs of an inward and invisible femininity (fig. 8). Again Ellen Grounds appears in the archive, dressed in Sunday clothes, seated now on a velvet upholstered chair, resting her elbow elegantly on the table with its decorative plant. This second series of photographs of miners in Sunday dresses tries to argue that working clothes are only that, a costume, garments placed on an essentially feminine body. This second image is offered as a truth but its artifice is less immediately evident for this is the prevailing fiction, a class ideal of a feminine body, without muscle, grime, or signs of labor. These two sets of photographs allow us to compare the equal but opposing fantasies which I suggested structured Clive Holland's much later text and which are constantly re-enacted across the Munby archive.

If we look at a series of the *carte-de-visite* photographs of Wigan women in their working gear (figs. 7, 9, and 10), we can identify a recurring rhetoric

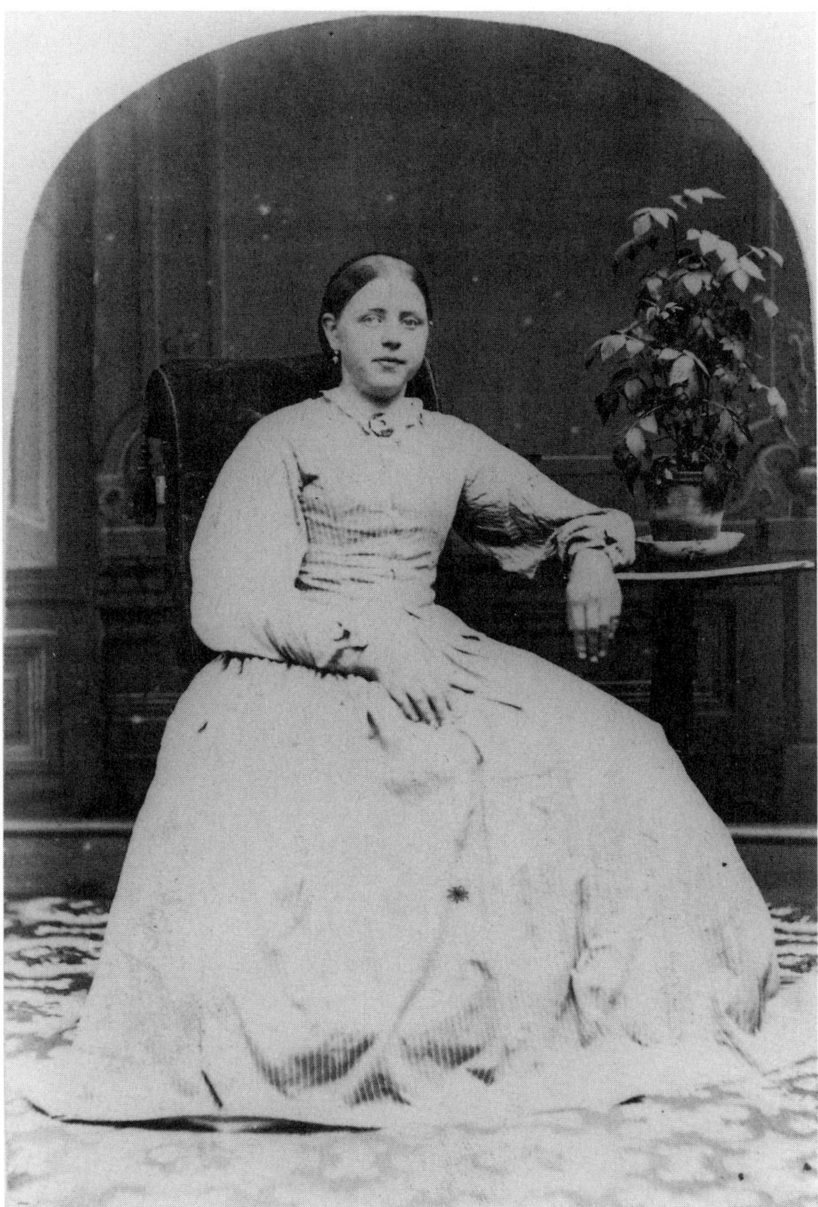

Figure 8.   Robert Little, *Ellen Grounds, Collier, in Sunday Dress*, 1866. carte-de-visite, Munby Collection (III-6-d). Reproduced by kind permission of the Master and Fellows of Trinity College, Cambridge.

in which the sitters are positioned for the viewer. Women stand or sit, always frontally posed, face to camera, with all its resultant awkwardness, legs planted firmly apart, holding studio props of shovels and sieves. Hands resting on shovel hilts, or arms on hips, the body is opened out for the viewer and its acquires a solid facticity as a body. Yet, in an important and historically precise sense, it remains hard to sex the body according to contemporary codes. In the Sunday photographs such as (fig. 8), the women sit in a quite different fashion, legs erased in the sweep of the flowing skirt, hands gracefully and inertly placed in laps, elbows elegantly resting on a table, bodies turned gently off-center to make inclined heads and arms a part of a continuous flowing line with softened contours. It is superfluous to talk frankly of bodies. These are the codes of the representation of femininity in which the body is absented and a more immaterial "condition"—femininity—is substituted through textures of fabric and the cut of costume, the fall of wrist and fingers.[28]

The specific appeal and pleasure of photography reside in its power to provide such credible figurations of fantasy by constructing with equal conviction such different bodies. In the one group, sexual difference is seemingly suspended by bodies which are known to be women's but which look like men's—muscled, direct, tough. The woman have bodies but no strong signs to sex them, that is, to make them signify a specific construct of sexual difference. I am perhaps overstating this, for the Munby archive contains many images which show women with earrings and frilly blouses or wearing a hat. But I suggest that we cannot now read these images at all as they would have signified in the nineteenth century for such combinations of what were once men's work clothes, namely jeans, with makeup and earrings are now a common feature of Western codes of femininity. We have to realize how very recently Western women began to wear trousers and how rapidly it has become normalized so that what we may be seeing in these images as clear indexes of feminine decoration and fashion were then overwhelmed by anomaly of their trousers and clogs or by something else about the combination of clothes, which I shall come to later.[29]

In the other set of photographs, sexual difference is confirmed, paradoxically through the evasion of the body and the proliferation of rhetorical signs of difference coded through costume, posture, gesture and overall harmonious effect which coalesces into the naturalism with which photography seduces us into accepting the world as transparently present: see, here is woman. The photographs from these two albums reveal that difference is an inscription on the body, a play of signs, and not a matter of given facts, or self-evident identity. It further shows that disordering a given system of inscription has unpredictable pleasures which need to be analyzed at the level at which they may be operating—psychosymbolically.

In twentieth-century psychoanalysis femininity has been theorized precisely as *masquerade*, that is, as not so much a veiling of a real or essential femininity, as an effect of signification of difference for men within a phallic economy of signs and bodies which make femininity always a pose, and a fiction. Femininity is defined in relation to the phallus which one can either pretend to be or to have, while of course never acceding to either condition. Woman disguises her lack *vis-à-vis* the phallus by appearing to be it for men, identifying with the lack it ironically signifies and hence becoming a signifier for masculine desire. Desire desires that which is impossibly lost, and it is occasioned by submission to the law which makes one subject to language and a sex. This account is the highly abstract and symbolic Lacanian reworking of Freud's thesis which, in fact, has a much more nineteenth-century feel to it. Freud writes of the absence and presence of a penis. The masculine subject's own sense of precarious subjectivity—his narcissism—is protected by a game played out on the body of woman whose apparent physical difference registered as a lack is disavowed by *fetishism*, the logic of substitution which allows the fetishist to maintain incompatible knowledges:

> A narcissistic relation to the male body image as phallic is at stake, but it is secured by reference to the mother's body. The fetish represents the desired but absent maternal phallus. It is a compromise formation between the traumatic perception that the mother has no penis and the continuing wish that she should have one.[30]

The fetish protects the son against narcissistic injury to his own body image as phallic—that is the obligatory acknowledgement of his own lack. The mother's apparent lack is itself fetishized so that the son appears to lack lack. Difference is, therefore, not a categorization, a, b, c, etc., but a relational effect, **a** and **non–a,** in which imaginary, symbolically inscribed bodies become signs within a system that is asymmetrical *vis-à-vis* a (masculine) and **non–a** (feminine) subjects, but which is no less traumatic for both **a** and **non–a** as a result of the precarious hierarchies it arranges. Its very instability and fictionality generates specific anxieties and intensities at the level of its constant repetition in representation. Whichever formulation of the masquerade one turns to, and there are several within the psychoanalytic debate, Freud, Lacan, Riviere, Johnston, Doane, the basic issue is that "woman"/femininity signifies what she is not—whatever that might be, for it is not assumed to be knowable within the phallocentric economy which uses woman as a means to erect a difference whose positive effect is the illusion of "man."[31] John Fletcher, summing up Lacan's contribution, concludes:

> In Lacanian theory a series of lacks and losses, of the object in the drive, of the subject in relation to language, are overlaid and signified by the phallus and the woman in so far as she assumes the position of the phallus. As man's missing part, as substitute for what he has had to sacrifice or mortgage to the Law, the woman-as-phallus for the man comes to signify in Lacan's terms "what he has to renounce, that is, *jouissance.*" Just as [Claire] Johnston's account insists on the woman's radical heterogeneity that is excluded or repressed by the phallic system of the male and the not-male, so Lacan's account recognises "a rejection of an essential part of her femininity" entailed by the woman's position as phallus-for-the-man. In his later formulations, her position as "not all" (*pas tout*) is supplemented by "something more" (*en plus*), a *jouissance* beyond the phallic function. The masquerade comes to signify the alienation involved in the substitution of "appearing" for "having".[32]

These photographs seem to give us some access to the anomalies of this process when confronting the emergent rhetorics and technologies of photographic representation. Heavily indebted to existing visual conventions and practices, photography, nonetheless, offered a new kind of visuality when it restaged those poses and gestures in its own, emergent semiosis. Through the index of a proper name, these images appear to give us simply two views of Ellen Grounds in 1866. Both—or some pair like them—lay on the table in the House of Commons, and both were then made part of Arthur Munby's private collection. Their use was in the movement of a gaze between them—and the impossibility of using either in the presence of the other to fix a meaning for what they purported to represent. The Sunday dress image provides the *appearance of femininity*, while signifying *femininity as appearance—masquerade*—which is as much a veiling and a displacement as any kind of showing. The poses and presentation of the women in their workclothes signifies a kind of blunt presence in which hands go out of shape as they are used to grasp shovel hilts and stretch to encompass wide riddles, as an apron is tucked up to reveal two legs ending in firmly shod large feet. These images are figuratively naked—revealing not the body of woman, as we wrongly assume the nude can do, but the prosaic conjunction of the signs of the artifice of sexual difference, since the conventional signs of both masculinity and femininity cohabit a single form. Can these details be managed as fetishes—to disavow the maternal lack by finding bodies that seem to promise to be both *pas tout* (the feminine lady as lack which ensures a coherence of masculine mastery of the phallus), and *en plus* (the phallic mother beyond the law of difference where the boy can also be the phallus for her whose desire he wishes to fulfill)?

It is impossible for us now to register an erotic if not pornographic charge in what were then shocking and exciting transgressions of the regimes of sexual and social order. If we were to see them only within the Foucauldian system of surveillance, exhibiting, as part of their utilization in parliamentary investigation, the disciplinary impulse in which a union of working men collaborated with the bourgeoisie to domesticate women, we would miss their productivity in relation to sexuality. The existence of these photographs in the Munby archive indicates not only their polyvalence but also the fact that they offer a much less stable visual field which was fractured by other—psychic—exigencies precisely because of their specificity as images, participating in what Jacqueline Rose has called "sexuality in the field of vision."[33]

fetishism, writing and drawing

Let us turn now to a diary entry which reports Munby's visit to the home of Ellen Grounds, Wednesday, 10 September 1873.[34]

> I reached Wigan ... and walked up to Scholes, the main street of the colliers'
> quarter of Wigan, to call on Ellen Grounds, the nearest of my friends, and
> learn from her the news of the pits ... Here I knocked: and opening the door

whom should I see but Miss Ellen Grounds, wiping the deal table in the middle of the brick floor. Miss Ellen who is now four and twenty, was in woman's clothes, this time: a decent brown stuff frock with sleeves, and a white apron: and her light brown hair was knotted up simply behind, and brushed smooth against her comely cheerful face. She looked up with a puzzled smile. "What, Ellen dun yo known ma"?—"Yea, Ah do—why yo' was here better than three years sin!" she answered: and gave me her hand, which was clean, and in spite of her manly work was neither coarse nor very hard. A fire was blazing in the grate, of course: and one side of it sat Ellen's father the brooman, who was fresh from work and was black; on the other, her handsome old mother, in a blue striped kirtle and a close frilled cap. And by the window with his feet on the settle, sat her younger brother, a collier; who never spoke a word the whole time I was there, except Yes and No—in answer to me. "Sit ye doon," said the damsel, handing me a woodenseated chair; and the old couple added "Aye, sit ye doon." But why did Ellen wear this *effeminate* dress? Why was she so *exasperatingly clean,* and the coal dust gone from her hands? Because she has been playing all week, stopping away from the pit, to attend her mother, who is unwell … And has Ellen got a sweetheart? "Naa, Ah lost him," said Ellen calmly enough." "He died o'smallpox," said her father: "but he's left her summat to remember him by." "What, that two-year-old child on the floor?" "Yah!" said Ellen taking up the lad and fondling him, which indeed she had done before: and added in reply to what I said, "But Ah never had a chance to marry him, yo know." Neither she nor her parents were ashamed of the matter, though they are all decent folks. Her father was evidently fond and proud of the child … Then we talked about being "drawed aht" [photographed]. Ellen said she had been "draw'd aht twice in my pit claes" and had seen her own picture hanging up for sale. It is not good however; and I asked her if she could not come tomorrow, as she is "playing." Her father and mother both concurred; and Ellen never thought of objecting to walk through the town in her pit dress; which indeed dozens of pit girls do daily, and go of their own accord to be drawed aht in that attire, in order that they may send the picture to absent friends. So Ellen promised to come tomorrow in her pit clothes …. The only question was, whether she should come with a black face or a clean one. She observed that one often looks just as well with *a black face:* I left the point to her discretion: but asked to see her working dress. "Here's t'bonnet," she said, bringing out of the scullery the pit girls' wadded hood bonnet, sound and fairly clean: "and here's mah bedgoon"; which was of pink cotton, patched with bits of blue. And the breeches? "Naa," said Ellen, with creditable shamefastness, "Mah breeches is oopstairs. Ah cannot fotch "em dahn." Her father and mother, however, both counselled her to bring them: and *I was glad of the opportunity of examining this unique garment.* So Ellen went upstairs, and came down with her trousers over her arm. "Them's mah breeches," she said: "they're patched that Ah connot tell t'maan piece on 'em: they was a pair o' men's owd breeches when Ah gat 'em, and Ah've wore 'em t'nahn year at Ah've worked at pits." And they were still good: a pair of trousers made up of patches of cloth and cotton and linen of various colors, but toned down by coaldust to a blackish brown. They were warmly lined and wadded, especially at the knees, to protect them when kneeling among the coals or crawling up the shoot: a garment well fitted to keep warm the legs of a woman doing outdoor work. *And (which spoke well for the fair wearer) the inside of the trousers was clean.* They had button holes round the top. How do keep them on? I asked. "Well," said Ellen in mere simplicity and not coarseness, "there's many a wench ties string round their waist: but Ah've getten a good backsahd, at keeps me breeches oop!" She who made this dreadful speech is a fair and comely English girl: homekeeping, industrious, and virtuous according to her lights.[35]

This passage merits more attention that I presently have time for. Its length is important, as is its detailed recreation of the setting and the dialogue. It is typical of the writing in the diaries about the women miners—tedious, detailed, anxious to miss nothing, mundane and yet, at moments, deeply shocking. As a text it reveals much through the pace of the writing. The time it took to write down, and then to be read, is what alone conveys the timing of the drama it *commemorates.* I use the word advisedly: Freud writes of the fetish:

> Something else has taken its [the maternal penis'] place, has been appointed its substitute, as it were, and now inherits the interests which was formerly directed to its predecessor. But this interest suffers an extraordinary increase as well, because the horror of castration has set up a *memorial* to itself in the creation of the substitute.[36]

I want to touch on a few elements which relate to the argument I have tried to develop here. Munby is disappointed to find Ellen "exasperatingly clean" and dressed in woman's clothes. He calls these *effeminate,* a significant inversion. Working clothes were condemned by the miners' union as being masculine, yet Munby treats them as the norm he desires while femininity in this space has become disappointing, if not deviant. Most crucial is the examination of Ellen's clothes themselves. Munby wanted direct, physical and visual contact, *on the spot and with my own eyes*. Fetishism is a necessary part of the process. The diary text in which the encounter is recorded is long-winded, and boringly so, preparing us for the ultimate sight by prolonged foreplay composed of professional observation, the socioeconomic discourse of facts and figures. The pattern is not dissimilar to that which I traced in Holland's prosaic tourist guide to Belgium. We are told what the clothes are made from and how they have worn; information here services an un-acknowledged erotic agenda. The discourse on cleanliness—his initial dis-appointment at finding her white and not black with coal dirt—now signifies in another, sexual, register when we are made witness to his peering into the crotch of her trousers for signs of dirt, which is, of course, a sign of sexuality, examining that area which would have touched the sexual parts of her body, looking directly at which might prove psychologically traumatic. The fact that they are clean, that is, without evident signs of sexual or other bodily functions, produces a prosaic relief following the excitement and danger of having dared indirectly to look at a woman's sex. "Nothing to see" is, paradoxically, comforting. We are thrown back to that moment in Freud's story of the little boy when he "first catches sight of a girl's genital region, he begins by showing irresolution and lack of interest; he sees nothing or dis-avows that he has seen, he softens it down, or looks about for expedients for bringing it into line with his expectations."[37] There are many levels in which fetishism operates here and I do not want to reduce all masculine sexuality and all problems of sexuality and vision back to this one process. In this instance of one passage from Munby's diary, there is fetishism in the dis-placement of viewing "woman" onto scientific investigation of the *inverted*, or inversion of the, masquerade of femininity, a woman's body and its mas-culine costume.[38] The trousers which metonymically signify the woman's sex by contiguity then become a fetishizing displacement of the absence that is in the end both so traumatic and yet necessary for this masculinity.

Another level of fetishism is, however, the writing, and in the writing. This involves a re-staging of this "*with my own eyes, on the spot*" proximity to the visual object, but softened down, muffled by expedients for managing the confrontation with a series of differences which are at once utterly threatening and yet the object of always unacknowledged yearning. Once he has peered and found no sign, he can reclaim his mastery, his fixity as

"Man," rational, speaking, naming, the subject of the discourse *but only through the act of writing which frames the "seeing" with the fetishism of discourse.*

Both writing in ink on paper and photography work by tonal contrast, producing what we call black and white. Black and white tonalities available to photography at this date, however, could not capture "dirt." We know this from another part of the Munby archive which involved Hannah Cullwick, who wanted to be photographed "in her dirt." She was advised that to "come out black" she should be rubbed with *yellow*.[39] It was hard for the photograph to signify the play on dirt and sexuality to which we have indirect access through the writing. This may mean two things: that the photographs function as an antidote to the dangers of proximity and seeing because they freeze and hold vision in a comforting opacity—a media grayness in which no cat is black or white, clean or dirty; or that there is another form of fetishism to be discerned in the photographs. If the latter were the case, scale would be the device.

On 11 September 1873, Munby went to Little's studio in Wigan, where he had arranged to meet Ellen Grounds for a photo-session (fig. 9).

"Hes yon wench coom?" "Yea, hoo hes," said Mrs. Little and she and her grown up daughter wore a puzzled smile, as if they were about to show me some *strange creature*. A moment afterwards, Ellen herself came out of the kitchen: and she was in her pit clothes, as she had promised. "Well, Ellen, yo've coom!" "Yah. Ah's coom, Sir!" said the collier-lass who looked vastly better and also *bigger* in her working dress than she did last night in her woman's clothes. She wore her wadded bonnet, the front part tied tight over her forehead, and the hood encircling her head like an aureole; her loose bluepatched cotton bedgown made her full bust and broad shoulders look *larger* still: below it came a striped skirt *gathered up round the hips*; and *under* that her breeches—the pair she showed me last night—and her iron clog-shoon. She had forgotten to bring her topcoat: and first she tried on a coat belonging to Mrs. Little's son, a big lad, but it was too small for her; so she tried a rough coat, like her own, of *Mr.* Little's; and it fitted her well. Then she was furnished with a spade to represent her great pit shovel. She shouldered the spade in workmanlike fashion, buttoned her coat, and stood readily and well, *as I posed her*; and she was taken, first in that guise, and then without the coat: I standing beside her, to show how nearly she approached me in size.[40]

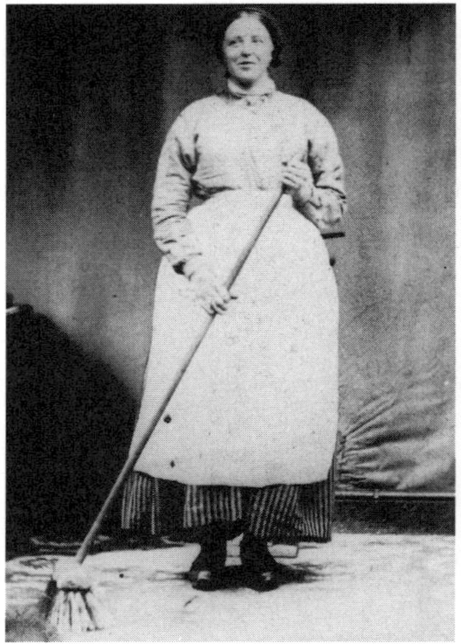

a

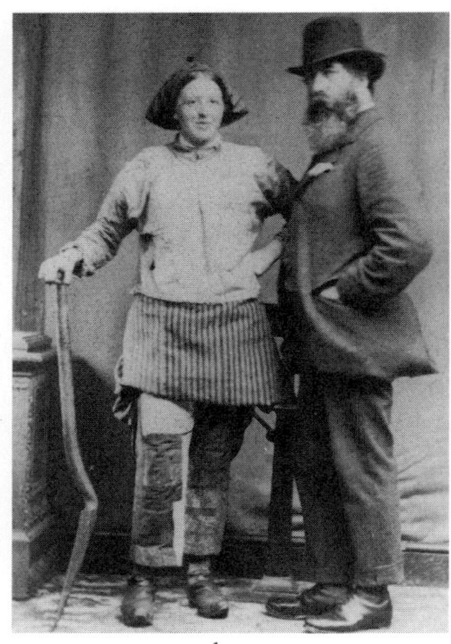

b

Figure 9.   a.b.c. Triptych
Robert Little

a) *Ellen Grounds, Collier Girl, 108 Scholfield Lane, Wigan, aged 22, taken in my presence, 1873, 11 September. Further annotated "Eh! It favours as Ah were sweeping the hahse."* Munby Collection (III-112-20-d). Reproduced by kind permission of the Master and Fellows of Trinity College, Cambridge.

b) *Ellen Grounds, aged 22 a broo wench at Pearson and Knowles Pits, Wigan, taken 11 September 1873 (and Arthur Munby),* 1873. Munby Collection (113-1-c), Trinity College, Cambridge. Reproduced by kind permission of the Master and Fellows of Trinity College, Cambridge.

c) *Ellen Grounds, taken in my presence, 11 September, 1873.* Carte-de-visite, Munby Collection (113-1-a). Trinity College, Cambridge. Reproduced by kind permission of the Master and Fellows of Trinity College, Cambridge.

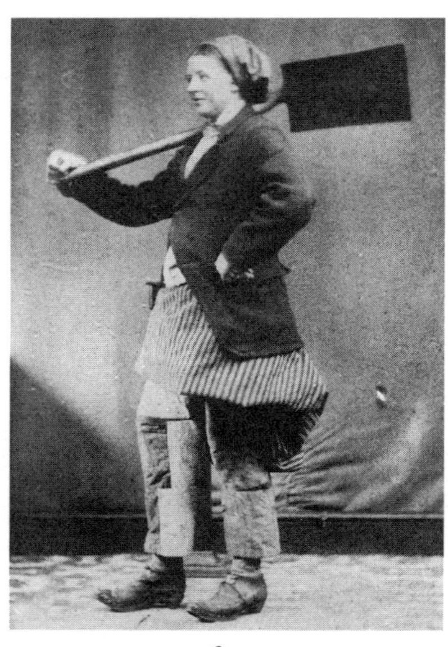

c

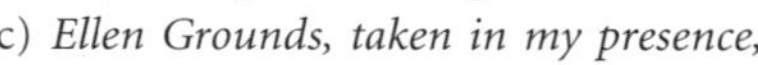

One other photo exists in the collection of Ellen Grounds in work-a-day woman's clothes holding a broom (fig. 9). The backdrop appears the same as in these last two suggesting perhaps Mrs. Little's studio on this same occasion. Her bonnet is differently tied and her striped skirt has been let down and covered with an apron. But both photographs make her seem very tall, by contrast to the scale of the photographs of Ellen Grounds in 1866 (figs. 7, 8). Either they have been cropped or Munby, choreographing the photo-session, insisted on this lowered position of the camera, and its proximity to the subject so that she fills the space while there are no objects to indicate scale.

This triptych of images creates an interesting narrative if we frame the duet between Munby and Ellen Grounds by her "workmanlike" image and her "effeminate" one—the two encountered over two days in real time but fabricated in discontinuous space by the photograph (fig. 9). The diary entry suggests a desire to see Ellen Grounds in her pit clothes. This is the locus of a pleasure, which is not to be found if the same tall woman wears a dress. Then she appears less large. The working costume has specific effects; it creates an illusion of size, which, in a sexual binary, we might say made her more masculine. But that is not said. Hard hands are described by Munby as "manly." It is probable that size signifies or allows the trace of another kind of body, the maternal body, that is a female corporeality marked in the dramas of sexual difference but registering a condition that is not yet subjected to the law of difference, castration symbolic or otherwise. What it is can only be hunted down through a disjointed series of moments of vision, through staged sites ("as I posed her"). These sights allow him to glimpse a fantastic body which is only poorly described by the Freudian term, the phallic mother.

> The pre-Oedipal, phallic or archaic mother must be understood as a Fantasy—the child's fantasy of an omnipotent, absolutely powerful, sexually neutral figure. Freud argues that the child (presumably a boy) bestows on the mother what he attributes to himself ... . The phallic mother is the fantasy of the mother who is able to grant the child everything, to be its object of desire, and in turn to be the subject who desires the child as her own object.[41]

In this diary entry the striped skirt is mentioned as "gathered up round the hips," giving an opportunity to speak of body parts. The description of the clothes is a displaced allocution of the body. It is not precisely the female body. Its confusion of strict codes of gender makes it a curious exemplar of something akin to the "sexually neutral body" that houses a longing for a specifically maternal body. It has a bust for sure which suggests this mature, maternal body. (Ellen Ground had had a child.) At the same time this gathered up skirt suggests that we redefine what the Wigan miner women were wearing. To say they wore trousers is to miss the point entirely. They walked about in public with their skirts hitched up—and although their legs are encased in rough men's trousers, these function as a sheath, like the tights ballet dancers and acrobats wore which drew attention to the legs while also veiling them—maintaining precisely the "almost but not quite" quality so essential to the structures of fetishism. In between these two bodies—one boringly veiled and contained and a parody of the femininity of women of his own class—the other partially revealed and transgressive of the strict codes demarcating sexual difference within Munby's bourgeois world—where is Munby, or shall I ask *what is he?* What is he trying to get at with this paradoxical proximity, this repetitious search for some kind of primal seeing? What's the point of having images like those of himself and Ellen Grounds in one frame, fixed as a matching yet disparate pair (fig. 1)?

But let me pause here. Whatever markers of difference I suggest we can read in these images will appear to be a willful reading in, or at best, a hypothetical reading of how these images may signify according to the theoretical models with which I have framed them. The photographs maintain discretion. They are as obvious as they are in the end opaque in relation to what motivated their production and collection and sustained their appeal to this one owner. There is another kind of evidence, however, upon which I can call. It is available precisely because it is so different from the deadpan of early photographic representation. That is in the album of sketches where Eliza Hayes is represented (fig. 2).

Drawing is closer to writing. It is also graphic. Yet drawing does not provide the fetishizing mastery produced in writing. Drawings invite a symptomatic reading of inclusions and exclusions, resistances and hesitancies, attentions and investments. Photography takes the prephotographic material, already coded by choices of pose, gesture, setting, lighting, usually framed by inherited conventions of picture making. It then "translates" it, which is at once a loss and a conversion. The result is quite different from the created drawing which registers pressures from the Imaginary in more inadvertent ways. [42] In the finished work, these become the very substance and effect. Drawing involves the body which traces on the fictive space of the paper fantastic bodies the drawing subject conjures up, often unconsciously through this activity. Through the movements of a hand, the drawing registers interest, anxiety, significance. Color, scale, size, proportion, pose and gesture are the result of decisions, in which conscious selection and intention are *overdetermined* by a multiplicity of unconscious choices and desires.[43]

If we go back to Eliza Hayes (fig. 2), might it be possible to suggest that this is what Munby "saw" in this Freudian version of the "mind's eye" when he looked at Ellen Grounds too? Are the other sketches of the women miners with whom Munby cultivated such "friendships" as his class and money permitted to be read also as a more revealing index of what motivated his observation of female labour *"on the spot and with [his] own eyes?"* Another named miner who appears in the album is Ellen Meggison, known affectionately in her community as "Boompin' Nelly," a mother of eight children. Munby first met her in 1853 and she is recorded in the diaries over thirty years. Munby drew Ellen Meggison seated, legs apart, elbows resting on her knees, while she holds the paws Munby has drawn as her hands (fig. 10). Her face and arms are black, and more, he has traced in her features the racist caricature of the facial type associated in nineteenth century Britain with colonial otherness, be it Irish or African.

I want to conclude with yet more extreme images from this truly riotous album (figs. 10 and 11). Despite their shared lack of signs of professional expertise, Munby's drawings are a frightful contrast to Van Gogh's beginner's exercise, as well as to photography's reassuring, freeze-frame stillness, its deadpan nonchalance. Munby's unschooled but striking drawings of Lancashire pitbrow women are charged by the evident intensity of the hand that held the pen to create on the page such vividly imagined faces and bodies. Unchecked by having internalized the rules of art, the aesthetic disciplines which regulate and manage the psychic drives which play across all tracings of the body, these images brutally create the components of a white bourgeois's repertoire of the fantastic body.[44]

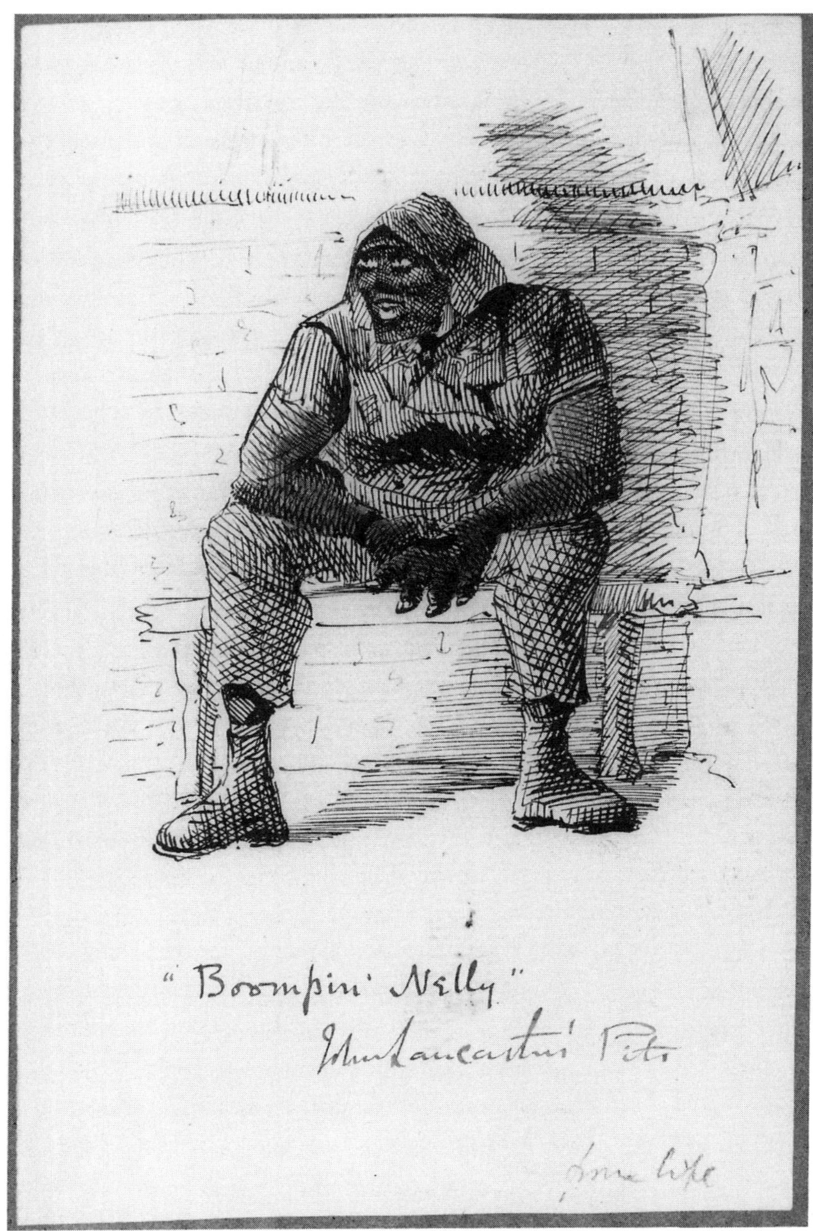

Figure 10.   Arthur Munby, *Boompin' Nelly (Ellen Meggison) John Lancaster's Pits, from life.* Munby Collection (110-17-folio-7-recto) Trinity College, Cambridge. Reproduced by kind permission of the Master and Fellows of Trinity College, Cambridge.

Nothing in the measured tones of the diary entries, with their careful recapitulations and verbatim record of conversations and encounters with generous, friendly, warmhearted and intelligent pitbrow women, prepares us for these raw and abusive visualizations of working class women. Grotesque racist caricature slips towards overt bestialization along a chain of Eurocentric signifiers from coal–dust–dirt–skin color–race–savage–beast–animal. My argument is therefore simply this: that the compulsive writing of the diaries and the notebooks, the collecting of hundreds of almost identical photographs, can now be read as a defense, indeed a necessity, a self-imposed submission to the safety of discourse and the opacity of the photograph. Here, in the sketches, we glimpse what they veiled, and thus at last see what "vision" constituted the secret that Munby wanted kept when he ordained that his diaries and collection were not to be opened for forty years after his death. Writing above all secured for Munby a stable subject position producing the distance of surveillance to control the dangers of proximity, which like the sleep of reason, produced monsters. The copious diary texts were a defence against the breakdown and excess incited by the proximity he obsessively sought all those years from 1853 through 1882 to these "not-quite-female-bodies" which appealed to him as transgressively indifferent, and yet would be aggressively punished in his own representations as indecipherably other. In the drawings, there is a vivid and almost literal figuration of what was verbally evoked in Holland's text, stunted prize fighters, with grotesque paws for hands and huge clubs for feet, with faces not merely hard from unfitting toil, but so other in relation to the white femininity they oppose, they can only be imagined in the racist stereotypes created by an imperial bourgeoisie for its enslaved and abused African other (fig. 11). Here, in terms of a visual shock that it is hard to tolerate, and cruel to inflict on the viewer who has any investment in African identity, we can see the interface of race, class and sexuality. While affirming the centrality of racism to the imperial bourgeois imaginary, this drawing indicates the transpositions and mutual inflections of race, class and gender in the constructions of white bourgeois masculine subjectivity in the nineteenth century.

Only as the subject of a mastering enunciation, as an author in a pseudo-scientific discourse of social investigation, was this white masculinity secure against itself, that is to say, only when "surveillance" mastered a psychically

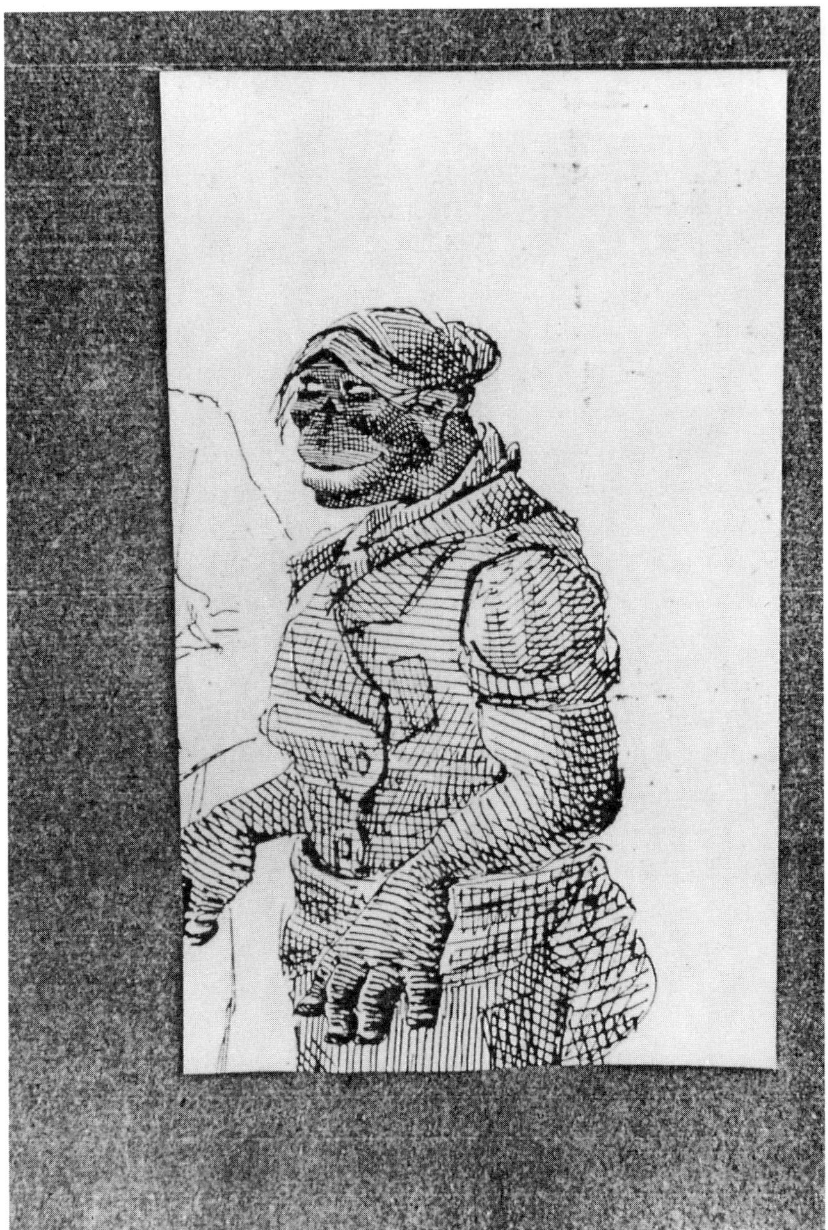

Figure 11.   Arthur Munby, *Untitled sketch*, Unpublished Album, Trinity College, Cambridge. Reproduced by kind permission of the Master and Fellows of Trinity College, Cambridge.

constructed "sexuality." Thus we find that a splitting of the subject, registered theoretically in the different concepts of the gaze in the work of Foucault and Freud, managed the superimposition of the one over the other and identified the gaze of mastery with the Oedipal formation of the Law while the gaze of desire ferreted out a way to hold onto a pre-Oedipal fantasy. There, in discourse, the man could verbally affirm what he found when his curious and eroticizing gaze *penetrated* beneath the coal dust, the dirt, the muscle: there, in *écriture*, he could conjure back again the maternal womanliness his look would pursue to the limits of visibility. In finding nothing to see, he saw the lack *vis-à-vis* his masculine seeing subjectivity that secured the difference upon which his sexual superiority, his social and self-mastery "as a man—a white, bourgeois man" depended. Yet in the encounter that had been risked, proximity to something *en plus*, something that had to be signified through size, through excess in relation to the fetishized image of the castrated feminine lady, could be momentarily glimpsed, offering a pleasure which almost created a space in which that "become-man" and that "lost-woman" were "alike," that is, where the rule of sexual difference and the expulsion of the male child from a universe made secure and dominated by a "maternal" figure could be fantastically and, for a moment only, joyfully suspended in an imaginary visuality. Yet finally, that law of difference had to be sadistically reimposed as the pen covered the page, drawing its "blackened" veil over such dangerous visions.

Language, being still so phallocentric, makes this difficult to articulate. Constant encounters with the images are necessary to keep in mind the kind of possibilities which only the different kinds of visualization could manage to keep in tension. The "maternal figure" is not a happy phrase. It is used here to try to signal a gap between a fantastic body, invented retrospectively by the child as it accedes to the Symbolic and thus acquires the means to signify both the loss and memory of plenitude, which the Symbolic inflicts and articulates. *The mother*, a linguistic term, is not the mother except in relation to the linguistic signifier, *the father*. These two terms are produced in relational difference by language which then articulates symbolically, as linguistic difference, a field of meanings, affects, fantasies and desires which were hitherto complex, transitive and unfixed and, in Lacan's terms "imaginary," that is, premised in the mirror image of visualized bodies and scenes.[45]

The maternal thus refers to an undifferentiated or pre-differentiated parent figure comprising many persons who fill that space in the early social and psychic life of a child. Parents of both sexes are part of this primary figure, and in social and historical conditions of childcare, non-related adults may participate—wet nurses and other class or race caregivers.[46] In my work on images produced by European bourgeois men in the later nineteenth century, Van Gogh or Toulouse-Lautrec, I have used the writings of another man of that generation and class, although socially and culturally differentiated by being Jewish in an anti-semitic Europe, Sigmund Freud.[47] In the problems some of his male patients experienced with their adult sexuality, Freud discerned the traces of the conflict initiated by the Oedipal crisis which forbade to them their primary sexual object: the maternal figure. The taboo against this incestuous choice was, however, fractured by the internal, social and gender divisions of the "maternal figure." In adult life the aggression inspired by the forced submission to the Law of the Father was displaced from the Mother through the idealization of an almost inaccessible, incorporeal femininity. The aggression and anxiety created by this prohibition and loss could be inflicted through sexual or other practices on the bodies of working-class women, which while female, and thus other, were not registered or treated as completely feminine. The feminine then signified the incestuously forbidden but idealized and "loved." In order to be desirable and sexually used, another female body was needed. To be erotic it had to be debased and it was debased by being eroticized. In the paintings and drawings by the artists mentioned above, this division is articulated clearly in terms of the quite distinct visual rhetorics which are used, on the one hand, for the representation of ladies, especially the artists' mothers, and, on the other, for prostitutes, urban working-class and peasant women. These "other" bodies are figured to emphasize not so much difference from men as difference from the lady— the Symbolic representative of the Mother with its unconscious freight from a pre-Oedipal relation to the son. Paradoxically this differencing occurred through exaggeration of maternal features such as hips and breasts, or through extreme difference from an idealized feminine face and phallicized body. The trope most often used was *bestialization*, which stands for both sexualization and sexual use. But bestialization goes beyond sexuality with the added weight of horror and abjection. In the drawing of Eliza Hayes (fig. 2), the male figure appears—on a conventional axis of difference—almost feminized with the delicate features, dainty hands and little feet. It is as if this figure internalizes aspects of the loved feminine as both class identification and a means of access to the forbidden bourgeois mother. Before him stands not an other, a working-class woman, but his psychic projection that is legible only in terms of the way it manages his, white masculinity's profound ambivalence. In characteristically fetishisinng fashion, all the signs work both ways. She is large and comforting; she is large and threatening. She is like me; she is repulsively different. She is like a man; yet she is not-woman, not the sign of femininity. She is a *neither-nor* figure in which the excess that the recalcitrant otherness which a non-phallically inscribed femaleness threatens to present to the precarious masculine subject—signified after Oedipalization as the phallic mother—is inscribed all over her body in color, in scale, in a face that sports only eyes and lips and a body with multiple nipples and a huge hand. Nothing I say can trap this fantasy within the mastery of language. As a Freudian reader of the image, I want what I say about it to sound odd, disturbing, rude, crude, excessive and extreme, shocking us by confronting us with what we try not to know about our fantastic psychic life. According to Freud, the unconscious works, in dreams for instance, by depositing its "hot" material into bland and puzzling images or scenarios whose meanings begin to unravel and proliferate as one is forced to "say" what you imagine you saw in the "mind's eye." [48] I am, therefore, not describing a supposed fact there in the drawing, but reading, i.e., verbalizing, the image's materials for the psychic ambivalence representation stages. This project for interpretation depends furthermore on placing what this mode of representation stages in sequence with other kinds of inscription—writing—and other kinds of imagining—photography—as part of the complex process of a historical but not idiosyncratic subjectivity to which the Munby archive provides access.

Munby's archive, as an example of the broader field of representation with which I have tried to link it, could, therefore, be read in Oedipal terms, except for compulsions which have so far been foregrounded in studies of Munby—the diaries and the photographic collection. These do not reveal as starkly either the contradictions or the sadism. Rather they instance the defenses against them. By setting the diaries and photographs in conjunction now with the overlooked album—or the repressed album, which has only selectively been reproduced—another trope can be identified for this paradox of white bourgeois masculinity: its self-definition and its conflicted structures of desire are premised **not** on a binary opposition man/woman which appears so publicly at the ideological level in Victorian discourses. A more intricate pattern of fractured femininities had to be constructed where difference was never only sexual. It was figured through the constant relay of social and racial difference, colonizing each other's tropes to visualize the psychic dramas of a historically specific masculine subjectivity and its confrontation with and formation by difference.

Munby's archive is riven with these fissures. In the diary writing there is frequently the moment when, however much he reports on his peering and seeing anarchic signs of many differences written in working women's bodies: they look like lads, they walk like sailors, they are as black as can be, their hands are hard as men's and so forth, he can ultimately reclaim what he calls "womanliness." This is always a relief because it signals the absence of sexuality, which, I suggest, signifies in his texts autonomous, female power where the phallic mother is not just his fantasy but what women really might be: more powerful—and "*en plus*" than men.

> Ellen flung herself into a chair and Jane leaned against the drawers, panting, and wiping the beaded sweat—and with it some of the blackness—from her red face … . those two young women in men's clothes, as black and grim as fiends and as rough and uncouth in manners as a bargee, and yet, *to those who looked deep enough* not unwomanly or degraded. (29 September 1860)

Womanliness, like femininity, has a comforting sound in most languages. Its phonetic largesse disavows the aggression toward and terror inspired in "men" by a naked "woman," woman in her female specificity, her specific (i.e., not phallically masquerading) corporeal presence which offers to phallocentric "vision" a field of radical undecidability, and thus defies its logic and its logos. Munby's figures are not nude, of course. But they registered as brute nature, uncivilized, unpolished, untransformed because they did not emit the signs of phallic culture—feminine deference and femininity as absence of an equal, contending power. They did not display the masquerade that is white bourgeois femininity. Trousered, these women disturbed the protective shield of costume which both aestheticizes and fetishizes sexual difference in a phallocentric culture. Without that artifice of fixed but veiled difference, the masculine imaginary ran riot, revealing some images of what such a subject desires, which the law forbids and the fetish disavows: the archaic phallic mother who, on this side of the Oedipal complex, can only be signified by men as raw, uncooked, unassimilable, abject and yet, beyond its law, it beckons as almost majestic. For while I would define fetishism as a process of containment within a semiotics of phallically defined gender, I want also to stress the pressure of what it tries to hold onto by freezing, substituting, displacing and yet commemorating. Fetishism is a memorial to another set of relations to and feelings about femaleness and its other, "unfeminine" yet irreducibly female and maternal bodies. The Munby drawings, however, expose a perpetual regress. Even if we find a condition in which the surveilling bourgeois man "desired" a controlled proximity to that which appeared to suspend the phallic law of difference, and liberate him from the social and sexual structures forming his gender and class, that imagined moment is itself censored. The contradictions of gender and class were visualized through yet another semiotics of power, the demonized fictions of the colonial imaginary which these images suggest were as critical to that psychsymbolic formation as those of gender and class. These matters were, it would seem, critically, black and white.[49]

notes

1 Arthur Joseph Munby was interested in many forms of heavy labor performed by women. In this article I shall focus on his major preoccupation—women in mining. Munby had trained as a solicitor but worked as a Civil Servant for the Ecclesiastical Commission in London. His investigations into "female labor" were both amateur and private. He was forced by circumstances to "come out" but very late on. For instance in 1887 he attended a delegation to the Home Secretary in defense of women's right to work. His papers were donated to Trinity College Library at his death in 1910 with the proviso that they were not to be read for forty years. Since that date interest has been attracted to this archive resulting in a number of publications: D. Hudson, *Munby Man of Two Worlds* (London: John Murray, 1972), which reproduces selections from the diaries linking Munby with

contemporary Victorians; M. Hiley, *Victorian Working Women* (London: Gordon Fraser, 1979), which focuses on the photographic collection of working women also using extracts from the diaries about Munby's amateur research; L. Davidoff, "Class and Gender in Victorian Britain" in *Sex and Class in Women's History*, ed. J. L. Newton (London: Routledge, 1983); and H. Dawkins "The Diaries and Photographs of Hannah Cullwick," *Art History* 10.2, (1987): 154–187. These last two develop a feminist analysis of the archive focusing on Hannah Cullwick, the servant whom Munby married, whose diaries and images form a major part of the collections.

2 T. G. Dugdale, Louisa Millard, Robert Little, John Cooper are the names that occur most in the Munby collection. John Hannavy and Chris Ryan, *Living and Working in Wigan* (Wigan: Smiths Books, 1986) give a complete listing of over thirty studios at work from the 1850s–1930s.

3 The theoretical and methodological issues have been discussed in "Feminism and Foucault," in *Theory and Interpretation in the Visual Arts*, ed. Keith Moxey Michael Ann Holly and Norman Bryson (Wesleyan University Press, 1994). A reading of Munby's "secret" and issues of the archive are discussed in "The Dangers of Proximity: The Spaces of Sexuality in Word and Image," *Discourse* 16.2, 1993–4 (published by Center for Twentieth Century Studies, University of Wisconsin, Milwaukee).

4 "Nineteenth century 'bourgeois' society—and it is doubtless still with us—was a society of blatant and fragmented perversion. And this was not by way of hypocrisy, for nothing was more manifest and more prolix, or more manifestly taken over by discourses and institutions." Michel Foucault, *History of Sexuality: An Introduction Volume One* (London: Penguin Books, 1978), 47.

5 Davidoff, 1983, see note 1.

6 The term and its further meanings are taken from Homi Bhabha's work, especially "The Other Question: The Stereotype and Colonial Discourse," *Screen* 24:6 (1983); 18–36. Bhabha develops a field of analysis in which Foucault's theories of power/knowledge and Freud's theories of fetishism are set into play to define the ambivalence of colonial discourse: "Nor would it be possible, without the attribution of ambivalence to relations of power/knowledge, to calculate the traumatic impact of the return of the oppressed—those terrifying stereotypes of savagery, cannibalism, lust and anarchy which are the signal points of identification and alienation, scenes of fear and desire, in colonial texts. It is precisely this function of the stereotype as phobia and fetish, according to Fanon, that threatens the closure of the racial/epidermal schema for the colonial subject and opens the royal road to colonial fantasy."

7 Mieke Bal, *Reading Rembrandt* (Cambridge: Cambridge University Press, 1992).

8   Peter Fryer, *Staying Power: The History of Black People in Britain* (London: Pluto Press, 1984).

9   I am working implicitly with Lacanian categories of the imaginary and symbolic. These constitute two registers of representation as well as two levels of subjectivity. For fundamental definitions see J. Laplanche and J. B. Pontalis, *The Language of Psychoanalysis* (London: Hogarth Press, 1973) and for an analysis of the terms relative to cultural theory see F. Jameson "Imaginary and Symbolic in Lacan: Marxism, Psychoanalytic Criticism and the Problem of the Subject," *Yale French Studies*, 55/56, (1977): 338–395. "The Imaginary may thus be described as a peculiar spatial configuration whose bodies primarily entertain relationships of inside/outside with one another, which is then traversed and reorganised by that primordial rivalry and transitivistic substitution of imagoes, that indistinction of primary narcissism and aggressivity, from which our later conceptions of good and evil derive." This quote from p. 357 captures the ambivalence of the many dualisms which characterized the fantasies shaped by the imaginary which is principally a spatial and visual syntax in contrast to the Symbolic's alienation of the subject in language—sequences, signifying chains, words, substitutions.

10   The Munby archive is in Trinity College, Cambridge. I am grateful to Diana Chardon of the Library who has catalogued the album of sketches.

11   This project is part of a book, *Sexuality and Surveillance: Working Women and Bourgeois Men*, Routledge in 1994.

12   Michel Foucault (ed.), *Herculine Barbin Being the Recently Discovered Memoirs of a Nineteenth Century French Hermaphrodite*, trans. Richard Dougall (New York: Pantheon Books, 1980). For a critical reading of Foucault's thesis, see Judith Butler, *Gender Trouble: Feminism and the Subversion of Identity* (London and New York: Routledge, 1990).

13   Foucault, *History of Sexuality*, 125.

14   In a remarkable undergraduate dissertation (University of Leeds,1982) Sally Walker, a costume historian, attempted to argue for the meanings of this working costume for the women who wore it in the political struggles around women's right to work.

15   These women have left little documentation about themselves—autobiographies, diaries, etc. At least in the 1842 Parliamentary Commissions we can find reported speech of women miners. But they are always spoken for in later texts and never called to give evidence in their own voice. Ironically, it is Munby's compulsive recording that gives us the only access to these women's account of their experience of work and family. This is the topic of another paper.

16   Two further psychoanalytical models should be noted: that by Lacan in which the body is achieved as an effect of the internalization of the imago, see "The Mirror Phase …" in *Ecrits*, (London: Tavistock Press, 1977) and that by Julia Kristeva, whose

thesis on the subject's relation to language is premised on the constant struggle between the semiotic—the remnants of the drives present through traces such as sound, rhythm, color, etc.—and the symbolic, the attempted fixing of meaning and temporary construction of unity by means of which the subject recognizes itself in the signifiers offered by language. Both theories suggest states of discontinuity and unity in constant play in which the body refers to both the grounds of representation and the represented. See Julia Kristeva "The System and the Speaking Subject" in *The Kristeva Reader,* ed. Toril Moi, (Oxford: Blackwell Books, 1986).

17   Emile Zola, *Germinal* [1884] Penguin Books, 1954. Page references are to this edition. Maheude is finally forced to return to work underground. Earlier in the text Zola repeatedly identifies her by her sagging breasts.

18   G. Pollock, *Van Gogh and Dutch Art: Van Gogh's Notion of the Modern* (London University, PhD, 1981) which will be published as *The Case Against Van Gogh: The Cities and Countries of Modernism* (London: Thames and Hudson, 1994).

19   Zola, p. 37.

20   Clive Holland, *The Belgians at Home* (London: Methuen & Co, 1911), 124.

21   A. Davis, *Women, Race & Class* (New York: Random House and London: The Women's Press, 1982).

22   A. Solomon-Godeau, "The Legs of the Countess," *October*, 39 (1986): 65–107.

23   Solomon-Godeau, 74.

24   *British Parliamentary Papers,* First Report of the Commissioners on the Mines 1842 XV, 24, Session 3 Feb.- 12 August, 1842.

25   *British Parliamentary Papers* XIII (1867): xiii.

26   *British Parliamentary Papers,* Evidence of P. Dickenson, 19 March 1866, question no. 651, n.p.

27   We should not minimize the gender conflict within working class politics. But we should also not ignore the class difference in the motivation of working-class men and bourgeois men in relation to the ideals of feminine domesticity. The point is that in both cases men abrogate to themselves the power to define women's social roles and identities in ways which effectively shore up their power and position as "men."

28   There is a detail in this photography which unsettles the image—her fingernails. I shall be dealing with that in another study of these images which relates to a different strategy of reading for class and gender focusing on an unexpected site of their signification: hands. See "The View From Elsewhere: The Politics of Female Spectatorship" about hands in Manet's *Bar* in *Media, Gender, Subject,* ed. Penny Florence and De Reynolds, (location: Manchester University Press, year).

29   Lisa Tickner, "Women and Trousers," Paper given at the conference *Leisure in the Twentieth Century* published by the Design Council, London, 1977, 56–67. Before the Second World War women wearing trousers fell into a few categories—

military (and these were often cross dressers), the stage, sport, the beginnings of the bicycle and glamourous evening or leisure wear. The major nineteenth century instance was "bloomerism" which has its own complex history in relation to middle class women's politics, dress reform and the suffrage. See Angela Kingston, *Bloomerism*, unpublished MA Thesis, University of Leeds, 1984, on the representations of women in bloomers in the British press in 1851.

30 John Fletcher, "Versions of the Masquerade," *Screen* 29:3 (1988): 50.

31 Claire Johnstone, "Femininity and the Masquerade: *Anne of the Indies,*" in *Einburgh Film Festival: Women's Cinema,* Claire Johnstone and Paul Willemen, (London: British Film Institute, 1975); Joan Riviere, "Womanliness as Masquerade" (1929) in *Formations of Fantasy,* Victor Burgin et al., (London: Methuen, 1986): 35–44; Jacques Lacan, "The Meaning of the Phallus," in *Feminine Sexuality,* Juliet Mitchell and Jacqueline Rose, (London: MacMillan, 1982), 74–85; Sigmund Freud, "Fetishism" [1927], *Pelican Freud Library: On Sexuality* (London: Penguin Books, 1977), 351–57; Mary Ann Doane, "Film and the Masquerade—Theorising the Female Spectator," *Screen* 23: 3–4, (1982), 74–87.

32 John Fletcher, 52–3.

33 Jacqueline Rose, *Sexuality in the Field of Vision* (London: Verso Books, 1986).

34 This is a long quotation but it is necessary to present the full text to stress the excess of "the scene of writing" where an event is restaged. The pace and detail of the writing indicates much more than a mere record of the visit. It is a dramatization, playing with delay and carefully building up to a final revelation and release of tension. And finally, only when it is read in its entirety does the full force of the fetishism of writing emerge. For a comparable analysis of diary writing, sexuality and the body, see Francis Barker, *The Tremulous Private Body* (London: Methuen, 1984).

35 *The Diaries of Arthur Munby* unpublished, Cambridge, Trinity College, Vol. 41.

36 Freud, "Fetishism," 353.

37 S. Freud, "Some Psychical Consequences of the Anatomical Distinction between the Sexes" [1925] in Pelican Freud Library, Vol. 7, *On Sexuality* (London: Pelican Books, 1977),336.

38 On the relation between fetishism and scientific investigation/curiosity and its socially acceptable sublimations, see Freud's writings on Leonardo da Vinci: S. Freud, "Leonardo da Vinci and a Memory of his Childhood," [1910] in Pelican Freud Library, Vol. 14, *On Art & Literature* (London: Pelican Books, 1985).

39 *The Diaries of Hannah Cullwick,* ed. Liz Stanley (London: Virago Books, 1984), 75–7 describes Hannah Cullwick's visit to the studio of Mr. Stodart of Margate in 1864.

40 Cited M. Hiley, op. cit., 92.

41 Elizabeth Grosz, *Feminism and Psychoanalysis A Critical Dictionary,* ed. Elizabeth Wright (Oxford: Basil Blackwell, 1992). This figure can also become the source of

persecutory fantasies. The difficulty lies in the terms in which this fantasy will represented remaining exclusively phallic so that the body of the maternal fantasy is still be articulated through Oedipal, castration anxieties. A more polymorphous sexuality seems to be insisting through the kind of body imagery we are discerning in the Munby archive—where size of hands, feet, shoulders and busts engages attention.

42 See Jameson, op .cit., on the Imaginary.

43 Overdetermination is a Freudian term: "Formations of the unconscious (symptoms, dreams, etc.) … [are] related to a multiplicity of unconscious elements which may be organised in different meaningful sequences, each having its own specific coherence at a particular level of interpretation." Laplanche and Pontalis, 292.

44 I am indebted here to Heather Dawkins's work on Degas for this concept of the "fantastic body." See H. Dawkins, *Sexuality, Degas and Women's History* (University of Leeds, PhD, 1991) forthcoming by Yale University Press.

45 Jacques Lacan, "The Mirror Phase as Formative of the I" in *Ecrits* (London: Tavistock Press, 1977): 1–7; for a useful account of Lacanian concepts and their use in cultural analysis, see Frederic Jameson, "Imaginary and Symbolic in Lacan: Marxism, Psychoanalytic Criticism, and the Problem of the Subject," *Yale French Studies* no. 55/56, (1977): 338–395.

46 I go into the role of the social division of childcare in relation to Munby and bourgeois masculinity in "The Dangers of Proximity," *Discourse* (1993). The discussion is indebted to Lee Davidoff's founding article on this archive, "Class and Gender in Victorian England" in *Sex and Class in Women's History*, ed. Judith L. Newton et al., (London: Routledge & Kegan Paul, 1983), 17–71.

47 "Fathers of Modern Art and Mothers of Invention," *Differences: Trouble in the Archives*, (1992): 4:3, 91–132 on Toulouse Lautrec. On Van Gogh see forthcoming *The Case Against Van Gogh* (city?: Thames and Hudson, 1995). The key text by Freud is "On the Universal Tendency to Debasement in the Sphere of Love" [1912], *Standard Edition* Vol. 11, 177–90.

48 S. Freud, *Interpretation of Dreams*, (Vienna, 1990), or for a more concise presentation of the theory, see *Introductory Lectures on Psychoanalysis* [1916] Penguin Freud Library, Vol. 1, (London: Penguin Books, 1973). Note that "unconscious representation … neither reflects nor signifies the subject and its objects. It is a pure cathexis of the word as such … the unconscious representation is only a text. But the text produces effects; since sexuality is organised as we have seen, not according to some instinct, some 'tendency,' but according to what has been said. Consequently, discourse makes impossible any direct and peaceable relation to the body, to the world and to pleasure. It turns away from *jouissance*; it is in this sense that is it castrating." Michele Montrelay, "Inquiry into Femininity" *M/F*, no. 1, (1978): 87–8.

49 Toni Morrison, *Playing in the Dark Whiteness and the Literary Imagination* (Cambridge: Harvard University Press, 1992) offers an extended analysis of the phenomenon in the formation of "American" literature.

on mary cassatt's *reading le figaro* or the case of the missing women

griselda pollock

Preamble: Eleven Thoughts about a Chair

She looked at the chair.

It was her chair, a personal chair, but not one you keep in a bedroom.

It looked a bit lonely. There weren't that many women sitting in these chairs. She had read somewhere that only 3% of professors are women. She wondered why and made a mental note to do some research some day.

She began to hear their voices—women's voices. Was this success they asked? Was this joining the establishment? Was it a political chair? She looked for the name. Social and Critical Histories of Art. What a mouthful! Whoever dreamed that one up she wondered? Was it a chair in art history? The plural changed that decisively. There were other histories to be told from that chair.

Was it his chair? Yellow matching the sunflowers…

Was it a chair in women's studies?

Was it a chair for women artists to rest in and be seen from?

Would it be the death of her?

Could she sit in it with feminists?

Who were the other women waiting to occupy this and other chairs?

She remembered one image of a woman in a chair, reading. She thought of the chair the woman who painted it had sat in. She looked at the audience seated in expectation of some kind of ordeal, though it was late and they wanted their tea.

She was not sitting but standing, ready to give a lecture to inaugurate her chair.

She would name it:

THE CASE OF THE MISSING WOMEN

And what I wanted from you mother was this: that in giving me life you remained alive.

Luce Irigaray "One Doesn't Stir Without the Other" (1981)[1]

memories of her

When I was a graduate student at the Courtauld Institute of Art in 1971, Anita Brookner gave one of her weekly lectures. It was a superb performance—as exceptional as it was to be relied upon to be so. There is one moment which I remember vividly—in what lecture I no longer recall. Anita Brookner flashed upon the twin screens two paintings, portraits from the mid-eighteenth century, and she remarked upon their utter dissonance. One was Van Loo's portrait of the *philosophe* Diderot (1767); the other was Liotard's portrait of Madame D'Epinay (figs. 1–2). Louise Florence Petronille Tardieu d'Escavelles Dame de la Live D'Epinay shared my birthday, 11 March 1726, and died 17 April 1783. Novelist and educational theorist, she became closely acquainted with Baron de Grimm, Diderot and Rousseau who composed *La Nouvelle Héloise* in a cottage *L'Hermitage*, on her estate, lent to him by Madame d'Epinay. Overlooked now, and used only for the information her letters and writings provide on the men of the Enlightenment, Madame d'Epinay gazes at us in Liotard's portrait coyly and coquettishly. Overdressed and fashion conscious, she appears to belong in another realm from the casually attired, busy, intense, alert and self-possessed male intellectual, Diderot as Van Loo represents the type of the new intellectual. Can Liotard's image be read as an image of a woman intellectual, a so-called *bas bleu* or bluestocking? Anita Brookner's passing comment on the assymetrical representation of gender and eighteenth-century intellectuals left a question festering in my nascent feminist consciousness. When I came to write an inaugural lecture for my own Chair twenty-one years later at the University of Leeds, I decided to take that incongruous pairing both as a way of paying homage to my women teachers in art history and as a means to explore contemporary feminist arguments about the necessity for a maternal genealogy to sustain women's contributions to culture as artists, teachers and intellectuals. The focus of this paper is one nineteenth-century painting of a woman

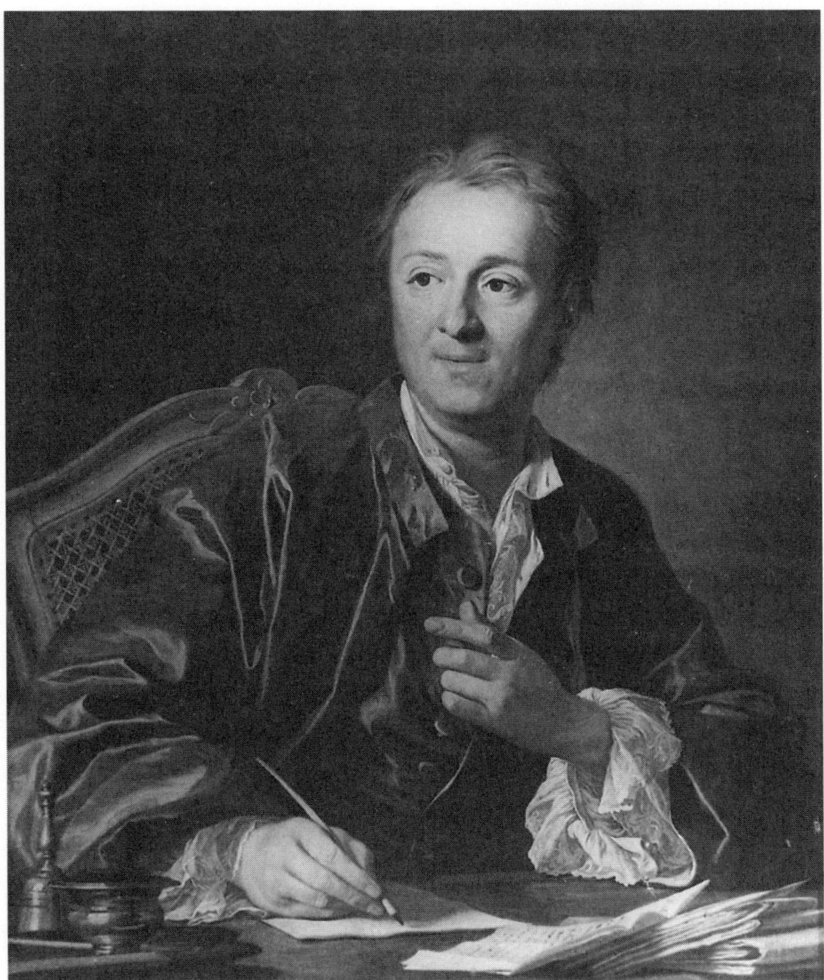

Figure 1.   Carl Van Loo, *Portrait of Denis Diderot*, 1767. Paris, Musée du Louvre.

in a chair, doing something intellectual, *Reading Le Figaro* by Mary Cassatt (fig. 4). Any reading of it, however, will depend upon our being able to transcend the opposition the eighteenth-century pair set up in order to find ways in which intellect and maternity, creativity and acknowledgment of the mother can be allowed to coexist, and more, to be the condition of intellectual creativity. To recognize what one woman artist painted in 1878, we have to re-cognize, re-define, re-theorize the mainstream culture that makes her

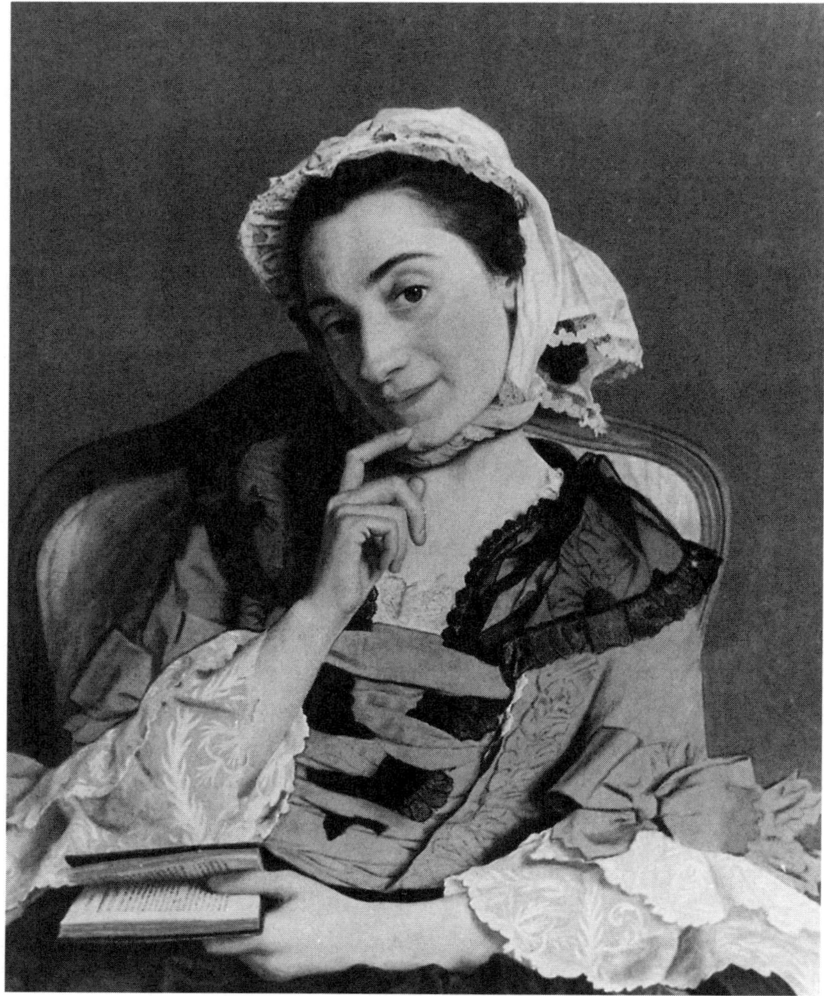

Figure 2.   Jean-Etienne Liotard, *Portrait of Madame d'Epinay*, 1768. Geneva: Musée D'Art et d'Histoire.

work unintelligible, that makes the portrait of Mary Cassatt's mother merely an image of a cozy middle-aged housewife.

Thus we are forced into an unexpected but historically overdetermined confrontation with modernity and its modernisms. There are, therefore, three starting points for this reflection which are both theoretical and historical: Marxism, psychoanalysis and a chapter in the history of the visual arts. All three are significant—if not always as acknowledged—faces of modernity: political Modernism, psychological Modernism, and cultural Modernism. Feminism was an inevitable response and challenge to all three—a Sexual Modernism or the modernization of sexual difference, to be more Kristevan. In the post-modern moment of reappraisal of modernity, a feminist re-reading is not only essential but also illuminating for the feminism that now claims a space to sit on one of culture's privileged chairs.

critical critics and their others

In *The German Ideology*, written in the 1840s, Karl Marx and Friedrich Engels imagined a future communist society free of the division of labor, in which we would no longer be contained within one domain of work. Not only shall we fish, hunt or rear cattle as we like—overcoming divisions between areas of work, but the manual/mental opposition will also be broken down—we may all be "critical critics" after dinner.[2] In this scheme no attention is paid to the sexual division of labor and no thought is given to the opportunities for women to participate in any or all of a society's range of productive and creative activities.

For far from being acknowledged as thinkers, critical women are usually called nags. They were punished or even burned for their attempts to claim knowledge and speech as women. By the nineteenth century the sexual genocide—witch burning—gave way to psychological warfare and young, critical women in trouble with their nonperson status within bourgeois society were either called hysterics or feminists; and they were incarcerated in either hospitals or prisons. Psychoanalysis was formed in the encounter with some of these young women[3] In 1882, Berthe Pappenheim, alias "Anna 'O'" created the "talking cure" during her treatment by Josef Breuer, in a case written up and published with his colleague Sigmund Freud.[4] Despite Freud's later retreat from this creative dialogue with female hysterics, and his final perplexity about femininity, psychoanalysis continued to attract women to it as both analysands and analysts.[5] Indeed by the early twentieth century, "new women" are to be found in significant numbers in (psycho) analysis, both being theorized and doing the theorizing.

In 1929, the year after British women were granted the vote on equal terms with men, Joan Riviere (1883–1962: fig. 3) published a major theoretical paper on female "critical critics," titled "Womanliness as Masquerade."[6] Herself one of the new psychological types she was attempting to understand, namely women intellectuals, Joan Riviere struggled to find terms in which to to explain the paradoxical phenomena of the new women professionals, admitted by legislation into public spheres whose psychological economies, however, allowed no acknowledgment of and psychic suppport for an active femininity. Father-identified as the world of public work is in principle, and populated by men in fact, the relation of the mother to the ambition and creativity of women professionals found no representational support (then as now). Women struggling with its social contradictions at the psychological level fell ill, exhibiting in their symptoms extreme psychic pain. Riviere did not articulate the problem of which she herself was a part in such terms. She offered, however, the insight that her patients' ambition and suffering resulted from an unresolved rivalry with *both* parents—with models of both masculinity and femininity. This implied that her patients had refused to adopt the required passivity of so-called normative femininity—defined in Freudian theory as an exclusively a *receptive-passive* mode. Radically for that moment, Riviere drew upon Melanie Klein's revolutionary new work on the emotional intensity of the very early mother-child relation and the significance of the aggressivity towards the mother long before the Oedipal moment, which suggests that the infant's psyche is powerfully shaped by fantasies about female corporality, especially about the contents of the mother's body which contains breasts, milk, babies *and* the father's penis. Riviere thus departed from the strict Freudian model of femininity as suffering from envy of the male/rivalry with the father, to argue that her women patients exhibited the persistent desire to *give to*, as well as to receive from *both* parents; that is, to harness the sadistic drives of the early fantasies Klein had identified and deploy them in socially validated activity and creativity as masculine subjects are conventionally allowed to do, thus ensuring through their social roles a certain psychic gratification of archaic feelings through sanctioned sublimations. But in the public arena in which that desire to be active was played out by women as lecturers and professionals in the early twentieth century, such activity and creativity became a source of

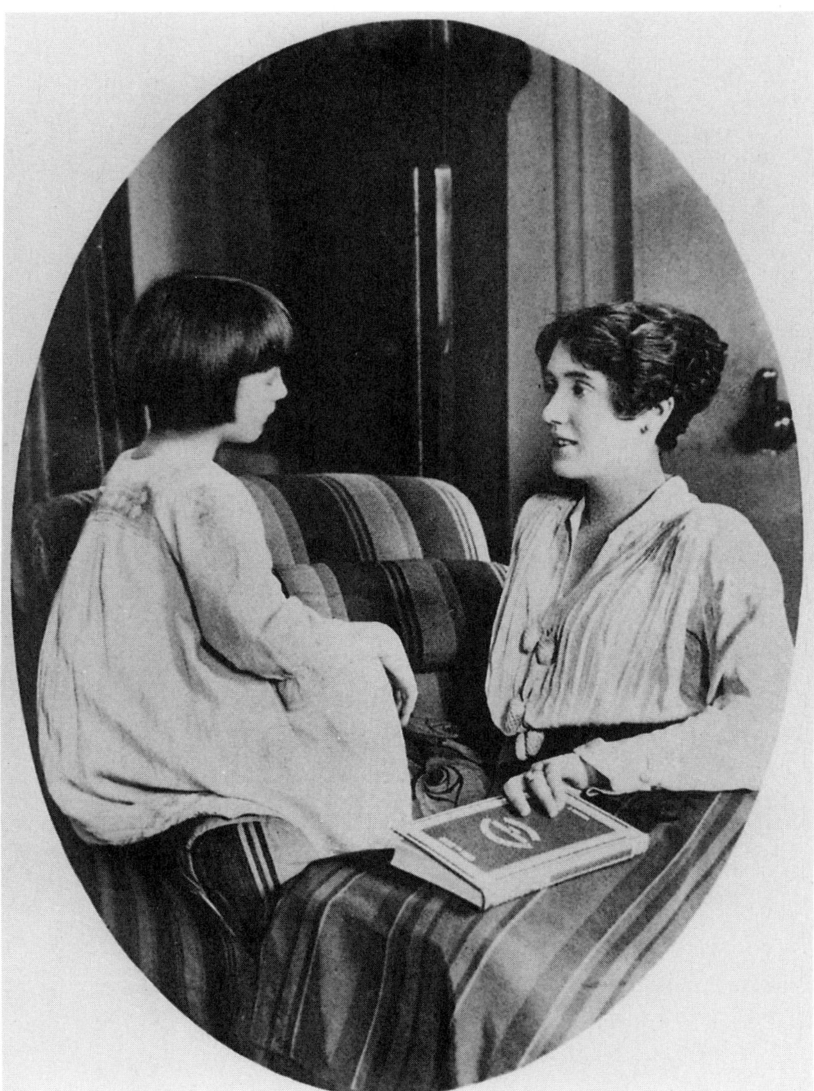

Figure 3.   Anon. *Joan Riviere and her daughter Diana,* c 1913. Archives of the British Psychoanalytical Society, London.

acute anxiety through fear of retribution from the *father*—whose surrogates filled their audiences and the public arena of professional life—for having appropriated *his phallus*—the symbolic key to giving, to "activity" within a patriarchal society. Riviere's explanation, however, in the end reasserted Freudian assumptions that activity is by definition only phallic, and those who act in this way are identifying with or rivalrous with the Father alone. Riviere's text ends up denying her own and Klein's insights both into the powerful role of and rivalry with a maternal imago, into the desire of the woman to appropriate the contents of the mother's body and, therefore, to *give* a symbolic child to the mother in the form of the daughter's intellectual achievement, in distinction from the socially normative idea that woman only desires passively to *receive* a child from the father, that is, to become, via the paternal phallus, a repetition of the mother.

Re-reading Riviere's text in the 1990s, from a feminist and a mother-seeking perspective, the partially admitted and then repressed references to the mother as a figure of both archaic and later Oedipal rivalry and desire jump off the page—helping us to resist its collaboration with both Freudian and general modernist tendencies towards matrophobia. Since Riviere can only admit a phallic reading of the neuroses of women intellectuals, she poses femininity as a masquerade for all women. The traditional woman assumes femininity as a masochistic but genuine form of enjoyment of passivity; femininity is donned by the new women as a mask to deflect paternal punishment and cover their own anxiety about being active in the public arena and thus appearing to challenge the father whose exclusive domain professional intellectuality appeared to be. Trapped between masochism and an anxiety-ridden exploration of sadism (the basis of rivalry and ambition), Riviere's "new women" fell ill through having no means to live their difference from their mothers in a manner consonant with a desire to be active, creative, intellectual *in relation to her as well as to the father.* Despite the fact that Riviere falls back under the sway of the father, lapsing into typical Freudian binarism by explaining her patients' intellectual ambition through either a masculinity complex or Freud's theory of female homosexuality, the very act of attempting to theorize the specific contradictions experienced so painfully by women intellectuals in the 1920s opens up the possibility of our taking up this critical issue. It shows us where the social conditions of women's work as intellectuals, that is the character of our universities, their curricula and their personnel profile, and the content of our academic work, intersect with the psychic dimension, revealing the psychological cost and affective impact of trying to work as women in contexts which repeat the founding crime of modern culture: **matricide**. I want to ask: can we in the 1990s, as a result of our current feminist theory, resist the masquerade by theorizing our desire to be women intellectuals beyond the phallic premise that still contained Riviere's ability to imagine a "cure"?

reading *reading le figaro*

In 1878, the American artist Mary Cassatt (1844–1926), age 34, painted a large and imposing picture of her mother, Katherine Kelso Cassatt, aged 62, in a white day dress, her dark hair drawn back in an informal bun, reading the daily Paris newspaper, *Le Figaro,* with the aid of pince-nez firmly set upon the bridge of her nose (fig. 4). It is a very nice painting, and despite its informal, domestic setting, it impresses us as quite a powerful image. Given our histories of Modernism, however, and the privileged—that is to say partial and paternal—terms of modernity which underpin our understanding of it, I am not sure that we can see it at all. Isn't this painting too cozy, too familiar, too mundane, too much part of the private, domestic, feminine sphere to function as a public image of the social consciousness of its time, place and epoch? How can a portrait of anyone's middle-aged mother reading the newspaper after breakfast compete with the canonized icons of European Modernism: Manet's grandiose *Olympia* (1863–65 Paris, Musée d'Orsay), or his *The Bar at the Folies Bergère* (1882, London, Courtauld Institute Galleries), let alone Picasso's *Demoiselles d'Avignon* (1907, New York, Museum of Modern Art), all images that categorically negate the mother and housewife in their staging of modernity as sexuality in the public domain of commodity and entertainment?

One might begin to make the case for Mary Cassatt's painting by stressing its apparent transgression by showing a white *bourgeoise,* or indeed any woman, engaged in intellectual activity. Katherine Kelso Cassatt is reading. Yet a woman reading was paradoxically one of the paradigmatic images of a negative feminine relation to modernity. From Fragonard to Van Gogh, women appear as novel readers in paintings of modern life. Indeed this trope is played through in one of Modernism's most categorical novels, *Madame Bovary* (1857) by Gustave Flaubert. Emma Bovary's relation to the

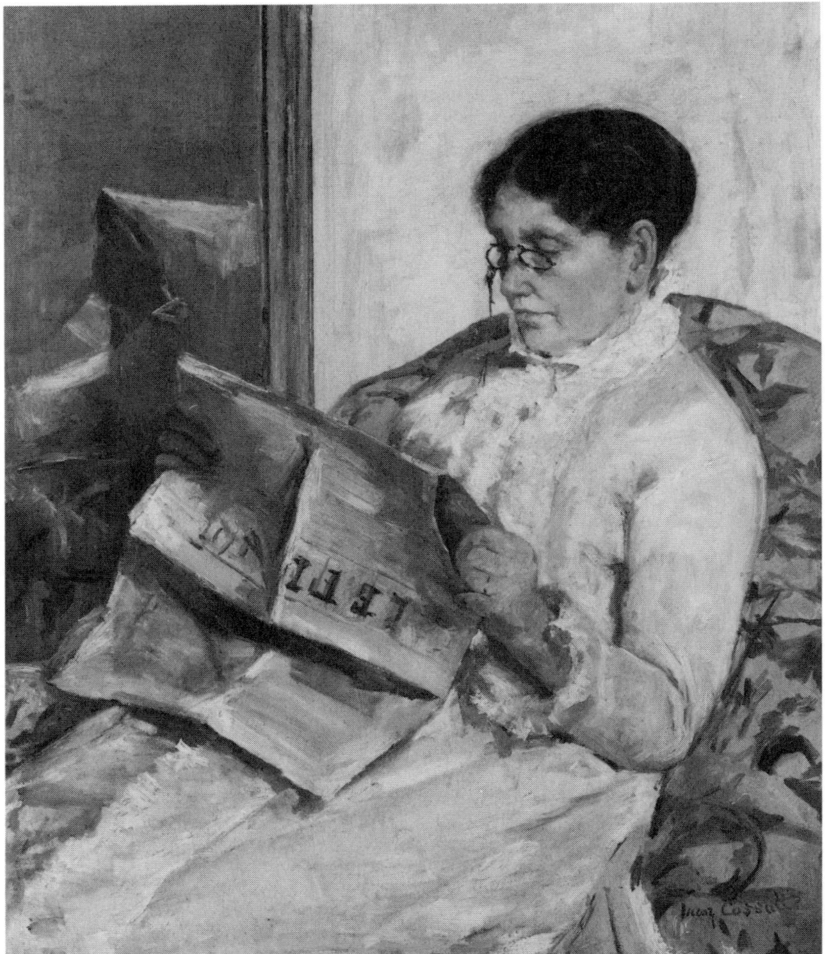

Figure 4.   Mary Cassatt, *Reading Le Figaro*, 1878. Washington, Private Collection.

world and her tragedy, such as it was, was the result of an undereducated petit bourgeois woman's susceptibility to the romantic fiction of her time, much of which was not only addressed to women, but written by women. The most male of authors, Gustave Flaubert, however, defined his Modernism precisely in the cruel distance his crafted prose would fabricate between his authorship and the contaminated world of popular culture synonymous with the women who passively and sentimentally consumed it.

Masculinity claimed as its own, and thus gendered, the intellectual high ground of Modernism through the self- imposed, rigorously antifeminine discipline which marked its difference from an utterly feminine, popular "other" associated as much with the working class, the masses, mass culture as with women.[7] Represented indeed, but as its very negative, "an internal exclusion," the woman reader is, therefore, a complex and contradictory site for Mary Cassatt's intervention into the emergent culture of artistic Modernism. The meanings of her gesture here are made clearer by relating it to a work realized in 1893, namely Mary Cassatt's vast mural on the theme of "Modern Woman" painted for the Woman's Building of the Columbian World Fair held in that year in Chicago.[8]

One of the organizers of the Woman's Building at the Columbia World Fair, Sara Hallowell, stated in a press release: "We women have eaten of the Tree of Knowledge and the Eden of Idleness has become hateful to us. We claim our inheritance and are become workers not cumberers of the earth."[9] In a letter of 11 October 1892, Mary Cassatt described the subject of her mural using similar imagery.

> Mr. Avery sent me an article from one of the New York papers this summer, in which the writer, referring to the order given me, said my subject was to be "The Modern Woman as Glorified by Worth"![10] That would hardly express my idea, of course I have tried to express the modern woman in the fashions of our day and I have tried to represent those fashions as accurately & as much in detail as possible. I took for the subject of the centre & largest composition Young women plucking the fruits of knowledge or science ... The occasion is one of rejoicing ... An American friend asked me in rather a huffy tone the other day "Then this is woman apart from her relations to man?" I told him it was. Men I have no doubt, are painted in all their vigour on the walls of the other buildings; to us the sweetness of childhood, the charm of womanhood, if I have not conveyed some sense of that charm, in a word, if I have not been absolutely feminine, then I have failed ... I will still have place on the side panels for two compositions, one of which I shall begin immediately is young girls pursuing fame. This seems to me very modern ... .The other panel will represent the Arts, Music (nothing of St. Cecilia) Dancing & all treated in the most modern way.[11]

When I first read this letter in 1978, Cassatt's affirmation of *femininity* was deeply disturbing, if not embarrassing to current feminist sensibilities. The term meant everything against which I was in revolt: it signified what Betty Friedan, in 1964 had called in her book of that title "The Feminine Mystique." It has taken many years of careful historical analysis to bridge the gulf between the late nineteenth-century feminism expressed in such unexpected terms by Mary Cassatt in this letter and the present moment of feminism so as to be able to enjoy Mary Cassatt's ease with a femininity that is so historically distant yet still psychically alluring.

Now lost, and only known to us through poor reproductions and extant but incomplete painted studies, Cassatt's mural *Modern Woman* reveals an articulated self-consciousness about the relations between women and modernity. Significantly it framed them through a repudiation of the Christian concept of femininity whose twin poles are a fallen, sexual Eve and the immaculately conceived passive Virgin-mother. Christian notions of Eve place knowledge and sexuality in a dangerous liaison of which Woman, as descendent of the Christian version of Eve, is the permanent *memento mori*. The full weight of this tradition's gynophobia becomes clearer by contrast with Jewish theology and a Jewish feminist understanding of the Eden Story. In the Hebrew Bible there is no Fall and hence no original sin. The human beings are disobedient and their punishment is that now they must do something. They are to be productive: work and procreate. They must live in time. The Hebrew word which is usually translated as naked can also mean wise. The same word is used of both the serpent and the people after they have eaten the fruit of the tree. Thus they did not only discover their sexual bodies, their nakedness, but also, like the serpent, they "fell" into wisdom or knowledge. In wisdom we are deprived of innocence and the irresponsible nakedness of ignorance. Significantly the woman, *isha*, a merely female word form of the Hebrew word for human, is only named, *Havvah*, meaning life-creating, "mother of all living beings," after the acquisition of wisdom, that is, after the humans find themselves newly naked in their knowledge, not so much of evil, as of time and personal responsibility for life and the coming of generations after them. That founding ethical moment of the encounter with the other for whom you are responsible (which few philosophers will acknowledge as fundamentally deriving from specifically feminine, maternal experience) is signified as the realization and naming of woman as mother, that is not in her relation to man, but to the action of making the future through her children. It is at this point that sexual differentiation takes on specific meanings. In Hebrew *Adam* is derived from *Ha'adamah* which means earth/matter, while the name *Havvah/Eve* is taken from the root word for Life. *Havvah* is that which dynamizes the earth, *Adamah* and gives it time, history, regeneration and generations.

There is an unexpected relation between this reading of the ancient Hebrew scriptures and later nineteenth- century feminism. For many feminists found it necessary to contest the patriarchal interpretations of *Gan Eden*, through which later Judaism, Islam and Christianity had laid down a deep ideological bedrock of "blaming woman," in order to reject the equation of female sexuality with evil and to rearticulate the relations between procreative sexuality and wisdom, which is fundamentally between the historical creativity of motherhood—for that is what Eve means—and knowledge/wisdom—for us, perhaps, theory.[12]

Mary Cassatt's mural *Modern Woman*, showing young women joyfully and guiltlessly plucking fruit from the Tree of Knowledge, marks an attempt to to conjoin the project of modernity with one of its major moments: feminism. Recalling it questions the selective memory of Western bourgeois societies by reasserting that women mounted one of the major ideological challenges and sustained political assaults upon them. This is still unfinished business. Cassatt's lost thematization of "modern woman" in terms of rewriting the ancient mythologies of the Garden of Eden exposes to us the continuing patriarchalism of modernity itself. Yet in a postmodern moment, we no longer subscribe to modernity's mythic claims, having lived through two centuries of genocides, enslavement and systematic exploitation and oppression enacted in the name of its enlightened rationality. As Zygmunt Bauman has argued, however, postmodernity refers not to the supersession of modernity, but to the living out of its underlying contradictions.[13] Our revitalization of the feminist project in the late twentieth century is indeed the product of one of modernity's profound contradictions revealed to itself. Knowledge and sexuality have been constructed antagonistically for women in order to sustain a hierarchy of gender whose power relations will only be challenged when the social and psychic ties binding power, knowledge and phallic masculinity are confronted, uprooted and transformed. The job of feminist theory now, as then in Cassatt's moment, is to provide access to the desires and fantasies that might make that revolution possible. It is at this point then that a feminist exploration of representations by women of women, especially of their mothers, becomes a critically useful archive.

educating mother and a poor semiotic legacy

Mary Cassatt painted her mother quite often. In a painting dated 1880, she is also shown reading, but this time a story book, and she is clothed in her grandchildren Robert, Katherine and Elsie. This later portrait of 1880 functions to underline the specificity of the earlier *Reading Le Figaro* (fig. 4). *Katherine Cassatt reading to her Grandchildren* (USA, Private Collection) operates within an iconography of the family, and a semiotics of motherhood specifically cogent in the French context of its production: *la mère éducatrice.* This was the novel and powerful ideology of the post-revolutionary French Catholic bourgeoisie. Moral responsibility for the social and religious discipline of children was ascribed to the mother. "The ideal mother was to be educated, cultured and confident enough to transmit religion, *politesse* and learning to her children."[14] While elevating the domestic sphere and maternal duties to the role of a divinely destined and socially exclusive calling for women, this ideology of educated mothering can scarcely mask what was otherwise the post-revolutionary defeat of women, their exclusion from whatever liberty, equality and fraternity survived the revolutionary Republics in the gynophobic legislation of Napoleon's imperial *Code Civile.*

By reading the signs of the times in late eighteenth-century representation, we could have seen the defeat coming, if only negatively. In the last days of the Ancien Regime, social élites had indeed allowed a space for upper-class women to participate in the exciting currents of learning that would ultimately destroy that old order. Aristocratic women ran salons.[15] Artists' daughters and their petit bourgeois sisters became academicians in the arts—Elizabeth Vigée-Lebrun (1755–1842), Adelaide Labille-Guillard (1749–1803), Angelica Kauffmann (1741–1807), Anne Vallayer Coster (1744–1818) and many, many others. Yet other women took up science and philosophy, for instance, Gabrielle-Emilie le Tonnelier de Bréteuil, Marquise du Châtelet, (fig. 5) the long-time companion of Voltaire who translated Newton's mathematical treatises and Leibnitz into French, winning prizes from the Académie des Sciences, here portrayed by Marie Anne Loir (ca. 1715–post 1769) dressed as an elegant aristocrat holding a pair of compasses, but also, and more prominently, a flower. The context of this publication does not permit the extended illustration which would emphatically make my point. Comparison of portraits of the women intellectuals of the Enlightenment with those of their masculine counterparts, such as those with which this text began, (fig. 1–2) suggest that there was no imagery through which to incorporate the female *philosophes* into the emerging visual iconography of modern Western humanity. [16]

The many stunning images by which women artists of the eighteenth century publicly asserted their presence as women and artists/intellectuals, however, expose a profound conflict of semiotic systems. What presence could modern femininity, itself a negative sign of the Enlightenment discourse on Reason and its natural association with masculinity, have which is not always a display of what Riviere would later define as the masquerade— the overcompensation of an excessively feminine appearance donned to deflect retribution for assuming what is being defined as a purely masculine prerogative?[17] (fig. 6) Mary Cassatt's intervention in this history of representations with *Reading Le Figaro* (fig. 4) needs to be read against this inherited semiotic inadequacy and the social and cultural conditions which made it impossible for these and later nineteenth-century women to image themselves as intellectuals precisely at the moments the distinct social identity or strata, the intelligentsia, consolidated its eighteenth-century initiation.[18]

reading for the
mother-daughter plot

Biographically, we know very little about Katherine Kelso Cassatt. No one would think to consider Katherine Kelso Cassatt one of the "new women" or even count her among the women modernists. At best she might be praised as the very model of the bourgeois ideal of *la mère éducatrice*, sharing her own privately acquired cultivation in the arts, literature and modern languages with her daughters. In 1877 she arrived in Paris to live with her

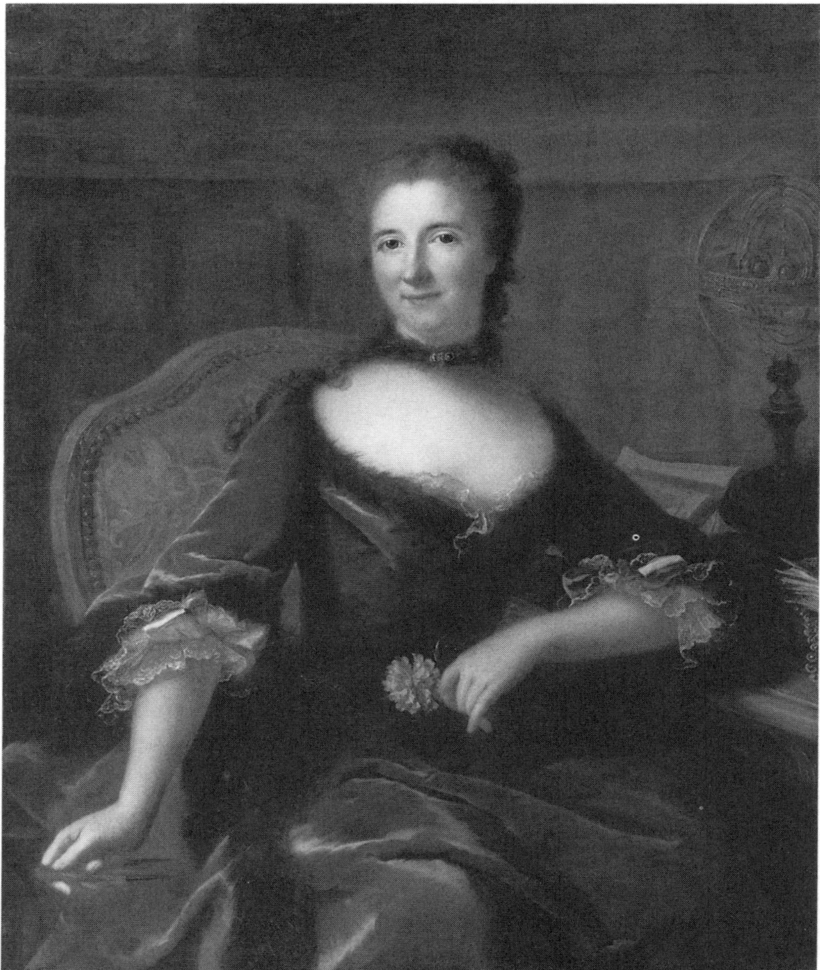

Figure 5.   Marie Loir, *Gabrielle-Emilie le Tonnelier de Bréteuil, Marquise du Châtelet,* 1745–49. Bordeaux: Musée des Beaux Arts.

younger daughter who had trained as a painter in Philadelphia but knew, that because she wanted to be a serious artist, she would have to live in Europe and probably in the city Walter Benjamin would name the "capital of the nineteenth century." There are about forty letters that Katherine wrote to the rest of her family about Mame (Mary) and her activities.[19] But because

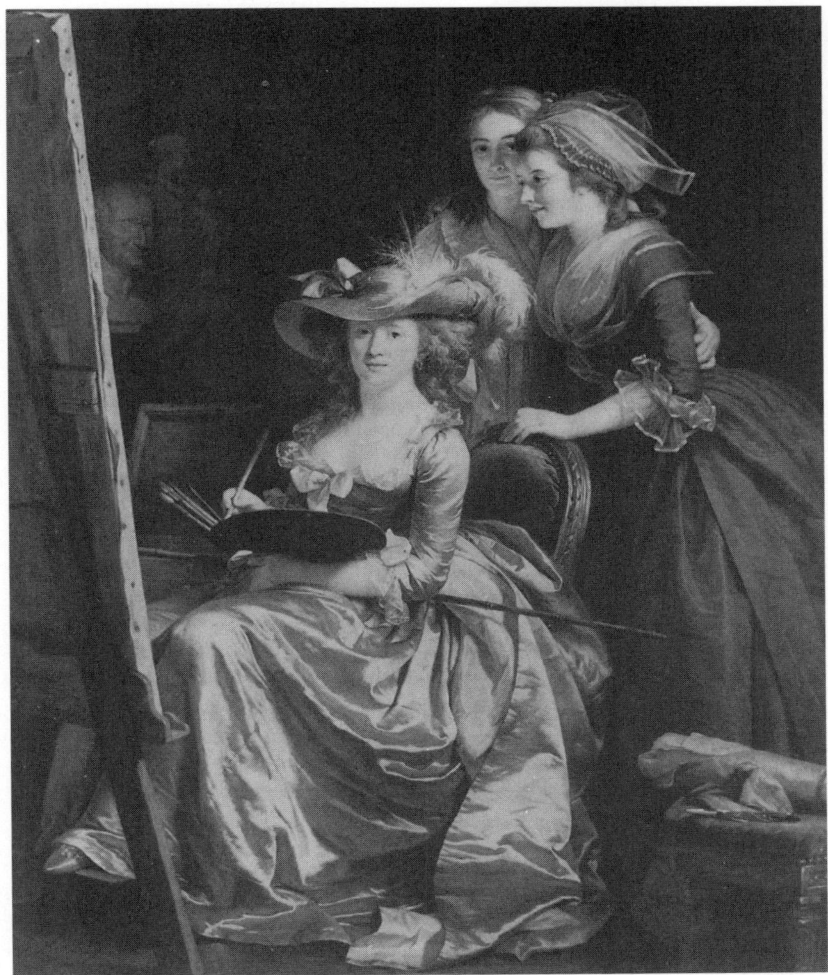

Figure 6.   Adelaide Labille-Guyard, *Self Portrait with Pupils*, 1785. New York: Metropolitan Museum of Art.

they lived together from 1877 until Katherine's death in 1895, there are none between mother and daughter to use as textual support for my hypothesis that Mary loved her mother, respected her, lived her adult creative life beside her, incorporating her within it in numerous ways—directly as in several portraits and obliquely through her recurrent address to the relation of an adult woman to a female child—a consistent displacement of Western culture's privileged imagery of motherhood—the passive Madonna and her son.

Mary Cassatt painted many images of the mother-daughter relationship, tracing the psychic space the maternal body outlines, inhabits and creates as the matrix of the infant and, as importantly, the later, adult subject. Never natural, always social, the relations of mothering and childhood are represented by Mary Cassatt as a semiotic system, the site of a social but also mutually constructing psychic exchange. Cassatt's fascination with the semiosis of mother/child interaction has so often been misread because there is no public discourse on the daughter's relation to the mother comparable with the pervasiveness of the father/son rivalry, or the son's fascination with the abjected or idealized mother which has colonized our Western social imaginary under the law of the patronym and filled our art galleries with a one-sided story.[20]

Desire, one of whose modes of existence and fields of representation is cultural creativity, is forged through the subject's recognition of its separation from the mother, from the irredeemable but haunting loss occasioned by the access to language, by our being precipitated across the cultural reef into a symbolic system—language—which is a defining character of human sociality. But while feminine desire, like its masculine counterpart, is precipitated by the *symbolic castration* of language, the enforced separation from an archaic world of flows, drives and things, feminine desire is articulated in a different relation to the lost body of the mother as both imago and object from that which our dominant culture of heterosexual sons has normalized. Women's desire—and its signification through a possible Matrixial reorientation of the Symbolic—has yet to be recognized in representations by women painters of a certain critical moment in the conjunctural histories of feminism and Modernism.[21] Perhaps the particularity of the formal language and semiotic content of Mary Cassatt's painting may be a point of departure for such a project.

Mary Cassatt's painting is of a mother, her mother. That specific relation to the maternal imago is signified precisely by absenting the child—the man child—which in patriarchal law is woman's only stake in the Symbolic, her only value in the uterine economy. Cassatt's painting depicts a woman alone but busy, reading, her mind actively working on the materials of her culture.

Relating a maternal figure not to a child but to a text prevents the maternal body from functioning stereotypically as container, the mere passageway between nature and culture, between being and language.[22] The woman-child is signified in the painting, however, as the gaze which caused this image to come into being and it is that look that the painting finally signifies. Thus the artist/woman creates upon the canvas a mirror/screen in which to read herself shaped in the measure of her desire as a daughter for a mother, as a woman in relation to a maternal imago of creativity and also to a feminine model of the intellectual. The mother is present but separate, over there, even though she is painted from so close at hand that her whole body cannot contained by the frame. Through this dialectic of suggested physical proximity and formally signified psychological distance, the painting can be read as both an image of profound attachment and a negotiation of deep loss. It thus enacts a process of complex recognition of the lineaments of a historically and socially specific femininity.[23]

But what of Cassatt's images in general as an orchestration of bodies and gazes—the very plane of visual re-presentation of the constituting moments of the subject? This painting stages what I have elsewhere been tempted to define as a specifically bourgeois feminine form of relational space within the dialectic of modernity and the city.[24] In later analyses of her paintings, I have argued that in many of the paintings we name "Cassatt," female figures, held tight to the frontal plane of the imaged space, look sharply away, their vision cutting through compressed and shallow plastic space, evoking another zone, offscreen. Women are shown to look for something beyond the field of vision revealed to the spectator so that their looks and their world of social being appear to resist being tamed within the frame of dominant culture and its signs. Or, as here, a woman is shown occupied with her own interests which reach via newspaper or a conversation with unseen others into the social sphere of her historical and social moment. The significance of the refusal to be framed through either of these strategies cannot be sufficiently emphasized. The viewer, occupying the place from which the painting was produced, has access to the privileged, analytical look of the producer while also feeling a latecomer, present but never able to appropriate a scene that, as a figurative image of a woman looking and thinking, and as a metonym of a feminine producer, is so clearly not replayed for the gaze of mastery. This positions the viewer relatively, allow-ing access to, but never domination of, the subject of representation as a subject of vision and hence both the site and object of desire.

Mary Cassatt's repeated representations of women and children together are often read as proof of the limited vocabulary of Western bourgeois women's art. For some, her interest in mother and child images reads as regression to an inevitable femininity, defined as forever trapped in a pre-Oedipal attachment to the mother. These are two sides of the same fantasy of unity which conflate woman with a primordial archaic femininity, the unitary abstraction, Woman, the genetrix whose underside is death, the loss of being. Attention to the precise structures of Mary Cassatt's images reveals a play of gazes which inscribes the force of the Symbolic—the law of separa-tion—and thus decisively puts the subject matter outside of regression and into the field of representation shaped by an adult woman's feminine psychic formation in the Symbolic by Oedipal, and *Jocastal*, desire. In many of her images of adult woman and female child, the maternal as *chora* (the refer-ence here is again to the work of Julia Kristeva who imagines the archaic mother as both a vessel and an envelope of sound and touch) is implied by the way in which the gaze of the mother is represented as almost tactile. In *Marie Looking up at her Mother* (1897, fig. 7), looking becomes a form of gesture, physically enveloping the small child in a visual embrace associa-tively represented through the materiality of the pastel used to form the sweeps of bodies and costumes in which the tiny child is lodged. Yet against this almost "choric" image of the mother as a containing space for the infant, there is, nonetheless, a constitutive sense of imminent separation, or rather of the "severality" of discrete persons coexisting within one space. The exchange of glances both intimates partition and proffers vision as the bridge on which to construct a compensatory relationship. How often is the young child represented in Mary Cassatt's *oeuvre*, like the old woman, in the pose of thought, an emblem of a young sphinx questioning the curious paradox of our human mode of being built on the juncture of singularity and relativity, an I and a non-I—who are separate yet neither to be assim-ilated nor negated?[25] The precise fact of a same-sex couple of infant and adult disrupts the binary opposition which sustains the phallacy of a patri-archy around its opposition human (man) and Woman ([m]other).

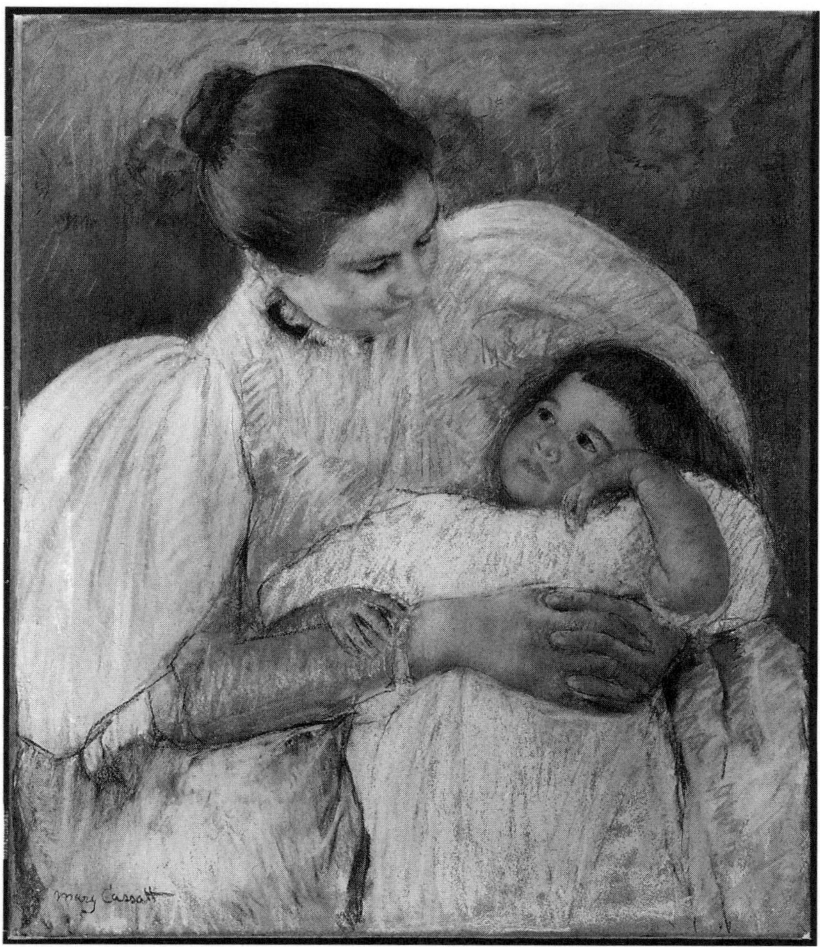

Figure 7.   Mary Cassatt, *Marie Looking up at her Mother/Nurse*, 1896–97. New York: Metropolitan Museum of Art; Gift of Mrs. Ralph J. Hines, 1960.

I suggest that the point of identification in such images by Mary Cassatt is not, however, the mother (the adult woman in her social destiny which Mary Cassatt, the historical artist born 1844 and died 1926, decided not to become) but the female child—the daughter. The paintings are the figuration, there- fore, of a daughter's relation to the mother and of a femininity based on this common, but also historically mediated and varying relationship. This fem- ininity—sociologically distinct, but not necessarily dissimilar at its deepest psychic levels, from that in which my generation was formed—is explored in the work of Mary Cassatt **against the grain of, yet it is also conditioned by** the terms of a modern Western bourgeois conflation of woman and motherhood. I would suggest, on the basis of my reading of some of Mary Cassatt's images, that this apparently unpropitious ideology of feminine domesticity and motherhood lodged in the separate sphere of the private home, could, however, function paradoxically as the support for a mother- acknowledging feminism which would challenge that very ideology. That is why its archaeology is vital to reorient the feminist project of today.[26]

From her research into the diaries and letters of a range of nineteenth-century middle-class American women like Katherine and Mary Cassatt, Carroll Smith- Rosenberg has identified what she calls "a female world of love and ritual."[27] This "world" was sociologically and psychologically based on the contradiction between a society of extreme gender polarization and the intimate female-to-female relations of mother and daughter it fostered. These often lifelong intimacies formed a striking contrast to the antagonisms and rivalry which are the expectations of contemporary mother/daughter dyads. The extremity of gender-role differentiation in the nineteenth-century bourgeois household and the enclosure of women in the domestic sphere created both the need for, and the possibility of, profound emotional bonds between women, founded in the intimacy of the daughter's often long-lived experience with her mother and her world of women relatives, friends and domestic employees. Indeed social historians Taylor and Lasch have argued that so extreme were the differences between men and women in the emergent American bourgeoisie that although men and women married and bred, emotionally and affectively, they inhabited radically different worlds.[28] Smith-Rosenberg's material furthermore underlines that the relations between women, many of whom were married, remained passionate, physical, long-lasting, loyal and jealous. Without denying the reality of lesbian desire and relations or assimilating all female interconnections to active homosexuality, this material reveals a specific configuration of women's identities and emotional ties which demands acknowledgement at the theoretical level as what Julia Kristeva called the "homosexual-maternal facet."[29]

This research might appear to reverse the normal terms of feminist history's reading of the bourgeois society as an unrelievedly negative space for bourgeois women, physically confined and intellectually impoverished. Both appraisals are accurate. Focusing, however, on the realm of affects and the forms of emotional life, I would suggest this: At the social and political level, nineteenth-century bourgeois and working-class feminism may have been a revolt against the dehumanization of women by a bourgeois patriarchy which denied its daughters, sisters, mothers and wives its own class privileges, namely social and intellectual rights, and refused women of all classes economic and sexual independence. At the psychological level, however, the women's movement, which was based upon the identification with and solidarity between women, could only have come into existence through the complex and powerful relations these women had with their mothers and a network of emotionally invested female others. Kaja Silverman, writing of our present feminism, argues that feminism is impossible "without activating this homosexual-maternal fantasmatic."[30]

Ironically, it is through feminist engagement with psychoanalysis, the discourse of psychological Modernism, that this historic and different configuration of the mother-daughter relation and its social effects can be rediscovered as a psychic condition displaced from view by social constructions of femininity characteristic of the liberal post-war settlement. Kaja Silverman, for instance, has returned to Freud's overlooked hypothesis that the Oedipus complex has both a *positive* pole and a *negative* pole. The *positive* refers to the socially normative outcome of gender and sexual orientation. The *negative* refers to the fact that the child not only identifies with, but Oedipally desires, its parent of the same sex. The ideological image of the mother and daughter as two facets of one entity, Woman, denies women this *negative* Oedipal **desire for the mother**, by implying that femininity is exclusively an issue of **identification with the mother** and that desire is forged only via the phallus leading to the displacement of the wish for a penis onto the desire to carry the father's child. The acknowledgement of the *negative* Oedipus complex allows us a way to imagine how what analyst and artist Bracha Lichtenberg Ettinger has theorized as a Matrixial space of difference (an I and a non-I) can be retrieved from the subject's earliest pre-history and raised to play a part in the Symbolic—the terrain of culturally validated meaning and subject—validating representation. The mother then is constructed **not** as a utopian space of infinite regress, perpetually condemned to the silence of the archaic chora or her pre-Oedipal role as lost object.[31] The Mother functions as an Other in the Symbolic, an Other whose desire the female child longs to fulfill, that is, to *give* her mother what she wants, to bear for her and to her a child, or, and this is my point about women intellectuals and the maternal, a symbolic, i.e., creative or intellectual, surrogate through professional or other activity.

Kaja Silverman's work on the *negative* Oedipus complex has suggested ways women can challenge the existing cultural and psychic economies from inside. Refusing to be positioned as the monstrous and baffling Sphinx, confined always outside the city gates with no one to assume that the answer to her riddle of humanity might be her own sex.[32] We can then "speak about a desire which challenges dominance from within representation and meaning, rather than from the place of a mutely resistant biology or sexual 'essence.' From thence we can develop strategies for activating that fantasmagoric scene which corresponds to maternal desire, one which the symbolic does its best to cordon off and render inactive by denying it representational support."[33]

The **missing women** of my title are thus the symbolically missing mothers: the maternal genealogy as a organizing image for feminist social relations and cultural production.[34] This is not a compensatory idealization. Each of us has individually to acknowledge the loss of our mother, and accept the fate of all humanity to speak at the price of sacrifice of her corporality to language and the Symbolic of our particular culture. But unless we find ways to acknowledge the continuing function of the maternal in the Symbolic as both generating body (life) and as intellect (knowledge)—that is the very combination read from the Hebrew Bible's *Havvah* and paradoxically acknowledged in *la mère éducatrice*—we will all be unable to tolerate difference, and thus the heterogeneity not only of sexual bimorphism but, by extension cultural, ethnic, sexual and social diversity.[35]

the mortal mother: life or death?

Phallic masculine culture projects onto Woman-as-image its own fear of human singularity, which is nothing more than the dread of being cast adrift

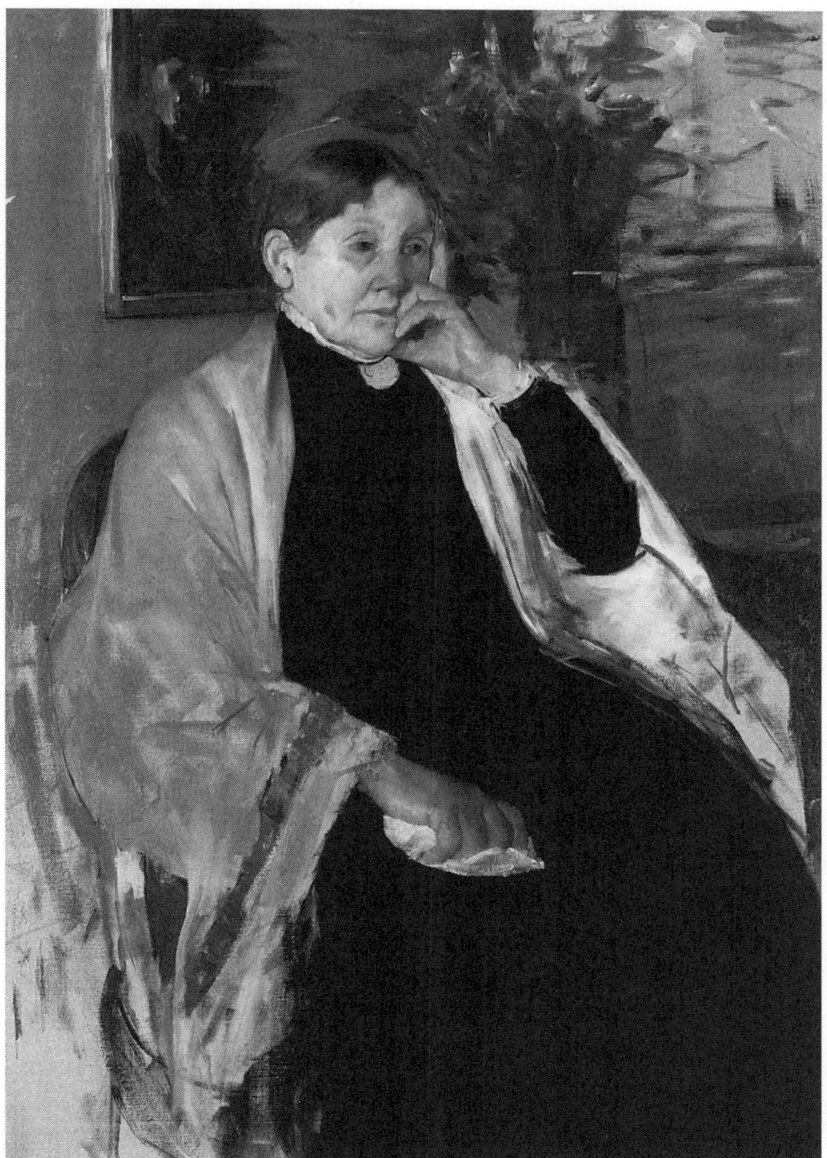

Figure 8.   Mary Cassatt, *Katherine Kelso Cassatt*, 1889. San Francisco: Fine Arts Museums of San Francisco; Museum Purchase, William H. Noble Bequest Fund, 1979.35.

from the founding mother. Masculinity denies its own endemic lack vis-à-vis the culture of both maternal and paternal authorities to which it must accede. What is most grotesque is that masculine culture then projects "Woman," who as mother was one and two at once, as nothing at all, as void, lack, death-bringer, castrator, the negation of being, only imaginable in an idealized abstraction as Beauty or as abjection—the silenced and forever lost (read banished) Mother of death, the end of being.

In 1889, Mary Cassatt again painted her mother, a drained and exhausted image of someone who had only survived near fatal illness in the 1880s (fig. 8). This painting is once again monumental yet utterly tender, the stark expanse of the black dress broken by her cameo broach, setting off one aging hand clutching her handkerchief, while the changed features of her stricken face are still patiently examined, its lineaments lovingly retraced. She sits in the posture of the thinker that is iconographically linked to melancholia and through that to death.

This is, perhaps, much more obviously a maternal image because the body conjoins these competing moments of life and death. Robert Graves traced the ancient forms of the white and black goddess, woman as the limit, the borderline between, and yet the carrier of, opposing forces of life and death.[36] *Reading Le Figaro* (1878, fig. 4) is all the more compelling and difficult an image precisely because it has avoided such cultural freight. It resists the citations, references, deference to the grand tradition of the seated portrait of the socially esteemed and elderly from Raphael's inaugurating *Julius II* through to the seventeenth-century matrons in Frans Hals's disturbing images of the patrician guardians of the poorhouse in which he spent his indigent old age and onto a group of paintings by various hands known as "Rembrandt's Mother" where an elderly woman is often shown both aged and reading. In these paintings, the text the "mother" reads is neither novel nor newspaper—anachronisms of course—but the Bible and thus the woman is assimilated iconographically to the prophetess Hannah, who is famous for the son she belatedly bore and gave up to the Temple, Samuel. In some cultures women who survive to pass through the menopause are allowed to fight or study. When their wombs are no longer in active social service, they revert to being honorary men so long as their studies remain within the patriarchal universe. If old women read, think or theorize beyond that text, they are prob-

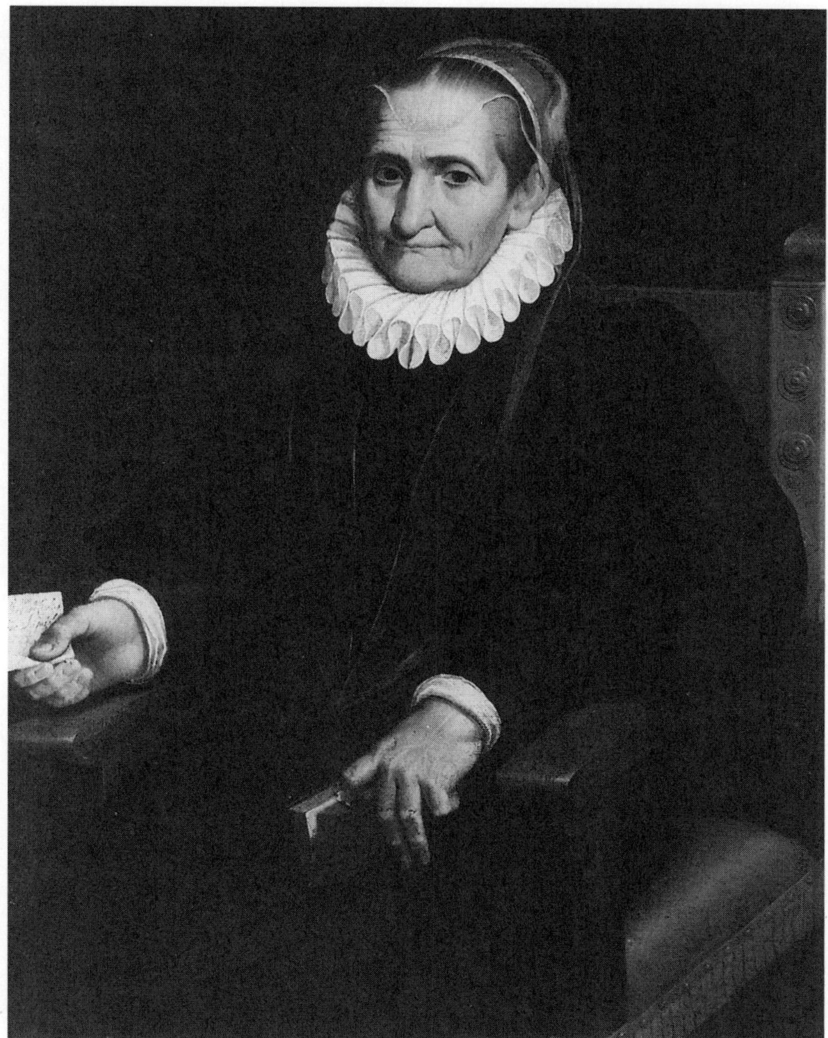

Figure 9. Sofonisba Anguissola, *Self Portrait,* ca 1610. Bern: Gottfried Keller Collection.

ably burned as witches or deemed mad. If, however, we use recent feminist research to follow the matriline and not the patriline of Western art's histories, we find a more relevant precedent—a self-portrait by an Italian painter of the sixteenth century, Sofonisba Anguissola, (1532–1625, fig. 9) who painted

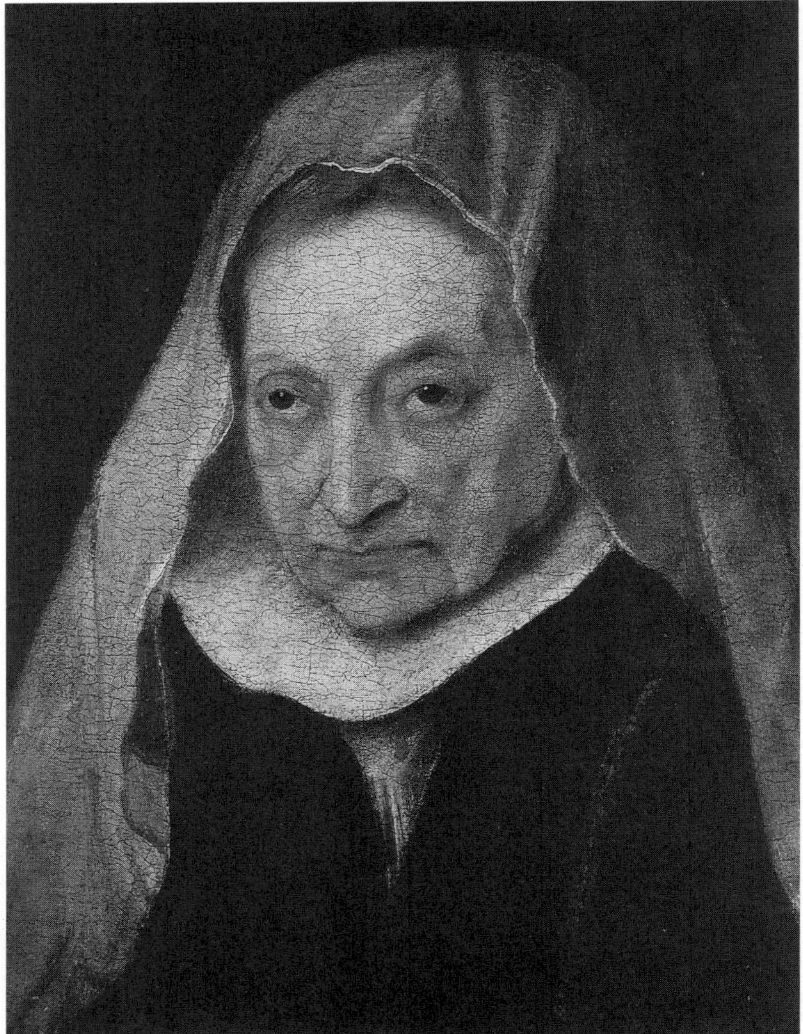

Figure 10. Anthony van Dyck, *Portrait of Sofonisba Anguissola*, 1624. Private collection.

herself throughout her life but also seemed to contemplate her aging self with pleasure and peace of mind.[37] Here she portrays herself in 1610, aged 78, her eye still sharp and her grip still firm. It was painted for Philip III of Spain who paid his father's court painter a stipend and this painting, like other notarized documents of this period, was undertaken to prove that she was still alive and thus still eligible to receive her royal pension. Contrast this to another painted homage to her, Van Dyck's portrait dated fourteen years later, 12 July 1624, when Anguissola was 92, still with a good memory and quick-spirited and kind, so Van Dyck, the artist, wrote in his notebook. Subtle are the details through which he inscribes his masculine anxiety as he contemplates her aged face. Note the position from which he paints so that she has to look up at him from under heavy lids while the slackened flesh of the lower lid reveals the troubling moistness of old age. His evident respect for a charming *grande dame* with great stories to tell of life at the court of Philip II of Spain is not translated into this slack-skinned brooding *memento mori*. Here is only the dark goddess—woman as death, not *Havvah* (fig. 10).

modernity and the
displacement of the mother

Reading Le Figaro (fig. 4) displaces such heavy iconographic freight partly with its self-conscious modernity of facture and color. Yet compare this modernist image of a parent reading the newspaper with another which delineates the difference of tradition-breaking and desire between sons and daughters. In 1866 Paul Cézanne painted the Aixois glove-maker and banker Louis-Auguste Cézanne in an armchair in his large chateau, Jas de Bouffan (Washington, National Gallery of Art). He is shown informally, with cap, smoking jacket and slippers, reading not his usual Republican paper, but a Paris newspaper. *L'Evenement* was where Paul's childhood mate, Emile Zola, was publishing bold defenses of Manet and the other artists Cézanne aspired to join as part of a radical new tendency in the Paris art world. While the painting is *of* his parent, the image is addressed, aggressively, *to* his father. The mixture of formal composition and informal posture allows Cézanne to inscribe his identity as an artist into this paternal space to which he will literally and figuratively accede. (He inherited the estate Jas de Bouffan and the fortune that sustained it on his father's death in 1886). This personal, biographical rivalry corresponds, however, with the cultural game, avant-gardism, which is all about displacing the fathers of culture and one's immediate older brothers.[38] Cézanne's heavily painted still life hangs above

Louis-Auguste's face while a similar manner of painting with bold use of the palette knife is used to refashion Louis-Auguste in terms of Cézanne's own fabricated persona—rough, workmanlike, dissident, self-exiling from his father's bourgeois place. The painting stages several complex maneuvers in the relations between son and father—recognizable and culturally normative. The signal difference is that while Mary Cassatt stages a similar kind of maneuvering about identity—personal, artistic, professional and social—in relation to a manner of painting her mother, it is not culturally normative because her painting is not about killing or displacing that parent. Rather she signifies the continuity between her presence and her mother's singular, adult and self-regarding intellectual identity by fashioning an image in which two subjects can be imagined co-existing, co-affecting, although only one appears to be pictured.

At the start, I suggested that *Reading Le Figaro* could hardly be a painting of modernity. Neither the image of a middle-aged woman nor that of a mother of adults has any place in the modernist imaginary. Indeed I would state it more bluntly now and suggest that Modernism defines its modernity precisely not only by the abolition of the mother but through the expropriation of her creativity. The figure which Modernism made its own sign—and indeed the body upon which generations of avant-gardists claimed their modernity was that of the prostitute—the public woman, the antithesis of the confined, domesticated reproductive femininity of *la mère éducatrice*. In her careful reading of images of the feminine in the writings of Walter Benjamin, Sigrid Weigel argues that the idealization of the prostitute and the lesbian in the discourses of the male modernists signifies the destruction of the mother, the procreator, and conversely, the appropriation of creativity to found a new myth of artistic origin: the autogenetic masculine artist.[39] In place of the Oedipal fantasy and desire for identification with the mother which for three centuries at least had obsessively produced the image of the Madonna and her son as a key icon of and for the Western artist, Modernism dethroned the Madonna, eventually making woman-mother redundant as even the residual, massacred body was abandoned for the virginal blankness of the canvas upon which the mastery of chaos would be gesturally inscribed.[40]

The work of a minor modernist and contemporary of Mary Cassatt, Comte Henri de Toulouse-Lautrec (1864–1901), perfectly narrates this peculiar trajectory. Toulouse-Lautrec painted several portraits of his aristocratic mother. These are decorous and still, producing a classed body held to the surface of the painting through the meticulous decorum with which she is represented, eyes downcast, a muted gaze folding back onto the encased corsetted and fully-clothed body seated in passive, deathly repose. In one case she is reading a small book—perhaps a prayer book; in another, she too appears in brilliant white set against a garden, which is enclosed and enclosing. In every way, however, the aristocratic feminine body, still, iconic and artificial, respected and distant, is the very antithesis of the mobile, exposed, rude bodies of prostitutes and public performers through which her son Henri would establish his artistic paternity and make the once-glorious name of Toulouse-Lautrec transcend the archaic anachronism of the French aristocracy to live on in the annals of Modern art.[41]

In locating the mother in the spaces of bourgeois femininity, Henri de Toulouse-Lautrec produces the necessary antithesis to the defining territories of his avant-garde Modernism: the café, the brothel and the prostitutional body created by the mutual inscription of masculine sexuality and money. A photograph of the ailing Toulouse-Lautrec and his elderly mother in her garden in 1901 shocks precisely because it is so incongruent with those images through which the myth of the modern artist as sexual dissident and social exile was fashioned. For Toulouse-Lautrec is the *artiste maudit* abandoned and rejected by society and family, forced in his physical and personal abjection to find a pseudo-home among the prostitutes of the Rue des Moulins. Recent scholarship has made us skeptical about such myths—but they are important, not as historically documented fact, but as integral parts of and signifiers for the myths of modernism—its myth of origin written into cultural history in a patrilineal genealogy of canonized images in which the masculine artist fashions his modernist identity in contest with a woman's body that is decisively not—or is it?—the body of the mother: from *Olympia* to *Demoiselles d'Avignon* and onto Willem de Kooning's more generic monsters of the 1950s called *Woman*. (fig. 11)

In her essay on "A New Type of Intellectual: The Dissident" Julia Kristeva cites de Kooning's *Women* paintings in the context of discussing the significance of sexual difference in modernity and its legacies.[42] Kristeva heretically places maternity at the center of this debate while identifying its

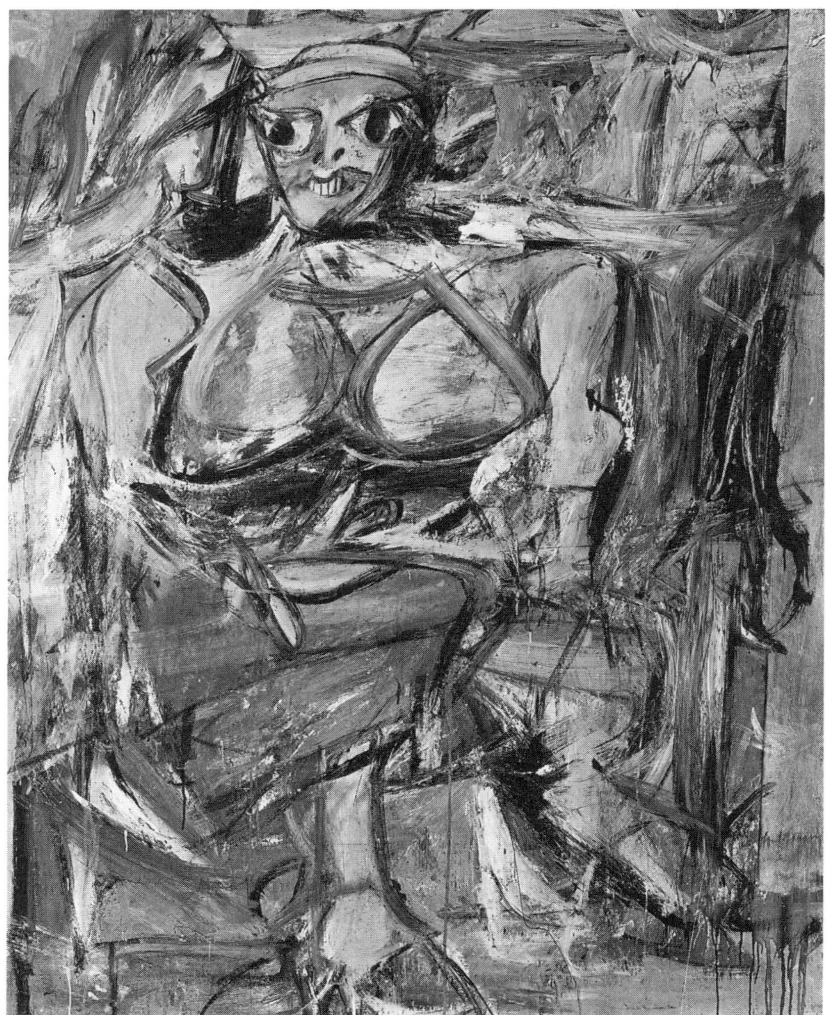

Figure 11.   Willem de Kooning, *Woman I*, 1950–2. New York: Museum of Modern Art.

evasion or apparent erasure in modernist discourse. She cites Mallarmé's poignant question: "What *is* there to say about childbirth?" along with Freud's late admission of perplexity in his more famous question "What does woman want?" and asserts the critical centrality of both questions.

> If pregnancy is the threshold between nature and culture, maternity is the bridge between singularity and ethics. Through the events of her life, a woman thus finds herself at the pivot of sociality—she is at once the guarantee and the threat to its stability."[43]

Julia Kristeva argues that while female creation cannot be taken for granted, it is only represented in a displaced form: "It can be said that artistic creation feeds on identification or rivalry, with what is presumed to be the mother's *jouissance* (which has nothing agreeable about it)."[44] Here she is summarizing what she had argued in her 1975 study of the relations staged in images of the Virgin and Child by two men of the Renaissance, Bellini and da Vinci, between masculine creativity and the maternal body as "the luminous spatialisation, the ultimate language of *jouissance* at the far limits of repression, where bodies, identities and signs are begotten."[45] The mother's presence in Western culture is thus a half-absent one obsessively retraced on the canvas of culture by her sons alone—that is, until now. Then Julia Kristeva refers to de Kooning's *Woman* series thus: "That is why one of the most accurate representations of creation, that is, of artistic practice, is a series of paintings by De Kooning entitled *Woman*: savage, explosive, funny and inaccessible creatures in spite of the fact that they have been massacred by the artist."[46]

Here Kristeva is implying what Luce Irigaray would put more bluntly, that paternal culture is premised not as Freud suggested in *Totem and Taboo* on the murder of a primordial father, but on **matricide**—where the sadistic rivalry Melanie Klein discerned in earliest mother-infant interaction becomes through cultural forms a deadly cultural norm.[47] Irigaray displaces the screen of the Oedipus story as the key masculine myth of the subject's origin to expose the more terrible legend of Clytemnestra. Clytemnestra is the mother of Iphigenia, sacrificed by Agamemnon so that he can go to war to retrieve Helen. Clytemnestra kills Agamemnon and is in turn murdered by her own son Orestes in alliance with her other daughter Electra. The patriarchal version of the legend is highlighted in the fact that matricidal son Orestes is exonerated by Zeus while no sympathy is accorded to Clytemnestra for the father's murder of her daughter.[48]

> The murder of the mother results, then, in the non-punishment of the son, the burial of the madness of women—and the burial of women in madness—

and the advent of the image of the virgin goddess, born of the father and obedient to his law in forsaking the mother.[49]

This Graeco-Christian legacy is, I suggest, passionately revived in the secular culture of Modernism which, in its hegemonic form in the twentieth century, allowed women access to liberal society only in the guise of Athena, "one of the boys." But then, Julia Kristeva poses an impossible question about de Kooning's images of the monstrous, mad, massacred modern *Woman*. What if they had been created by a woman?: "Obviously she would have to deal with her own mother, and therefore with herself, which is a lot less funny."[50] No Cixousian laughter of the Medusa breaks out here.[51] Herein lies the complexity and paradox of woman's relation to herself within modern intellectual culture—premised as it is on the murdered mother, her expropriation, her own decapitation[52] by the establishment of binaries in which the feminine is a complex of negated, mastered, devalued terms. The antithesis of the social, the historical, the intellectual, the cultural—to be part of any of them requires that woman too murder her mother and identify, like Athena, with the Father, or with the boy-child of that other Virgin Goddess, the Madonna, valued only for her son.

Julia Kristeva challenges this economy by arguing outrageously that maternity and creativity are not incompatible—as our culture has for so long attempted to assert (on condition that economic constraints are not too heavy, for the poorest of the poor in most societies are working-class mothers and their children). Maternity is posited as a system of Imaginary and Symbolic psychic relations and images and not just a social experience in the gendered division of labor. Maternity is categorically disruptive of the formative oppositions in patriarchal culture—indeed of the possibility of any opposition—because it can be reread paradigmatically, as Bracha Lichtenberg Ettinger has argued, by stressing the severality of the prebirth moment as the site of duality, dialogue and process—an irreducible moment of a non-antagonistic relation between an I and a non-I, a subject and several others, inside and outside, cyclical time and historical time.

Maternity is, however, not synonymous with women. Its importance emerges from social practice of child-rearing only when it is appropriated by thought: theorized, i.e., when "critical critics" and artists get hold of it. The understanding of maternity is, therefore, as much a necessity for men as it is a project for women. It is an intellectual issue, by virtue of its being a hybrid, a trickster, a sport, a pollutant, in the Symbolic laws of phallic culture.[53] In categorical opposition to the one, the phallus, and to the discrete and agonistic difference the phallus signifies, maternity can hardly be thought unless we produce a new kind of intellectual—a practice of analysis which can find its own formal and logical equivalents to that heterogeneity, that contaminated, impure and disruptive web of bodies and words. It is in this sense that Julia Kristeva can posit "women" i.e., thinking, political creators of our moment, **feminists**, as a new form of intellectual: one of the four types of contemporary dissident she identifies: the rebel, attacking political power; the psychoanalyst, dealing with death and discourse in place of religion; the writer, challenging the law through language; and "*sexual difference, women—which is only specific in terms of its relation to maternity.*"[54]

This does not mean that women who do not bear children are not women, or that only in becoming a mother can female persons be such dissidents. By virtue of being born, we are all in relation to the maternal body, and in potential relation to her desire, to giving her what she wants. Luce Irigaray puts it more complexly:

> It is also necessary for us to discover that we are always mothers once we are women. We bring something other than children into the world, we engender something other than children: love, desire, language, art, the social, the political, the religious, for example. But this creation has been forbidden to us for centuries, and we must reappropriate this maternal dimension that belongs to us as women. If it is not to become traumatising and pathological, the question of whether or not to have children must be asked against the background of another generating, **of a creation of images and symbols.** Women and their children would be infinitely better off as a result.[55]

For these French feminist intellectuals, feminism is the simultaneous invention of an Imaginary and a Symbolic in which to articulate the maternal-feminine by means of which sexual difference can mean something other than death. In a sense they are posing the feminist—modern woman in her intellectual mode—as a mother-acknowledging, mother-recognizing theorist—as the intellectual of postmodernity whose existence depends upon and, it is hoped will bring about, the necessary revolution in the signification of a subjectivity whose possibilities in modernist culture have been foreclosed.[56]

I see Mary Cassatt's *Reading Le Figaro,* a portrait of her mother, in middle age, no longer at the point of procreation and still long before her own mortality has begun its active claims on her aging body, as a extraordinary moment in which a historically created matriline was given a semiotic form, and was signified in a radical cultural language which, in process of emerging, in 1878, seven years before even Freud came to Paris to work with Charcot on hysteria, allowed one daughter of an educated mother to create herself as an artist without killing her mother.

I envy Mary Cassatt her middle-aged mother.[57] She lived and worked in her mother's presence and with her company until she was 51. When I was 14, my mother died.[58] I grew up to bear children in the absence of a mother's esteem. I became involved in the Women's Movement without her opposition or support. I developed feminist theory without her conversation or critique. I progressed to occupy an academic chair that felt half-empty in the absence of her maternal acknowledgment. Neither my infantile rivalry nor my Oedipal desire ever found its resolution in our mutual recognition as adult women. Yet my feminism began as a revolt against my mother, or rather against her experience of post-war white Western femininity. Reclaiming in the later 1960s the legacy of nineteenth-century women's political activism was a direct refusal of what bourgeois femininity had been reduced to by the pyrrhic victories of the "liberal" emancipatory legislation and the post-war project for the re-domestication of women. The feminist theory so many of my generation are now developing, however, twenty years after that renewed revolt by women, has focused increasingly on the figure of the mother, on the need for the maternal metaphor.

But, in one final twist, I must ask, what if I identify for a moment with the seated mother and not her creative daughter. In a major installation, *Interim 1984–1990,* based on the feminists of the generation of 1968, Mary Kelly has explored women's complex relations to power, money, history and the body. Specifically working from the experience of women in their 40s and 50s, she examined the disjunctive relation of women to middle age—the time between: to a body and mind out of synch with culture's limited and limiting repertoire of images of femininity. In Section Two, *Pecunia,* Kelly plots the iconography of femininity in the popular imagination through the greeting cards which signal the culture's definitions of the female life- cycle: wife, mother, unmarried sister, daughter/bride. These are, in fact, kinship positions as ancient as they are still part of the modern and they are defined across the axes of sex and death. They function exclusively in relations, positive or negative, to procreativity via the phallus in a nexus from which creativity, art, science and the intellect are excluded. Kelly's work addressed the question: what happens to women when they are no longer "bright young things," virginal brides, young mothers and before they become old bags? In a critical project that is not utopian, Kelly posed a historically revitalized feminism as the struggle to forge languages and semiotic spaces in which to ask specifically feminine questions about identity and power, to represent our desires and to pose the riddles of existence without having Oedipus imagine that the only answers must be framed exclusively in terms of Man.

Mary Kelly thought of dedicating *Interim* (see Ch. 4) to perhaps one of the most famous and yet unnoticed middle-aged mothers in Modernism, a contemporary of Katherine Kelso Cassatt, the woman known to us only as "Dora's mother". "Dora" was the pseudonym given to Ida Bauer, the patient in one of Freud's most important case studies of hysteria, published in 1905.[59] It is currently argued that the failure of this analysis—Dora abruptly walked out on Freud after three months—resulted in part from Freud's failure to consider not only the patient's mother but his blindness to the active "homosexual-maternal facet" in "Dora's" psychic life. Freud never bothered much with the mother but that did not stop him from conjuring up a picture of her in his text which aligns his writing with the larger culture of modernity I have been outlining:

> I never made the mother's acquaintance. From the accounts given me by the girl and her father I was led to imagine her as an uncultivated woman and above all a foolish one, who concentrated all her interests in her domestic affairs ... She presented the *picture* (my italics), in fact, of what might be called the "housewife's psychosis."[60]

Freud later admitted in marginal footnotes the major oversight of "Dora's" attachment to a mother-surrogate, Frau K., who was the source of her considerable "sexual" knowledge, but he never understood her passionate attachment to, and sense of loss vis-à-vis, her mother expressed in her adoring vigil in front of Raphael's painting, the so-called Dresden Madonna. For all Freud's insights, as this extract chillingly reveals, this text is a monument to the epistemological genocide that resulted in the repression of the mother within classical psychoanalysis and the ignorance of the desire that structures mother-daughter relations in the psychic life of women. It was only in the work of the modernist women who sought and found intellectual creativity in the profession of psychoanalysis, Helene Deutsch, Karen Horney, Anna Freud, Melanie Klein and, of course, Joan Riviere (fig. 3), that psychoanalysis was expanded to incorporate the function of the mother Freud so cruelly negated.[61]

In a typically feminist move, attentive to what is pushed to the margins of patriarchal culture, what falls below the threshold of its male intellectuals' desire, Kelly delivers "Dora's" mother, the middle-aged housewife, from the prison of Modernism's negative imagery to make her the questioning voice.

> In a sense she underlines the dilemma for the older woman of representing her femininity, her sexuality, her desire when she is no longer seen to be desirable. She can neither look forward, as the young girl does, to being a woman, that is having the fantasised body of maturity; nor can she return to the ideal moment of maternity—ideal in that it allows her to occupy the position of actively desiring subject without transgressing the socially acceptable image of the woman as mother. She is looking back at something lost, acknowledging that "being a woman" was only a brief moment of her life.[62]

If woman is only defined in some relation anticipatory or actual to procreativity, can it be that woman in middle-age or as intellectual or professional is "not woman"? Does this question not suggest that while we acknowledge that we live beyond the limits of the mythic term, Woman, we are also in the process of redefining what it signifies so as to make unnecessary the hybrid neologisms: woman artist, woman intellectual—where the second term, by the fact of needing the gender qualifier, does not in itself include women? Following the French analyst Michèle Montrelay, Mary Kelly is suggesting "the adult woman is one who constructs her sexuality in a field that goes beyond sex" (procreation?).[63] This means finding the means of making female sexuality pass into discourse—giving it symbolic representation. Women are confined not by sex, but by men's cultural use of their sex, namely the masculine image of the mother as vehicle and cipher, lost but longed for and hated. Thus it is argued that women's own sexuality—the specificity of their own corporeally founded and psychically organized energizing libido—is suppressed. Only by entering discourse can women experience the necessary sublimation of sexuality into an extended form of creativity. (This is basically Freud's notion of libido as men experience it.) In addition to sexual representations which make us sexually active, libidinal energy is socially harnessed through being attached to a range of representatives—power, money, work, fame, social altruism and so forth, as well as creativity. The crucial advantage men therefore enjoy in a culture fashioned to the measure of their psychic formation is the correlation of their desire to discourse, to speech, to intellectual activity and to these sanctioned rewards. Women cannot merely claim access to these pleasures by joining in existing institutions, cultures and languages, as the liberal politics of modernist equality has wrongfully suggested. Only through the combination of theorization and visualization, suggested here by the work of Mary Kelly, and indeed by Mary Cassatt, through dissident intellectual and artistic creativity, will we forge a system of different representations adequate to support the articulation of women's humanity in its psychic, social and cultural specificities.

an epilogue about chairs and processions

What happened to my own mother, and the generations of "new women" between Cassatt's moment in the late nineteenth century and mine after 1968, from Riviere's neurotic professionals of the 1920s to Friedan's depressed housewives in the 1950s, to the feminist theorists of the post-1968 era, was the erasure of a culture premised upon the possibility of mother-daughter alliance. The feminist movement and the work of women artists at the end of the last century are evidence of that culture, which was, however, already being compromised by men in what have become the hegemonic articulations of Modernism from Marxism to psychoanalysis and modern art. Therefore, Cassatt's image, now that it can be read for both its lost, i.e., historical, moment of production and for the still-pertinent psychic formation in which it was founded, provides a way to have access not only to my own lost mother, but to a historical and cultural "maternal genealogy" as one of the critical representational supports for contemporary feminist theory as it struggles to reframe the cultures and politics of modernity in terms which allow that ancient figure of *Havvah* what Cassatt called an occasion of both acknowledgment and rejoicing.

But, on this occasion, an inaugural lecture when, because of accession to a Chair I am allowed to state the conditions of my occupancy, I must pause, like Virginia Woolf in 1938, on the verge of the war against fascism, to question my assimilation to a position inside a key modernist institution. Virginia Woolf used the images of uniforms and processions to represent the social hierarchies and élites which the undereducated bourgeois sisters of educated white men had struggled to join only to find that their procession was turning into feet marching to war. "There they go, our brothers who have been educated at public schools and universities, mounting those steps, ascending those pulpits, preaching, teaching, administering justice, practising medicine, transacting business, making money. It is a solemn sight always—a procession."[64] But for the last few years, Virginia Woolf notes that, as admirals and professors, judges and civil servants go by, that "there, traipsing along at the tail end of the procession, we go ourselves." At the moment "we" wear white with green and purple, the suffrage colors as our public dress for procession, but who will say if "we" will not don their uniforms, strap on swords and inverted coal scuttles and try to hide the dresses of the private house in the veil of public liveries? Thus the ambitions that drove bourgeois women of the nineteenth century to claim their space within the civil society of the male bourgeoisies must be firmly scrutinized when it looks as if their procession leads not to liberty but to war:

> The questions we have to ask and to answer about that procession of academics during the moment of transition are so important that they may well change the lives of all men and women forever. For we have to ask ourselves, here and now, do we wish to join that procession or don't we? On what terms shall we join that procession .... Let us never cease from thinking what is this civilization in which we find ourselves? What are these ceremonies and why should we take part in them? What are these processions and why should we

make money out of them? Where in short is it leading us, this procession of the sons of educated men?[65]

Virginia Woolf's question is still timely but the world in which she formulated it was clearly élite and upper-class. Yet I I found this passage quoted by a contemporary feminist, the working-class child of an immigrant, part-Jewish family, Adrienne Rich, in a powerful critique of the androcentric university written in 1973–74: "Toward a Woman-Centred University."[66] I believe her essay and its call should be compulsory reading for anyone genuinely concerned with democratizing education. Democracy does not go well with liberalism which says "We are the best, and have what you desire. Come, join us if you can but on our terms, which, surprisingly, you can't ever quite match. Come at least and join the parade, but disguise your cultural, social or sexual specificity in our gowns and at our tables, or at least have the decency to don the necessary masquerade as you sit in our chairs." Democracy means really addressing and meeting the needs of the heterogeneous communities who have the right to an education that does not undermine their integrity and, as importantly, that of their mothers and fathers, that does not "deracinate," declass or degender them, which does not make it hard, as bell hooks so poignantly argues, to go home and still talk to Mum or your sisters.[67]

Do not be mistaken. This is not a call for an easy-going populism or a facile anti-intellectualism. For I am sure few Mums or Dads let alone any of you much enjoy the taxing demands of concentration and theorization inflicted on you by this paper. Like Marx and Engels, some of us want to overcome the division of labor which segregates the intellectual and the manual worker. And beyond what they hoped, we want us all to be able to be critical critics, after the washing up and childcare. To achieve this, we must seriously question how intellectuals will function when we have destroyed the remnants of the Kantian mystique of Pure Reason and the deceit of liberalism which universities sustain by being unable to take on board the full dimension of dissident difference, of difference as a necessary and creative dissidence; by their inability to hear the full meaning of the historical critique now framed by intellectuals who philosophically as well as affectively love and respect their mothers.

notes

1 Luce Irigaray, "And the One Does not Stir without the Other," trans. Hélène Vivienne Wenzel, *Signs*, 7:1, 1981, 60–67.

2 K. Marx and F. Engels, *The German Ideology* [1845–6] ed. C. J. Arthur, (London: Lawrence and Wishart, 1974), 54.

3 L. Appignanesi and J. Forrester, *Freud's Women*, (London: Weidenfeld and Nicholson, 1992).

4 J. Breuer and S. Freud, "Case Histories: Fraulein Anna O.", *Studies in Hysteria* [1893–95], International Psychoanalytical Library No. 59, trans. James and Alix Strachey, (London: Hogarth Press, 1956), 30.

5 This point was made by Carol Gilligan in her paper given at the symposium at the Institute of Contemporary Art in London, 12 December 1992, held to mark the publication of Lisa Appignanesi and John Forrester, *Freud's Women* (London: Weidenfeld and Nicholson, 1992).

6 J. Riviere, "Womanliness as Masquerade," *International Journal of Psychoanalysis* 1929, vol. 10, reprinted in *Formations of Fantasy,* ed. V. Burgin et al, (London and New York: Methuen), 35–44.

7 A. Huyssen, "Mass Culture as Woman: Modernism's Other," in *After the Great Divide:Mass Culture and Postmodernism* (London: MacMillan, 1986), 44–64.

8 J. D. Kysela, "Mary Cassatt's Mystery Mural and the World Fair of 1893," *Art Quarterly* 29:2, 1966: 129–155.

9 M. Howe Elliott, *Art & Handicraft in the Woman's Building of the World's Columbian Exposition Chicago 1893* (Paris and New York: Boussod et Valadon, 1893).

10 Charles Frederick Worth (1825–1895), English couturier working in Paris.

11 N. M. Mathews, ed. *Mary Cassatt and her Circle: Selected Letters* (New York: Abbeville Press, 1984), 237–38.

12 For further discussion of texts such as Elizabeth Cady Stanton's *Woman's Bible* (1894) and current feminist re-readings of Eve, including those by Mieke Bal (1987), see Ilana Pardes (1992).

13 This analysis is argued extensively in Zygmunt Bauman's recent writing, see especially, *Intimations of Postmodernity*, (London: Routledge, 1992) and *Modernity and Ambivalence* (Cambridge: Polity Press, 1991).

14 B. Corrado Pope, "Revolution and Retreat: Upper Class French Women after 1789" in *Women, War and Revolution*, C. R. Berkin and C. Lovett, ed. (New York: Holmes and Meier, 1980), 231.

15 S. G. Tallentyre, *The Women of the Salons and Other French Portraits* (London: Longmans, Green and Co., 1901).

16 In lecture format I could present the striking iconography that emerged with portraits of Diderot (painted by Van Loo in 1767) or Fragonard, Winckelmann (portrayed by Angelica Kauffmann in 1764), Joshua Reynolds (Zoffany: 1772, Kauffmann. 1766–67, Reynolds: 1778/9), Vincent (Labille Guyard: 1780s), Robert (Vigée Lebrun: 1789) and contrast the rhetoric of professional commitment, reason and self-determination with images of women such as Madame du Châtelet (Loir: 1745–49), Madame D'Epinay (Liotard: 1840s), Cornelia Knight (Kauffmann), Madame de Pompadour (Boucher: 1756, Dourais: 1763–64) and countless self-portraits of women of this time: Labille Guyard, Vigée Lebrun, Kauffmann exquisite and significant but clearly different.

17 What difference would an interested feminist re-reading of these images produce? Isn't there a significance in Labille-Guyard's decision to image herself as a creative mother figure surrounded if not by daughters then female pupils, or in Marie Victoire Lemoine's homage to the exiled Elizabeth Vigée Lebrun, showing her self, the elder by one year, as a child drawing at the feet of the renowned artist (exhibited Salon 1796)?

18 The concept of the intellectual is first defined by Zola at the time of the Dreyfus affair, that is concurrent with Mary Cassatt's practice, but its historical roots lie with the *philosophes* and *bas bleus* of the eighteenth century (Bauman, 1987).

19 Mathews, 1984, op. cit.

20 I am indebted to the work of Marianne Hirsch (1989) for both her insights and her extensive research into feminist writing on this suppressed relation in women's literature.

21 The term "matrix" is introduced by the psychoanalyst and artist Bracha Lichtenberg Ettinger to signal the possibility of other strata of subjectivity than those defined by the phallus, the signifier of the one which can only confront another as its other. The matrix imagines a moment of subjectivity that is already plural, several in a contiguous space, such as is metaphorically represented and actually experienced by the mother and child duo in the late term pre-partum period. See her important text on this major feminist rethinking of psychoanalysis, "Matrix and Metramorphosis," in the special edition I edited of *Differences* 4:4 (1993): 176–207 (titled *Trouble in the Archives*).

22 This refers to the theories of the maternal chora and male artists' privileged access to maternal joy proposed by Julia Kristeva in "Motherhood According to Bellini" [1975] in *Desire in Language* ed, L. Roudiez (Oxford: Basil Blackwell, 1980), 269.

23 See my "The Gaze as a Question of Difference" in *Dealing with Degas*, ed. R. Kendall and G. Pollock (London: Pandora, 1992).

24 G. Pollock, "Modernity and the Spaces of Femininity," in *Vision and Difference: Feminism, Femininity and the Histories of Art* (London: Routledge, 1988).

25 The debt here is again to the propositions of Bracha Lichtenberg Ettinger, 1992, op. cit.

26 The femininity in question here is specifically white, bourgeois, though in no simple way heterosexual. I am not generalizing feminism from it so as to make its social specificity hegemonic. Hortense Spillers work on the sociopsychic complexities of the African American family in relation to the respective roles of mother and father indicate a distinct line of enquiry within a common field directed by the historical particularity of each community which is developing feminist theories congruent with historical experience and social situation. (H. Spillers, "Mama's Baby, Papa's Maybe: An American Grammar Book," *Diacritics* 65–81. 1987 17:2).

27 C. Smith-Rosenberg, "The Female World of Love and Ritual 'Relations between Women in Nineteenth Century America'," *Disorderly Conduct: Visions of Gender in Victorian America* (New York and Oxford: Oxford University Press, 1985), 53–76.

28 W. R. Taylor and C. Lasch, "Two 'Kindred Spirits': Sorority and Family in New England 1839–46," *New England Quarterly,* Vol. 36 (1963): 23–41.

29 Kristeva, 1980, op. cit., 239.

30 K. Silverman, *The Acoustic Mirror* (Bloomington: Indiana University Press, 1988), 125.

31 For those unfamiliar with debates in feminist theory and recent redefinitions of psychoanalysis, these statements may make little sense. In classical Freudian theory, the mother is a major figure in the early life of the child but has to be separated from and it is the emergence of the Father as a third term which dissolves the apparent unity of the mother/child dyad and precipitates the child into its Oedipal drama in which the mother is redefined as lacking and lost. Thus within a masculine psychic economy the Mother is both the representative of a lost object to be replaced by later surrogates, but she also represents a lost moment of plenitude before the child itself had to acknowledge his/her lack and, through this, its own vis-à-vis the world whose order and law the Father represents. The role of the castration/Oedipal complex is fundamental to this account. Feminists have wanted to understand the specificity of the feminine pathway through this process of subject/gender formation and have explored the continuing significance of the so-called pre-Oedipal phase and the female child's relationship to and identification with the mother and the fantasy of that primary mother, the so-called maternal body associated with nurturance, life, food, sound, rhythm, early speech and so forth. The main debate in feminist circles at the moment is between those who pursue theories of femininity in a privileged relation to the the archaic and pre-Oedipal mother and those who argue that this condemns femininity to a marginal place in the Symbolic, the rules, values and symbols of the culture. Thus to argue for the Oedipal mother, a figure around whom sexuality and desire is articulated for women, locates the mother in the

Symbolic. It is the absence of acknowledged (as well as to-be-invented) feminine elements of the Symbolic (which on this logic will be associated with and therefore named as maternal) which confounds women's place in culture and denies their linguistic and social life a representational support. The arguments about women's language and its vicissitudes in relation to the psychoanalytical formulation of the subject's entry into language (the symbolic based upon the imaginary [Lacan] or the semiotic [Kristeva]) have been explored in what is called "French" Feminism, associated with the writings of Julia Kristeva, Hélène Cixous, Luce Irigaray, Annie Leclerc and Monique Wittig.

32 M. Hirsch, *The Mother-Daughter Plot: Narrative, Psychoanalysis and Feminism* (Bloomington: Indiana University Press, 1989), 2.

33 Silverman, op. cit., 124.

34 The concept of the maternal genealogy has been forcefully argued by Luce Irigaray, "The Bodily Encounter with the Mother" (1981), D. Macey, Trans., in *The Irigaray Reader,* ed. M. Whitford, (Oxford: Basil Blackwell, 1991), 34–46.

35 To return briefly to political Modernism's struggle against class and race oppression, I am suggesting the relevance of these feminist theories of the Matrix and maternal genealogy for a politics that includes and extends beyond issues of gender. This reverses the reduction of women's struggles to limited and partisan interests of white middle-class women without denying the class/race located and historically specific psychic and social terrain on which emerged the formation which allows this theoretical elaboration through the interplay of feminism, Marxism and psychoanalysis.

36 R.Graves, *The White Goddess* (London: Faber, 1948).

37 The first monograph on this artist, first recorded by Vasari, has been written by Ilya Perlingieri, *Sofonisba Anguissola* (New York: Rizzoli, 1992).

38 See G. Pollock, *Avant-Garde Gambits: Gender and the Colour of Art History* (London: Thames and Hudson, 1993).

39 S. Weigel, "The Construction of the Feminine in Walter Benjamin," unpublished paper given at the Benjamin Conference, London, Birkbeck College, 17–19 July 1992; published as "From Gender Images to Dialectical Images in Benjamin's Writings" in *The Actuality of Walter Benjamin, New Formations,* Summer, 1993, no. 20, 21–31.

40 I am thinking here of Jackson Pollock's work of late 1940s and early 1950s, the so-called drip paintings. See Pollock, "Feminism, Painting and History" in *Destabilising Theory,* ed. M. Barrett and A. Phillips (Cambridge: Polity Press, 1992), 138–176, and Chapter 5 in this volume.

41 G. Pollock, "Fathers of Modern Art & Mothers of Invention," *Differences,* 4:3, (1992), 91–132; revised in G. Pollock, *Differencing the Canon: Feminist Desire and the Writing of Art's Histories,* (London and New York: Routledge, 1999).

42 J. Kristeva, "A New Type of Intellectual: The Dissident" [1977] in *The Kristeva Reader*, ed. T. Moi, (Oxford: Basil Blackwell, 1986), 292–300.

43 Ibid, 297.

44 Ibid, 297.

45 Kristeva, 1980, op. cit., 69.

46 Kristeva, 1986 op. cit., 297.

47 Irigaray, 1991, op. cit., 36.

48 The mother is killed but not revenged. The sisters are either sacrificed (Iphigenia) or sent mad (Electra). The Furies—the women seeking to avenge the murdered mother-queen—are buried, like the wicked witch of the North, under the temple on the Acropolis, which was of course the imperial Athenian treasury, its bank, the Temple dedicated to the virgin goddess Athena who was so very male-defined and father-identified that she claimed she had been born from her father's head.

49 Irigaray, 1991, op. cit, 38.

50 Kristeva, 1986, op. cit, 297–198.

51 H. Cixous, "The Laughter of the Medusa" [1975], in *Women, Gender and Scholarship*, ed. E. Abel and E. K. Abel (Chicago: University of Chicago Press, 1983) 279–297.

52 H. Cixous, "Castration or Decapitation?" *Signs*, 7:1 (1981), 41–55.

53 See my forthcoming book on women and images of poverty in the nineteenth century, *Sexuality and Surveillance :Bourgeois Men and Working Women* (London: Routledge).

54 Kristeva, 1986, op. cit. 295–96.

55 Irigaray, 1991, op. cit., 43.

56 I am using this term in both its colloquial and technical senses. In psychoanalysis foreclosure denotes a specific mechanism which lies at the origin of psychosis which results from the primordial expulsion of a fundamental "signifier" from the symbolic realm of the subject. In this sense the refusal of signifiers of the maternal in the symbolic casts women into a kind of generic psychosis—unable adequately to articulate their subjectivity because of the lack of signifiers of their specificity as opposed to the phallus which consistently signifies only their difference. (Laplanche and Pontalis, *The Language of Psychoanalysis,* (London: Karnac Books, 1973:166).

57 Mary Stephenson Cassatt (1844–1926), American painter, resident in Paris, feminist, socialist, lifelong supporter of independent movement in art, member of Impressionist exhibiting society. Katherine Kelso Johnston Cassatt (1816–1895), mother of Mary and of Lydia Simpson Cassatt (1841–1882), married to Robert Simpson Cassatt (1806–1891), moved to Paris from Philadelphia to live with Mary, 1877.

58 Kathleen Alexandra Sinclair Pollock (1913–1964).

59 S. Freud, "Fragment of an Analysis of Hysteria ('Dora')," in *The Penguin Freud Library*, Vol. 8, *Case Histories* (London: Penguin Books, 1977).

60 Freud, ibid, 50.

61 J. Sayers, *Mothering Psychoanalysis* (London: Penguin Books, 1991).

62 M. Kelly, "Invisible Bodies: Mary Kelly's *Interim*" *New Formations,* 1987, No. 2, 11.

63 M. Montrelay, "Inquiry into Femininity" trans. P. Adams, *M/F* (1978), No. 1, 94.

64 V. Woolf, *The Three Guineas,* (London: The Hogarth Press, 1938), 70–71.

65 Ibid, 72.

66 A. Rich, "Towards a Woman-Centred University" [1973–74], in *On Lies, Secrets and Silence* (London: Virago Books, 1980), 125–156.

67 bell hooks, *Talking Back: Thinking Feminist, Thinking Black,* (Boston: South End Press, 1989).

part iv
cinematic moments

crows, blossoms and lust for death—cinema and the myth of van gogh the modern artist

9

griselda pollock

van gogh, film and mythologies

IN 1990 A VAN GOGH FILM FESTIVAL WAS organized in Amsterdam. It revealed a range of films which constitute a "difficult genre" as Gertjan Zuilhof called it in his introduction to the catalogue. On concluding his survey of films ranging from documentary to parody and opera, he comments: "A great and intriguing artist such as Vincent van Gogh does not intrinsically make an interesting film; on the contrary, the subject demands better-than-average courage, intelligence and cinematic quality to arrive at an acceptable product; Van Gogh has a lesson to teach the cinema."[1]

Most films are lazy. They lean heavily on the artist's biography, extracts from letters read in ponderous tones, and paintings lovingly filmed with romantic musical accompaniment. Zuilhof identifies a few noteworthy treatments, but notes the repetitiveness and predictability of so many versions of Van Gogh's life and work.

Not only do these patterns betray a lack of intelligence or individuality, but they are signs of the power of a mythology for which a nineteenth-century Dutch painter has become a key signifier. It is not so much that these films are about Van Gogh's life, work, and death, but rather that the materials available in the biography of that historical figure are locked into a structure of fantasy deeply embedded in modern Western culture.

Vincent van Gogh shot himself on Sunday 27 July 1890, and died two days later from blood loss and untreated infection. His demise, however, is figured in representation through a recurring mise-en-scene: the artist shoots himself while painting the *Wheatfield with crows* (fig. 4), or in a wheatfield suggested by the painting. In Kurosawa's *Dreams* (1990) an American director Martin Scorsese played Van Gogh in a vignette of the *Wheatfield with crows*. Robert Altman produced a feature-length film entitled *Vincent and Theo* (1990), marking a departure in its focus on the relationship between two brothers, one of whom happens to be Vincent van Gogh, the painter. The older brother, Vincent, shoots himself while painting in a wheatfield. These films, each of them distinct in its emphasis and attitude, reveal how clearly certain images of Van Gogh are imprinted on our cultural imagination. Furthermore, they both show how powerful an earlier film, *Lust for life* (1955), remains in shaping the myth of Van Gogh, in providing the abiding terms of its visualisation. Several scenes in Altman's *Vincent and Theo* seem purposely to quote, or knowingly repeat the mise-en-scene of Minnelli's reconstructions of Van Gogh locations and paintings. One film alone manages to resist the lure of the mythic death in the wheatfield. Made in 1989 by Christoph Hübner and Gabriele Voss, *Der Weg nach Courrières* focuses on three moments in Van Gogh's Dutch period, creating a dialogue between past and present by filming contemporary locations in Belgium, Drenthe and Nuenen in documentary-cum-travelogue style, and juxtaposing the poverty or economic reality of these actual communities with extracts from Van Gogh's letters. There is no death, no progressive development, no encounter with French modernism. Instead, the film makes a serious attempt to create a sense of the historical and geographical specificity of the Dutchman's artistic beginnings. But all this is undone by the final citation of Pastor Bonte's reminiscences to Louis Piérard in 1924. While filming a self-portrait which the artist painted in Paris, Bonte's words are read: "One is greatly surprised that he became a real painter."

The film is anti-mythical, for it gives social depth and historical meaning to art as a dialogue with a lived and experienced social world. But the unfamiliar Van Gogh it produces is merely the foil to its structuring absence. The mythical Van Gogh of the *Sunflowers* and *Wheatfields*, the canonical modernist, is invoked at the end of the film to render its scrupulous and original approach cinematically remarkable but culturally a footnote. It reconfirms the teleological schema which Van Gogh's constant moves from place to place have come to represent, namely, his evolution from sombre Dutch social realism to his modernist self-consciousness as an expressionist and colourist. In most narratives, the shift was prompted by his encounters with painters in Paris. Hübner and Voss's film ends just before the critical moment when a Van Gogh most people don't know or like is transformed into the painter of the most expensive flowers in the world.

Van Gogh is a mythical artist, the stuff of legends, the paradigm of the modern artist.[2] Art-historical literature has played a major part in fixing the meanings of this myth which structures the ways in which people understand "Van Gogh." Roland Barthes argues that myth is a form of communication but it is "depoliticised speech [...]. Semiology has taught us that myth has the task of giving an historical intention a natural justification, and making contingency appear eternal [...]. What the world supplies to myth is an historical reality, defined, even if this goes back quite a while, by the way in which men have produced and used it; and what myth gives in return is a *natural* image of this reality."[3]

Barthes's essay "Myth today" is the most extended analysis of the role of myth as a form of signification in contemporary culture. It belongs to the realm of both semiology—how meaning is produced through signs—and ideology—what motivates and fixes meaning in the interests of dominant social forces. Barthes examines the way in which myth "naturalises" its contentious meanings.

Myth is not distortion, propaganda, but a semiological process which takes over previously constituted meanings, first-order signs, which are marked by their social and historical moment. These are made into the signifiers of a second order system or signs. A sign is composed of a form (signifier) and a concept (signified). In their union a meaning (the sign) is produced. B-l-o-s-s-o-m as a graphic or acoustic form is married to the mental idea of flowering trees to form a sign, a denoted meaning. Myth appropriates this first order of signs, empties it to make the sign a signifier, a form for a signification at a second level. Its original meaning is both absorbed and distanced. Its contingency in time and space is erased all the better to lend its seeming literalness to the myth it will signify.

Barthes's Model:

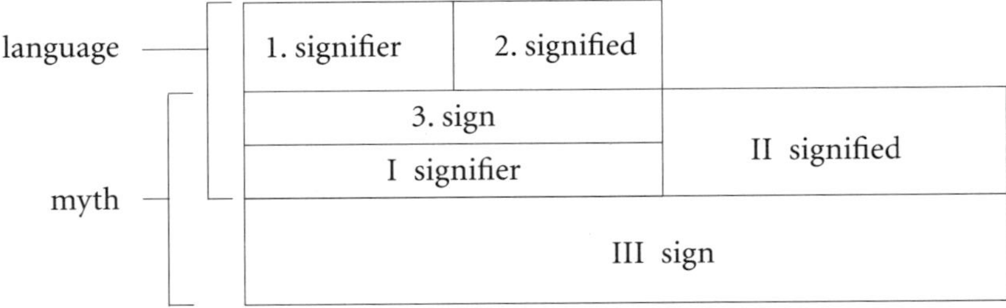

Myth takes over forms (signifiers) from already constituted signs. This, however, creates a dilemma for myth when it is being received. Barthes provides the example of a photograph on the front cover of *Paris Match*—this is 1957—of a North African soldier in French uniform saluting the French tri-colour. "The form of the myth is not the symbol; the Negro who salutes is not the symbol of the French empire; he has too much presence, he appears as a rich, fully experienced, spontaneous indisputable image [a first order sign]. But at the same time this presence is tamed, put at a distance, made almost transparent; it recedes a little, it becomes the accomplice of a concept which comes to it fully armed, French imperialism; once made use of it becomes artificial."[4]

But myth has problems at the level of its consumption. This is what distinguishes it from ideology in its obvious form and yet makes it paradigmatic of how bourgeois ideology functions through appropriation and naturalization.

It is possible for the viewer/reader to focus on the signifier, and the meaning becomes literal; the African soldier becomes an example or symbol of French imperialism. Focusing on the new concept makes the meanings obvious; the soldier is the alibi of French imperialism. Barthes therefore concludes: "In one word, either the intention of the myth is too obscure to be efficacious, or it is too clear to be believed. In either case where is the ambiguity? This is but a false dilemma; myth is neither a lie nor a confession; it is an inflexion. Placed before the dilemma which I mentioned a moment ago, myth finds a third way out. Threatened with disappearance if it yields to either of the first two types of focusing, it gets out of this tight spot thanks to a compromise—it *is* this compromise. Entrusted with 'glossing over' an intentional concept [i.e. ideologically motivated meaning], myth encounters nothing but betrayal in language, for language can only obliterate the concept if it hides it, or unmask it if it formulates it. The elaboration of a second-order semiological system will enable myth to escape this dilemma: forced either to unveil or liquidate the concept, it will *naturalise* it. We reach here the very principle of myth: *it transforms history into nature.*"[5]

The life and work of a Dutch painter, Vincent van Gogh, who was active between 1880 and 1890, poses historical questions. But his life and work have been appropriated to function as the signifiers in a second-order discourse—or several. Van Gogh becomes a signifier of discourses on the modern artist, the avant-garde, expressionism, artistic nature, creativity and madness, existential alienation and so forth. The concepts have changed in the course of the twentieth century, and in different communities and critical contexts.[6] But when I argue that "Van Gogh" is a mythical artist, I am not suggesting that these uses are wrong or wrongly motivated. I am pointing to ways which they can be read in order to see how the mythic meanings are secured by appearing to be simply the transparent reality of the artist's life and the works. They are made to *seem* to be what is *said* of them, and through them.

In the case of Van Gogh, the process Barthes calls myth has made the biography exceptionally significant. Many art historians now complain that "the life" has come to replace appreciation of the works. Art history has made a considerable effort to dispel what now seem to be excessive or outdated mythologies. Instead of the fascination and identification with a suffering victim, which inspired many psychiatric studies, as well as popular *vie romancée* like *Lust for life* from 1934, a new myth is being manufactured, the myth of Van Gogh the diligent and conscientious craftsman.[7] It is reasonable to suppose that this sanitized—sane—and more controlled, competent and professional painter blends better with the huge investments made in his works. In the popular mind, Van Gogh's fame now rests less on his ear and his death than on the price tags attached to his floral arrangements.

Films have played a special role in the manufacture and dissemination of the mythic "Van Goghs," partly because the formal characteristics of cinema correspond with the imperatives of mythic signification. Firstly, they are apparatuses of "naturalisation," through their photographically contrived realist form. A filmed reconstruction of Van Gogh's painting of his bedroom in the Yellow House literally brings both the past as well as art itself to life. Secondly, the narrative drive of film as it moves through time, tying its viewers in to the stories and scenes that unfold through the agency of the camera/projector, retraces the biographical trajectory of which Van Gogh is a paradigm case. Ten short years of artistic activity, marked by numerous ruptures, radical rethinks, new departures and back-tracking, are typically represented as a logical development. Ten short years are mapped onto the model of early years and apprenticeship, followed by tentative discoveries of new and modern directions, flowering into maturity, fading into decline, and ending in death. Ten short years become a microcosm of a whole life cycle and of art history's monographic patterning of artistic production.

Hollywood films are defined as examples of the classic realist text.[8] Realism is based on a model of knowledge as the direct apprehension by a conscious subject of the world, the object. Narrative is defined as a complement to this process, for it is the device by which contradiction and complexity in the Real are denied. It suggests that all we need to do in order to know is to look and see. Gill Davies elaborates on this theme: "Narrative in both the novel and the film has the same effect. It creates a sense of inevitability and closure, in that the action is felt to be predestined, tidy and without contradictions. The basis of most Hollywood stories is a forward-moving plot—the rise and fall of a gangster, a tycoon, a movie star [...]. A problem, a question, a deficiency or a violation of order is posed in the opening sequence, and the end of the film coincides with the problem's solution."[9]

Formal symmetry and rhyming are additional devices which ensure the resolution of whatever problem is established as the precipitating disorder which drives a narrative through its temporal unfolding to a conclusion which is experienced as a closure. Yet another force in narrative, which gives its sequence a dynamic, is based on a structure of oppositions, which have such thematics, relevant to bio-pics in general and "Van Gogh" sagas in particular, such as Individual versus Society, City versus Country, Life versus Death, and so forth.

In this essay I want to re-examine Minnelli's *Lust for life* (1955), which is in many ways *the* mythic film about Van Gogh. It appears to rehearse the major components of the legend of the suffering genius and mad artist, and lodge them in the popular imagination through the powerful visual images it creates for the legendary story. I would argue, however, that Minnelli's film is much more than a rehearsal of the twentieth-century myth of Van Gogh. It is a critical text, which provides a more complex reflection on the meanings of the artist and of modern art itself then most of the subsequent films on the artist, which endlessly repeat the major tropes of the psycho-biographic literature and minimize any context for considering the success or failure of Van Gogh's project. Minnelli's authorship and his experience as a director of major Hollywood melodramas inflected the bio-pic and transformed it into something which, according to the review in *Time* magazine, "falls midway between being a first-rate art film and a high-pitched melodrama."[10] The reason given for this assessment provides a key to our reading of *Lust for life*: "… because the Hollywood story builds relentlessly to Van Gogh's ear-slicing for its climax […]."[11] It is because the film undoes its own narrative drive, the impulse to get the viewer through to the death which marks both the end of the artist's life and story and the conclusion of the narrative form, the closure of its biographical saga, that this film can be said to *work* the ideological or mythical materials out of which it was formed.

The film took on the "Van Gogh" legend as it was in the mid-1950s, a myth which inhabited the historical persona of Vincent van Gogh.[12] In ways which outrun Minnelli's intentions and MGM's purposes, it reworks the legend and thus permits us to raise questions and note contradictions which the myth had made unthinkable: What kind of artist was Van Gogh? Was he a modernist at all? Was he a tragic figure or was he what Minnelli's Gauguin implies in the film, a financially-protected, insipid sentimentalist?

T. J. Clark argues that the social history of art seeks to explain the links between historical processes and artistic forms, without reducing either to being merely the reflection or unitary cause of the other. While attempting to identify the many factors that shape a work of art or a film, we must also recognize an active, productive relation between a text and its historical, social or aesthetic materials. "A work of art," he writes, "may have ideology (in other words, those ideas, images and values that are generally accepted, dominant) as its material, but it *works* that material; it gives it a new form and at certain moments that new form is in itself a subversion of ideology."[13]

When formally analyzed, is Minnelli's and MGM's *Lust for life* an example of such a critical reworking, or is it a case for Barthes's analysis of myth? What does the semiotic form of a narrative realist film do to the already mythic story? Can this entertainment form of popular culture articulate questions which are silenced in élite modernist art history? Is it inflexion in a mythic sense, or in a subversive fashion? What knowledge does the viewer gain from it?

who killed van gogh? or lust for death

Vincente Minnelli, the director of MGM's 1955 production of *Lust for life*, recalled in his reminiscences the haste with which the film was finally made. MGM's option on Irving Stone's romanticized biography, first published in 1934, was due to expire in December 1955, and Stone refused to extend the option because he himself had plans to make a film. According to Minnelli: "Nature wasn't going to wait for Metro-Goldwyn-Mayer [...] and Metro couldn't wait for Minnelli. It was late July of 1955, a time when flowers had lost their first innocent blooms [...]. Members of the company crew, on location in Arles for the past two months, were trying to fool Mother Nature by using chemicals to keep a wheatfield alive until my arrival. I would be forced to shoot Van Gogh's suicide scene first, and though few pictures are shot in sequence, starting out with the culminating action presented a problem I hoped wasn't insuperable. What if the preceding action didn't logically build?"[14]

Minnelli's film ends with Van Gogh (Kirk Douglas) painting the *Wheatfield with crows* (Amsterdam, Vincent van Gogh Museum) before shooting himself and retiring to his bed to die. But, interestingly, the film began with this scene; it was in fact shot first. This production schedule and its dependence on local agriculture, however, have a mythic significance.

minnelli's ending

The finale of the film builds up to its fatal climax by a temporal elision. It is the fourteenth of July, and Auvers is boisterously celebrating Bastille Day. The *pompiers* brass band is out in force, and a funfair has been set up in the square. Van Gogh wanders into the village café, overwhelmed and alienated by the noise and merriment. Then, with a violent gesture, he sweeps out of the café, and the film cuts to a close-up of wheat swaying in the wind. Suddenly, a flock of crows comes hurtling out of this calm sea of yellow. The film cuts back to Van Gogh at work on the famous painting. The crows descend on him menacingly. He adds a few ominous black shapes to the canvas and, with mounting frenzy, savagely changes his sky from a sunny, pale blue to a foreboding tone, hissing: "It's impossible!" He abandons the painting, turns towards a tree, and hangs on its branches for a moment, before writing a note which concludes: "I can see no way out." Taking a gun from his pocket, he again drapes himself over the tree. The camera cuts to a farmer crossing the field in his cart, and the sound of a gunshot shatters the silence. Cut again to Van Gogh in bed, attended by his brother Theo. His life is ebbing away. "I want to go home," he implores, and then dies, while Theo sobs: "My own dear brother." Vincent's painting of the *Reaper* fills the screen, and the image is accompanied by a voice-over of his conversation about death with one of the nuns at the asylum in Saint-Rémy.

> Nun: But the mower? Is he an imaginary figure?
> Van Gogh: That's just a man struggling in the heat to finish his work. It's the figure of death.
> Nun: It doesn't seem a sad death.
> Van Gogh: Oh no, it's not, sister. It happens in bright daylight, the sun flooding everything in a light of pure gold.

Finally, the camera moves back to reveal a display of Van Gogh's paintings. Across them are the words: "The End," followed by "Lust for life."

The film's job was to lead its audience up to these scenes in such a way that the viewer experiences them as the conclusion to the narrative. Minnelli expresses a director's anxiety about achieving this conclusion. This is in some ways ironic.

the ending of the myth

By the mid-1950s, a single painting—the *Wheatfield with crows*—had come to represent the endpoint, the full stop, indeed the final testament of the modern artist "Van Gogh," a persona gradually fabricated over the sixty years following the painter's death in July 1890.[15] In books, exhibitions and art-historical studies, the painting he had produced in mid-July came at the end, the last plate, the last work. An image wrongly associated with his "suicide," it came to be the signifier of the "Van Gogh" myth.

Filming this scene first reveals its culturally defined place as the climax of the story. A filmed biography must close where the life ended. This can only be signified through the one painting which had come to express the suicidal moment: "I can see no way out," writes Van Gogh/Douglas, echoing Meyer Schapiro's sentiments about the painting in 1946: "The canvas is already singular in its proportions [...]. And this extraordinary format is matched by the vista itself, which is not simply panoramic but a field opening out from the foreground by way of three diverging paths. A disquieting situation for the spectator, who is held in doubt before the great horizon and cannot, moreover, reach it on any of the three roads before him [...]." And later, commenting on Van Gogh, the artist who painted this image of his own desperation: "It is as if he felt himself completely blocked, but also saw an ominous fate approaching."[16] The painting thus marks the point at which art history traditionally kills off the artist.

Death is a major component of both the popular and the art-historical "Van Gogh." By the mid-1950s, millions of people all over the world had encountered "Van Gogh" through exhibitions of his work, arranged chronologically and accompanied by excerpts of the artist's letters.[17] The superimposition of a strict art-historical chronology on a seemingly auto-biographical documentary, recounts a cathartic journey through haunting and sombre images of old age, poverty and despair (the Dutch period, from 1880 to 1885), on to the luminous, pantheistic exuberance of sunflowers and blossoms (the French period, especially 1888 and 1889). But just as "life" seems most vividly confirmed in the ecstatic productivity of these imaginary visions of a southern European landscape, the viewer must encounter and accept death in the wheatfield (1890). Such a potentially traumatic loss was negotiated by the fact that Van Gogh could be assimilated to a major trope of Western culture, the sacrifice of Jesus. The artist dies so that his art may live on for others. At once a revival of Christianity's key theology of sacrifice and redemption through death, and a secularized sacrifice to the demands of the capitalist art market (the dead artist), "Van Gogh" became a paradigm of the popular and fundamentally christological concept of the modern artist, dramatized in a Passion play for modern times. The symbolism of a "light of pure gold" links the two together.[18]

Van Gogh's art was presented in exhibitions and framed by art-historical narrative to sustain this mythic figure, the modern artist as a secular Christ, which Van Gogh's own brief career as an evangelist can be employed to enhance. Religion and Art converge in the figure's biography to condense in the mythic figure of the modern victim, "Van Gogh." A particular, historically contingent suicide is "naturalised" by its appropriation better to obscure the precarious conditions of private production in the market system of the late nineteenth century.

Minnelli could thus rely on his audiences' preconceptions of Van Gogh's symbolic *death*. The image of Van Gogh/Douglas draped around a tree just before shooting himself is a fairly explicit allusion to the Crucifixion. This emblematic scene is confirmed by the decision to begin the film with Van Gogh's abortive yet heroic experience as an evangelist in the mining district of the Borinage. The audience's first image of Van Gogh/Douglas is of a man seated beneath a Christian symbol. Of course, the rhyme works in reverse order when we view the film, so that Van Gogh's struggle to be a Christian missionary among the poor, wronged miners, his rejection by the Church authorities, and his increasing alienation, first from his middle-class family, presided over by his pastor-father, then by the artist community, symbolized by Gauguin, borrows even more powerfully from the life of the Christian figure of Jesus.

Returning to the death in the wheatfield, it is significant that we do not actually witness Van Gogh's action. It occurs only on the soundtrack, in a manner which echoes the other major climax and moment of self-mutilation, the ear-slicing, which I shall discuss in detail below. On both occasions, the viewer is shielded from directly witnessing an assault on the artist's body, and in that absence, meaning is supplied by mythic knowledge already in circulation, which amounts to Van Gogh being known as "the artist who cut off his ear and killed himself."[19] It also allows the emptied frame to be filled with other culturally-authorized images of sacrificial death, enabling the mingling of the Van Gogh/Christ legends to occur in the viewer's imagination, where such connections have been tactically lodged by visual rhymes and emblems throughout the film.

Yet, the practical matter of filming the final scene at the beginning of the production process worried Minnelli, for he could not foresee how the rest of the film would actually work towards this conclusion. He knew it would stop there, but he could not be sure that this would indeed be the end—the point to which the film would drive, the objective which the narrative would have to achieve, the place where all contradictions dynamically established to keep the film moving along, would find their resolution.

the murder of the myth

This represents some difficulty. Like biography in general, the bio-pic of a famous person's life attempts to manufacture a unity. Caroline Merz writes: "The contract of biography is to deliver up a life—and whatever methods are used, whatever the personality described, its success or failure, is judged on whether it creates a coherent personality."[20] A filmed biography must also engage the viewer in identification with the hero, so that the ups and downs of a life as it passes through its early years to maturity and success engage the viewer with a personality re-created as a hero. An untimely or tragic death, while making the personality more remarkable and exciting, is difficult to manage. The loss of the hero cannot be too tragic, as the audience should not go home too distressed. While in a biographical sense Van Gogh's self-inflicted death will inevitably be the conclusion of the film, it must be managed so that the audience can bear it. Minnelli's filming of the final scenes employs a number of devices to ensure this. Van Gogh/Douglas is placed in a reconstruction of one of Van Gogh's paintings, and is shown painting it and then altering it, the better to express his state of mind. Hence the landscape functions as a projection of his inner, mental world, while he becomes a figure in his own landscape. As an artist he is thus distinguished from ordinary people, who observe but do not share this mental turmoil.

His suicide is motivated by nature's assault on him in the form of the birds, yet they are also extensions of his own paranoid feelings. The overall effect is to denaturalize the scene, and to distance the viewer from the figure of Van Gogh, seen on the verge of disintegration. He becomes a kind of "abject." [21]

Minnelli's film in fact prepares the viewer for the murder it will commit—the killing off of Van Gogh—by detaching the viewer from identification with the bio-pic's initial hero. This is achieved through a splitting of the hero mid-way through the film. Writing of this phenomenon in Hollywood Westerns, Laura Mulvey draws on Vladimir Propp's analysis of the function of the hero in folktales, who usually achieves symbolic integration into society after undergoing an ordeal. She further sees the conclusion of the hero's quest or ordeal, usually in marriage, as a conclusion to a psychic narrative, the Oedipal complex. Failure to submit to social law, which Western heroes such as John Wayne in *The searchers* make into a virtue, can be read as a "nostalgic celebration of phallic, narcissistic omnipotence." Indeed the mythic character of the modern artist, which both Gauguin and Van Gogh can be seen to personify, is another form of this masculine nostalgic fantasy. [22] Mulvey writes that the "tension between two points of attraction, the symbolic (social integration and marriage) and nostalgic narcissism, generates a common splitting of the Western hero in two, something unknown in the Proppian tale." [23] In her case study, *The man who shot Liberty Valance*, Tom Doniphon (John Wayne) represents the man who, at the height of his powers, must bow out of history—the film opens with his funeral—while Ranse (James Stewart) is the man inscribed in history as the financially and politically powerful lawyer.

Mulvey's analysis of the Western's splitting of the hero, with the accompanying death of one of the irreconcilables whose conflict animates the narrative and enacts a potent fantasy for the masculine viewer, is not directly analogous to a film about modern artists. All artists in this mythology are Doniphons, hence their assimilation to Christian sacrifice. Van Gogh bows out of history: Theo the married man in his integrated social place remains, as do the paintings. Theo is the Ranse of this story, the surrogate for art lovers, dealers, art historians. So too are the viewers, who are allowed an imaginary identification with a nostalgic fantasy, and yet are returned in the end to social integration.

Therefore, what happens between Gauguin and Van Gogh is more narratively significant than the Vincent/Theo opposition. Minnelli's film dramatically hinges on their encounter in the Yellow House at Arles. At the end of this sequence a new hero is established and Van Gogh is put beyond viewer identification so that the death is acceptable as the necessary conclusion, even though the last few scenes leading to it are increasingly tedious. When Van Gogh declares that he wants to go home, the audience feels much the same. This means in effect, that the climax of Minnelli's film is not the suicide, but, as the *Time* critic commented, the disaster in Arles.

These scenes establish a series of oppositions whose effect is to estrange the viewer from Van Gogh, because he is represented in Kirk Douglas's performance, with its exaggeratedly physical, if not hysterical, representation of mental turmoil and emotional excess, as simultaneously bestial, feminine and insane. As a result of the Yellow House episodes Van Gogh is invalidated—literally he becomes an invalid lying in a hospital bed, and, figuratively, he is delegitimated as a heroic figure.

modernism and mania

Minnelli was therefore right to have been worried about beginning his film with the ending, for the narrative drive of *Lust for life* culminates dramatically in the conflict between Van Gogh and Gauguin. This has major consequences for what the film is finally about. The dynamic of the film is not so much Van Gogh's anguish as the debate about modern art and the nature of the artist who can withstand the modern conditions of production. Van Gogh, seemingly the paradigm of the creative victim, is displaced by the much more compelling characterisation of Gauguin, who manages to maintain both masculinity and aesthetic integrity. No wonder that Anthony Quinn, who played Gauguin, and not Kirk Douglas, received an Oscar. Gauguin is characterized as a loner, a man forced to declass himself and leave his role as pater familias in order to follow his vocation as an artist. It comes as a surprise when viewing the film to recognize that Gauguin assumes the mantle of the modern artist at the climax of the film, after which Van Gogh rushes headlong towards his filmic death. It is Quinn's

Gauguin who preserves art against the increasingly feminised emotional and psychological excesses of Douglas's Van Gogh.

Minnelli was well versed in the literature by and about Van Gogh, and in the history of modern art.[24] Hollywood had its fair share of prominent collectors of modern art. The actor Edward G. Robinson and his wife, the painter Gladys Lloyd Robinson, acquired substantial collections of modern paintings, which were exhibited in Washington in 1953 and in Los Angeles and San Francisco in 1956–57. The Robinsons owned two Gauguins as well as Van Gogh's *Portrait of Pére Tanguy* [F364] from 1887 and *The old willows* [F520] from 1889, both in the Stavros Niarchos Collection. Indeed the script is full of direct quotations, especially in the scenes in which Gauguin and Van Gogh compete intensely through "electrical" discussions about their art.

Minnelli's description in his reminiscences of the way he imagined Gauguin's visit to Arles, however, reduces it to a banal saga of *jalousie du métier* stemming from Gauguin's uncomfortable discovery that Van Gogh was emerging as a serious artist just when he himself had hit a dry period. Referring to them as the "original odd couple," Minnelli indicates that he saw them as polarized opposites. Gauguin, fastidious, intellectual, self-disciplined, and yet a libertine; Van Gogh, ascetic and asexual, yet an untidy and emotionally-smothering slob.

What happens on the screen is shaped by what the director and script mapped out, but it works these materials into a dramatized conflict of what was in fact decisive in the formation of early modernism: sensibility, sensation, perception and temperament on the one hand, rooted in naturalist theory and associated in practice with Impressionist painting, while on the other hand, the rationalisation of painting practice, a desire for order, system, method or at least a structure, be it revamped academic idealism, or a confection of fashionable German philosophies and other less respectable pseudo-religious and occult theories.

Let us face this surprisingly serious aesthetic debate through the filmic drama. Gauguin arrives to be enveloped in a Van Gogh bear hug. He is led into a room decorated with pictures of sunflowers, which he strokes gingerly, surprised by their texture. Following Van Gogh to the kitchen, he is astonished at the sheer number of paintings strewn about, but his amazement gradually gives way to disgust at his friend's pathetic attempts to cook. The chaos of the kitchen, littered with dirty brushes and paint-stained rags, is swiftly cleaned up, and we cut to a scene of homely serenity as the two men puff their pipes at a table covered with Hollywood's chief signifier of domestic bliss—the checkered tablecloth. But the friends are soon at loggerheads, arguing out opposing views on art. Gauguin categorically states the modernist case: Art is an abstraction, not a picture book. He paraphrases Maurice Denis's observation: A picture [...] is essentially a flat surface covered with a certain pattern of colours arranged in a certain order.[25] Gauguin argues that he will disregard the order in nature and seek after harmonies of pure colour, deliberately composed and carefully calculated, that move you as music moves you. However hackneyed such definitions sound when spoken in an imagined dialogue, they clearly articulate that modernist practice involves a rupture between what is represented in art and the means of representation. Modernism privileges the procedures and process of its own making. Painting is about colour, surface, flatness and an autonomous, aesthetically contrived and evaluated order, independent of nature, whatever references it may make to it or not.

Van Gogh/Douglas interrupts Gauguin with a list of artists of the past from Rembrandt to Millet, who, he argues, capture the human spirit and express the dignity of toil. He thus adopts a humanist, romantic-naturalist position, associated with the mid-nineteenth century. Gauguin is filled with scorn. "Millet! That calendar artist with his dun-coloured tones and sentimental insipidity." If Millet had a message, he says he should have been a preacher. "Painting is for painters." Balanced as this argument appears from the philosophical point of view, it identifies Gauguin as the modernist and Van Gogh as the romantic realist. The final conflict in this scene swings the balance. Van Gogh advocates Millet, and states that he is not afraid of emotional responses (in obvious contrast to the sophisticated response of the kind Gauguin imagines through his analogy with music), linking himself with feminine excess and an empathetic, almost bodily vision of art's communicative power, which in the twentieth century has been more closely associated with popular culture than with the avant-garde. Gauguin argues that Van Gogh needs to learn control—to manage what he feels through aesthetic forms, which move us as music does, suggestively, abstractly.

Picking up one of Van Gogh's paintings, Gauguin insists that "it's bizarre, disordered, the paint's slapped on. You paint too fast." Enraged, Van Gogh replies: "You *look* too fast".

This exchange confirms Van Gogh's identification as a spontaneous painter, filled with the desire to make his paintings immediately convey to his viewers the actual experiences and forces of nature. His ideological baggage includes the popular realist artists—Millet, Lhermitte, Israëls and Breton—loved by museum-goers in the twentieth century, yet disdained by scholars.[26] Gauguin's advocacy of craftsmanship, self-criticism and the cultivation of an aesthetic order distilled from nature and nourished by the imagination and intellect, provides a convincing alibi for modern art. Not just art of the modern period, however, which is of course heterogeneous and in which realism, both conservative and radical, has been a major tendency, but what museums and universities popularly conceive of and art-historians celebrate as modern art—cubism, futurism, abstraction.

The debate had its origins in the late nineteenth century, but the immediate political climate of the Cold War returned the issue of avant-garde versus kitsch to the ideological agenda. The conflict erupted in the 1940s and achieved a high political profile when Congressman George Dondero of the 17th congressional district of Michigan, an associate of the more infamous Senator Joseph McCarthy, attacked modern art, both within the Congress and outside, claiming that it was un-American and a Bolshevik conspiracy to destroy American values. Trotsky's friend, Wassily Kandinsky, had unleashed on the Czarist government the black knights of the "isms"—all of them deadly. Cubism aimed to destroy by "designed disorder," Futurism "by the machine myth," Dadaism "by ridicule," Expressionism "by aping the criminal and the insane," Abstraction "by the creation of brain storms," and Surrealism "by the denial of reason."[27]

Un-American because it had originated in Europe, modern art was dubbed Communistic because it seemed distorted and ugly, because it did not glorify "our beautiful country, our cheerful and smiling people, and our material progress." Dondero argued that art which did not exalt America in plain, simple terms that everyone could understand bred dissatisfaction. It was opposed to the American government, he felt, while those who created and promoted it were enemies of America.[28] The defenders of modern art—

museum directors and critics—replied by pointing out how totalitarians both of the left and right, Stalin as well as Hitler, had hated modern art and persecuted artists, "insisting on hackneyed realism saturated with nationalistic propaganda."[29]

In this wider context of the ideological struggle known as the Cold War, films about modern artists would inevitably rework debates about realism and modernism, which were couched as a conflict between a popular and an élite culture, Europe and America, national masculinity and foreign effeminacy and degeneracy. In 1954, the Museum of Modern Art in New York celebrated its 25th birthday with a statement by the Republican President Eisenhower, who chose from the speeches the museum had prepared for him one on the theme of freedom of the arts: "Freedom of the arts is a basic freedom, one of the pillars of liberty in our land [...] as long as artists are at liberty to feel with high personal intensity, as long as artists are free to create with sincerity and conviction, there will be healthy controversy and progress in art."[30] Such a statement ambiguously uses freedom to allow all practices, setting personal expression and individual conviction above the highly politicized and conflicted arguments about modernism staged by Dondero and Barr.

Lust for life woud be open to different readings according to how Van Gogh and Gauguin signified for different constituencies. Both were played by American actors in a British and European cast. Yet Van Gogh was identified with the nationalist realist populist tendency against the more cerebral and semi-abstract modernist painter Gauguin.

Let us return to the text of the film. Up to the argument scene, Van Gogh and Gauguin are established as holding opposing positions. Since Gauguin is the newcomer and not the ostensible subject of the film the odds are still on the audience's identification with Van Gogh. In passing, however, the script reveals that Van Gogh had very little understanding of modern art as it was being developed by artists like Gauguin. Van Gogh is characterized in this dramatisation closer to what he fundamentally was—a romantic realist entrenched in mid-nineteenth century literary and artistic culture. The film thus articulates what is carefully repressed in art history's assimilation of Van Gogh into its canonical story of modern art: the question of whether his was a modernist practice at all.

Whatever the balance which the device of dialogue and argument allows the film to hold up to this point, it is shattered by the visualisation of the breakdown between Gauguin and Van Gogh. But before analyzing this scene in detail, we need to recapitulate that beginning/ending, asking what killed Van Gogh, and we need to frame the Arles climax in the film's discourse on Van Gogh as the Natural painter.

nature/culture or art and death

Minnelli films his conclusion so that it appears that what kills Van Gogh, a man already isolated by society, is Nature. Up to this point, Van Gogh the artist has been construed through his unmediated contact with Nature, which was both his personal refuge from social alienation, and the source of his art. In the final stage of the film, Nature, in the form of the birds, aggressively turns against both the man and the artist. There can be no more, no place to go for the man portrayed as a victim of society's hostility to the avant-garde artist who nourished his creativity through imaginative identification with the forces of Nature.

The problem which the film aims to resolve is Van Gogh's lack of a place in the world. The sequence of scenes in the film shows a progressive exclusion of Van Gogh from all communities. His assimilation into nature and art compensate for this. There are many scenes of Van Gogh painting outdoors, looking and painting. A pictured world is invested with this symbolic gaze, which becomes the writing of the sign of personality upon nature to produce Art. The film thus creates a fundamental opposition at both the literal and symbolic levels between social space and the surrogate space of Art.

The opening sequence functions as a preface to the story of the artist, showing his failure to be admitted to the Church and his failure to be legitimated even in his most vigorous efforts on behalf of the miners. This creates a significant configuration:

| *Church* | Van Gogh | Miners |
| *Society* | Individual | People |

This section ends with the arrival of Theo, which establishes an Other to whom Van Gogh can speak himself.[31] This Other, Theo, becomes a critical mediator, a surrogate for the spectator who both receives Van Gogh words and images, but stands between the audience and the artist as the bearer of the emotional burden of proximity and involvement with the artist; yet he reassures us by being socially integrated. Theo lights Van Gogh's pipe and says, "Let me take you home." This of course rhymes directly with the deathbed scene, pipe and all, when Van Gogh asks to go home—and thankfully dies. Both moments are linked with and by the scene of Theo's visit to the bandaged Van Gogh in the hospital at Arles, when Theo again offers to "take him home."

There is no home for Van Gogh: this is a figure which cannot be accommodated within the film's frame or within the ideological system. The pathetic outsider, the social failure, is momentarily redeemed, it seems, by his art, for which he must inevitably die. The overpoweringly negative aspects of his impossible, anti-social outsiderness are counter-balanced by his identity as an artist, which is built up through a direct relationship with Nature. Minnelli's film presents a particular interpretation of Van Gogh as a naturalist, who pursues his untrammelled, unschooled, and spontaneous creativity through flowers and fields, through painting labourers whose lives are spent close to nature. (Of course, this is already a mythic version of the Countryside, which ceases to be the site of agricultural labour and its economic and social relations.) Such a construction of Van Gogh has some historical evidence to lend it support in Van Gogh's choice of Millet and not Manet as the leader of modern art, in the pantheon of naturalists with which he peopled his own *musée imaginaire*—Rembrandt, Ruysdael, Rousseau, Daubigny, Mauve, Israëls. It also echoes Van Gogh's own statements about his desire to be a peasant painter, to live a simple life in the country, and it corresponds with his repeated attacks on the corruption of the city and its urban economy, on merchants and dealers, and on the dangers of excessive refinement and civilization.

However much the trope of nature versus culture is derived from Van Gogh's own ideological programme, it can also be located as a theme in the oeuvre of Vincente Minnelli. Here we need a momentary digression into a key element of contemporary film theory, authorship or, more correctly, *la politique des auteurs*. *Auteur* criticism developed in the 1950s and 1960s as a critical device for the study of films by commercial Hollywood directors who

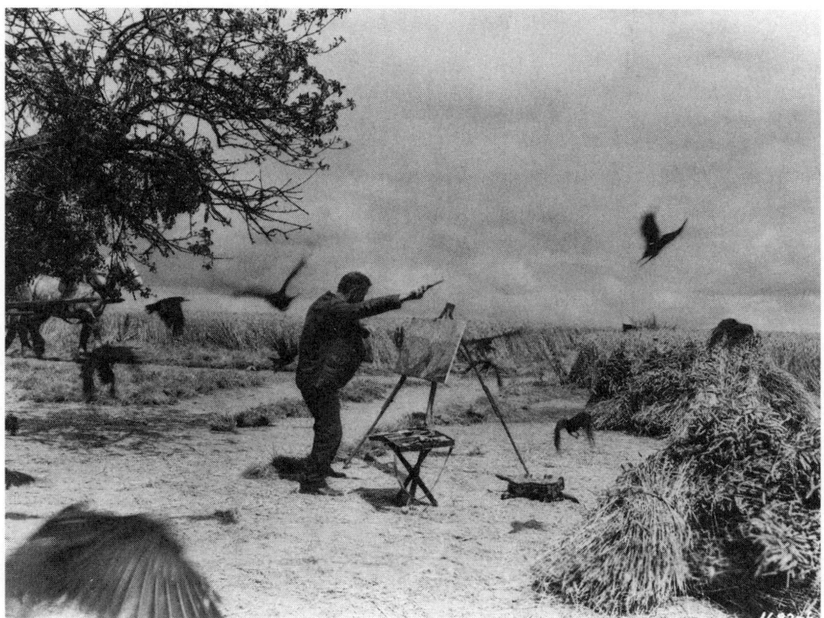

Figure 1.   Vincente Minnelli, *Lust for Life*, film still, MGM 1956.

distinguished themselves as *auteurs* through the pattern of themes and stylistic characteristics which could be discerned, not as the product of intention, but as recurring tropes and features of a body of work. Minnelli's films have been subjected to auteurist analysis and certain key motifs emerge which have prompted critics to write of his "moral vision", the "unity of his themes." Here is Thomas Elsaesser, writing in 1972: "Minnelli's films invariably focus on the discrepancy between an inner vision, often confused and uncertain of itself, and an outer world that appears hostile because it is represented as a physical space littered with obstacles. Life forces upon the characters a barely tolerable sense of rupture and the Minnellian universe has its psychological raison d'être in a very definite and pervasive alienation. But instead of commenting upon this modern condition, nearly all his films concentrate on portraying the energies of the imagination released in the individual during this period of decomposition [...]. Two types of hero come to symbolize this situation: the artist and the neurotic, two ways of dealing with the actual which are obviously not unrelated. That he sees them as intimately connected states of being constitutes the coherence of his moral vision and the unity of his themes."[32]

In addition to *Lust for life* Minnelli made many films about the artist, among them *An American in Paris* (1951), and *The cobweb* (1955). Elsaesser's *auteur* analysis of Minnelli's oeuvre provides significant clues to the way Van Gogh's story is spatialized in *Lust for life*. There is an obvious tension between the inside and outside, what is the real man and what is the man others see. Art functions as a means of externalisation, hence the stress on expression, and a means of access to an inner landscape—hence the painting's function as paranoid vision. Furthermore the film reconstructs spaces in which Van Gogh's drama unfolds across a series of scenes which are at once geographical locations, social sites, and visual emblems of the conflict between the individual and a social world. The crows are not exactly obstacles, but they rise out of the country space and attack. Everything signifies on at least two different levels. One is literal, hence the loving reconstruction of a credible environment for Van Gogh, complete with historical detail derived from the evidence of the paintings, and climatic conditions such as the mistral and the sun. Another level inscribes this actuality with signs of the Minnellian universe, for it is an imaginary setting for both the inner struggle of the creative person in the process of decomposition, and the conflict between the alienated individual and the obstructive social environment. The only means to cut through the resistance of the world around him is his gaze as an artist. Vision thus provides a moment of lyrical liberation when the artist looks at nature. In relation to nature there seems to be a directness of being and a spontaneity of expression. Art is therefore an ambiguous figure, as it is, of course, a cultural, creative and imaginative defence against disintegration and social pressure. But it is also virtually synonymous with nature—through a landscape painter, through this spontaneity of looking, seeing, painting, signified by the name "Van Gogh."

It is interesting to compare the discourse on nature/culture in *Lust for life* with another Minnelli film, which incidentally also articulates another of *Lust for life's* key themes, the relation of the popular and natural to the cultural and élite. Though set on Broadway and dramatized by actors and singers, *The bandwagon* (1953) provided a vehicle for Minnelli to explore the relative values of popular entertainment and élite art forms. In this "debate," the issue of Nature versus Culture functions as a key axis for plot, romance, and thematic content. Cyd Charisse plays a classical ballet star (Gaby) who is cast as a dancing partner to Fred Astaire, playing a one-time vaudeville song-and-dance man now in decline (Tony). Their difficult interaction dramatizes the conflict between a highly stylized form of dance and the spontaneous and cheerful movements of Tony Hunter's popular art form, which he breaks into at any time and any place. The moment of romantic reconcili-ation, and thus ideological realignment, comes with a walk in Central Park, when Gaby and Tony watch couples dancing to a band. They themselves, however, wander on, but slowly and subtly find their walking turns into an expressive and naturalistic dance. In the park, close to Nature, without choreography, true art is presented as something which is neither commer-cialized popular dance nor formalized high art, but a direct overflowing of feeling into freely expressive movement.

On the basis of such comparisons one might then argue that Minnelli's characterisation of Van Gogh was not merely an attempt at historically accu-rate reconstruction, but that it stemmed from his own position in the key debate of modern times, between modernism (avant-garde art) and mass culture, which produced a yearning, apparently satisfied by "Van Gogh", for some artist or art form which seemingly bridged what Andreas Huyssen has called "the great divide."[33] "Van Gogh," the outrageous modernist, mis-understood and persecuted to death in his own times, the Christ-like avant-gardist, can also seem accessible and authentically popular without being tainted by associations with mass, manufactured culture, namely what Theodor Adorno referred to as the "culture industry." Van Gogh introduces Nature back into Culture. This trope makes it possible to raise obliquely the politicized contemporary debate on the nature of modern art, its contradic-tions personalized in a single figure. This is the work of myth, for in so far as it appears merely to recreate before our eyes the being of Van Gogh, the conflicts of both early modernism and mid-twentieth century debates about the politics of official modernism are conjured away. Nature thus replaces History at many levels simultaneously.

For the first half of *Lust for life*, until the end of Van Gogh's period in Paris, he is set apart from all other artists. He works in the fields, wearing a rustic's sheepskin *gilet*. This separateness functions in part to explain even his departure from Paris, the mecca of modern art, where he meets Seurat, Bernard, Pissarro and Gauguin. However, the logic of the film demands that he return to nature for the real flowering of his individual genius, because the film establishes Van Gogh as a naturalist, and art as a means to Nature. This trope is realized in the film's sequence of his arrival in the Provençal town of Arles at nightfall and his awakening to the beauty of Provence. Having found a room, Van Gogh retires. Day breaks through tiny cracks in the shutters of a darkened room. From a point inside the room, the camera tracks the artist making his way to the window in the dark. This creates suspense, and the viewer, in the position of Van Gogh, is promised something to see when the shutters are thrown open. Suddenly the screen is filled with blossom, a filigree network of branches and blooms against a background of intense blue. The space is as shallow as any proto-modernist painting should be. All-overness is also achieved by the suspension of any precise point of view for what is being shown on screen. The unintelligibility of this immersion in blossom and sky is narratively secured by the filmic device of the reverse shot, which establishes Van Gogh/Douglas at the window, looking. But there is total disregard for all the rules of film's use of shot/reverse shot sequences, eyeline match and the 180-degree limit on the camera turning. For when the camera then cuts once again to the field of blossoms, music breaks in to accompany a visual essay of tracking, panning and zooming camera work.[34] The viewer is transported up and down these flattened screens of flowering trees in a way that bears no logical or perceptual relation to the spectator (either Van Gogh inside the film or the viewer outside). The camera's movements feed a nostalgic fantasy of the total freedom of the eye, suturing the viewer to a notion of the artist as at once both eye and "I". The images on screen then dissolve into painted images while retaining the same upward and downward movement. The photographic vision of the blossoms yields to the (photographic representation of the) artist's vision, seemingly directly registered on the canvases painted by Van Gogh. Pure perception slides effortlessly into art, signifying by this sleight of photographic representation that art is merely the optical register of pure individual perception. Or that Van Gogh's art is not only his vision of nature, but Nature itself, captured by the innocence or intensity of his artistic vision. The filming and viewing mechanism of the camera/projector is the condition for a display of sights which appear independent of the observer—seeming to make Nature herself directly present to Sight—the ultimate trope of realism.

What is elided is, of course, the fact of both film as production—shooting, developing, processing, editing, adding scores etc.—and art as a graphic and material production process. Why is this important to note? In a film, the photographic process, which is peculiarly liable to efface its own status as manufacture, lends its fetishistic structure to become a metaphor for art as pure unmediated vision. Represented by filmic codes, art seems not to be representation at all, and hence not to warrant historical or social analysis. Instead the film effaces all the traces of the working body, productively and calculatingly engaged with a culture, the socially-authorized materials and ideologically-determined conventions of representation which produce historically specific definitions of art. Van Gogh worked, as the dramatized discussion with Gauguin affirmed, at a period when a realist definition of art was in the process of contested transformation. Modernism was not the product of a succession of individual geniuses, but the complex response to a period of social transformation that precipitated a cultural crisis from which certain tendencies ultimately emerged as the official progressive culture of the Western bourgeoisie.

The legend of Van Gogh as a direct, spontaneous painter of his own vision of nature obscures that historical condition of modernism's existence. Turning history into nature, the legend is corroborated by the film's own mechanical means of representation. The camera mimics a single eye, and seems to function as a surrogate for the artist's perception. The silver nitrates merely register through light an image on celluloid in the way the retina registers an image on its surface. Of course this is not an accurate description of either perception or photography, which is a highly rhetorical procedure. Nonetheless, photography so effectively disguises the facts of its manufacturedness and coding that the viewer, in a darkened cinema and in a state of suspended animation, is permitted, indeed solicited, to participate in a fantasy of pure voyeurism, identifying with the eye of the camera while almost displacing it as a mechanical instrument to become the sole master of a visual field. The shot/reverse shot is the classic site of this so-called suture of the spectator to what seems a pure act of vision. Van Gogh/Douglas is shown looking. The artist signifies the gaze, the subject who looks. The viewer is then shown what he sees so that nature becomes the direct and simple object of vision, an object therefore of knowledge through that direct appraisal.

In the dichotomy created in the film—artist/object, Van Gogh/blossoms—the mediation of the filmic process disappears. The third term, the paintings, then function as the synthesis of both artist and nature. Art is effortlessly produced through looking. Art is at once natural and more than Nature, without becoming artifice or Culture.

But there is a difference between the filmed blossoms and the painted ones, which function as the signature of the artist on nature. Art is the trace of personality, giving rise to an expressionistic rendering of the scene, while personality is art, that which modifies what the photographic process has come to define as nature. Thus a muted commentary on modernism is introduced, signalled by the discrepancies between the blossoms we see as what Van Gogh sees when he opens the window, and the painted blossoms into which they dissolve. Art is at once direct visual experience and the personal filter through which nature passes. In some senses this is the filmic realisation of Zola's naturalist idea that "art is nature seen through a temperament," an idea Van Gogh himself knew and rehearsed in his letters, without any real appreciation of the polemic from which it stemmed.[35]

By the time we reach the final scene in Auvers, the audience is overfamiliar with the image of the artist with his easel at work on site. But this time Van Gogh is clearly located in one of his paintings. This has happened once before, with the *Night café*. Van Gogh is in Nature, here signified by billowing yellow ripeness, fertility and bounty. The crows appear, but instead of going for the ripening grain, they launch themselves at the artist and his painting—preliminary skirmishes for Hitchcock's later horror film, *The birds*. The crows represent the aggressive side of nature turned against Van Gogh, whom we have already seen turn aggressively against himself. Therefore they also read as projections of his own disturbed condition. The scene thus changes dramatically into a moment of intense paranoia, and Van Gogh becomes at once the victim of that which alone has sustained him and his art, and of his own destructive drives. The shooting is actually off screen, and the audience, like the peasant rumbling through the fields on his cart, only hears the ringing shot. So, who killed Van Gogh?

unravelling the subject:
disintegration and castration

Gauguin is the chief suspect at two levels. The police question him when he returns to find a bloodstained Van Gogh after the ear-slicing episode. The film also endows Gauguin with a deadly gaze.

Van Gogh and Gauguin are trying to paint in the vineyards in a howling mistral, which is too much for Gauguin. He wants to leave but bitterly snaps that he hasn't got the money. He goes home to the Yellow House. An apologetic, indeed sickeningly anxious Van Gogh returns later and starts snivelling about everyone needing love. Eventually Gauguin explodes and tells his friend some home truths about his sentimentality, contrasting Van Gogh's idealisation of Millet and toil with the real hard labour that he, Gauguin, has had to do in order to be able to paint, because he did not have a brother to support him. Infuriated by the taunt, Van Gogh hurls a glass at Gauguin's head. His guest fixes him with a long, chilling stare, and then leaves. He walks off through the dark alley-ways towards the brothel they used to frequent, with the sound of running feet behind him. Van Gogh suddenly appears, razor in hand, shot in soft focus and appearing to be looking up. Reverse mid-shot to Gauguin, reverse to an even softer focus close-up of the face of Van Gogh looking across and upwards in a way that signifies his being looked at by a Gauguin who is next shown in distinct close-up for several seconds. The screen is thus filled with the "castrating look" which stops Van Gogh in his tracks, and he crumples, arriving home through the linking shots of lamps—the street lamp, the house lamp and the lamp in his painting of the *Night café*.

By using the term "castration," I have purposely introduced psychoanalytic notions as a means of analysing what happens at this point. Freud explained the legend of the Medusa's gaze—Medusa turned her victims to stone by looking at them—in terms of castration fears which are typically projected onto the female figure who is herself castrated and hence threatens castration.[36] Nevertheless, the Medusa is fetishistically endowed with phallic snakes for hair, combining both fears of castration generated through discovery of female difference, and dread of the father who will castrate the boy who fails to submit to the law. The gaze is phallic and castrating, and is assumed to be masculine. Turning the gaze punitively on a man thus feminizes him as the object of the gaze. In this filmic exchange the twin and incompatible forces of masculinity, which its dramatisation has unleashed, battle it out, with the law, victory and life on the side of the potent, masculine, rational and imaginative artist—Gauguin. Van Gogh literally disintegrates, grimacing at his own reflection in the mirror, pulling at himself in a representation of mental pressure and breakdown which mimics the actions of small children. But it is intensified; that is to say, this action reverses the sequence by which the human body is initially incorporated, made into a bodily whole through the integration of all parts into a single gestalt, the imaged body providing a psychical boundary within which a self can be located and recognized. The fact that the scene takes place before a mirror invites reference to Jacques Lacan's thesis on the formation of the subject through the "mirror stage."[37] Arguing that the human subject is not born with a sense of self or a given identity, psychoanalysis locates key stages or phases through which the "little omelette," as Lacan describes the human infant, gradually develops into an "I"/ego. The mirror is a metaphor for the fact that we can only achieve sufficient psychic unity to emerge as an ego, an "I," by internalizing an externally generated image. The image in the mirror provides a figuration of bodily unity with which we identify. Thus the sense of self comes from outside as a physical gestalt through which is realized a psychic unity. This process takes place in early childhood, at the age of six to eighteen months, but it gives rise to a mode of understanding which Lacan calls the Imaginary, which is characterized by the process of identification and misrecognition. The Imaginary, however, remains a structuring element in human subjectivity even though the subject must enter the Symbolic and accept the law of the culture, taking its place as a man or woman and in language.

Minnelli's film traces the struggle of an individual vis-à-vis society, which is at once a mythic struggle between the masculine subject and the law of the Father (Church, actual Father, Society). Art provides a temporary escape through nostalgic fantasy, which Minnelli represents as the momentary release of imagination in the process of subjective decomposition. The climax of the film turns on the collapse of all strategies for subjective integration. Art thereby appears as only a temporary mirror for Van Gogh, which promised a unity in the image of the artist. The breakdown at the personal level of friendship and professional companionship with Gauguin is exacerbated by the absolute denigration of his artistic project through the debates about realism and abstraction. This is dramatized, or shall I say, this crisis is figured and given a bodily form on screen for the viewers, functioning as an imaginary identification for them, by means of the final fight between Van Gogh and Gauguin. The destruction of Van Gogh—his castration and death as a viable subject—is visualized through an amazing crisis which seems registered on the body of the film itself. At one point the film/time stands still. The aggressive gaze of Gauguin is internalized and turned against Van Gogh by himself as the man and his mirror image confront each other in hatred and hostility. And then the mirror goes void. The empty mirror (with a trace of Van Gogh's painting of the *Night café* in the background) remains on screen, and for six long seconds the film seems to stop. There is silence until a bloodcurdling scream is heard and a blood-stained figure flashes across the mirror. The combination and sequencing of the petrifying gaze of Gauguin, the Father who assimilates Art to himself, the encounter, or rather replay of the mirror phase, the visual void, the acoustic silence, the screech, and finally the blood, constitute a vivid figuration of the sacrificial drama of masculinity submitting to castration. Yet these elements are, as it were, running against the normal temporal sequence. The time of the subject is running backwards, unravelling the subject which these moments—the imaginary and the symbolic—typically constitute. Van Gogh is thus symbolically castrated as a man and as an artist. Since masculinity figures itself as rationality, its opposites are Woman and Madness—to which Van Gogh is now consigned as hysterical, wounded, invalided and mentally disabled. Viewer identification is detached at the point at which the mirror empties and Van Gogh's image goes off screen, prefaced by a horrific image of the grotesque and the bestial.

The last fifteen minutes of the film taking us to Saint-Rémy, Auvers and the wheatfield, now function as a coda. They comfort the viewer with several alibis. One is mythical: it's not a bad death in the sunshine and the wheatfields, because it is a natural death, part of the cycle of seasons (reprise of the *Reaper*). Another alibi is theological: the Crucifixion motif, the artist struggles and gives his life that others may enjoy his art. Hence the screen filled with the paintings, a comforting surrogate for the artist whose murder the film has enacted and the viewer is asked to sanction.

Van Gogh did not, however, die of the myth. His botched suicide attempt succeeded only because Dr Gachet failed to get him adequate medical attention. Van Gogh was a Ronald Reagan, shot in the chest, and not Pope John Paul or John Lennon with a life-threatening stomach wound. But the myth of Van Gogh is a deadly one which makes us all collaborators with capitalism's purposes. Art has become a hugely valuable commodity, and the artist's death a component of the manufacture of its value. The Van Gogh story tells us that it is in the nature of the artist to struggle, suffer and often die by his own hand. But now the market is changing, its needs and hence alibis are different. This may be also determined by the fact that an increasing number of the leading buyers of modern art come from Japan, where the cultural mythologies of sacrifice have different formations, and where western Christian theology is less profoundly rooted in a popular or élite imaginary. Many contemporary artists are extremely rich and well integrated. The historical conjuncture of modernism's legends of the artist and its economic conditions of entrepreneurial venture capitalism have been overtaken by post-Modernist economics and its culture. *Lust for life* was a film of its moment, and it is not coincidental that it achieved such popularity, like Van Gogh himself, in the 1950s. Its release coincided with the contemporary death/suicide of Jackson Pollock and the high point of Abstract Expressionism's fame as the culmination of modernism and the final avant-garde.

It is therefore unsurprising that the films made about Van Gogh for 1990 seem tame, repetitious or overblown in comparison with the ambition and the dramatic and symbolic cogency of Minnelli's film from the 1950s. *Lust for life* deserves scrupulous analysis precisely because it crystallized the myth which it took as its resource, while at the same time exposing what the myth achieves. No film was less aptly named. The Van Gogh myth is about Death. The Van Gogh myth refutes any discourse on sexuality, desire, and the complexities of subject formation within regimes of sexual difference. Minnelli's film spoke of death, and revealed modern art to be a deadly contest. Most of all, it showed that Van Gogh was culturally expendable, an artist of the past, locked into Victorian sentimentality and a naïve notion of realism, which was being overtaken by modernist concepts of art-making he never fully

grasped. Yet the chance coincidence of an unhappy life with deeper imperatives of Western culture and society rendered his story ideologically
significant. Van Gogh, like the African saluting the tricolour of imperial
France, became material for myth. Appropriated, emptied and reinvested,
the very spontaneity and naïveté, everything that refutes his place in modernism's calculated strategies of picture-making, became the key elements to
accomplish the *naturalization* of his place as the paradigmatic modern artist,
a depoliticization which is the signature of myth.

notes

1 Gertjan Zuilhof, "The Van Gogh films. A critical sketch of a difficult genre" (translated by Beth O'Brien), *Vincent van Gogh on film and video. A review*, Amsterdam 1990, p. 33.

2 See my study, "Artists, mythologies and media: Genius, madness and art history," *Screen* 1980, vol. 21, no. 3; reprinted P. Hayward (ed.), *Picture this. Media representations of visual art and artists, London, John Libbey 1988.*

3 Roland Barthes, "Myth today," *Mythologies* (1957) London, Jonathan Cape 1972, p. 142.

4 Ibid., p. 118. Comments in square brackets are by the author of this article.

5 Ibid., p. 129; this author's italics.

6 See C. Zemel, The Formation of a Legend: Van Gogh Criticism 1890–1920, Ann Arbor: UMI Press, 1980.

7 The catalogues for the exhibitions of paintings and drawings held in Amsterdam and Otterlo in 1990 were exemplary in this respect.

8 C. MacCabe, "Realism and the cinema. Notes on some Brechtian theses," *Screen* 1974, vol. 15, no. 2, pp. 7–27.

9 G. Davies, "Teaching about narrative," *Screen Education*, 1978/9 no. 29, p. 59.

10 Vincente Minnelli, *I remember it well*, New York, Doubleday & Co. 1974, p. 309.

11 Ibid.

12 The book I am writing at present, *The cities and countries of Modernism. The case against Van Gogh*, London, Thames and Hudson, will contain a full documenta-tion and analysis of the manufacture of Van Gogh's reputation in the cultural politics of the twentieth century.

13 T. J. Clark, "On the social history of art," in *Image of the people*, London, Thames and Hudson 1974, p. 13.

14 Minnelli, op. cit., p. 298.

15 For further documentation of this process, see my forthcoming book, *The cities and countries of modernism. The case against Van Gogh*, London, Thames and

Hudson; see also my study "Artists, media and madness ..." in *Screen* 1980, vol. 21, no. 3. I use the form "Van Gogh" to distinguish between the historical character Vincent van Gogh and the persona manufactured through art-historical writings, critical interpretations, exhibitions and other media products. "Van Gogh" is the effect of both the works produced by the artist Van Gogh and the subsequent readings of them in specific discursive practices. The usage derives from *auteur* theory developed in film criticism. See J. Caughie (ed.), *Theories of authorship*, London Routledge 1981.

16   M. Schapiro, "On a painting by Van Gogh. Crows in the wheatfield," *View. The modern magazine*, vol. 7, no. 1, 1946, pp. 9–14, reprinted in B. Welsh-Ovcharov 1974, pp. 158, 161.

17   The first major exhibition to do this was organized by A. H. Barr at the Museum of Modern Art in 1936.

18   It is impossible not to recall Clement Greenberg's caustic comment on the avantgarde being tied to the bourgeisie by an umbilical cord of gold. "Avant-garde and kitsch", in *Art & Culture*, Boston, Beacon Press 1961, p. 38.

19   On the widespread media coverage of these incidents, see Russell Lynes, *Good old Modern. An initimate portrait of the Museum of Modern Art*, New York, Atheneum Press 1973, p. 135. Lynes comments that by the time the MOMA's exhibition of Van Gogh opened, in 1935, "every suburban housewife knew about Van Gogh's ear." Ibid.

20   C. Merz, *An examination of biography in film and television*, University of East Anglia, Ph. D. 1981; cited in *Screen* 1983, vol. 24, no. 405, p. 146.

21   The notion derives from the work of Julia Kristeva, *The powers of horror. An essay on abjection*, translated by Leon Roudiez, New York, Columbia University Press 1982. Kristeva writes: "There looms, within abjection, one of those violent, dark revolts of being, directed against a threat that seems to emanate from an exorbitant outside or inside, ejected beyond the scope of the possible, the tolerable, the thinkable. It lies there quite close but cannot be assimilated." p. 1.

22   G. Pollock, "Feminism and Modernism" in R. Parker and G. Pollock, *Framing feminism*, London, Pandora Press 1987, pp. 85–87.

23   Laura Mulvey, "Afterthoughts on visual pleasure ...," *Framework* 1981, vol. 15/16/17 p. 14.

24   "Before Corwen's script was delivered, I was doing research on my own, so that I could approach the picture with an educated eye. Van Gogh's five volumes of letters to his brother Theo were of enormous help. I pored over them ...," Minnelli, op. cit., p. 301.

25   "It is well to remember that a picture—before being a battle horse, a nude woman, or some anecdote—is essentially a plane surface covered with colors assembled in a certain order," Maurice Denis, "Définition de néo-traditionalisme," *Art et*

critique Paris 23, 30 August 1890, reprinted in Maurice Denis, *Théories 1890–1910*, Paris Rouart et Watelin 1920; cited in H. Chipp, *Theories of modern art*, University of California Press 1968, p. 94.

26 In 1934, the Art Institute of Chicago's *Song of the lark* (1884), by Jules Breton, was voted "America's most popular painting." As soon as the *Century of Progress* exhibition was over, however, the museum's director had the work put in storage, calling the exhibition of the picture a moment of weakness and an exhibition of America's poor taste. See Hollister Sturges, *Jules Breton and the French rural tradition*, Omaha, Nebraska, Jocelyn Art Museum 1983, p. 95.

27 *Congressional Record* 81st Congress 1st Session (1949) p. 11584, cited in J. De Hart Matthews, "Art and politics in Cold War America," *American Historical Review* 1976, vol. 81, no. 4, p. 772.

28 Ibid.

29 A. H. Barr, "Is Modern Art Communistic?" *New York Times Magazine* 1950, September 17, section 2.

30 Cited in Russell Lynes, *Good old Modern. An intimate portrait of the Museum of Modern Art*, New York, Atheneum press 1973, p. 350.

31 This is perhaps the point of sharpest contrast with Robert Altman's *Vincent and Theo*, 1990, which juxtaposes the two brothers and increasingly has to render Van Gogh/Tim Roth an ominous silent presence.

32 T. Elsaesser, "Vincente Minnelli," *Brighton Film Review* 1972, p. 20; also in R. Altman, *Genre The Musical*, London, British Film Institute 1982.

33 Andreas Huyssen, *After the Great Divide. Modernism, mass culture and postmodernism*, London, MacMillan 1986.

34 The film was made in cinemascope, which is singularly unsuitable in its ratios to represent the shapes of Van Gogh's paintings. Minnelli overcame this problem by using a moving camera panning over the paintings. The device can be explained from a technical point of view, but its effects have to be assessed semiotically.

35 E. Zola, *Les oeuvres complétes. Emile Zola Mes Haines*, ed. M. LeBlond, Paris 1928, p. 24; Van Gogh read Zola's *Mes Haines* in 1879 (LT 139); see also LT 297, 355, 399; LR 38.

36 S. Freud, "Medusa's head," in P. Rieff, *Sexuality and the psychology of love*, New York, Collier 1963, p. 212.

37 J. Lacan, "The mirror stage as formative of the function of the I," *Ecrits. A selection*, translated by A. Sheridan, London, Tavistock Press 1977.

10

empire, identity and place: masculinities in greystoke: the legend of tarzan[1]

griselda pollock

prologue

THE PRE-TITLE SEQUENCE OF FERID Boughedir's documentary on twenty years of African cinema, *Caméra d'Afrique* (France, 1983) serves as the preamble to my analysis of the pre-title sequence of Hugh Hudson's *Greystoke: The Legend of Tarzan* (USA, 1984). I am interested in this film particularly because it dared to recycle in the 1980s "The Legend of Tarzan," arguably an irredeemably racist trope from the era of high imperialism derived from Edgar Rice Burroughs's eugenicist novel *Tarzan of the Apes* (1912) which had inspired a whole series of egregiously racist films during the 1930s, most famously starring Johny Weissmuller in the 1950s. Not to frame this film by the politics of representation in African cinema would be to compound the way the film *Greystoke* displaces the overt racism of its heavily colonial reference texts by effecting an almost more disturbing erasure of Africans. What I shall want to suggest is that the film is a critical project insofar as it distances us from the "old order" variously embodied in a number of key male characters. The distancing takes place through separating the Tarzan figure off from the colonial social Darwinist world of its origins, representing him not as its ultimate expression but as a divided and contradicted figure seeking to find his own integrity as a man in the aftermath of its decline. This Tarzan is closer to the topic of other films which took on the theme of children found in the wild, or brought up separated from human society, such as *L'Enfant Sauvage* (Truffaut, France, 1969) and *The Enigma of Kasper Hauser* (Herzog, Germany, 1974). But the imaginary field of that extremely contemporary struggle for understanding humanity through its origins, heredity and environment is the appropriated spaces of a mythical Africa which is even less inhabited and less historical than that over which Johnny Weissmuller's inarticulate muscle-bound Tarzan lorded it. The very gesture that updates "Tarzan" as a hero for our times nonetheless exposes a specifically *post*-colonial racism that can only be truly grasped when confronted with the speaking discourse of Africans on the politics of cinema itself. Contrary to authorial intentions claimed on its behalf, the film *Greystoke* realizes a specific relation between a representation of a masculine quest and the colonial imaginary which is as structural in the 1980s as in the early 1900s. It is this which qualifies the question of "man's search for identity" (Hugh Hudson speaking of his film) as a matter of a whiteness that is all the more telling for never imagining that it needed to be addressed.

Ferid Boughedir's film begins with an extract from another, from Med Hondo's *Les Bicots Négres*. That film opens with a procession of women and children across the landscape moving from left to right. On their heads they carry calabashes or modern aluminium buckets with equal grace. They pass by a bright yellow JCB and a large truck with a tank—for water or oil—on its back before joining a seated assembly of people of all ages, resting under the shade of a few trees in this dry, bright and used landscape. From this representation of both community and work, technology and craft, we cut to a half-length figure, placed against a background of huge film posters. Behind the man's head we can read the words *Sophia Loren—Technicolor—Anthony Quinn* in bold letters. The man, an African, speaks in French, directly addressing the audience: "You have come to see a film. In Africa we also love the cinema ... . But what does cinema signify to the people of

Africa, of the Third World?" In an ironically jovial discussion, the speaker implicates the presence of film and its exhibition technologies in Africa in relation to colonial penetration and economic exploitation of the continent. The cinema, originating in Europe and America, is historically a way of the First World being in and "worlding" Africa and defining Africa to Africans.[2] As he speaks about this equal industrial and ideological colonization the camera moves back to allow us a glimpse of a neighboring poster. It shows a woman in abbreviated skins for a costume. We read the words *Johnny Weiss* … and finally, the careful and primed spectator will notice the huge slashed blood red letters of the word *TARZAN*, glimpsed before a close-up of the African mouthing the word C-I-N-E-M-A.

This brief but telling scene poses the contradictions to be negotiated by a cinema generated in Africa, by African filmmakers, contesting their post-colonial fate of "being represented" or "being represented to" by Western cinema. They must thus both claim the technologies of production and critique the existing imperialist legends of Africa in order to represent themselves in their own vision and voice back to the First World. Africa has not only been economically exploited but the effect of the specific cultural representations of Africa that were part of the colonial project has been a profound crime of erasure, brilliantly exposed by Chinua Achebe in his reading of Joseph Conrad's novel of a colonial journey into Africa, titled *Heart of Darkness* (1905):

> Africa as setting and backdrop which eliminates the African as human factor. Africa as a metaphyisical battlefield devoid of all recognizable humanity, into which the wandering European enters at his peril. Of course, there is a preposterous and perverse kind of arrogance in thus reducing Africa to the role of props for the breakup of one petty European mind. But it is not even the point. The real question is the dehumanisation of Africa and Africans which this age-long attitude has fostered and continues to foster in the world.[3]

Action movies of the kind associated with heroic actors like Quinn supplemented by lusciously desirable and often distressed heroines played by Loren schematically stand for a regime of sexual difference in the cinema so precisely characterized by Laura Mulvey—the masculine subject as figure in the landscape, the narrative's agent in space and time: the woman as icon and object of gaze, possession and punishment.[4] Beyond both figure and icon is the setting, the landscape that is their European field of action and never imagined as an already inhabited and worlded space occupied by competing communities and cultures. Contrast this formula with the recurring trope of African cinema: women who walk across the landscape, inhabited but not plundered, used but not mastered. In the procession that opens Med Hondo's film, cited above, the women turn to look at the camera which then films them looking back, not imprisoned in its frames but questioning its presumptive presence in their place. But while the unnamed Loren/Quinn movie in Technicolor is clearly the telling emblem of Hollywood cinema where man/woman reads also as an implicit colonial gesture, the oblique reference to Tarzan is also powerfully significant of what is hard for the African to enunciate: the horrific mis-representation of Africa coded in the Rice Burroughs novel and its offshoot Tarzan movies that is at once a total *worlding* and appropriation of Africa in cinematic representation for the West's imaginary as its field of adventure and self-discovery. Significant too is the fact that the only image allowed in this sequence is that of Maureen O'Sullivan as Jane, costumed in total defiance of traditional African dress—which is woven cotton, richly dyed and patterned and worn in skin-protecting full length swathes.[5] Ragged and partial covering with wild animal skins is eloquent of the West's denial of African technology and craft production let alone trade while at the same time it makes the body thus clothed bespeak the masculine subject of which Jane is always a complementary sign, Tarzan, man-the-hunter. It also casts the whole mis-en-scène and thus Africa itself back into pre-history.[6] The visible sign of that mytheme which Tarzan signified from Rice Burroughs to the long series of Hollywood B movies is the body of woman. It is her image and the sexual ideology that it "embodies" that is the antithesis to the speaking African subject, himself framed by a completely different representation of African femininity and the land of Africa which preceded his address to the audience. The worlding of Africa thus also occurs through this inscription onto its landscape, emptied of all specific and local social and kinship systems, but over-inscribed with a Western regime of sexual difference. In this movement the countries and people of Africa disappear behind the mythic signifier of [European] Woman. Africa thus both ceases to be a social and cultural entity while it is also appropriated as a "virgin territory" and "dark continent," that is, it is feminized—awaiting the white man's mastery and determination.[7]

time and the other

It would be possible to read *Greystoke* as a self-conscious return to the myth whose aim is to distance itself from the gross colonial ideology of the original in order to draw out from the story other general themes, universal issues around the question of man's identity.

> It's the *themes* that interest me. Man's origin and continuous search for that origin. The haphazard nature of our birth. Tarzan-Clayton is born into what we call a noble family. But he doesn't live in that environment, he lives in an environment in which he has to struggle like the man in the street has to struggle. The place he's born into is no different from being born in Notting Hill Gate or the South Bronx—a ghetto.[8] And he's got to fight to survive.
>
> And then the white man comes in, and in his arrogance, D'Arnot … makes the great error of saying "You don't belong here" …. And so he persuades him, he corrupts him, he's like the serpent in the Garden of Eden. And Tarzan is brought back from the jungle and plonked down in the "civilized world." And what happens is very tragic really. For he's very intelligent, very sensitive, and he realizes that it's not the place for him. And the penality he pays for not conforming… is that his surrogate ape father is killed. And that finally drives him back to the jungle. The real power of the story is that he won't conform, he's his own man. He's not going to be put into a mold and told to obey the rules. Same as the characters in *Chariots*, in fact.[9]

What is interesting about this film is the ways in which it exceeds, undermines and contradicts the statements made on its behalf by those, like the director, who obviously had a clear conception of the film's project and intended meanings.[10] The film received much more critical attention in the French press than in Britain or America and was treated as an auteur film. These interviews with Hugh Hudson reveal a director with a developed literary conception of the meanings carried by his story. Warner Brothers, the producers, may have anticipated an action picture in the mold of *Raiders of the Lost Ark* (Spielberg, USA, 1981). What they got was a meticulous costume drama with more affinity with Truffaut's philosophical reconstruction of Jean Itard's experiment with Victor, the wild boy of Aveyron, in *L'Enfant*

Sauvage: asking what makes humans human—language, morality or something innate? Can a child brought up apart from human society ever be fully socialized? Is there human nature or is being human by definition the process of socialization via language? How important is the family to the structures of humanity? Where does the animal end with homo sapiens and the specifically human begin? Is the issue language and what relation is there between language and sexuality? What is the price of becoming human? Is the animal the name of the freedom humans fantasize for themselves when they contemplate the cost of human socialization?

The quotation above from Hudson is exemplary of such concerns, the question of individuality and social conformity, the Oedipal issues around the family and identity, and questions of paradise and the "castration" of civilization through language:

> *Cinematographe*: Once he has left paradise, he can never return?
> *Hugh Hudson*: It's finished. Once one learns language, there is no more paradise. D'Arnot is the serpent in the Garden of Eden. From the moment Tarzan who was in a state of pure innocence, receives words, he is lost. On the one hand he cannot do anything without language. It is the ambiguity of history: D'Arnot comes and gives Tarzan the apple. Once the apple is bitten, it is the end, but it is also the beginning. It is knowledge and all that comes with knowledge. The problem of identity. The dilemma of Tarzan is that of all men. We are in a terrible void. No one has roots any more. We do not know how to communicate, everything has become electronic .... At the end, Tarzan appears to be saying to the world: "I am like you, I do not know anymore what to do.... I am a lost soul. I acquired knowledge and self-consciousness and I kept my instincts and I do not know what to do. The serpent appeared in my garden and now, I am lost."[11]

These statements reveal a confusion between a general theme—*man* and *his* search for origins and identity,[12] and a superficial sociological application which turns out to be as uncritically if more disguisedly racist as the overtly imperialist story by Rice Burroughs of which the film presents itself as an updated revision. In both cases the socioeconomic experience and environment of bourgeois white men's cultural and social others become an imaginary landscape in which the white men can mythically explore their quite specific dilemmas around identity while misrecognizing their own cultural specificity through the naturalization process achieved by the mytheme of white man in the "jungle" or "paradise"—in fact another's landscape which is projected back in time as the mythic pre-history or sub-history of the West. The film raises the issues, therefore, of empire, identity and place.[13]

In Eurocentric Western culture such questions get posed exclusively in the masculine and through a masculinity that is "white under erasure" by virtue of being signified through its relation to an equally universalized white under erasure feminine other. In the new version, *Greystoke*, the feminine other is almost displaced by the opposition: the human versus the animal. Man-the-hunter and his embodied prey, woman, displacing Africa itself which is the trope of the Rice Burroughs novels, is updated by the existential self-exploration of the masculine subject. This involves a reversed journey to the heart of [Western] "civilization" accompanied by scientists and soldiers across a series of spaces which equally dramatize masculine mastery—not over woman, but over his own nature projected onto a landscape and embodied in the animal. Through the application of contemporary primatology and its studies of "man's nearest relatives," the primates become an embodiment of "human nature" in its wild, or pre- or sub-social state. Insofar as Africa is the site of Tarzan's "jungle paradise" and his apes, i.e., man in a primal habitat, the Africans can only be themselves erased or worse, elided with this base, wild, uncivilized, evolutionarily lower pre-human nature. This happens in *Greystoke* not through colonial application of social Darwinism as in Rice Burroughs' novel, but through a liberal intent to avoid social specificity and dramatize only the "themes." The inattention derives from the imperialism of Western universalism.

For those unfamiliar with this film a short synopsis is in order at this point. The film tells the story of the accident by which the infant son, "Johnnie" [Tarzan figure], of Scottish nobleman Lord John Clayton and his wife Lady Alice, themselves shipwrecked on the coast of Africa, comes to live among a community of apes—a cross between chimps and gorillas—in equatorial West Africa. He is discovered by a survivor of a scientific mission from the British Museum, a Belgian, Capitaine Phillippe D'Arnot. D'Arnot is nursed back to life by Tarzan/Johnnie after being wounded and pursued by the African people living in the area who are represented as almost without language and with the implication of cannibalism. D'Arnot teaches his wild man to shave, to speak (French and English), to experience via the mirror of imagery his difference from the animals around him and to understand the concept of the Oedipal family and descent. There is no space for comparison with back-skinned humans—the opposition is white/black: human/ape. "When did you last see a white ape?" asks D'Arnot. The presence of hairless but dark-skinned tool-making and tool-using, speaking bipeds—i.e., other humans in the same forest—is simply erased. They exist only as dangerous aliens in their own world. Taken back to the ancestral estate in Scotland, Greystoke, Johnnie (he is never called Tarzan in this film except in the titles when Christopher Lambert is introduced as *John Clayton, Tarzan, Lord of the Apes*) is claimed by his grandfather, the aging Earl of Greystoke (Ralph Richardson). He becomes involved with his grandfather's ward, a young American woman called Jane (Andie McDowell) who teaches him to dance and conjugate Latin verbs. Granddad dies. Jane and Johnnie have sex and become engaged.[14] The climax of the movie takes place in the Natural History Museum when "Johnnie," now Earl of Greystoke, opens a new gallery dedicated to the principles of Charles Darwin, full of stuffed and mutilated animals—a scene of concentrated death and destruction which overpowers the social (human?) veneer the Earl has acquired, driving him outside to a laboratory in which he discovers in a cage his "ape-father," the silverback known as Greybeard. Liberating him, they romp together into Kensington Gardens where the chief scientist Sir Evelyn Blount (John Wells) orders the shooting of the escaped gorilla. In a cry of rage and despair, "Johnnie" cradles the dead creature wailing to the assembled onlookers, "Il est mon pére," and then "He was my father." In the chaos of grief and confusion following this episode Johnnie decides he must "go back." His decision is supported by Jane who says "I want him to be whole" and the film returns from the darkened mansion of death and desolation in Scotland to the lush vegetation of equatorial West African. There, clothed in colonial whites, D'Arnot and Jane painfully bid farewell to the half-naked Johnnie who leaps and bounds and hoots his way back to his gorilla community, while the soundtrack carries D'Arnot's voice saying that he hopes one day the world will turn to make it possible for the two of them, Jane and Johnnie, to be together in this place.

This "difficult" ending reveals the distance between the Weissmuller/ O'Sullivan Tarzan movies and *Greystoke*. Clad somewhat skimpily, the Jane of the 1930s found no problem being the little housewife in Tarzan's inventively mechanized jungle home just upriver from the local trading post. Everything in *Greystoke* leads to the point at which Africa cannot be the site of a heterosexual union of Europeans "gone native." Its spaces are not colonized territories and appear hardly inhabited at all; they signify in fact temporally—and the time-scale is the history of the masculine subject. (This is underlined in Hudson's comments above in which the "jungle" is a Garden of Eden and there is a male serpent which alone traduces the innocent Adam in a garden completely without Eve.)

The landscape carries the connotations of the different temporalities and registers of the masculine subject caught between maternal and paternal regimes of identification and subjectivity acquired only through the loss and repression of a part of the subject's own history. In order to explain why the film ends with a spatial return that is a temporal regression to masculine narcissism, I shall have to start at the beginning.

The film's opening sets up its two key spaces, "equatorial West Africa" and "Scotland" (see Chart 1) and it would be easy to identify them as representations of a founding binary of Western culture: nature (Africa)/Culture (Britain—itself represented by aristocratic rural Scotland and metropolitan scientific London.) In fact this thematic, which is present, is a blind. It is profoundly reconfigured through the actual construction of the the film's rhyming use of place and articulation of identity across its spaces. Before proceeding to demonstrate this, however, it is first necessary to consider how marginal is the opposition man/woman as a variant of the binary nature/culture. What is really significant about this version of the Tarzan story is peripheral position of "Jane." The film is not articulated through the relation of Tarzan to a feminine other.[15] Its treatment of masculinity is interesting precisely because it foregrounds what the final heterosexual union veils—the complex negotiations with competing masculine others and the continuing power of the realm of the pre-Oedipal mother.

This film reworks the Tarzan legend precisely in its displaced relation to the feminine. It marks its difference from the Loren/Quinn, or O'Sullivan/Weissmuller, Me Jane–You Tarzan model precisely by downgrading the function of Jane as that which lures Tarzan from his animal life and from Africa.[16] She is not the object of desire, the prize, the possession of which will constitute the masculine subject's wholeness or self-mastery. Jane is not the figure of desire on which hinges Tarzan's pre-history in the world of animals and his emergence into humanity, as in the book. The ramification of this shift puts "Tarzan" in a different frame and suggests that we have to ask of this film: what status does the figure of Tarzan almost without Jane have in such a radical reworking of the legend?[17] I would suggest that the film becomes a specific dramatization of a contemporary masculinity and its crises in which Hudson's notions of "man's search for his origins" and the "struggle for survival" in "an environment" in order to be his own man actually indexes to more than banal existentialism and social Darwinism. It bespeaks a fantasy of masculine narcissism in which the phallus is imagined to be possessable. This involves a series of complex imaginary moves in relation to the maternal body and the genealogy of the father but without Woman (the symbolic representation of the phallus which the masculine subject will in fact pretend to repossess, hence the impossibility of a sustained adult sexual union).

Laura Mulvey has pointed out in her analysis of the divided hero in some Westerns (her case study was *The Man Who Shot Liberty Valance*) that certain kinds of action films which structurally depend upon an emblematic use of landscape, figure and housing (as homestead, salon, church or town) play to a phallic narcissism in which one fantasy of the male subject receives embodiment in the form of a hero who resists submission to the castrating law of the father, forgoes love and never enters domesticity or social position. John Wayne in the finale of John Ford's *The Searchers* (1956) provides a classic example of this excess of masculine narcissism which does not enter the home as the symbolic site of castration.[18] In *The Man who Shot Liberty Valance*, the story is told in flashback by Ranse Stoddart (James Stewart) who is now a married man and respected Senator (society, law, rule of the father, etc.). He recalls his rivalry for his wife Hallie with Tom Donniphon (John Wayne) who in fact does kill the rampaging criminal Liberty Valance while making it appear that Ranse was the hero. Tom never marries and remains an outsider to society. He dies and the film's story is occasioned by the mourning at his funeral.

> This narrative structure is based on an opposition between two irreconcilables. The two paths cannot cross. On one side there is the encapsulation of power, phallic attributes, in an individual who has to bow himself out of

history. On the other, an individual impotence rewarded by political and financial power, which in the long run, in fact, becomes history. Here the function of "marriage" is as crucial as it is in the folk tale. It plays the same part in creating narrative resolution, but is even more important in that "marriage" is an integral attribute of the upholder of the law. In this sense Hallie's choice between the two men is predetermined. Hallie equals princess equals Oedipal resolution rewarded, equals repression of narcissistic sexuality in marriage.[19]

The interest of *Greystoke: The Legend of Tarzan* lies in the implicit presence of this structure of the narcissistic hero. It works to install Johnnie, not as Tarzan, the action hero, master of the jungle, Lord of the Apes, but as a regressing idealization of this masculine narcissism who cannot submit to the law of society, sexuality and marriage. The figure thus constructed has extremely contemporary ramifications as a combination of sundry politics of wholeness and escapist organic restoration of an ideal, safe world: environmentalism, animal rights and liberal individualism which were both the product of Thatcherism and its liberal but muted and impotent reaction.

With the death of the old order, represented as a paternalist aristocracy by the aged Earl (Ralph Richardson), who owns all he surveys (a landscape of equal depopulation figured only by animals he trains and rides), and the emergence of the new bureaucratic and scientific order represented by Sir Evelyn Blount (John Wells), who lords it over a mausoleum of dead and dissected animals, there seems to be no place to be "whole," as if, by stretching the analogy, the current social and ideological order is too constricting or impossible for the realization of a young self-seeking but responsible masculinity. The son revolts against rather than contests for the father's mastery. Unlike *The Mosquito Coast* or even *Crocodile Dundee*, which have important resonances with this legendary material, the opposition is never between urban jungle where people are the problem and another simpler way of life, a kind of "back to basics," however complex and dangerous it turns out to be. *Greystoke* is not constructed on that axis.

There are, therefore, two threads to track through the film from its significant opening. The first is the paradoxical position of Johnnie as a negated Tarzan, as a figure who defies castration and exits from the symbolic—which can be traced through the application of structural analysis of the narrative as myth. The second is the extended array of masculinities represented in the film from which the one that is desired but remains impossible is retrieved by the final scene with Johnnie reversing the temporal sequence of his accession to human subjectivity—language, family and sexuality—and escaping back into the dense green womb of a primordial Africa where lie the bones of both his mothers. (Hudson describe his opening as "the jungle—the Earth, Paradise, Mother Earth …")[20]

in the beginning . . . .

In an interview on the release of the film in 1984, Hugh Hudson complained bitterly that his artistic conception of the film as a whole had to be sacrificed to the necessities of exhibition programming. Thus a considerable amount of the film had to be edited down to allow more playing times per day at the cinema. The video release of *Greystoke* restored the film to Hudson's original full-length cut. This includes a long pre-title and title sequence, which, with the final scene, will be the topic of this short paper.[21]

The film opens by juxtaposing two tableaux.

The first scene is indicated by a title: Equatorial West Africa, 1885. Despite the specific and loaded dating, putting the action right in the middle of what is called "The Scramble for Africa," the scene we see is, in effect, the beginning of the world. Coded by a huge panoramic shot of an uninhabited landscape (compare the opening of *The Last of the Mohicans*), we see the world before time.[22] A volcano threatens and a streak of lurid red snakes across the horizon. Birds call as we hear the rumble of thunder. Cut to a high crane shot of a single ape, locked in the dense greenery, raising and beating a huge stick—in a manner reminiscent of the great scene of discovering tool use in Kubrick's *2001* as well as true to National Geographic Natural History Films showing recent research on chimp behavior and their use of clubs as threatening gestures.[23] Visually, acoustically and by action, this scene defies its dating to suggest a primordial moment, a genesis, Africa as the place before time, before history, a space on which time and history are not yet inscribed.

There is, however, a population of primates. Through modern understanding of their behavior and assumed hierarchies, which appear to mirror some aspects of Western ideology, there emerges the possibility of narrative, which does imply time and history. Narrative is precipitated by an event that

Chart I

LOCATION	SOUND	TITLES	ACTANTS	EVENTS	MYTHEME
PANORAMAS volcano and jungle river, waterfall precipice	bird song	Equatorial West Africa 1885	none	none	before time Eden Africa
close shots of jungle scenes	thunder animal noises	....	single male ape group females & babies	Storm Natural Disaster	Male Violence
chase of mother and infant	distress animal noises Kala's cry grief	....	Greybeard (F)1 Kala (M)1 dead infant 1	chase of mother and infant	Mother 1 - **Family 1 -** **Death**
PANORAMAS L/S mansion in landscape, ploughed field sunshine on house	Elgar's First Symphony	Scotland Ten Months Earlier	none	none	History Tradition Europe Civilization Time
M/S mansion in grounds	music	Warner Bros.	none	none	Nature Controlled
C/S mansion	music	Greystoke Legend of Tarzan	none	none	Architecture Dynasty
C/S Woods and Parkland	men's voices geeing up horses conversation	credits	Earl in phaeton and his son on horseback racing	Father and Son competition & communication	Family Separated
House various interiors and exteriors rain	dialogue music thunder discord		Earl, son, Jane & Alice	departure of son & daughter-in-law	**Father -** **Family 2-** **Lack**

Chart I   *cont'd*

LOCATION	SOUND	TITLES	ACTANTS	EVENTS	MYTHEME
Coastline Shipwreck	discord	none	dead bodies Alice, Capt. Lord Clayton	Natural Disaster	Scotland in Africa Shipwreck
Interior Treehouse	Clayton's voiced over diary	none	Alice, Clayton Baby	Birth Death	**Family 2 + child + Family 2 - mother -**
Interior Treehouse baby cries	animal noises		Clayton (father) Greybeard (father) Alice (Dead Mother) Kala (Mother) Ape infant (dead) Human infant (alive)	Battle Clayton dies Kala takes Baby	Animal-Africa Human-Europe conflict *exchange* **Family 2 - Death Family 1 + (Hybrid)**

Chart II   **TARZAN CHILD AND DEATH**

AFRICA	*COAST/EDGE*	*SCOTLAND (IN AFRICA)*
Storm/Animal Violence = Death	Storm/Shipwreck = Birth Natural violence	Animal Violence = Death DEATH OF MOTHER 2 DEATH OF FATHER 2

CHILD

Human violence DEATH OF MOTHER 1		*SCOTLAND* DEATH OF [GRAND] FATHER 2 Human violence DEATH OF FATHER 1

can set the two in motion in this otherwise timeless space. The "event" is the anger and violence of the great silverback, Greybeard, who, maddened by the sudden storm that ravages the peace of this primordial state of timelessness, chases a young mother ape, Kala, with her tiny babe clinging desperately to her damp fur. She has to make a huge leap to escape Greybeard, and in doing so her baby falls to its death. History begins with loss—an image which manifests the latent structures of subjectivity itself and creates the

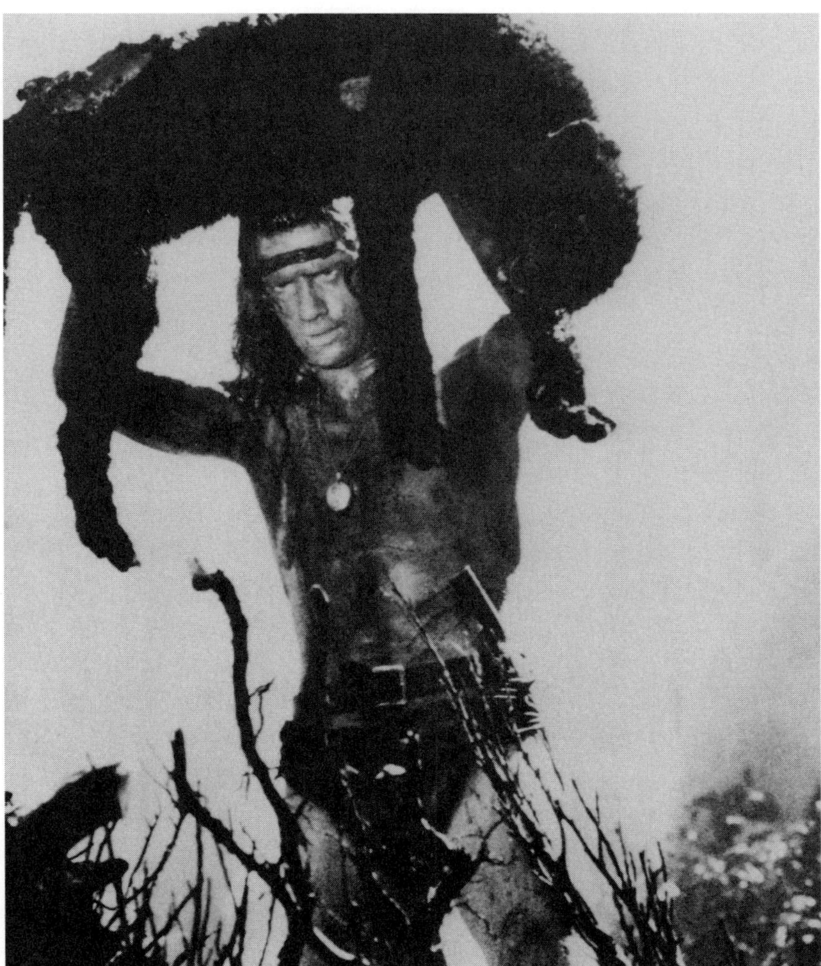

Figure 1.   Hugh Hudson, *Greystoke*, film still, Warner Bros., 1984.

very gap into which the human child will later be inserted. This creates a narrative function for the human child other than as hero.

The animals in this landscape introduce the notion of community, of family, of sexual difference and through this death, lack. They provide, unknowingly, all the necessary elements of narrative. What subverts stasis is a loss towards the resolution of which the narrative will be driven. The mourning ape mother's cry screams out across the landscape that becomes now also an acoustically marked environment that has moved beyond noise to a primary but powerful articulation that is communication and expression. The crescendo of vocalized grief is cut off as the film replaces this space with darkness.

A second panorama fills the screen, but not green and red. A gentle yellow morning sunlight bathes a huge mansion nestling in the rolling hills of cultivated landscape artisitically framed via Claude and Constable. The title printed over a rich brown ploughed field reads "Scotland Ten Months Earlier."[24] A cut and we see the grand mansion more dominating of its surroundings. This is the space of history and a way of controlling time: tradition, accumulated narratives and a succession of deaths and substitutions. There is control over the landscape, agriculture. Architecture protects the living beings from the excesses of nature which poured down and maddened the primates of the cinematically earlier and chronologically later scene just discussed.

Then action interrupts the stillness as a man on a horse and a man in a two-horse phaeton come thundering through the landscape racing each other as they urge on their galloping steeds. Humans and animals are juxtaposed in a landscape in ways in which control over the animals and the managed worked land become "landscape" laid out for mastery through possession rather than labor, mutually reinforcing the meaning of the men who control both animal and land.

The titles roll over this landscape to the sounds of Elgar's First Symphony with all its heavy overtones of British Empire and heritage. Where there was bird song and thunder, there is orchestral music (Edwardian English). Where there was animal hooting and growling, there is language (upper-class English). This dialogue that now comes across on the soundtrack reveals that the younger man, a son, "is going" and so is his wife Alice. Their destination is not stated, apart from it being "no place for her." It is on the one hand, "over there," the other place, the destination since the fifteenth century of Western man's imaginary tropical journey.[25] But, on the other, the viewer will quickly assume that "there" is the place we have just been, ten months later! The other space is evoked within this landscape, introducing the film's problematic not as alternating spaces of difference, but interpenetrated spaces.

Departure scenes follow as the young couple take their leave for a journey to the Tropics. As they leave, it begins to rain and the music suddenly becomes disturbed—warning us as well as underlining the visual image of the elderly Earl's grave foreboding. He is left in solitary melancholy possession of the screen, behind a rain-washed pane of glass. A sudden dissonance jars across the scene on the music track.

It would be easy at this point to set these two opening scenes up as simply Nature/Culture. Undoubtedly they lend themselves to this and lean upon its possibility. But the film is more complexly inscribed around the question of time and relies on the relay between the two spaces rather than on their pure opposition. For what follows the setting in place of the Greystoke mansion is not entry into it, but rather a scene outside it, another kind of confrontation with nature and relations to animals which signifies measures of human control over the animal and masculine self-production in that relation to landscape as its setting. Film sets up for the viewer not only the sequence of scenes but a pattern of memory. This opening scene of the old Earl and his son will repeat with Johnnie/Tarzan in his father's place forging a link between the two masculinities via dynasty and identification that transcend the difference of the spaces, while the Earl's son will soon be found in another confrontation with animals which he loses at the cost of his life, a scene that his own son will re-enact victoriously to establish himself as the dominant male, Lord of the Apes in the same "African" space. Thus the opening two set-ups establish corresponding, if alternating, spaces of masculinity rather than any simple opposition of nature/culture a superficial reader might immediately mistake.

Music forms the bond which allows us to bridge space. The next scene is a shipwreck off the coast of Africa, with the same dissonant notes playing across the scene of wreckage and death. Scotland is deposited in Africa where all of it will die save the baby that is to be born there. For Lady Alice Clayton gives birth to a son and dies of malaria shortly after his birth. Lord Clayton dies soon after in a struggle with Greybeard when the apes finally penetrate the tree house that he has built from the ship's wreckage. The silverback has been followed into the cabin by the grieving ape mother, still carrying the corpse of the infant who fell from her grasp during the mighty storm with which the film opened and with which the film has only just caught up fifteen minutes into the movie. She hears the human infant boy's cry and drops her dead baby to claim and comfort this human one. Thus Scotland represented as a family/dynasty experiences death and lack: the Earl has lost both his son and daughter-in-law. Scotland produces a child which is taken over to make good the loss in the animal family of Africa which was the narrative precipitating event of the first scene—the beginning of the world, of time and of the story.

The coincidence of Africa's loss (family 1 –) with Scotland's gain (family 2 +) inverts to produce a loss for Scotland which becomes *family 2 –* while Africa becomes *family 1 +*.

The child—the Tarzan figure—thus will function as a token that circulates between two spaces which it not only relates to each other but in some way incorporates as the problematic of identity. His meaning is loss and restitution for others. The child/boy/man can move between the two spaces but at whatever pole he rests he will know only loss because the drama is established fundamentally not as Nature and Culture but Oedipally, that is the structuring framework is composed of two families, two systems. The loss which the first scene narrates produces a childless mother who can be restored to her motherhood only by creating another loss to a family signified fundamentally only as a male genealogy. Two families are put into conflict in a way which overdetermines the impossible identity of the child, whose narrative will in all its contingency narrate the predicament of the masculine subject per se forced to pass from a maternal space within which he experiences unity and later a fantasy of total omnipotence to the paternal law at the price of submission to the "castration" of language and the law of the Father.

The pre-title and title sequence suggest therefore not a simple nature/culture binary. The chief opposition which structures the narrative as it is set up here is between man versus nature and a "natural man"—an impossible neologism which Darwinism and Existentialism combined in Thatcherite Britain and Reaganite America alone might momentarily conceive. Tarzan is to be the figure at once at home with the animals in their unhistorical space, and yet belonging to a different order, humanity, yet not at home with its culturally specific and historical articulation in late-Victorian or 1980s Britain. As a hybrid of sorts, this figure must mediate and negotiate aspects of a male human dilemma about its own status. Nature (a feminized originary maternal space including an archaic father figure) could be inside him as the child raised in it, and he could represent man dominant in a natural habitat without being nature (i.e., the mother). The relation of this human figure to the nearest relatives among the animals, the communal and communicating apes, becomes the crucial siting of the story of a fantasy of escape from patriarchal into phallic masculinity, rather than the backdrop to the colonial project of the original Tarzan narrative which was the installation of an imperial masculinity.

I am forced into making this somewhat unusual distinction. Of course patriarchal masculinity is orchestrated around the phallus and is thus phallic. But in a culturally applied psychoanalytic reading of this film, I am suggesting that we can use the term phallic as in "the phallic phase," a period prior to the resolution of Oedipal complex and the submission to "castration" (to which masculinity must submit even if it is fantastically disavowed through the figure of the Woman as Other and lacking). The phallic phase involves fantasies by means of which the male child believes either that it can be all that the mother desires, i.e., the phallus, believes that the mother is phallic, as it were all-powerful, and believes through the state of primary narcissism that he has the phallus, i.e., is omnipotent. These fantasies are all highly defensive against the continuing drip of loss, separation and emptying out which is the trajectory of the subject en route for speaking sexed subjectivity. So I use the term patriarchal masculinity to refer to submission to the law, and phallic masculinity to signal the continuing pre-Odeipal regressive masculine fantasy, what Laura Mulvey calls Oedipal nostalgia, "an internal oscillation of desire, which lies dormant, waiting to be 'pleasured' in stories of this kind."[26]

Furthermore, I would suggest that rather than then placing Africa/Scotland as merely the specific form of the nature/culture opposition, we should read this juxtaposition for a series of rhymes about various states of nature and control over nature and the effects of violence, both natural—storms which lead to the death of a child and cause shipwrecks—and social—the maddened ape and the confrontation between man (Lord Clayton) and ape which lead to the former's death.

Africa/Nature/Timelessness/Family **Peace**
– Africa/Nature/Family Disordered **Storm** =[**birth**] **death**

Scotland/Managed Nature/History/Family **Peace**
– Scotland in Africa/Loss of Control/Family Extended **Storm** = **death** (**birth**)

From this initial setting up of the human child's origins in a displaced *Scotland in Africa* and its adoption by the animals and subsequent finding and relocation as *Africa in Scotland*, Tarzan becomes a hybrid figure in mythic discourse who can, however, only be an impossible solution to the lack experienced by both Africa and Scotland and figuratively by the narrative. The events which set the narrative in motion are doubled so that the loss to one is the gain of the other. While he restores Kala, the ape, to her motherhood, his existence also anticipates the restitution to the Earl of his lost son. Insofar as Scotland and Africa are imaginary settings for the playing out of questions of [?] Man's identity—an identity that masquerades as generically human but is specifically European—the narrative drive of depleted families and misplaced children, of loss and lack, will be played out across the body of Tarzan. He is not a hero, a master of the landscape, but a token of exchange that moves between contradictory poles of a doubled system that is narrative itself. This structural positioning of the main male character thus transgresses the position cinema has established for masculinity especially in its heroic narratives like the Western of which Tarzan stories are a kind of subgenre.

In this revision of the myth, Tarzan functions as a mediating figure, the trickster, that can, by "the accident of his childhood" experience both places, families, worlds which have been set up as not so much absolute oppositions with the implication of progression from one to the other, or mastery by the one over the other, but as poles of oscillation of desire which, nonetheless, imply a temporality—time before history and the time of tradition, which is hegemonic imperial and patriarchal history. They set the terms and parameters of his being, externalizing aspects of its possibility, being at the same time signifiers of his "nature," i.e., human nature. It is this term with its contradictory ideological burden rather than the pair nature/culture which this film seems to dramatize in a contemporary form. Is the nature of a man conflicted or a matter of oppositions that might have to be sublimated? Is the nature of a man a matter of a past or a future and how will the one be reconciled with the other? Can it be imaginarily enjoyed by its refusal? Faced with the decline of a political order premised on masculine dynasties and supplanted by science and technology and its apparatchiks, does masculine fantasy regress to boyhood stories with their servicing of those infantile fantasies of a phallic omnipotence? Does not the idea of wanting to be "whole" signify implicitly the refusal of the castration, the subject realized only in splitting, division and loss of the real to the symbolic?

The meaning of Tarzan in this film is set, therefore, by his entry into it as a child, which was Hudson's and Austin's specific reorganization of the original script. Such a beginning could merely suggest that the subsequent narrative will chronicle his development "to manhood"—the thematic of a kind of historical biopic. But that temporal drive is mediated by the other aspect of this entry as infant. For he is the desired but lost object of two incompatible family systems, two clans, two dynasties. The one in Africa and somehow outside time and thus beyond society turns the space of Africa into the figuration of one kind of pre-historic (and pre-Oedipal) community with a specific kind of egoistic individual realization within it; the other in Scotland makes that space signify the constraints and demands of social conformity, submission to history and to the law of the Father to whose place the endless line of male offspring of an aristocratic dynasty literally accede, each in turning bearing the same name, Earl of Greystoke, and having to bear the burden of that "place in society," whatever individual impulse may be. This is articulated in the chaotic scenes that precede the ending of the film when Johnnie has wept over the dead silverback calling him "my father." Sir Evelyn Blount argues that Johnnie must overcome the accident of his childhood and "take his place in society," confirming the social system by embodying the name, the tradition, the law of history. Johnnie's reply is that part of him is the Earl of Greystoke and part of him is *wild*. The term twists with different meanings: wild as in wild animal— *fauve* in French, or wild as in wild card, something that upsets the apple cart and throws the system out by its unexpected character. One could also read this as: part of me has acceded to the Symbolic and literally accepted the Name of the Father, masculinity as the temporary occupancy of the Father's place, while part of me remains a child, pre-symbolic, pre-Oedipal with fantasies of narcissistic omnipotence intact—not borrowing the place of the unattainable Paternal Phallus, but believing through the rituals of primate battles for dominance that I have the phallus, and I refuse to accept castration and your law. That is very wild, and it is usually only imagined in the *Wild* West.

In the Rice Burroughs original the function of growing up "wild" is to prove that the natural aristocracy or superiority of the white race—eugenicist heredity—will out whatever the environment. In *Greystoke*, that childhood is raised to a symbolic function as the permanent alternative to castration and symbolic masculinity. It is in the play of the two families, two identities, two possible places for his "manhood" which is set up by the film's spatial alternation between Africa and Scotland that raises the possibility for the film to stage the contradictions of masculinity. The film, like many a Western, thus opens the route to regression as if it is the final heroic affirmation of masculinity. Misrecognized as an existential choice of personal freedom and individual integrity, the figure of Tarzan as Johnnie reclaims the narcissistic dreams of phallic omnipotence by refusing to submit the law of the father and by winding the clock of subjective development backwards.

From the the point at which D'Arnot took on the task of teaching "Tarzan" language—significantly through a scene with a razor and a mirror "Johnnie" was on a journey towards socialization that would clothe him, marry him off and locate him in society. What he experiences in the course of this entry is sexuality and death—the castration against which he revolts. Significantly in the hysteria of his grief after the shooting of "Greybeard," Johnnie rides around the castle grounds whipping the horses before the carriage he is wildly driving through the night of rain (an interesting compounding of images of his father/grandfather racing horses and his silverback father going wild in a thunderstorm), shrieking "Mother—Father—Family" the words D'Arnot would chant to him to insist upon his humanity. The final scene of the film shows the grown man going back—"I'm going back" he declares when he comes into the castle after the horse driving scene just mentioned. (Note the same lack of specified destination as in the opening scene when Lord Clayton states to the Earl "I've decided to go.")

Back to a place is also back in time. The spatial journey offers us a literal level on which to graft the metaphoric rejection of the Symbolic. The end of the film's narrative is most ambiguous because is does not end where narrative should with heterosexual union. That is balked as he abandons language, and reclaims his hooting; abandons bipedalism to bound over the hillside; and leaves behind D'Arnot and Jane as the bereaved figures representing Mother—Father—Family as he reverses time and reclaims both his childhood and his utter omnipotence as Lord of the Apes, rather than as the "castrated" and therefore human Earl of Greystoke.

What of his sexuality now? The literal-minded viewer may legitimately worry that the film has not dealt with this aspect, now that he has been initiated by Jane. I do not think that the scriptwriters thought this through. But my reading of the film at the level of the fantasy that it is "pleasuring" might suggest this solution. Sexuality is a construct composed out of component drives that are only Oedipally focused on genital activity. Thus the film also offers the escape from sexuality as another effect, indeed, price, of the acquisition of subjectivity. Tarzan might simply be imagined to revert to the polymorphous perversity of infancy following Freud's sense that sexuality as we think it—genitally-focused pleasure—is a late construction of the component drives precipitated by language and organized by the castration complex. Unravel those and "sexuality" is also undone. Who needs it if one imagines one has or even is the phallus?

Theoretically, of course, no one has or ever is the phallus which is we are told merely a signifier—a means to organize meaning around lack. Its paradoxical capacity to signify power lies precisely in its inaccessibility as the nothing which stands, therefore, for the lost everything. I am using the imagery here to signify fantasies arising in the imaginary phase in which initial negotiations of the fate of being lacking operate unchecked by reality and by social convention. Thus the story of women being found to be castrated must be read as a later legend by means of which the lack that all subjects, masculine as well as feminine experience, is projected retrospectively by masculine subjects away from themselves. Thus they acquire masculinity Oedipally through the replacement of one fantasy—that they are the phallus or have it, infantile notions of omnipotence—by another, namely that by accepting the "castration" of the law they will accede to the Father's place, "assuming" a phallic position while never having it or being it through relations to sexual others male or female. I am suggesting that under certain historical circumstances the narcissistic fantasy based in and on the boy's own body and its phallic pleasures find expression in a range of cultural forms … Boys' Own Adventures, so to speak. This film, *Greystoke*, straddles two key moments in which this became culturally pervasive in the colonial west and yet which would appear to be in opposition: late Edwardian Imperialism and Thatcherite Modern Toryism. What intrigues me is the relation between that latter cultural and political context and the emergence of the possibility of using a trope from the former moment to articulate the dilemmas of the 1980s. Because of the impossible task the film was set, it could never be a box office hit: as a narrative it could achieve no resolution because the film literally ends by going backwards. If the film breaks down as a narrative, it is nonetheless available for a different kind of reading that comes closer to the way Freud would construct his case studies; a kind of layering of memory, fantasy and retrospectively imposed signifiers. This film can be read chapter by chapter, tableau by tableau, following the pattern of accumulating rhymes and repetitions. This produces an archaeological figuration of the fiction that is the subject in masculinity. The film text's structuring of the contradictions it posed and those it exposed make *Greystoke* an important site for examining the return of the masculine repressed as it were, and the relations between cultural stories, legends and myths and their continuing potential to stage culturally particular, politically specific yet psychically persistent dramas of the subject. What remains disturbing, however, for all the disruption of Oedipal narrativity, is that the condition for this dramatization is still the dehumanization of Africa. This is what makes the Tarzan legend ultimately and irredeemably a figure of a persistent colonial foundation to contemporary psychic structures.

notes

1 1984; dir. Hugh Hudson; prod. Warner Bros. Starring Christopher Lambert, Ian Holm, Ralph Richardson, James Fox, John Wells and Andie McDowell.

2 The term "worlding" derives from the work of Gayatri Spivak, especially "The Rani of Sirmur," *History and Theory*. 1985, vol. xxiv, no. 3, 247–272.

3   Chinua Achebe, "An Image of Africa," *Research in African Literatures*, 9:1, (1978): 9. See also Patrick Brantlinger, "Victorians and Africa: The Genealogy of the Myth of the Dark Continent" in *Race, Writing and Difference*, ed. Henry L. Gates (Chicago: University of Chicago Press, 1985), 185–222.

4   Laura Mulvey, "Visual Pleasure and Narrative Cinema," *Visual and Other Pleasures*, (London: MacMillan, 1988).

5   I am endebted to conversations with Joanne B. Eichler on dress and textiles in West Africa. See *Dress and Gender: Making and Meaning*, ed. Ruth Barnes and Joanne Eichler (Providence, R.I., Berg Publishers, 1993).

6   Remember Raquel Welch in a skin bikini in *2 Million Years B.C.*

7   For a detailed analysis of the meaning of "Africa" in Western discourse since antiquity, see Christopher Miller, *Blank Darkness: Africanist Discourse in French* (Chicago: University of Chicago Press, 1985).

8   In this context we cannot avoid the implication that certain urban areas are like a "jungle" and that the nature of this jungle is related to the nature of the people living there: Notting Hill and South Bronx are culturally black neighborhoods. This is the kind of inattention to the implications of statements made in the register of the "man in the street" which characterizes the liberal text with a specific kind of unexamined racist structure.

9   Harlan Kennedy, "Interview with Hugh Hudson: *Greystoke.*" *Films*, May 1984, 22.

10 The film originated in a script written by Robert Towne who wanted to direct it. His original script begins with a scene in a trading post and the revelation of the almost super-human strength of the mature Tarzan accompanied by D'Arnot. It begins at the derelict outposts of colonial civilization and Tarzan's adult encounter with it. The radically revised script in fact filmed produced a radically different agenda as expressed repeatedly by Hudson in these interviews.

11 "*Enfants Sauvages*: Entretiens avec Hugh Hudson," *Cinematographe*, 1984, 8.

12 The automatic use of a generic masculine for human explorations of origins and identity has been cleverly disputed in its own mythic territory by Elaine Morgan in *The Descent of Woman* (London: Souvenir Press, 1972). She challenges the masculine bias of evolutionary anthropology through a feminist reading of theories of the aquatic ape.

13 These are the themes of a major film, *Territories*, produced by Sankofa in 1985 which posed the questions on the streets of Notting Hill Gate and articulated them across gender and sexuality so signally unexplored and unimagined though certainly still present in *Greystoke*.

14 I want to acknowledge the work of Amanda Phillips as an M.A. student in the Social History of Art, who first analyzed the extraordinary character of the love scene in this film and identified the dislocated position of Jane and thus woman in the narrative. She wrote a paper on this topic for a seminar on the film.

15   I should point out that the word Tarzan is never used in this film. The main character is known as Johnnie, John, Lord Clayton or Lord Greystoke—for the film does not make Rice Burroughs' mistake of imagining the animals as speakers with their own language; "Tarzan" means "white ape" in the language of the apes in the original book. I refer to this character in this way to signify the continuing operation of the myth thus named in the original book and dispersed in popular culture through this signifier.

16   In the first Rice Burroughs novel, Jane is shipwrecked on the coast of Africa with her father while hunting for treasure which will release her from a promise to marry the American man to whom her father is in debt. Tarzan spies upon her and eventually has to rescue her from assault by his arch ape rival Kerchak. His "gentlemanly behaviour and honouring of her virtue" during this rescue and sojourn in the jungle is used to prove his innate artistocracy in contrast to the "black brute" he overcomes to save Jane. On her return to America with her father, Tarzan resolves to follow her to Baltimore … even though there he does not declare himself the real Lord Greystoke and leaves her to marry his cousin who currently bears the title. He does return to Africa to carry on the adventures which made Rice Burroughs wealthy. The core of this drama is his sexuality and its management in relation to a feminine object.

17   Jane Porter does of course occur in the film, at Greystoke, but everything about these scenes indicate their lack of intensity and ideological investment.

18   Laura Mulvey, "Afterthoughts on 'Visual Pleasure and Narrative Cinema' Inspired by *Duel in the Sun*," *Framework* 15/16 (1981) and reprinted in *Visual and Other Pleasures* (London: MacMillan, 1989) 29–37.

19   Laura Mulvey, Ibid., p. 14

20   *Films*, May 1984, 23.

21   I am writing a book analyzing the whole film.

22   Thomas Pakenham, *The Scramble for Africa 1876–1912* (London: Weidenfeld and Nicolson, 1991) chronicles the campaigns of European imperial ambitions which carved up the African continent.

23   The film makers studied in particular the work of Jane Goodall on chimp behavior in Tanzania while also using Dian Fossey material on mountain gorillas. The key National Geographic documentary is *Monkeys, Apes and Man*, 1971.

24   I will come back to this extraordinary inversion of film time in due course.

25   See Cleo McNelly, "Natives, Women and Claude Levi-Strauss: A Reading of Tristes Tropiques as Myth," *Massachusetts Review*. 16, (1975): 7–29.

26   Mulvey, op. cit., 15.

part v
autohistories

11

territories of desire: reconsiderations of an african childhood
dedicated to a woman whose name was not really "julia"

griselda pollock

Travellers with closed minds can tell us little except about themselves.

Chinua Achebe[1]

It is not difficult to transpose from physics to politics [the rule that] it is impossible for two bodies to occupy the same space at the same time.

Johannes Fabian[2]

the voyage out, and back

FOUR HUNDRED YEARS AFTER COLUMBUS'S notorious voyages in 1492 to the so-called "Americas," one hundred years after Captain Cook sailed to the "South Seas" in 1792, that is so say, one century ago, in 1892, a painting travelled from Tahiti to Paris with a stopover in Copenhagen. Art was globe-trotting on colonial ships. The painting had been made in the South Pacific, but it had been painted for Europe (Fig. 1). Its European producer, Paul Gauguin, was an artistic tourist travelling through colonial space in order to traverse time—both historically and psychically. Tourism has been identified as one of the key structures of consciousness associated with modernity. The anthropologist Claude Lévi-Strauss searched the "savage mind" for the fundamental structures of human thought by travelling to South America to record the mythic tales of what television names "the disappearing tribes." He argued that modern society was too complex, and its structures were too smashed by rapid economic, social and psychological change to yield to comparable analysis. Dean MacCannell has, however, claimed that it is possible thus to analyse modernity. Tourism provides just such a typology of modern consciousness and he argues "that tourist attractions are precisely analogous to the religious symbolism of primitive peoples." MacCannell goes on to suggest that "the deep structure of modernity is a totalizing idea, a modern mentality that sets modern society in opposition both to its own past and to those societies of the past and present that are treated as pre-modern or underdeveloped."[3]

Tourism requires a territory on which this temporal ellipsis can occur. It creates a spatial encounter in what is always a fantastic landscape populated with imaginary figures whose difference must be construed and then marked in order that the sense of loss, lack and discontinuity characteristic of metropolitan modernity can be simultaneously experienced and suspended by a momentary vision of a mythic place apparently outside time, a "before-now" place, a garden before the fall—into modernity. This experience, therefore, becomes a classic example of fetishism, a repetitious experience of knowing loss and disavowing it by substitution.

The painting that travelled and marked the voyage out and back of one of art history's paradigmatic tourists was given a title in pidgin Tahitian: *Manao Tupapau* (Fig. 1). This translates as merely: "Spirit: Thought." Generously, this has been interpreted as Gauguin trying to say "The Spirit of the Dead Watches." A black-faced specter stands watch over the naked body of a young Tahitian woman lying on her stomach, her head turned towards the spectator and her hand lies rigid on the pillow. The painting is by Paul Gauguin. The model was Gauguin's 13-year-old Tahitian wife. Yes, I did say

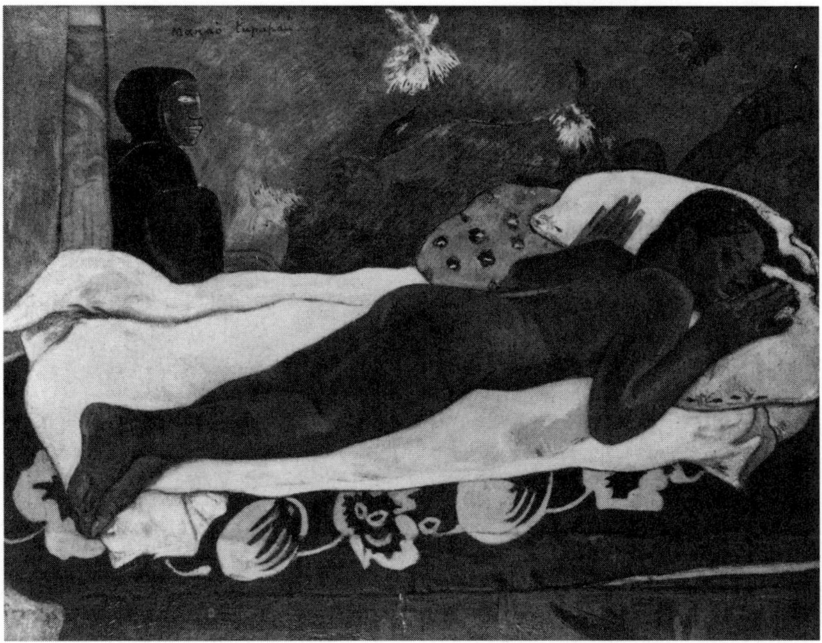

Figure 1.   Paul Gauguin, *Manao Tupapau*, 1892. Buffalo Albright Knox Art Gallery.

wife. Her name was Teha'amana, Bringer of Strength. The painting was sent first to Gauguin's Danish wife. Yes, I did say wife. Mette Gauguin was the mother of his five children from whom he had lived apart since 1887. He had come to Tahiti to earn enough money to finance the possible resumption of their marriage.[4] He had married Teha'amana within the rituals of patriarchal exchange governing the island's current kinship systems and marriage customs. Two wives, two systems, two places, two female figures in the painting whose viewing apex is one man—the apex of a triangle between two wives, two systems, two places.

Two women, therefore, mark a geographical but also cultural distance which is traversed by the masculine, European artist—a point for ethnographic transactions between cultures and genders. The trope of displacement and attempted reconnection via a triangulated structure of one man and two women, each coloured as white or dark, is the tropical journey as sexual quest for which Cleo McNelly has identified a genealogy from the beginnings of Europe's colonial invasions—the Renaissance—to one of the most compelling of contemporary anthropological texts which is at once autobiographical, and frankly autocritical. The text is *Tristes Tropiques* by Claude Lévi-Strauss, published in 1953.[5] She states that an analysis of the tropical journey as myth reveals one of its key problems: "the objectification of the other, the native, the woman that lies at the very heart of structuralist thought." Note the conjunctions: woman, native, other. They are the title of a series of texts produced by the Vietnamese film-maker and critic now resident in the US, Trinh T. Minh-ha which aim precisely to challenge and re-explore these overdetermined synonyms.[6] Which is the signifier, which is the signified—or are they all part of a pure significance—sliding down the chain of deferred meanings? Or do they all signify that which utters and is uttered by this historically precise chain, the power of privileged men of the West who are represented by indirect signification, by constituting themselves as speaking or enunciating subject in opposition to spoken or enunciated woman, native, other? I want to suggest that *woman/native/other* is the sign of a fantastic journey enacted on a cultural map whose cartographer is the violence of imperialism. Women—privileged and Western—are, however, not absent from either the map or the journey. For where there was Teha'amana, there was Mette and her daughter Aline—to whom Gauguin addressed his letters and notes about this painting and its subject, contrasting the things girls of her age would do in Tahiti and not in Copenhagen.

While claiming this signifying cluster *woman/native/other* as a trope which can be identified in Western literature since the Renaissance, Cleo McNelly connects contemporary anthropologist Lévi-Strauss to his cultural predecessors in nineteenth-century modernity, to the poet Baudelaire and the novelist Joseph Conrad, for whom the "native girl" combined the otherness of both race and sex to become the prime object of the tropical quest into the heart of imaginary darkness, which was, as Stuart Hall has remarked, always part of the European traveller's own baggage.[7] Thus "the tropical journey, with its cargo of sexual adventure and questions of identity" are structured through the oppositions: here and there, home and abroad, light and dark, safety and danger, famil(iarit)y and sexuality, seeing and touching, thinking and feeling.[8] These antimonies converge to be embodied through the contrasting figures of geographically dispersed but mythically interdependent femininities: "At either end of this journey stand two figures, each of whom has a profound mythological past: the white woman at home and her polar opposite, the black woman abroad" (ibid.). In the European imaginary, the white woman is mother, sister, wife opposed to the negative mirror-image of the black woman, "the dark lady of the sonnets, savage, sexual and eternally other. At her best she is a 'natural woman' sensuous, dignified and fruitful. At her worst she is a witch, representing loss of self, loss of consciousness and loss of meaning" (ibid.). It is her irreducible strangeness which gives her value and makes her an object of white man's fascination but never a subject of historical acknowledgement or recognition of her cultural, historical and psychological status as a subject.

Gauguin's painting was produced within that antimony. But it also contains within its space an internal doubling which juxtaposes the two aspects of the "dark lady" in awkward and menacing combination. The one promises a warm, lovable "naturally" sensuous young woman on the bed, her sexuality not so much offered to, as sadistically anticipated by the viewer. She is watched by the other—a dark forbidding figure conjured up by Gauguin aesthetically as a pastiche of a carved ancestral figure culled from several cultures indiscriminately, whose aesthetic order this European man can only perceive as so strange and other that it is like death itself. It is this duality which in fact reflects what I have called Gauguin's "avante-garde gambit," which the painting was meant to enact on his professional behalf when it took its place in the gallery showrooms of Durand Ruel in Paris in 1893. Gauguin's painting relies upon intended reference to, but also a calculated displacement of a major avant-garde representation: Manet's *Olympia* painted in 1863, but reinserted into the cultural politics of the 1980s by its purchase for the French nation and accession to its museum of modern art, the Luxembourg, in 1890.[9] There Gauguin had made a copy of it, a canvas also exhibited in Paris in 1893 at another gallery from that in which *Manao Tupapau* was being shown. Like *Olympia*, Gauguin's painting juxtaposes two female figures. Manet's painting, I suggest, can be read as a critically *anti-Orientalist* project, which not only redefines the culturally heterogeneous female body in art—the nude—as site of a distinctly modern sexuality, commercial and classed, but inflects the specific colonial phrasing of that trope with a demythicizing reference to modernity in the person of the African attendant/partner.[10] She wears both a turban and an ill-fitting European dress. In *Olympia,* therefore, two stock characters from the Western artistic imaginary, the nude white woman at her toilet or in her boudoir attended to by an African woman (examples are by Nattier, *Mlle Clermont at her Bath* 1733 (London, Wallace Collection) and Debat-Ponsan, *Massage* 1883 (Toulouse, Musée des Augustins)), are set into a proletarian working relationship to each other, and *against* the spectator, who is challenged by the armed and self-arming stare of the reclining woman, and is resisted by the preoccupation of the other woman with her own other. "Laure" looks to "Olympia" to whom she is presenting the flowers. Gauguin's painting misrecognizes the politics of his reference text, the Manet, and, in that state of semiotic insensitivity or ideological blindness, his work re-orientalizes its theme.[11] Both Gauguin's figures are "other," doubling the image of dark lady and juxtaposing but also linking her youthful sexuality to age and death. The look of the reclining woman is "disarmed" by the exposure of her body in this vulnerable pose. Gauguin wrote to his Danish wife about this painting, omitting details of the marital arrangements which had made the painting possible, in order to "arm" her (Mette) "against the critics when they bombard you with their malicious questions."[12] The weaponry he supplied to deflect the recognition of an overt display of a colonial erotica was a spurious tourist fabrication of out-of-date ethnography peppered with invented notions of ancient religions and current superstitions which displaces his, Gauguin's sadistic voyeurism on to her, Teha'amana's culturally specific paranoia. Tahitians, he "explains," are afraid that spirits of the dead stalk you in the dark. His own "tourist attraction" (in the dual sense of what attracts and that which is the attraction) leans cynically upon "the religious symbolism of primitive peoples," confirming MacCannell's supposition about modern tourism.

The mundane restaging of the cultural trope of woman/native/other by Gauguin's painting and the sexual, personal and professional transactions it was produced to perform serve to illustrate my point of departure (*sic*) in the overdetermined relations of woman to territorialized otherness, whether in the cultural texts or the texts of their critical analysts. I want to disorder the standard narratives of the tropical journey by inserting *woman-to-woman* narratives in feminized geographies. These confront issues of difference which cannot be reduced to this sliding system of signifiers down a phallocentric chain of eternal pairings. Here contradictions and desire do not figure themselves on the bodies of the other, of woman as other, as native, as difference. Instead they propose an intersubjective locus for complex psycho-social transactions which expose the racism installed in the structures of subjectivity as part of the very cultural identity of the white child, and specifically the colonial child. I will draw here upon the transforming feminist conceptualization of a symbolic shaped by the matrix advanced by Bracha Lichtenberg-Ettinger, who argues for another model to that of Self and Other, proposing a stratum of subjectivity based on the coexistence in space of the several, an I and some non-Is, unknown to me in some dimension, and yet not Other.[13] These disorderly thoughts and images will keep circling back to the problem of the territorialization of desire—the question of the native reframed as a matter of nativity, and its elective displacement, of the impossible fantasies of belonging and identity confronted by the telos of nativity, death. I want to explore the historical and political nature of the migration between the two.

I have started with Gauguin's painting not because its hallowed place in art history's complicity with the tropical journey and its imperial foundations needs to be challenged—that has been begun at least in my recent book on *Gender and the Colour of Art History*.[14] The painting and the art historical analysis to which it gave rise allow me to establish the visual track of this essay: triangulation between two women and a man, images of doubling, of returned gazes, of coloured oppositions, of pairs and, eventually, alliances and "elective affinities." An unexpected exchange can occur between the past being studied and the present in which it is studied, between an art historical icon and its critical analyst. What makes my reading not only possible but urgent, for me at least, are the traces of my own placement in a history I can find shadowed within the doubles, triangles and circuits of desire enacted in the cultural forms of another moment of that historical trajectory. And the traffic runs both ways. My own subjective formation within another legacy of colonial tourism creates a position from which the Gauguin painting can be read to yield meanings that counter and indeed refuse art history's collaboration with the painting's founding, colonial myths. This, far from collapsing back into a self-indulgent kind of *ego-histoire*, the subjective moment of one history becomes the objective gaze that can read another history of the subject, of historically framed masculinities and femininities in their specific and unanticipated connections.

Given the growing fashion for postmodern suspension of both the etiquettes and even the concepts of historical research and writing, I must make one further qualification of this project. The movement in this essay involves several voices: art historian, storyteller, personal reminiscence, feminist critic. These are all "me", the enunciative subject of this discourse. My subjectivity informs unconsciously and consciously all that is noticed, attended to, considered significant and then written. But at specific points that implicit condition of all discourse becomes the explicit object of analytical enquiry in which the "author" acts as both analyst and analysand. The tactic is not to centre this rhetorically "personal" self, to make the autobiographical subject the ultimate referent of the text—a truly colonial move—but precisely in order to decolonize the texts by analysing in order to displace a specific historical subject and subjectivity, that of the white woman, from the picture. In contradistinction to the collapse of historical perspective into the autobiographical circle, I aim to create the space for a politically sensitive project: autohistory, in which avowing all aspects of the self becomes a necessary part of a reflexive and responsible acknowledgement of the historicity of all subjectivities. Thus autohistory can refuse the ideological delusion of a separation between the public and the private, the professional and the personal at all levels of the text, and in terms of its writing strategies as well as its contents, since the two are inextricably involved. I want to use this paradox and dare to traverse the polite boundaries that maintain a symbolic distance between the territory of history and the desire of the historian.

migration and return: a time for telling tales

I want to move to another register of story-telling, which will serve, despite the disjuncture it effects, to stage an alternative model of both doubled woman-to-woman relations and a triangulation which is decidedly non-Western and non-Oedipal. It also suggests other, feminist ways to read the "religious symbolism of primitive peoples."

Let me tell a story about some economic migrants, a family driven by the terrible famine in their own land to seek food and survival in a neighboring country. A mother, her husband and their two sons travel around a landlocked sea to the mountainous regions they have watched from afar. Disaster, however, soon befalls the family. The father dies. The two sons marry local women, going against a deeply held prohibition in their home culture to mingle with the women of their adopted land. They pay a price for breaking the taboo, for "sleeping with the enemy," for they too fall ill and die. The relicts of this sad tale are thus three women: a bereaved widow, and two childless daughters-in-law. The widow decides to go home and bids her two daughters-in-law return to their own mothers, to their blood kin. Eventually after protest, one does. But the younger refuses to abandon her mother-in-law. She then says:

> Do not urge me to leave you, to turn back and not to follow you.
> For wherever you go, I will go.
> Wherever you live, I will live.
> Your people shall be my people.
> Your God shall be my God.
> Where you die, I will die and there I will be buried.
> Thus and more may the Lord do to me if anything but death parts me
> from you.

This is a powerful affirmation of personal loyalty. Item by item, the daughter-in-law identifies the typical criteria of our belonging, of cultural identity and its relation to matters of location, of religion and, significantly if surprisingly, of death. It poses a shift of identity as primarily one of movement, a journey ("Where you go, I will go"). This relocation is consolidated by settling in a place ("Where you live, I will live"), followed by a entry into a community ("Your people shall be my people"), the acquisition of the culture signified through its God/gods, its belief system. The declaration is sworn, like a marriage vow, until death do us part.

The story, which some of you will have recognized, comes from the Book of Ruth, included in both the Hebrew and Christian Bibles. Within the Jewish context of its origin, it is read annually on the early summer festival which celebrates *the* covenant. The delivery of the Law at Mount Sinai is defined as a covenant between God and his chosen people, who at the time were landless exiles, fugitives from slavery in a powerful empire, from which they had escaped but seven weeks before. In the wilderness of total social abjection, this motley stateless crowd was to be constituted as a people/culture by the Law providing for ethical guidance in every social, moral, economic, legal and ritual area of life. This episode marks an important shift in the history of human religions. Religion, here represented as an ethical and social code taken on as an agreement between two parties, makes a major break from contemporary ancient religions and cultures which were seen to be literally geographical. Most gods were territorial, associated with bits of land or even special features of the landscape. Judaism is the religion of choice and covenant made with a wandering tribe in a desert.

Paradoxically, it is the foreign woman who *chose* to be Jewish: Ruth, who has become the symbolic figure of the covenant between a people and their God. Yet the Jewish people were given choice at the symbolic moment at the foot of Mount Sinai, and it is this idea which defines Judaism's theological distance from the notions of race and nation which since the late eighteenth century have framed anti-semitism, and popular misconceptions of Judaism and the Jewish people. Ruth was, however, not only a non-Jew. She was a Moabite, and for the historical Israelites, that meant she was a prohibited other, *the* stranger. Yet she became the most famous proselyte to Judaism, a moment of acknowledgement of the stranger as someone who can be assimilated and not as that which can only induce either aggression and violent resistance or fascinated and ultimately disfiguring desire. The Greek word "proselyte" is often seen as a mere synonym for the Latin term "convert." In fact, proselyte means immigrant. Conversion implies change from one currency or substance to another, while the concept of proselyte as immigrant involves displacement and admission in a way that may uproot the immigrant from a native culture, but provides other ways of transacting outside of the native/other dichotomies.

The promises Ruth makes to Naomi involve movement, relocation and cultural transformation, but above all, they signify a covenant between two people, formed in difference, able to resolve that difference without self-annihilation. Although this text is usually used as an example of someone choosing Judaism, it places God neither first nor last, but only as the penultimate change in a longish list which primarily stresses person-to-person loyalties. The last sentence is often paid scant attention, yet it is crucial: "Where you die, I will die and there will I be buried." This statement will resonate profoundly for small and battered migrant communities for it acknowledges the obligations on family members to secure appropriate burial for relatives. To die childless and without relations is to die alone, unprotected and forgotten. Thus this text introduces the vitally important question of memory. The continuity of a people is composed of its many acts of particular remembering. What is vital is not so much its nativity, but its history, which is a continuous and living act of collective memorial which does not depend necessarily on the land of origin or birth. Ruth's reference to death and burial is symbolically necessary to complete the transition from being a native through the process of migration to a new—I almost use the word—patriation. I want to indicate a changed relation to the territory—the land of one's birth, of one's ancestors, versus the adopted community amongst whom one may choose to die and rest. But in this case it cannot be a matter of patriation for the transaction is between two women and it thus becomes the model of a matrixial relation: the insider and the outsider—the migrant who returns with another migrant, going in the opposite direction—who form a mutually acknowledging alliance.

Cultural identity is hinged on how we refuse death through cultural memory, living in the presence of tradition and historical change. Modernist tourists were in the act of refusing the space and time of their own cultural death while inflicting it on everyone else. Modernity appears to uproot, deracinate, detraditionalize societies. It thus makes difficult, if not impossible, the sense of belonging which could only be found by a migration in time and space backwards to the pre-modern pasts where other peoples's memories, or the fictions of them, could be "colonized" to do service for what the Western moderns felt they had lost; to arm them against what they felt they were experiencing, a living death. Travel thus becomes a fetishizing activity, journeying as disavowal of both the present and of death.

What I want to stress is that the cultural displacement Ruth chooses is stated as allegiance to a person, namely Naomi. It is an astonishing act of *woman-to-woman* covenanting. Yet in the history of Western art, for which the Book of Ruth has served as a source, there is no visual representation of this transaction. Instead we find many paintings of the harvesters of Naomi's rich kinsman, Boaz, in whose fields Ruth was sent to glean. The text itself also displaces the matrix and the matriline, created by Ruth and Naomi's alliance, so that it would seem that two quite different narratives inhabit this one text.[15]

The subsequent chapters of the Book of Ruth dramatize the Jewish law of the levirate (when a kinsman must take up his deceased kin's land and line) as the means of Ruth's integration into the Bethlehem society. This law is adamantly patrilineal. For in this second narrative, it is only by virtue of her status as the widow, the relict property of her husband and thus of her father-in-law Elimelech, that Ruth enters this community. She has no status except as she is an adjunct to the father-in-law's land which, like her womb, has been left unharvested and barren. Jewish law provides for the redemption of this wasted land by calling upon the next of kin to take up the inheritance and make it fruitful again in the name of the deceased. The claiming of the property inheritance involves any other relics of the dead kin. Ruth the Gleaner is also Ruth the Gleaned. The text is inconsistent even here. For at times Ruth appears as owner or inheritor; at others she is merely part of the inheritance: "When you acquire the property from Naomi and from Ruth the Moabite, you must also acquire the wife of the deceased so as to perpetuate the name of the deceased upon his estate."

I am drawing attention here to this contrary position of the figure of Ruth within this narrative. In its patriarchal form she is woman, the sign to be exchanged, the body whose potential to labour and give birth is acquired as part of a property. Reduced to her female body, woman forms a continuity with the land as property, as attribute of man, lacking the phallus to make her productive by planting of his seed. Like his land, she must become the conduit for his line and name.

The conflict between the patrilineal and the matrilineal narratives in this text is resolved by the birth of a male child.[16] The local women of Bethlehem proclaim, however: "a son is born to Naomi"—thus replacing the lineage of the father (-in-law, Elimelech) with that of the mother (-in-law, Naomi). And yet, the sentence structure is ambiguous, for it is as if Naomi gave birth to the said son, and thus had her maternal desire gratified. The child can be seen as the gift of the loving woman who has chosen to be with her. Thus birth ceases to function merely as timeless cycle of female biological reproduction in which one woman can more or less stand in for another in a constant replication. Instead the child registers as part of a symbolic activity. Furthermore, Ruth enacts what Kaja Silverman has argued is one crucial and underexplored aspect of specifically feminine desire, namely the wish to fulfil the desire of the mother, by giving her a child. These transactions utterly displace, for a moment, the typical phallic economies that govern women and children in the fulfilment of masculine desire and patriarchal law.

The transitivity—or heterogeneity—of the text is continued in the next sentence. For having had the child proclaimed as hers, Naomi puts the child to her own breast. She thus suckles her "grandson", forming a completely non-phallic triangle composed of the two mothers and their son. The maleness of the offspring doubles as the signifier of desire under the sign of the phallus and as the gift between mother and daughter which marks the terms of their union. The restoration to Naomi of the power of life is utterly at odds with the imagery of the patrilineal narrative of Naomi's barren state and Ruth's function as unfertilized property. I want to suggest that this triangle of bonded women of different cultures connected via a nativity, via the son one bears to ensure matrilineal continuity of the other, offers this relation as a matrixial model directly counter to that enacted in modern, patriarchal tourist fantasy of the tropical quest.

The patriline has the last word, however, for tacked on to the end of the book is a seemingly bizarre listing of the genealogy of the house of the future King David, Ruth's great grandson, from whose lineage she and her mother-in-law-in-love are completely absented. The son who binds the mother and daughter-in-law (two women) can also function as their stake in the other, patrilineal system which effectively excludes them at the level of the signifieds but uses their female bodies at the level of its signifiers. Thus we arrive at these incompatible yet coexisting equations: phallus as property; nativity as connection. I want to use the story of Ruth and Naomi and their child as the "matrixial" axis on which to pivot us into a feminist perspective on migration, nativity, death and alliance in both a post-biblical and a postcolonial era.

another time, another place: an african childhood reconsidered

A photograph from a family album—a necessary reference to and moment of respect for Jo Spence who alerted us to the historical and the ideological in the everyday and every family archive—registers a social and political complex across the bodies of two women and several children casually framed in a photographer's viewfinder (Fig. 2). It is a scene on a beach. As such it could be anywhere. I know it was taken in December 1950 at a popular holiday resort called St. Michael's-on-Sea, near Durban on the Indian Ocean coast of South Africa. It is a poor photograph, messy, badly composed, with too much extraneous detail. Yet the amateur's weak compo-

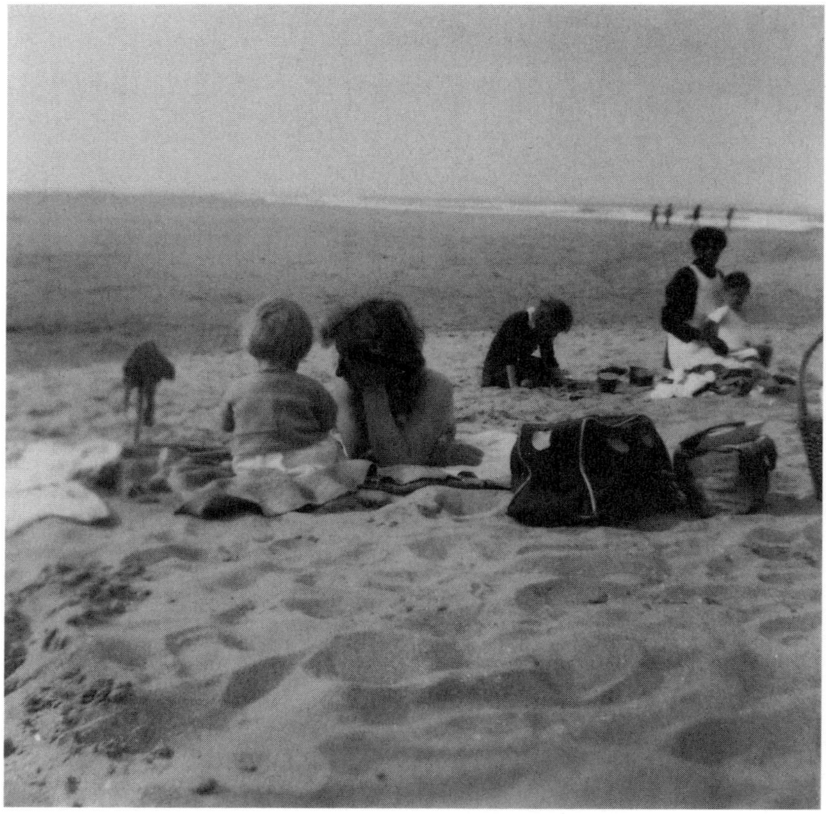

Figure 2.   Family photograph taken at St. Michael's on Sea, South Africa, 1950.

sitional skill has made the photograph an unexpected document of its place of origin which resonates far beyond the reaches of its casual occurrence in a family album. Including what is typically off-screen yet foundational in constituting the social and historical specificity of the scene and of the seeing, the photograph emerges out of its archive as a document both political and personal. In the middle ground a European mother and child are caught in an almost emblematic moment. It would not take Victor Burgin or Mary Kelly to tell us what fantasy was activated in the person carrying the camera by that moment of transient intimacy—a sturdy toddler busy with some newly acquired skill practised under the quiescent attention and enveloping gaze of its attentive mother (Fig. 3).

The photographer was too far away from what had made him take out his camera (the photographer was surely the father) and so his object of desire

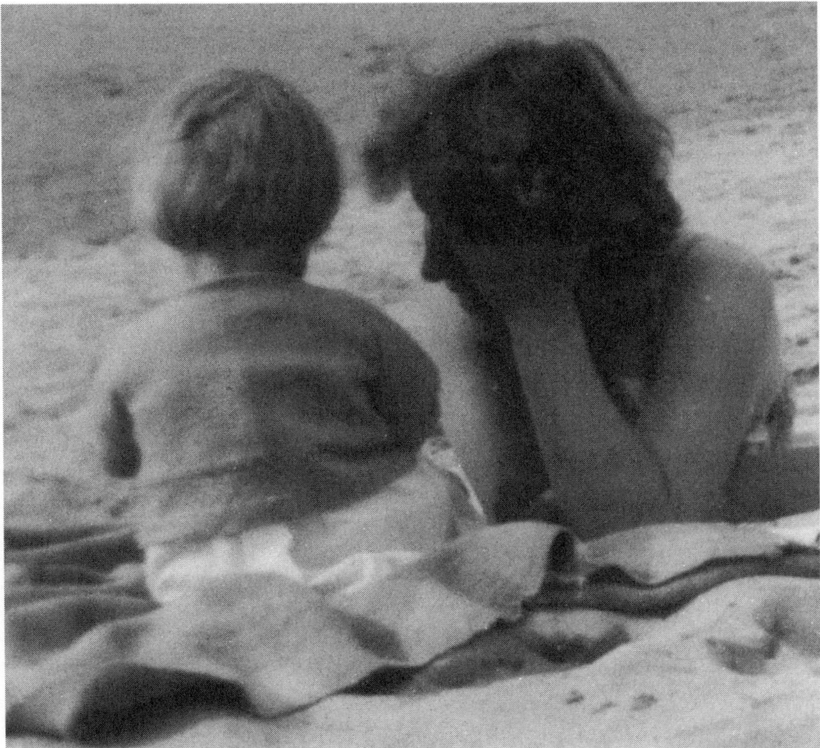

Figure 3.   Detail: *Dyad.*

is encumbered with extraneous tote bags and other people. Stranger still, his activity has become the object of a gaze within the photograph. The picture thus looks back at him, from a point off-centre (Fig. 4). That steady gaze makes him a pure Lacanian subject—"photographed".[17] He is a picture for the unconsidered but not invisible other in the field of vision he does not control. The man photographing his little family is being watched by a woman who halts her work to look across at his leisure—his tourist snap (Fig. 5). She is an African employed to look after a European child whose mother is absent. While the coupling of adult woman and child pretends to simulate the dyad at the other side of the scene, it refutes that unity of mother and child, representing instead its socio-cultural antithesis or underside. Furthermore the African woman is the third figure in the triangle which appears in the photo only in its ideal, and idealized, holiday form as the maternal dyad.

The dark lady and the white wife/mother occur in the same space and time of the photograph, their relations and contradiction not, however, contained by the mastering gaze of the masculine tourist/artist/ photographer we encountered in first section of the chapter. Two mothering women

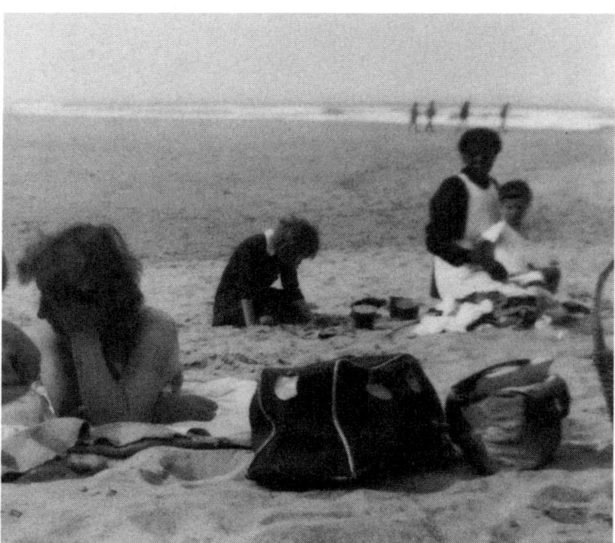

Figure 4.   Detail: *The Other Looks Back.*

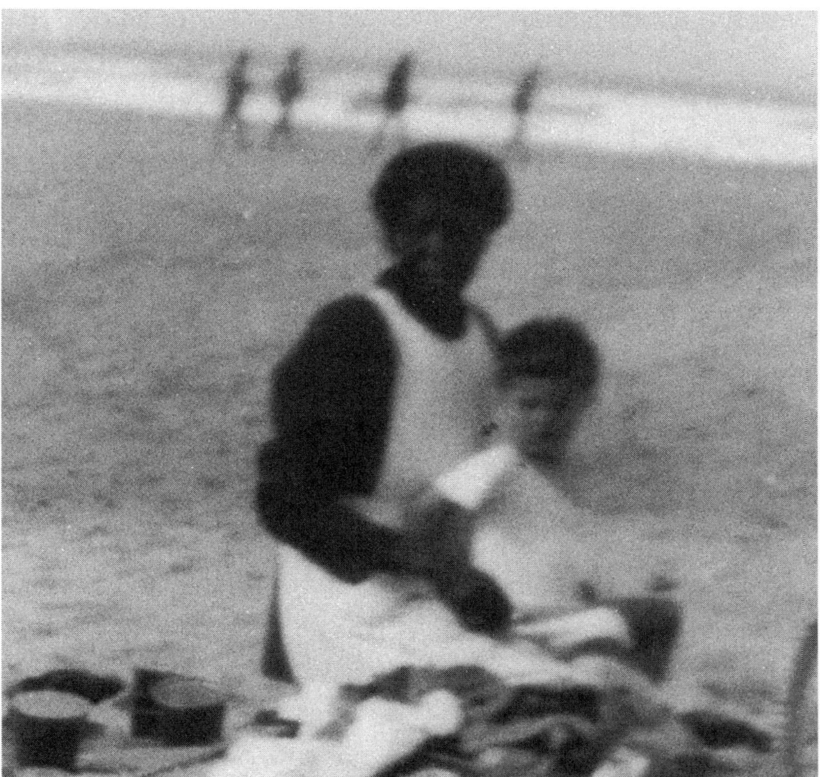

Figure 5.   Detail.

coexist but not in any chosen covenant or alliance such as occurs in the biblical story of Ruth and Naomi. Across the times and spaces of their production and uses, unexpected transactions emerge between an utterly mundane family snap and one of the icons of Western modernism—*Olympia*. I note the sorority between the African women in their borrowed costumes of servitude caring for the white woman, or her children, while acknowledging the shocking incongruity of the comparison within our normal codes of academic divisions between the historically relevant and the personally mundane. In Manet's case, the figure of "Laure" is raised by his calculated strategies of proto-modernist disruption to being a critical signifier in a way that cannot seriously be claimed for the chance concurrence of the two women in a family snap. Here, in the photograph, however, instead of the containment of a black woman's gaze—or its murder and exploitation in the Gauguin painting (Figure 1), where it became the gaze of death in the place of sexuality—we unexpectedly encounter a returned and critical look. In Barbara Kruger fashion, this gaze puts its other—the absent European gaze which, *pace* Linda Nochlin, is the real meaning of the Orientalist project— on the spot.[18] Her gaze punctures the space which should frame and contain the European dyad as simply and universally "mother and child". Yet because of what Richard Dyer has suggested is the racism imprinted in the technologies and lighting codes of Western photography itself, her African face threatens to dissipate into what Christopher Miller, writing of French Africanist discourse, has called "blank darkness".[19]

A final observation—in my developing theme of the polarized woman as the axis of the tropical journey, this photograph contains within one frame both white woman and dark lady, although syntactically and politically, they are rigidly separated (except, perhaps, in the tiny mind/imaginary of the white Euro-African child). I recognize the critical danger of what I am saying—a self-indulgence perhaps to focus on my white self—a fulfilment of Lubaina Himid's astringent remarks about how white people keep seeing themselves at the centre of other people's pictures where they absorb the efforts and energies of others. I cannot speak for the African woman in that picture as I cannot even speak for the African woman, whose real name was not "Julia", who normally cared for me on that beach and at home in South Africa. I can speak to and about my white mother, who played her part in that woman's servitude. I can also admit that my desire— forged in the series of psychic losses which are always historically textured—is "territorialized" upon a black woman's nurturing body.

I, placed now as the viewer in and yet not in the place of the photograph's producer, can therefore respond to her African gaze, which once was as comforting to me, the colonialist/economic migrant's child, as that of the white mother with her own child which occupies the intended foreground of the image.

Childcare is labor and mostly the labor of women. It is a matter of class, of gender and of race, as here. Some privileged women pay others to do their childcare. It is one of the major employer–employee relations between women—a class system at the heart of the socially permeable bourgeois household.[20] In South Africa, African women are employed by European women to look after the latter's children, while their own black children are left at home with relatives—in the townships if they are lucky, in the homelands if not. The child in the photograph was thus cared for seven years. Emotional bonding and psychic formation took place in the socially and culturally permeable household of the Western bourgeoisie as postcolonial economic migrants. My parents left England in 1947 to escape postwar cold and rationing for a tropical journey that was a quest for somewhere better to raise a family. The white child born into this situation is the perplexed meeting point—a subjective nexus—of the social and cultural contradictions which are resolvable neither by sexuality nor by conversion (Fig. 6).

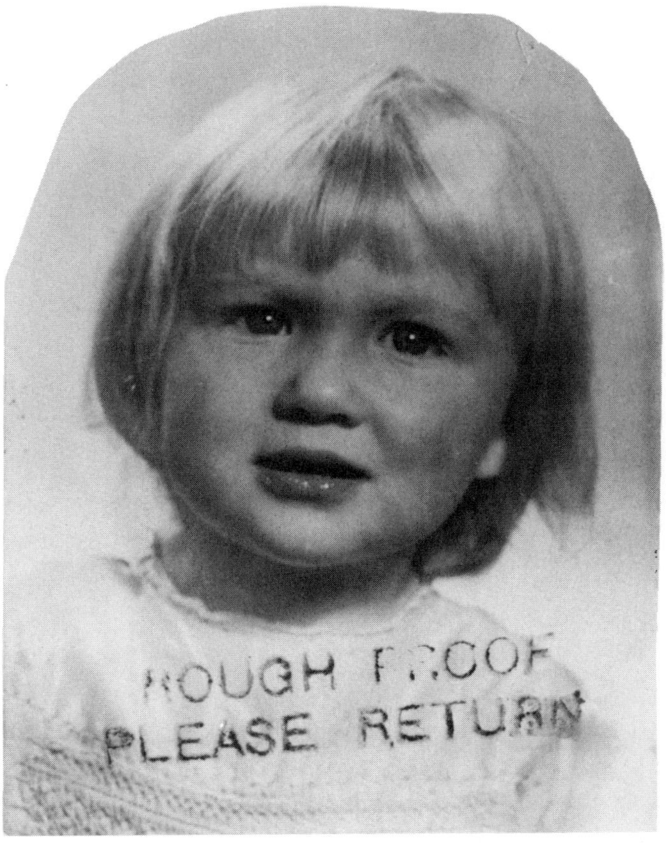

Figure 6. *Rough Proof,* Childhood portrait.

The child, however innocent, is being formed as a bearer of the dominant order of *whiteness* through an Oedipalization which is profoundly historical, social and, I am arguing here, racial. The situation is not neutral but one in which differences of culture and class are being patterned as hierarchy because the economic relations between the leisured mother (white), who displaces her child, and the working mother (black), who is robbed of her own—i.e. between employer and servant—are enacted at the level the child grasps as a series of affects, complexes, loyalties and losses. The white child is a token of unequal exchange which infantalizes the adult African woman because what she does as an adult identifies her with the realm and status of her childish charge. The servant/employee's paid work makes her stay "at home" with the child, thus freeing the white mother/employer to enjoy the personal freedoms the leisured bourgeoisie usually allows to its men: to meet with friends, to play golf or bridge, to do voluntary work, or indeed to be a journalist, to be politically active against apartheid, to belong to women's organizations like Black Sash, to travel, to take lovers, to write—to create herself as a bourgeois individual.

Liberation for some women in this situation is gained at the price of another's servitude and personal pain. But the point is that the freedom this white mother achieves is a version of what we typically associate with the bourgeois man in our accounts of the metropolitan bourgeoisie at home. He is the privileged traveller through and occupant of public spaces of money, exchange, leisure and power. In the mid-twentieth century, the post-colonial racist society allows some women access to his privilege but only by overlaying the gender of African women with the multiple subordinations of race and class.

In writing his biography of Flaubert—another of the tropical travellers of the sexual quest—Sartre discusses the formation of class consciousness in the child of the bourgeoisie by suggesting that class is invisible within the family, following Marx perhaps who wrote:

> Upon the different forms of property, upon the social conditions of existence, rises an entire superstructure of distinct and peculiarly formed sentiments, illusions, modes of thought and views of life. The entire class creates and forms them out of its material foundations and corresponding social relations. The single individual, who derives them through tradition and upbringing, may imagine they form the real motives and starting point of his activity.[21]

It takes a historical but always social moment of crisis or conflict for that individual—the child of my discourse—to see its parents in the eyes of others, for class consciousness to be forced upon the child; just as Sartre argues a Jewish child only recognizes himself or herself as Jewish in the eyes of the anti-semite other. In the images by which Sartre attempts to explain his thesis on social identity and the role of the other, which Franz Fanon elaborated in relation to the postcolonial experience, and which recurs in Carolyn Steedman's analysis of class and subjectivity, *Landscape for a Good Woman,* there is often a "castrating" moment in which the black or working-class child is the traumatized witness to the revelation of a social lack in the parent, who, up to that point, has been imagined as a figure of authority and power.[22] The child has to recognize, with the resultant injury to its own narcissism (since its identity is formed through identification, i.e. introjection of the imago of its parents), the death of omnipotence and plenitude in the figure with which the child identifies. It is thus wounded by the authoritative gaze of the empowered social other, which reduces her/his own beloved caretaker. In one sense this "castrating" moment is the social re-enactment, or staging on the plane where social and psychic realities interface, of the Freudian schema of the male child's trauma at the site of apparent female, i.e., the mother's genital insufficiency which is symbolic of her want of power and authority. I want to combine both models—or rather map the social and the psychic on to each other to extend both—in the triangulated structure within the family. The typical triangle of the Freudian story is between a son and his sexually differentiated parents. The one I want to overlay is that between a female child and two women, a mother and a nanny who are by this "moment" inscribed differentially in terms of class and race. What the "white" child (or rather the one who will become "white" by this lesson) learns is a structure of difference and authority relative to which she must take up not merely a gender position (she could potentially identify with both women because they are both of her gender) but also one of class and race. Or, we could put it thus, she must adjudge between two positions, one in which privilege comes to be inscribed through a differentiation of power that is represented linguistically as a physical and cultural difference, as race. This difference is thereby not recognized as the result of class, of social relations, cultural exploitation and so forth; rather here, like

Freud's schema, anatomy—skin color, voice, looks—seems to give the difference a natural origin.

In the situation of colonial childcare within the colonizer's household, the (white) child, abandoned by its mother, and the (black) mother, deprived of her child/ren, are thrown together across the rifts of class and culture into a potentially compensatory dependency in which they may both, in a state of loss and deprivation, find surrogate bodies to cuddle and be cuddled by. Their world is already one of metaphors and metonyms. For each is the substitute for that for which each "really" longs. This dyad is triangulated not by the father so much as by the economically and culturally empowered white mother. She represents for the white child the desired but distanced ideal, whose attraction as a figure of identification is intensified precisely by her mobility in the world, her difference from the "beloved" *native* surrogate mother, confined by her and with her to the realm of the domestic, the infantile, the powerless.[23]

The typical Freudian model of Oedipalization has offered a means of explaining the formation of human infants in sexual difference (limited as its effectivity was to the male child). In its postcolonial situations, the white girl child, in whom I am primarily interested here, is positioned simultaneously in two hierarchies: as a child subject to the power of the mother who appears free to come and go, to be absent and to determine access to her increasingly idealized person; and, secondly, she is identified with what remains behind at home, in the thus "subordinated" realm. The African nanny belongs there with her, but also *to* her, creating for the child a fantasy of control sanctioned by the conditions of employment and artificially created poverty. The child is thus "empowered" *vis-à-vis* a figure whose adulthood and authority should—but by this token does not—maintain her in a position of authority towards the child, her charge.

The colonialist's child has a stake through which to traverse the division, namely her physical similarity to the mother which is signified not as gender but as *whiteness*, as race. The child can thus imagine an identification with the power and authority the mother represents *vis-á-vis* the African nanny. Thus, like the penis in the system of phallic sexual difference, an insignificant physical detail—skin colour—is invested with the power of signification, signifying within the colonial symbolic its racism. Not to identify with the mother and her culture—her gods, her people, her lodges and her death (to recall the terms of Ruth's cultural identification) is to be infantilized and blackened, to be like the *native* and the *other* and, in all its patriarchal negativity, *woman.*

Colonialism colors gender, and gender inferiority can be displaced by cultural power expressed through race, in a way that then makes the articulations of a specifically feminist consciousness in South African struggles seem utterly diversionary from the overwhelming obscenity and violence of that society's racism. It should be noted, none the less, how important debates about women's rights have become in the arguments advanced by African women in the formulation of a new constitution for South Africa, in ways that demand reconsideration of the double legacy of sexism through both traditional and colonial patriarchies.[24] The question of white women's implication through the very fact of gender identification in the psychological formation and perpetuation of racism needs also to be acknowledged—opening the way for woman-to-woman alliances in the struggle against a racism that white women may actually carry inside them as part of their sense of being "women" and being "white" in such a culture.

I am playing a dangerously loose game of analogies, trying to imagine ways to discuss the formations of a white colonial/bourgeois femininity in terms that echo those used to explicate the paradoxes of "masculinity" in difference theory. It is argued there that the distance forced between men and their mothers—discovered to be lacking the phallus as signifier of social power and authority—generates the profound contradiction between the desire for the lost object and the compulsion to debase and punish the body which seems a constant reminder not so much of *its* deficiency, as of the lack within the masculine subject, as a result of its being outcast from the maternal space. Masculinity is the psychic journey with these two faces of a lost and desired but dreaded and often punished femininity at its poles—the dark and the white ladies of the tropical journey that is always taking place inside the white man's head. If psychoanalysis has allowed us a psycho-political theory of the contradictions of phallocentric sexist societies and their masculinities, might it also provide terms to analyse the formation of the white child girl as well as boy in colonial societies—to grasp the formation of racism as a contradictory pressure of divided maternal images produced in societies where the gendered division of childcare is further patterned through race as well as class?

As the little white girl I was, born and formed in this socio-psychic complex, I know the twin forces that conflict between identification with the white mother and its possible freedoms for a woman in a still bourgeois world, and the lost fantastic identification with a black woman, who, whatever her own pain and desperate sense of exploitation and loss, generously gave me her care and nurtured me at the cost of her own daughter's need for her mothering. In the racist formation of the white child—whatever the politics of her later years—there is a danger of being trapped in the psychic time and space in which a mythical Africa and its landscape, colours, textiles and music become an imagined but forbidden native space, the metonymic image of the woman whom she the once-child imagines was one of her lost mothers. In her autobiography and celebration of black South African women's courage and creativity, *Call Me Woman*,[25] Ellen Kuzwayo records her meeting with a white woman, Elizabeth Wolpert, who came to Soweto in search of African women's self-help groups in order to establish a trust in memory of a black woman named Maggie Magaba who nursed her as a child. Elizabeth Wolpert translated that childhood debt into an alliance, a covenanting for social activist struggle which brought traditional strangers into political alliance in the manner of Ruth and Naomi. I was deeply struck by Elizabeth Wolpert's action. I thought, "That's a way to turn from the trap and engage in the political struggle for change." But then, I couldn't do anything like it. I do not even know "her" name.[26]

When I was younger, people would ask: Where are you from? Identity is so often a matter of origins. As a white child of a postcolonial twentieth century, I honestly could not answer the real question: Who are you by birth? Of what place are you a "native"? I could, by way of trying not to be rude, give as a reply the itinerary of my childhood. Born in Bloemfontein, I grew up in Johannesburg, then moved to Toronto, Canada, and later settled in Francophone Catholic Quebec until, in my mid-teens, I was brought to England. I had two nationalities (South African and Canadian), dropped one (South African) and picked up another (British). Then I used to alter this disjointed story a bit and say simply I was born in Africa and hoped no further revealing specification would be necessary. It was, I realize now, not mere embarrassment about having to admit to being by birth a white South African, though that was real enough. I now recognize that I was expressing the *territorialization* of my desire, a formation of desire in childhood and in specific social relations whose only links with actual people I once loved was, typically, displaced on to a land, a landscape, a territorial signifier: Africa. The word "Africa" became a signifier not of property but of loss and permanent exclusion, and thus functioned not dissimilarly from the woman/native/other modality of Western masculinity. It was a signifier of the lost mother(s) of a particular, historical femininity. I cannot go back to this "Africa" for it is not a spatial but a temporal journey. It is to be hoped that I can never go back to that "Africa"—politico-economic configuration of colonialism and apartheid whose destruction is being actively struggled for in this our present.

I am using these stories of locations, identities and beginnings to reconsider the question of nativity, nationality and migration: to fracture the notion of origins as the source of identity both in the colonial discourse on "natives" and in its own fantasies about nativity, i.e. relations to a "fantastic" maternal space and sign. Shall I be like Ruth and affirm loyalty to a chosen national identity—to Britain, to Canada? Or do I remain a South African by "birth," a "white" by acculturation, and thus a "racist" by psychological formation in such a society? At what point can we make these issues political, a matter of covenants, alliances and chosen realignments which involve rejection of original formations and the refashioning of new, painful but negotiated affiliation? But to what South Africa could I want to belong—that of my childhood written in my desire and memory, or to a new and painfully struggled-for democratic space to which I cannot claim any connection? Or can we, like Ruth, throw off a culture, a formation, a tradition and an upbringing, and decide negatively: that is, *not* to belong to any myth of origin, in terms of time or space? Rather the project is to enter into dialogues, political transactions on the symbolic territories of the international women's movements. A critically self-examining feminist project allows us the possibilities both of escaping from the political hysteria—hysterics suffer from reminiscences—of colonial formations and of producing futures, new lives for our "children" or our political and cultural progeny based on acts of alliance.

I suspect that, in the words of Janina Bauman, writing of the complex choices in her life as a Jewish survivor in postwar communist Poland, that we all have "a dream of belonging," made acute not because of tourism but precisely because of the twentieth century's epidemic condition of migration, refugeeism, diaspora.[27] Can we be proselytes without a claim to a land, to nativity and its correlate nationhood, or worse nationalism? The moral of my tale, my own story, as well as Gauguin's story, is that we need to resist and disrupt the territorialization of desire—all forms of nationalism and identity politics, and join Lubaina Himid's well-travelled modern women, in breaking up the maps and in talking strategies of revenge on the power structures that are the bringers of death across the whole of the earth. In her powerful painting *Five* (acrylic on canvas, 5′ × 4′, 1991) shown in her major 1992 exhibition, *Revenge*, at the Rochdale Art Gallery, two black woman sit at a round table (Fig. 7). They are engaged in energetic dialogue in an interior in which 1920s Paris (international modernism) vies with ancient African

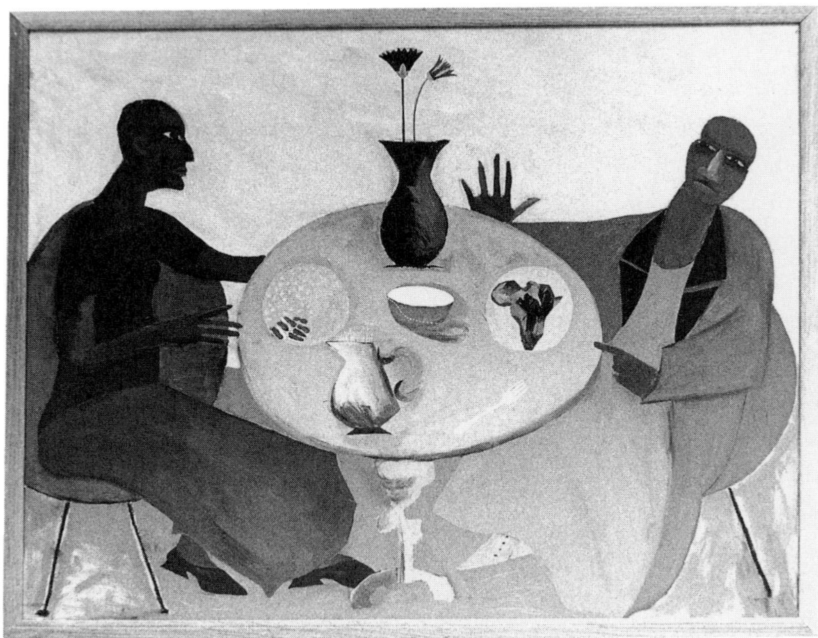

Figure 7.   Lubaina Himid, *Five*, 1991. Leeds, City Art Gallery. Collection Griselda Pollock.

Egypt, signified in formalized papyrus flowers (writing, culture, history) and a luminous and intense yellow (the lightness an antidote to that colonially invented "blank darkness"). On the table is a jug of water which appeared in several paintings. Water is used thematically throughout this exhibition. It connotes both the water of the most terrible journeys, the middle passage, endured but not survived by over 20 million African people in the era of European enslavement and early capitalism. It is also a celebratory reference to the water beloved and creatively used by Islamic civilizations in Africa in their gardens and architecture. Lubaina Himid's work ambitiously creates a figuration of the historical politics of contemporary cultural practice: where black women take the initiative to focus on the immediate historical dangers and dilemmas in which the cultural forms of canonized Western and male modernism are revealed to be profoundly implicated as having provided an imagery and an aesthetic for the colonial and postcolonial touristic projects of the Western bourgeoisies.

She takes over the color which Gauguin used as his avant-garde gambit, the colour that made a "brown Olympia" according to one leading critic, the colour that made Tahiti exotic, strange, edenic. She gives it a historical articulation, makes it articulate concrete histories of art and cultures. But the colour axis she refuses is the black/white opposition—the white and the dark lady. She had tried to intervene in this in a major installation, *A Fashionable Marriage* (1987), which critically reworks its referent text, Hogarth's *The Countess' Morning Levée*, from the series *Marriage à la Mode* (1743). The African slave serving coffee to the eager listener is replaced by a self-confident black woman artist, yet she still finds herself upstaged by the keen white feminist artist into whom she keeps pouring her energy. In the *Revenge* series there can only be black women in the picture for that is the only way to resist the power of the colonial trope which makes the black "woman, native and other." But as a white woman, I can be party to this dialogue, if I am prepared to listen and participate in a space that is not a matter of doubles and triangles. For the space is open in the painting, and the table is round, and we all need to discuss strategies of revenge for what Gayatri Spivak calls the "abject script modern western history has bequeathed to us."

I am wrenching Lubaina Himid's painting from its original place in a large and major exhibition where its meaning was created as a part of complex artistic syntax of women journeying to rewrite the travels of Columbus in 1492, perhaps loosening it from its own act of artistic decolonization and reconstruction of a new cartography written to the measure of black women's desire. I am asking of it to mark a break with the doubling of women so far encountered within the culture of colonial and post-colonial Europeans, be it in the work of Gauguin or my own childhood album. Perhaps I am hoping it can be connected to the story of Ruth—to woman-to-woman covenants across cultures, to reciprocal tenderness between "strangers," to created loyalties and constructed solidarities, to dialogical moments of reciprocated gazes and listened-to voices. "After Mourning comes Revenge," Lubaina Himid has written.[28] Against modernity's spatial travels—colonialism in all its forms and legacies—in order to return in time, we need a present, which is here and now, and it is between us. So I end with an image that utterly displaces from sight both the white man and the white woman, but creates a space at the table of political strategizing for anyone who will listen and form not an Oedipal or any other kind of triangle, but the matrixial space of the several in which singularity and similarity, difference and divergence can form the basis of negotiated connection and political covenant for transformation bound neither by nativity nor by death.

notes

1 Chinua Achebe, "An Image of Africa." *Research into African Literatures* 9, 1978, p. 12.

2 Johannes Fabian, *Time and the Other: How Anthropology Makes its Object*, New York. Columbia University Press, 1983.

3 Dean MacCannell, *The Tourist: A New Theory of the Leisure Class*, New York, Shocken Books, 1976, p. 8.

4 Bengt Danielsson, *Gauguin in the South Seas*, trans. Reginald Spink, London, George Allen & Unwin, 1965, gives a full account of Gauguin's time in Tahiti, and his incomplete grasp of the language. I want to mention here Amanda Holiday's film called *Manao Tupapau*, which explores the experience of Teha'amana modelling for the painting. The film is distributed by Cinenova.

5 Cleo McNelly, "Nature, Women and Claude Lévi-Strauss," *Massachusetts Review* 16, 1975, pp. 7–29; Claude Lévi-Strauss, *Tristes Tropiques* [1955] trans. J. & D. Weightman, New York, Athenaeum, 1975.

6 Trinh T. Minh-ha, *Woman, Native, Other: Writing Postcoloniality and Feminism*, Bloomington, Indiana University Press, 1989.

7 McNelly is thinking of Conrad's *Heart of Darkness* (1902), in which we read of a "dark lady." "She walked with measured steps, draped in striped and fringed cloths, treading the earth proudly, with a slight jingle and flash of barbarous ornaments. She carried her head high; her hair was done in the shape of a helmet; she had brass leggings to her knees, brass wire gauntlets to the elbow, a crimson spot on her tawny cheek, innumerable necklaces of glass beads on her neck; bizarre things, charms, gifts of witch-men, that hung about her, glittered and trembled at every step ... She was savage. And wild-eyed and magnificent; there was something ominous and stately in her deliberate progress. And the hush that had fallen suddenly upon the whole sorrowful land, the immense wilderness, the colossal body of fecund and mysterious life seemed to look at her, pensive, as though it had been looking at the image of its own tenebrous and passionate soul." (Penguin edition, 1973, pp. 100–1). For a feminist reading of Baudelaire's involvement with the "dark lady," see Angela Carter *Black Venus*, London, Picador Books, 1985, for a short story told in the persona of Jeanne Duval.

8 McNelly, op. cit., p. 10.

9 For discussion of the avant-garde as a game of reference, deference and difference, see my *Avant-Garde Gambits 1888–93: Gender and the Colour of Art History*, London, Thames & Hudson, 1993. This section of the chapter draws on the longer discussion in that book.

10 Orientalism, initially theorized by Edward Said in *Orientalism*, London, Routledge & Kegan Paul, 1978, has been widely used to analyse the visual imagery of Europe's cultural transactions with its colonial others, specifically, but not exclusively in the Islamic world of North Africa and the near East. Linda Nochlin's article "The Imaginary Orient," reprinted in *The Politics of Vision*, London, Thames & Hudson, 1991, reviews recent exhibitions of such paintings and provides a critical reading of them to which we are all indebted.

11 I am indebted to Mieke Bal, *Reading Rembrandt*, Cambridge, Cambridge University Press, 1991, for her analysis of iconography and both critical uses of reference texts and failures to do so: see Ch. 5, "Recognition: Reading Icons: Seeing Stories."

12 Paul Gauguin, *Letters to his Wife and Friends*, trans. Henry J. Stenning, London, The Saturn Press, 1949, Letter 134, pp. 177–8.

13 Bracha Lichtenberg Ettinger, "Matrix and Metramorphosis," *Differences* 4: 3, 1993, and her essay included in this volume.

14 Griselda Pollock, *Avant-Garde Gambits 1888–93: Gender and the Colour of Art History*, London, Thames & Hudson, 1993.

15 Two famous examples are paintings by Nicholas Poussin *Summer* (from his *Four Seasons*) and J. F. Millet, *Harvesters Resting*, 1852.

16   My thinking about this part of the text is indebted to Naomi Segal, "Reading as a feminist: the case of Sarah and Naomi," *University of Leeds Review* 32, 1989/90, pp. 37–57.

17   I am thinking about Lacan's later formulations on the constitution of the subject: "In the scopic field the gaze is outside. I am looked at, that is to say I am a picture. This is the function that is found at the heart of the institution of the subject in the visible. What determines me, at the most profound level, in the visible, is the gaze that is outside. It is through the gaze that I enter light and it is from the gaze that I receive its effects. Hence it comes about that the gaze is the instrument through which light is embodied and through which … I am photographed" (J. Lacan, *Four Fundamental Concepts of Psychoanalysis* [1973], ed. J. A. Miller, trans. A. Sheridan, Harmondsworth, Penguin Books, 1979, pp. 95–6). For further commentary on this concept see K. Silverman, *The Acoustic Mirror*, Bloomington, Indiana University Press, 1988, pp. 161–2.

18   Linda Nochlin, "The Imaginary Orient," in *The Politics of Vision*, London, Thames & Hudson 1991, pp. 33–59.

19   The reference to Linda Nochlin is from Nochlin, op. cit., R. Dyer, "White," *Screen* 29: 4, 1988, pp. 44–65; C. Miller, *Blank Darkness, Africanist Discourse in French*, London and Chicago, University of Chicago Press, 1985.

20   Feminists have done a lot of work on the critical importance of the working-class women who cared for and contributed to the formation of bourgeois children at both social and psychic levels, for instance L. Davidoff, "Class and Gender in Victorian England" in *Sex and Class in Women's History*, ed. Judith L. Newton *et al.*, London, Routledge & Kegan Paul, 1983; J. Gallop, *Feminism and Psychoanalysis: The Daughter's Seduction*, London, Macmillan, 1982.

21   K. Marx, 'The Eighteenth Brumaire of Louis Bonaparte' [1852], reprinted in *Marx and Engels Selected Works In One Volume*, London, Lawrence & Wishart, 1968, p. 117; J.-P. Sartre, "Class consciousness in Flaubert," *Modern* Occasions 1: 3, 1971.

22   F. Fanon, *Black Skin White Masks* [1952], London, Pluto Press, 1986; C. Steedman, *Landscape for a Good Woman*, London, Virago, 1987. Steedman writes about two such scenes: one when her mother is criticized by a middle-class social worker, the other when her father is chastized for picking flowers in a public park by the park warden.

23   It is very rare that white children in these situations ever see their black nannies in their own contexts, for both servants' quarters and trips to the African workers' homes are severely prohibited. The restrictions are of course broken, but for me, the memories of visiting Julia in her "shack" hidden in our garden, with its bare walls and floors, its bed up on bricks, its utter contrast to the luxury in which my family and I lived were painful moments—a confusion of feelings about the awful conditions in which someone so loved and needed by me was

made to live by others whom I also was meant to love and respect. Responses to this situation as a child are limited—political activism later may be a result of this other kind of "witness" to social "castration." But this unacknowledged body of feelings which are carried by children raised in these circumstances can have other outcomes—in the case of the male child, sexual uses and abuses, enacted upon African women, which parallel the formulation of bourgeois masculinity in the European household with its working-class nannies and child minders, which Freud analysed in his paper "On the universal tendency to debasement in the sphere of love" [1912]. *Freud Pelican Library: On Sexuality* Vol. 7, Harmondsworth, Penguin Books, 1977.

24 Thandabantu Nhlapo, "Women's rights and the family in traditional and customary law," and Frene Ginwala, "Women and the elephant: the need to redress gender oppression" in *Putting Women on the Agenda*, ed. Susan Bazilli, Johannesburg, Raven Press, 1991.

25 Ellen Kuzwayo, *Call Me Woman*, London, The Women's Press, 1985.

26 African women employed as domestic servants are often, like working-class women in the metropolitan countries were, given names by their employers. African identity is thus eroded by the employee being known only in the household by obviously European names, like Julia, Daniel, Pius, Sarah and so forth.

27 Janina Bauman, *A Dream of Belonging*, London, Virago, 1989.

28 Lubaina Himid, *Revenge*, 1992, Rochdale Art Gallery, Rochdale, England. Catalogue edited by Jill Morgan and Maud Sulter.

griselda pollock

THIS TEXT PRESENTS A SELF-PORTRAIT OF a feminist intellectual haunted by death.

It was first presented as part of an installation: a filing cabinet, a TV monitor and two armchairs with headphones linked by leads snaking back to the image box. A hard, metallic body formed a memory cabinet, trying to keep things in order and classified in separate compartments. The video monitor offers a glimpse into the mind—a place of thought, imagination, fantasy and trauma. It is silent. The witness must hear the words that struggle with and against the images. The witness must hear them in her own body and space. In performance, the audience hears my body speak the words I publicly reclaim and own. As written text, the unspoken sound runs through the reader's mind. The piece is in seven parts—moving in, frame by frame, from cultural texts—a painting and a play—to two Jewish theorists of modernity hunted by fascism: Walter Benjamin and Sigmund Freud—to men mourning their parents—Paul Bryant and Roland Barthes and, at the center, there is the "dark core" of my dead mother and my bereaved motherhood.

deadly tale no. 1   1636

The art historian stood up, adjusted her half-glasses to a precise point on the bridge of her nose, clicked the remote and craned her head awkwardly to check the focus on what she hoped was the correct slide. She began:

In 1635–36, the English painter John Souch painted *Sir Thomas Aston at the Deathbed of his Wife.*

Set in an imaginary bedchamber, the painting divides into distinct compartments.

These generate a web of meaning.

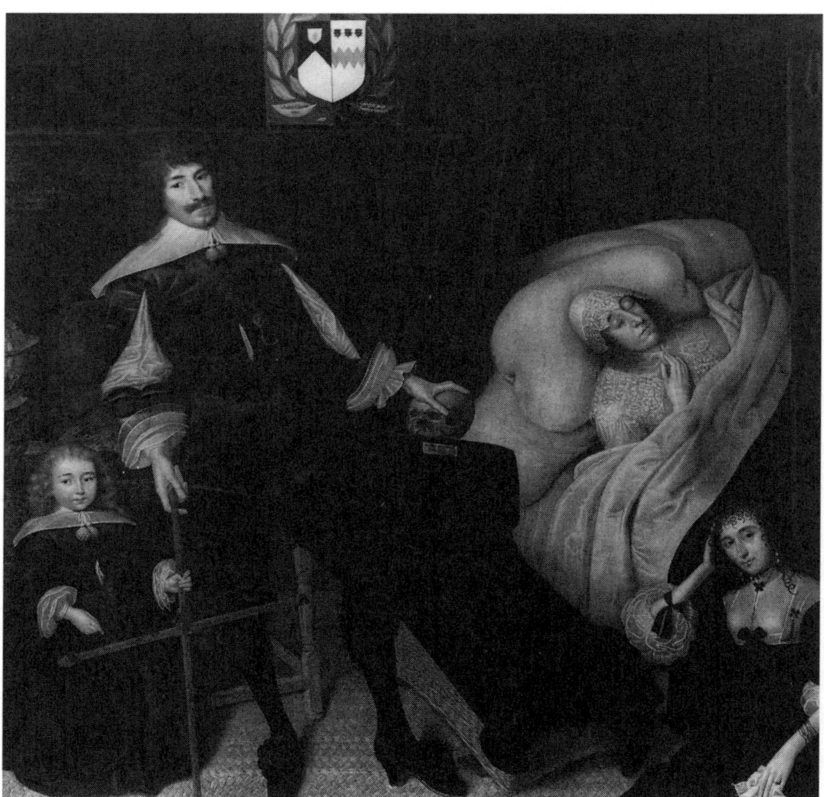

Figure 1   John Souch. *Sir Thomas Aston at the Death Bed of His Wife,* 1635–6. Manchester City Art Gallery.

Magdalene Aston died in childbirth 2 June 1635 leaving her husband Thomas and young son, Thomas,

who would himself die but two years later.

The draped cradle surmounted with a skull signifies another, recently deceased child.

Its sombre darkness—creating a central void in the painting—

contrasts dramatically with the pallor of the laid-out mother who has died in childbirth.

It is perhaps a little unnerving, if inexplicable, to find this same Magdalene Aston represented a second time in the painting, appearing to be alive, elegantly seated in the classic posture of melancholy at the foot of her own deathbed.

This curious doubling is a feature of the sixteeenth century theory of "two bodies," the natural, which dies and decays,

and the social which should be preserved in an elevating representation as "an element in collective memory." [1]

The painting can also be read in relation to the historical concepts of the family.

The body of woman is positioned iconically as the instrument not merely of procreation but of dynasty.

Madeleine Aston's body is the point of passage between Sir Thomas Aston and his offspring, a prospective Sir Thomas Aston.

Different bodies, same names, they would by succession keep the social body of the Aston family in a continuous present.

The painting exposes Magdalene Aston's failure to repeat and thus secure this patriarchal lineage. The draped cradle-cum-catafalgue occupies the center of the painting as a sign linking femininity and death.

It serves as the dark hinge between the erect masculine, symbol-ladened lineage of father and son and the languid, deadly, "feminine" domain of life and natural death, with its secondary existence in representation but only in the emblematic form of female melancholy.

The art historian removed her glasses and shuffled the papers back into a neat rectangle, looking up at the audience in the expectation of a question.

deadly tale no. 2   1940
walter benjamin 1992—1940

Diary Entry for an overworked academic.

16 July, 1992. I am at the Birkbeck conference to celebrate the centenary of Walter Benjamin.[2]

31 July 1992. Told A on the phone about the conference on Benjamin that he had missed. He replied with great satisfaction that, by pure chance, he had found himself on the very day of the anniversary of his birth, in Port Bou, the Spanish village in the Pyrannees where Walter Benjamin had committed suicide on 26 or 27 September 1940.

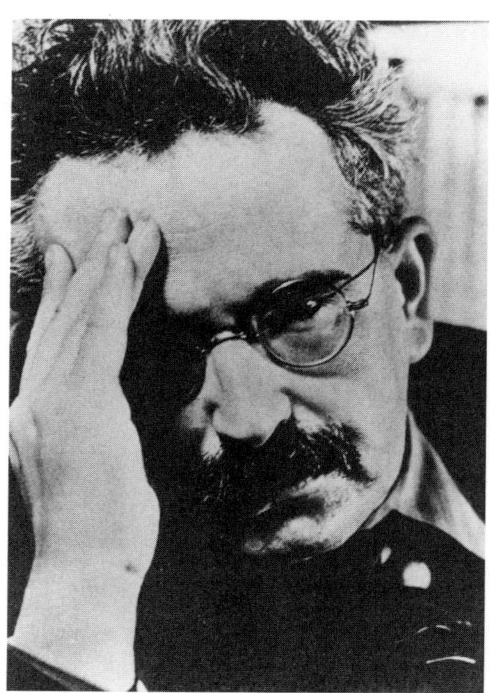

Figure 2   Gisele Freund, *Walter Benjamin*, Paris, 1939.

4 August 1992. Ever since the conversation with A I have found myself wondering, belatedly and yet for the first time, about the details of what I had frequently taken simply as a symbolic caesura in the history of critical theory rather than a concrete event enacted on a real body. How did Walter Benjamin die? At what time of day? Did he suffer? What happened to his body?

I got my copy of Gershom Scholem's story of his friendship with Walter Benjamin down from the shelf and checked the index entry under death. Sholem writes that he learned of his friend's death (on 26 or 27 September 1940) only on 8 November from Hannah Arendt who had visited Port Bou but found no trace of a grave. He reprints a letter which provides the only firm information about Benjamin's self-administered overdose of morphine, and the disposal of the body in a grave bought for five years by Frau Gurland, one of Benjamin's travelling companions. No trace of this grave has ever been found—Hannah Arendt went to seek it. I decided to write out the conclusion Sholem draws.

> Many years later, in the cemetery that Hannah Arendt had seen, a grave with Benjamin's name scrawled on the wooden enclosure was being shown to visitors. The photographs before me clearly indicate that this grave, which is completely isolated and utterly separate from the actual burial places, is an invention of cemetery attendants, who in consideration of the number of inquiries wanted to assure themselves of a tip.[3]

I am struggling with the relations between the suicide of Benjamin and his apocryphal grave and the much huger, more terrifying and indeed almost unimaginable collective experience of death that he killed himself to avoid: the murder of over 6 million people in what is known as "The Event," "That which Happened," and simply "The Destruction: Ha-Shoah."

Note for future lecture: Benjamin's use of Koestler's half-portion of morphine inflicted death by his own hand on his natural body, but the circumstances leave us with no social body to traverse that terrible darkness that opens up between the dead and their memory.

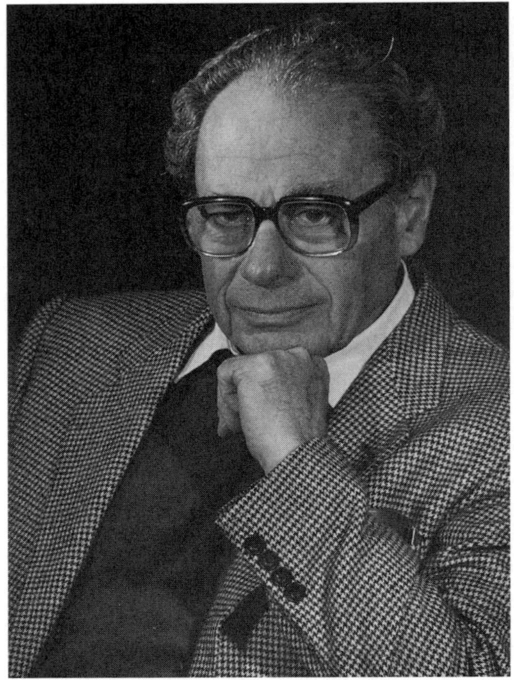

Figure 3 Zygmunt Bauman, *Paul Bryant*, 1983.

deadly tale no. 3 1992
pavel blumenzweig 1913–1992

Letter written to a friend, 26 June 1992.

Dear B,

Thank you for your letter of condolence. Yes, it is hard to believe. Pavel Blumenzweig, born in 1913, in Teplitz, in what is now the Czeck Republic, known after 1940 as Paul Bryant, has died at the age of 79. His is not a name curated by collective memory, yet I think he was, nonetheless, a historic figure because he was a figure of that history, although he escaped the Nazi invasion of Czechoslovakia in 1939 and survived to die of disease in old age in Leeds in May 1992.

He survived.

We say: "He escaped" and "He survived."

He was not untouched, however, for he was condemned to live with the experience of that monumental twentieth-century death.

He was sentenced to carry with him the knowledge that his own parents did not die of disease,

of old age,

of an accident,

but had been callously destroyed.

Old and trusting people, who could not believe what he told them about the threat against them because it surpassed imagination, even in a world where anti-Semitism was an everyday habit and part of the national culture.

They were horribly put to death, poisoned and suffocated by gas, and their bodies were burnt.

This manner of extinction changes the very ways we, who come after, forever contemplate that most singular of life-events, death.

I keep coming back to Benjamin's associate, Theodor Adorno, who wrote in his famous and disturbing essay, "After Auschwitz":

> The administrative murder of millions made of death a thing one had never yet to fear in just this fashion. There is no chance anymore for death to come into the individuals' empirical life as somehow conformable with the course of that life. The last, the poorest possession left to the individual is expropriated. That in the concentration camp it was no longer an individual who died, but a specimen—this is a fact bound to affect the dying of those who escaped the administrative measure.[4]

After Paul's death, as part of the curation of his social body, his memory for us, the collating of his papers, we found a short letter in his files, a letter from the International Red Cross Tracing Agency dated 1957. The letter bleakly informed Paul Bryant of Middlesex, England, of the exact date and precise number of the transport which had carried his parents Emily Ornstein and Berko Blumenzweig from the ghetto of Terezin (Theresienstadt) to Oswieçiem, better known in its German name, Auschwitz. The letter provided a date from which we could determine their certain destruction as elderly people who would have passed direct to the gas chambers, there to die a cruel, naked and unrecorded death.

My father-in-law "survived" and he lived to be stolen from his family by an undiagnosed cancer.

Cancer is a thief.

It silently crept upon us and snatched him away in ten days.

On the last night, I was the one who was visiting in the early evening. He had had sudden pain at the weekend and we were forced back to Leeds from our birthday weekend for him in the Lakes. They thought it was appendicitis and operated on Sunday evening. It was soon clear that it was something else. But they never say. The consultant just said we *must* see the surgeons, again, soon. None had come by five so I flew across the hospital to the ward where he had been for the operation and demanded a surgeon come over to see him. After half an hour, they came, a flock of doctors, white coats flapping, and I knew things were bad when they asked whom we should send for—and any relatives that might want to come. On the last evening, I sat by his hospital bed and I saw, it. I saw death creep over him. Death seemed like a pillow slowly suffocating a struggling man. It was visible. Before me was a dear friend, reduced by illness to a biochemical system being poisoned by systemic failure which an already weakened heart could not withstand. After a last-minute attempt to save him by surgery, he died the next day. They laid him out in intensive care. We took our leave of him. In death he looked like a great warrior on his funeral bier—for the poison had been swift in its devastation and the outer corporeal envelope betrayed no trace of the organic breakdown within.

His death screens from me the death of my own father six years before. He died in his sleep, from emphysema. Suddenly I got the phone call too early in the morning for it to be good news. This time, I experienced the coming of death, the tenderness of caring for a person whose body pains and fails them, the intuition and knowing that it cannot be stopped and the rage against the secret thief that changed all our lives.

What to do?

Yours, ...

deadly tale no. 4   1964
kathleen pollock 1911—1964

Text of a Talk to a Feminist Group on Autobiography and Grief.

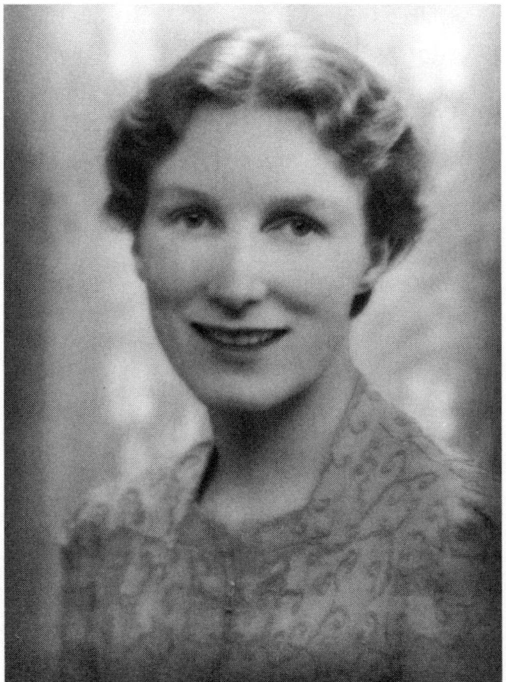

Figure 4.   Anon., *Kathleen Sinclair Pollock*, 1940.

"This is the second time cancer has robbed me.

My mother died on 30 January 1964 of cancer of the colon which had spread into her spine. She was 52.

Undiagnosed by doctors, her symptoms were misattributed to menopause—to middle age and femininity.

Not unlike me in size and build, she weighed less than 40 pounds at her death.

She was both horrified and fascinated by what the deadly disease had done to her. Stick-like legs protruded below a distended belly, like some Oxfam victim of famine—or an adolescent pregnancy.

Here was an outrageous morphology: the shape which promises life contained the ghastly growth that signaled imminent death—something within that natural body was gnawing away at whatever the social body is meant to encase: humanity, personhood. I have never come to terms with this death.

Its physicality was too outrageous.

The distortion of the maternal body was too grotesque to allow recovery and re-internalization of the beneficent image of the mother as either an imago of identification or as a memory of plenitude and desire.

All other traces of her were traumatically cauterized by the final victory of the diseased natural body over all that, in life, makes the body a social being, and the stuff of dreams.

The only moment of relief from terminal loss occurred when I was to become a mother myself.

Innocently, naively, I imagined it that it would be an easy and complete antidote to death—

fullness instead of emptiness,

presence in place of absence.

I miscarried.

In that, my first pregnancy, I dreamed the transitivities of feminine identity.

I oscillated between the maternal and the infant, between recreating my own mother, reaching out to her again, and imagining the joys of being a child cradled lovingly in the safety of another's body.

I created an imaginary realm of comfort which promised to bind a traumatized past to a healing future, offering restoration in an experience of maternal plenitude and power through the new life which was developing within the matrix of my own body—a singular space of doubling, oneness and otherness, where an I and a non-I co-exist harmoniously.

Pain exploded this dream.

Instead of life within the uterine matrix of severality, inner death led to a parody of birth as the no-longer-maternal body contracted to rid itself of dangerously decaying physical matter.

I did not know who was being mourned.

With pregnancy, I had once again become the child to be nurtured a second time round through the surrogacy of my own nurturing of my child.

I was also my mother.

I was also giving birth to her again.

I was being given, in the female child I was sure I was carrying, another chance to love her better so that she would not die through any act of omission on my part.

I failed again to defeat that history.
Doubling life gave way to redoubled grief.

Julia Kristeva talks of pregnancy as an almost psychotic state, a confusion of subjectivity as "cells combine, redouble, proliferate; size grows, tissue is distended, moods change their rhythm—speed up, slow down: within one body an autonomous other grafts itself. And within that space, both double and stranger, there is no one to signify this. The impossible syllogism of motherhood—"*It* is happening therefore *I* am not there" or "I cannot think it, yet it is happening."[5]
Julia Kristeva asks: Who is the subject of gestation?
I ask—who is the subject of death?
"It happened, therefore I am not there" or "I cannot think it, yet it happened."

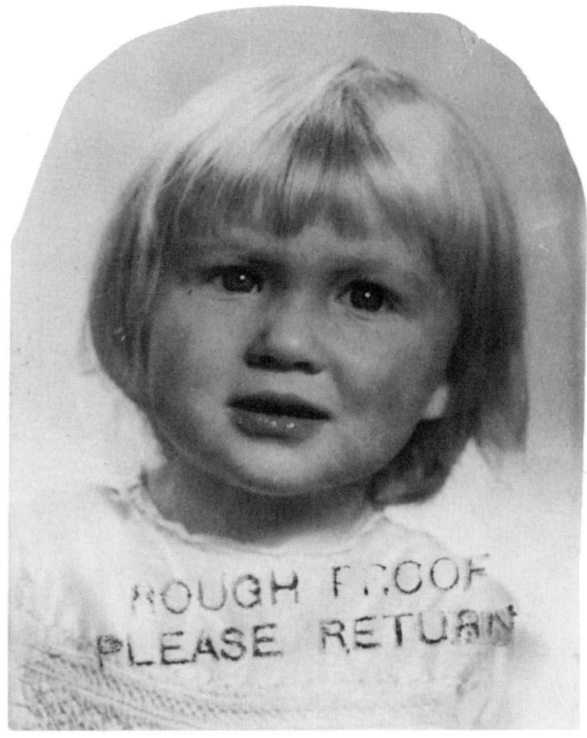

Figure 5.   Anon., *Rough Proof: Please Return*, 1950.

For the dying and dead, death annihilates subjectivity.
The living are the subjects of death. The living bear the event that happens elsewhere to another, to a natural body. The bereaved are its social body. This is why the philosophers never get it. They talk of death as human finitude. But I talk of death as something that happened to me who is not its living witness, the carrier of its memory, but its subject.
Can death then be gendered?" (fig. 5)

deadly tale no. 5
roland barthes 1915–1980

Extract from article by C.D. on "Death and Its Gender" (1992)

In 1992, I belatedly read with care the central sections of *Camera Lucida* (1980). While I was gazing helplessly at photographs of my own dead mother, hoping to pierce the utter fixity of the photographic image and

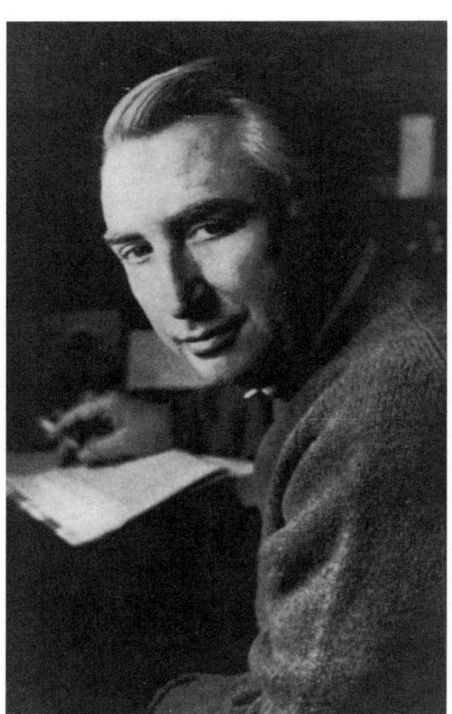

Figure 6.   Jerry Bauer, *Roland Barthes*, 1974.

reclaim some grain of recognition from its aesthetic freeze, I found Barthes had elegantly been there before me. Or had he?

> There I was, alone in the apartment where she had died, looking at these pictures of my mother, one by one, under the lamp, gradually moving back in time with her, looking for the truth of the face I had loved. And I found it.

He's writing about a photograph of his mother at age five, taken in 1898, in a conservatory or winter garden and in this childish prefiguration of her adult face, Barthes found **the** image of his mother. This photograph—which he will not show—is the heart of the book, its navel, says Elisabeth Bronfen. His mother is kept safe from our eyes; she's kept safe for his only.[6] Barthes tells us about the last period of this five-year-old child's later life, by which time she is his mother: she has no name, no being in this text except as "my mother"—Barthes' self-consolidating Other.

> At the end of her life, shortly before the moment when I looked through her pictures and discovered the Winter Garden Photograph, my mother was weak, very weak. I lived in her weakness … . During her illness, I nursed her, held the bowl of tea she liked because it was easier to drink from than from a cup; she had become my little girl, uniting for me with that essential child she was in her first photograph … . Ultimately I experienced her, strong as she had been, my inner law, as my feminine child. Which was my way of resolving Death. If, as so many philosophers have said, Death is the harsh victory of the race, if the particular dies for the satisfaction of the universal, if after having been reproduced as other than himself, the individual dies, having thereby denied and transcended himself, I who had not procreated, I had, in her very illness, engendered my mother. (72)

Death seems, therefore, to stage the oscillations between mother and child, trapping us into imaging once again a correspondence between life and death, or at least life-giving and death. No, this is not what is happening here, for this death is a radical rupture, in Barthes's case, from a dyad of mother and son to the perplexing unity of male mother and ancient daughter, a shift to the feminine significantly recouped by the use of the verb *engender*. *Engendre* in my French dictionary is defined as to beget—which has overtones of biblical narratives where a male genealogy is aligned down the generations through a lot of father/son begetting. Does this bring us back to the left side of the Souch painting with Barthes strung out across its different spaces and registers, his mother occupying that empty cradle atopped by the skull?

Barthes tells us that he nursed her, feeding her like a mother would a child. The mother became his *feminine* child—*enfant féminine* is the phrase used so she is not merely, matter-of-factly his daughter, his offspring. That feminine child is also him, my child, the child within me, the desired space of being a woman child to a mother, rather than a childless son to a dying woman.

In psychoanalytical narratives—another mother-killing death narrative?—a stake is important. Michèle Montrelay says women are the ruin of representation because they don't have a stake, something to mortgage to the Symbolic and language. Their sexuality and fantasy life retain the stamp of that archaic, precocious femininity entangled in the maternal body. With the son's bereavement, and no child created through his passage into and beyond a woman's body, Barthes lost his stake: except in being an intellectual.

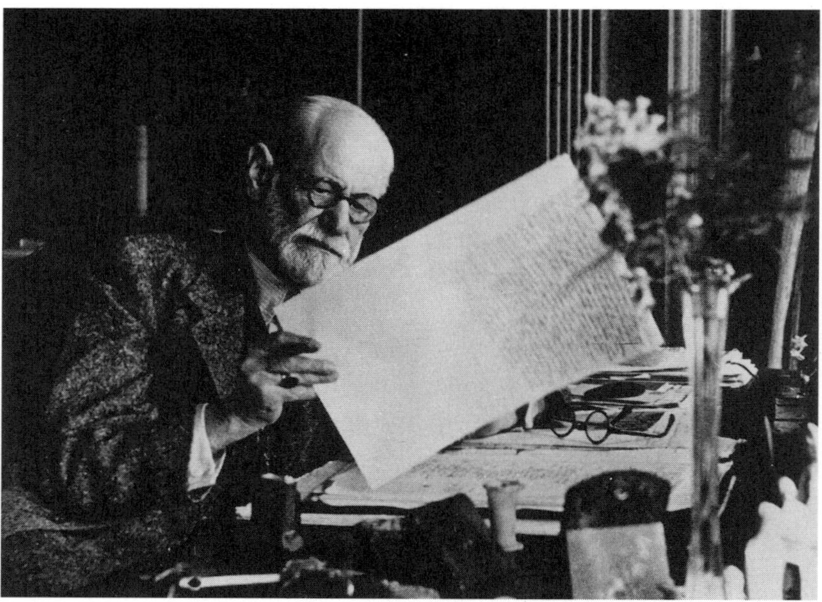

Figure 7.   *Sigmund Freud at his desk reading his Abrisse der Psychanalyse,* 1938. Mary Evans Picture Library.

deadly tale no. 6 oedipus-smoedipus—so long as he loves his mother

Diary Entry of a Feminist Academic, E.

21 April: You know I have come to the bizarre conclusion that Freud was not really writing about Oedipus and the castration complex. He used the Greek legend as a cover for too dangerous an idea to speak about openly. He was talking about another myth about death and the generations: about Isaac and the father/son death complex. The founding contract of sociality and the submission to the paternal law is better told in the Bible story of Abraham, called by his God to sacrifice his by then only son—the belated first fruit of Sarah's aged womb. The human social contract is established when Abraham's one unnameable God lets Abraham off killing his (legitimate) son with a big knife, displacing the actual sacrifice of the child of Sarah's womb, by substituting a *symbolic* act, the killing of a ram, which will stand as a metaphor for what God actually wanted from Abraham, namely his obedience to the Law. In a sense, God demanded Abraham's being which is what we concede to the Symbolic, to language, finding ourselves reformed and displaced through its signifiers.

This biblical narrative concludes with no further discussion of Isaac—named so because he made his mother laugh—but ends with the death of Sarah, the mother. The maternal process of creating the child was symbolically overtaken by the divine act of threatening its life and restoring it but only in an exclusive lineage of father to son.[7] The Greek version of such mythic material, the Oedipus legend, within which Freud disguised and thus disfigured his profound understanding of the symbolic contract of the binding of Isaac, is much more overtly about sexual organs, and desire itself—and the mother becomes the major figure screening the revenge of the son on the father, Laius, whom Oedipus unknowingly slays on his way to Thebes.

Instead of dying, out of sight, like Sarah, Jocasta acquires the characteristics of the Sphinx, the animal world over which the Greeks imagined man triumphed by his reason and unique self-recognition. Jocasta the mother becomes the figure of Death who can equally never escape being the lure of a masculine desire.

But what of Roland Barthes, the Protestant, not surrounded in childhood with that Greek and ever-older pre-Judaic image of the Mother and Child which has persisted in western Catholicism? After recounting his begetting of his feminine self/child in the mortal image of his lost mother, he writes his own suicide note:

> Once she was dead I no longer had any reason to attune myself to the progress of the superior Life Force (the race, the species) My particularity could never again universalise itself (unless utopically, by writing, whose project henceforth would become the unique goal of my life). From now on I could do no more that await my total, undialectical death.
> That is what I read in the Winter Garden Photograph.

It is quite clear that art will always enact death because it is the compensation for the creativity which, denied to men, allows women a dialectical relation of both self and other and life and death. The philosophers to whom Barthes refers sound pretty local, probably Lacanian, to me with all that junk about the race and the species, the particular and the individual. It is because they are allowed to get away with such utter banality and abstraction that Barthes can write *out* such a fantasy which so clearly delineates the uses and abuses of the female procreative and maternal body as the hidden center, the absent structure of phallic surrogate creativities.

I want to talk about death without too many of my own metaphorical delusions.

I want to talk about it in terms of blood, shit, bloating, gas chambers.

I want it to be embodied.

I want to be able to speak and think about my mother, her death, my mourning, my dead babies, those bloodied surgical dishes with the remnants of possible beings, sacs containing almost formed little limbs, who were not my stake in the race, my contribution to the species, but fully formed figurations of my own desire and themselves, real, physical life.

I do not want my body to be the passage through which men may beget themselves and their progeny.

I want it to be the site of a sexually specific and particular subjectivity which is a subject of gestation and of mourning.

Touched as I am by the poignant frankness of Roland Barthes's sharing in public of his feelings about his mother and her death, I see in his text the quintessential forms of the Western masculine narratives which embrace death rather than acknowledge the humanity of women. The female body—as opposed to its feminized death as enshrined in our culture—remains a terrifying hybrid—just as shocking to those of us who live inside it yet lack a signifying system to speak it. Even to mention my mother in public lacks, I feel, the validation of social collective memory which attaches to Barthes's lovely, silent, mother to whom he never spoke, in whose presence he admits he never discoursed for there was just "the space of love, its music." I am sure that the term "my mother" uttered by another woman signifies in our culture someone or rather something quite different from the image evoked if those words emerge from masculine speech. It risks the decline into senti-mentality, autobiography, not philosophical reflection on time, history and the text. That is why no image of her, captured in the obvious signifying systems of culture, moves me to recognize her—my mother. For the rela-tions of woman to woman via the maternal body and imago are sexually specific and, in the words of Kaja Silverman, endemically melancholic, that is, akin to a state of perpetual mourning. Mourning involves the withdrawal of libidinal investment in an object which is lost or has disappointed and this retraction is complete only when the object is discarded, having been rendered valueless by the success of forces of hatred over those of love which seek to maintain the cathexis. In the formation of feminine subjectivity, Silverman argues for an overlooked Freudian theorization of the negative Oedipal complex, i.e., a situation in which the mother is the desired object of the female child as well as the figure of identification in the construction of a gendered positionality in culture. The negative Oedipal attachment must be overcome, but the process will induce melancholia and a kind of mourning in the child because she is asked to devalue that with which she is also identified—in a sense she must lose herself. The cure—devaluation of the object—a detachment from the mother—is not possible or desirable. Femininity is condemned to a permanent and incomplete mourning which perpetually betrays its own ambivalences which can only be worked out dynamically, in other relations, such as joining the women's movement or having a child, that is, in activity rather than the passivity which masculine narratives impose on women, dead or alive.

deadly tale 7. last tale—a play reading from 1964

Towards the end of the lecture, the speaker suddenly stopped, took off her glasses and looked directly at the audience. Speaking as if she had decided to abandon her lecture on "Death in Shakespeare's Plays," she began in a weary voice. As she spoke, she became more animated, assuming the characters from a play.

"A long time ago, shortly after my mother died in 1964, I was taken to the Old Vic to see Tom Stoppard's play *Rosencrantz and Guildenstern Are Dead*. At the very end of the play, itself a playing out of themes from margins of Shakespeare's *Hamlet*, the leader of a band of actors, The Player, declares:

In our experience most things end in death.

A truism so banal, yet an ironic insight into patriarchal culture.

A comment about the deep structure of narrative, about the ever-present death drive. Stories end with death or marriage—much the same thing, traditionally.

Death becomes the figure of stasis, fixity, finality.

It is not.

Stoppard makes Guildenstern say so:

Death is not anything. Death is not.

It is not in the realm of being; like woman, it cannot be.

But it leaves a trace:

No one gets up after death—there is no applause—there is only silence and some second hand clothes ....

So true—all those poignant remains of daily life. What do we do with clothes:

Wear them, sell them, give them to strangers? Can we bear to part with what had once touched the missing body and graced its social presence?

The Player pretends to die, then gets up and takes his bow. He lists the kinds of death he and his actors can perform. Guildenstern can't bear it.

No ... . No ... . not for us, not like that. Dying is not romantic, and death is not a game which will soon be over.

Death is not anything.

Death is not.

It's the absence of presence, nothing more … . the endless time of never coming back …. a gap you can't see, and when the wind blows through it, it makes no sound.

The absence of presence,

The absence of presence

The presence of absence,

The presence of absence,

The endless time of never coming back

The endless time

of never

coming back

of never coming back

of never, never, never,

being there.

Endless neverness is real and constant, and makes a hole in a life that cannot be repaired and yet it creates a gap—a wound—*you* cannot see.

When the wind blows through it, it makes no sound.

I wanted to give that gap a sound.

I wanted to speak the endlessness of living with a grief that cannot be assuaged.

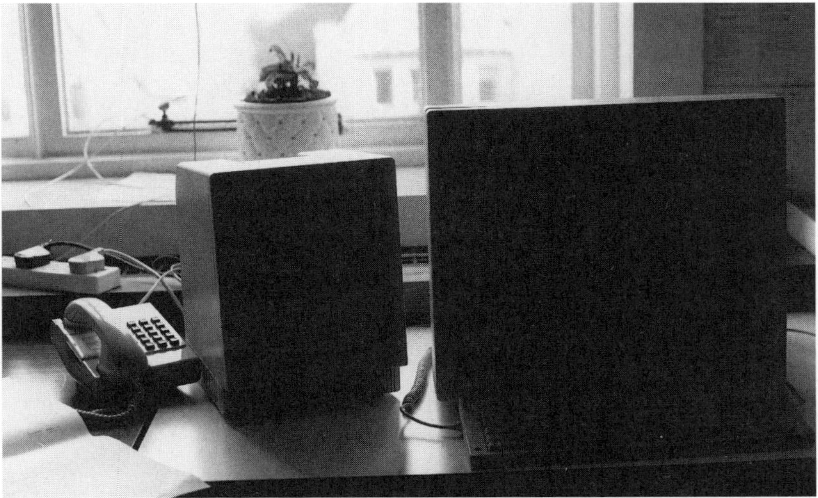

Figure 8.   Griselda Pollock, *The Death of Writing*, 1992.

Death lives with me and I live in it.
And I have tried to speak it, yet ….

afterword

However hard I have tried to find aesthetic forms through which to shuffle my pain and grief, to fix death to an image which contains and yet defers it, to pacify it, I cannot in all honesty pretend that the photograph or any sequence of images I might manipulate and call art, can stop that endless time of someone being missing in daily life as well as in my psychological stagings of my own formation. The millions of people today who are dying are leaving people who are terminally bereaved and there is, in our culture, as yet no adequate narrative which can stay, stop, halt or freeze that process, for me, and I dare to suggest for most. Why is this?

notes

1   Nigel Llewellyan, *The Art of Death : Visual Culture in the English Death Ritual c. 1500–1800* (London: Reaktion Books, 1991), 47.

2   Proceedings published as *The Actuality of Walter Benjamin*, ed. Laura Marcus and Lynda Nead, *New Formations* (1993), no. 20.

3   Gershom Sholem, *Walter Benjamin: The Story of a Friendship* (New York: Shocken Books, 1981), 226.

4   Theodor Adorno, "After Auschwitz," [1949] *Negative Dialectics*, trans. E. B. Ashton (New York: Continuum, 1973), 362.

5   Julia Kristeva, "Motherhood According to Giovanni Bellini," *Polylogue*, (Paris: Editions du Seuil, 1977), trans. Claire Pajaczkowska, in *M/F*, Nos. 5 & 6, (1981), 158.

6   p. 73. Something like an essence of the Photograph floated in this particular picture. I therefore decided to "derive" all Photography (its "nature") from the only photograph which assuredly existed for me, and to take it as a guide for my last investigation … . I had understood that henceforth I must interrogate the evidence of Photography, not from the viewpoint of pleasure, but in relation to what we romantically call love and death.

7   See Naomi Segal, "Reading as Feminist: The Case of Sarah and Naomi," *University of Leeds Review*, vol. 32, (1989–90), 37–57.

commentary:
griselda pollock
and feminist
critique:
post/modernism
in the fourth
dimension

penny florence

Thus my practice as a writer is concerned to refashion the historical knowledge of modern culture. I want to comprehend in one, dialectical movement the specificity of women's participation in its production and the conditions of the repression of knowledge of it.

Griselda Pollock
Critical Positions

preliminary
a critical situation

THE DRIVE OF ALL GRISELDA POLLOCK'S work over recent years, perhaps especially as it is represented in this volume, implicates readers beyond their responsiveness, however complexly that notion of "reader-response" is understood. The reader is conjoined as a *producer* of culture and of meaning. So it is that as you, the reader, to approximate the words just quoted at the head of this essay, gain a historicized sense of women's participation in the production of modern culture, you also participate either in its development or in the "repression of know-ledge of it." In approaching this commentary on Pollock's work, therefore, the reader may usefully pause to consider her/himself as a Subject and as a thinker and as a producer of meaning. As commentator, I myself am trian-gulated with her text and your text as part of that dynamic: triangulation is indeed only the basic ligature, since the spaces of this intertext are also inhabited by the visual works around which the words move and by the self-identified critical positionings it both negotiates and challenges. This could not be a commentary in any traditional exegetical sense. Such a position is no longer available.

This stimulating if difficult state of affairs is symptomatic of the philo-sophical crisis that has clearly been playing out through the last decades of the last century, but whose full trajectory, I would argue, extends right across it. What I shall attempt to do here is to make conscious use of the productive intertextuality set up in the *Critical Voices* series in order to situate Pollock's work and the feminist discourses and female-produced art which she has contributed to developing in the overall cultural kinesis. But the reader should make no mistake: even in those moments when the text that follows seems furthest away from any explicit reference to the Pollock of the rest of this book, an engagement with that work is its primary source.

I hope to demonstrate how Pollock's work may usefully be read as bodying forth in relation to the discourses of art and its histories the general crisis described just alluded to, and described for example by Rosi Braidotti as indicating a philosophy which is "both critique and act of creation of new forms of thought. It calls into question the very foundations and premises of what we recognize as 'thinking'" (Braidotti 1991, 3). Because most of Pollock's references are to works of the Modern period, and because the Modern (ist) Subjectivity is a nodal point in this crisis, "Modernism" has some prominence in what follows. But Pollock's work is premised on a more nuanced understanding of Modernism than that which is often declared to have been superceded by an illusory post-Modernism. This is not to say that the signifier "post-Modernism" is empty, as will become clear. Rather, it is to recognize in her critique of Modernism her creation of new forms. Braidotti notes that modernity as a philosophy has as its subtext the decline of the paternal metaphor. This is crucial to psychoanalysis: "The project of thinking the subject as a corporeal entity is one of the key events of the philosophy of modernity" (17). If this is what Pollock means by "the project of modernity," discussed below, I can only agree that it is essential not to abandon it. Braidotti also provides a clue in Nietzschean terms as to the development of Pollock's critical voice over time, which has become increasingly experimental, incorporating subjective and/or autobiographical material, not as arbiter or appeal to simple experience, but as another kind of evidence: "autohistory" (see especially "Territories of Desire"). It is urgent that the consequences of understanding that the subject of modernity is not identical to "self-reflecting consciousness" are not dissipated in a fog of imprecise neo-humanism. Braidotti points out that theoretical thought, "institutionalised as philosophy" is fundamentally incompatible with the body, since it is based on a misreading of the corporeal basis of subjectivity. Pollock's recognition of this alongside her understanding of art as a reticulated set of material practices the very least puts into question the authoritative voice of even "new" art histories. This is also one reason why her interest in the work of Bracha Lichtenberg Ettinger as theorist of the maternal (there are by now, after all, several) is deeper than the surface fact that she is an artist-theorist-analyst. Another is surely the directness of the link she forges with modernism as a racialised, sexed discourse and its historical consequence in the Holocaust and continuing holocausts. In this, reference to the real is emphatically not abandoned. But it is never assumed simply to be; the real is no more discrete that the imaginary or the symbolic or whatever set of terms you choose for kinds of relations between the self, the sign and the world under analysis. Nobody can afford to ignore the materiality of the sign in this dynamic, but given the kinds of the material control that have been exercised through the representation of women, people of color and those perceived to be of lower class, most especially no feminist.

I am well aware that objections will be raised to some of the directions I would wish to take this, especially in relation to Pollock's blend of materialism and psychoanalysis. Perhaps I might anticipate some of them by foregrounding potential compatibilities where it is usually the incompatibilities that are communicated. Lisa Tickner's position, that psychoanalysis and marxism are incompatible, also queries the possibility of any all-embracing theory of the subject and social relations in history, and queries the benefit to women of seeking one. I agree with this, but understand it as leaving space for non-unitary model which might frame the insights of marxism and psychoanalysis as not incompatible with each other and with yet other ways of desiring and knowing. Such problems arise not only from the failure to rethink impossibilities such as a search for the all-embracing, but from a common assumption that even to say that much is to be understood to adopt a kind of nihilism often named postmodern, and to be "against" broad theorising; you must be for or against grand narratives, generalisation is taken to be some kind of absolute. And to argue as I just have is to be a hopeless liberal. This prejudging stifles at birth the urgent work of finding new ways of understanding "the subject and social relations in history." What I have to say about where Pollock's work is situated should be read as countering the kinds of philosophical move that lead even to the formulation "humanist desire" in the first place, as well as the all-encompassing conceptualisation that might be its end. The work of finding a way forward so that the discourses of the subject and of social relations in history are not placed opposite each other has begun in earnest. But there is, or appears to be, large-scale cultural denial, symptomatic at the least of a time-warp between areas of cultural theory, as in culture at large, and visible, for example, in repetition. Repetition in a fast-changing culture is a multivalent phenomenon, and is not necessarily negative. By the same token, it is not necessarily positive either. But the current situation requires that serious attention be paid to the wider meanings of at least two prominent kinds of repetition, themselves not singular, which are those consequent on the closure of theoretical frameworks and on a selective appeal to the dominant past as "tradition" or determinant. Connotation at the level of reception is vital here; or to put it another way, anyone wishing to break with obsessive returns has to consider as a priority how well their remarks will travel in the face of them.

In what follows, I shall explore how Pollock's work impacts both upon the progressive and the regressive elements of this crisis, and upon developments and forms in visual art from which it is inseparable, but to which it is not limited. I have organized this exploration into three interrelated sections, each focusing on another aspect of the crisis. The first, "The world as material-semiotic actor" situates Pollock within the materialism/idealism debate in various manifestations; the second, "Neither from nor towards Modernism or post-Modernism" argues the fundamental coherence of her sometimes apparently contradictory statements about them; and the third, "Knowledge and Space" brings both into relation with the "Matrixial." The sections are of course artificial, sacrificing some continuities in favor of repositioning Pollock's work, and the feminism with which it is imbricated, to point towards their inseparability from contemporary debates. This is to insist that they cannot be marginalized as concerning women only or even perhaps primarily (in terms of implication rather than orientation).

the "world as material-semiotic actor"

There is no necessary opposition between materialism and radical philosophies of difference.

All major areas of (cultural) theory are to some degree working through the conceptual legacy of the assumption that there is; any list would have to include Deconstruction, Feminism of all shades, Marxism, Psychoanalysis, Modernism, post-Modernism, New Historicism, and do I have to invent something for Deleuzian-Butlerist New Corporealism? "Necessary" is doing a great deal of work in my statement, as are "materialism" and "difference"; a great deal of secondary-level matter stands in the way of either understanding what is at issue, or even being prepared to contemplate it. The fact that these difficulties are derivative and historical has no bearing on their importance and power.

I want to set the scene for a consideration of Pollock's position in contemporary debates in the light of this re-statement of a situation which in some form is so well known and repeated that it risks ceasing to signify in any strong sense. It is a formulation which belongs with several related oppositions together with which it installs a formidable dynamic or four-dimensional force-field. Prominent in this specific context as intersection with Modernism/post-Modernism are psychoanalytic/Marxist theory, which maps both onto subjectivity/collectivity, idealism/materialism, and to some extent onto the by now usually sterile discussion of French vs Anglo-American feminism.

This seeming-detailed point is one which, Chaos-like, ramifies because it is structural, if I may use that word without implying total absence of agency. What happens if a start is made from the philosophy formerly known as idealist on the assumption that this does not entail denial of the philosophy formerly known as materialist, or from the construction of Subjectivity and/or the Sign while holding open whether this entails denial of Historical Materialism any more than starting from Feminism necessarily means abandonment of masculine tradition? It is not that the differences in the materialities of thought, sexed subjectivities, corporealities, the physical world, economics, history and societies are elided. Rather they are fore-grounded in their specificities. They all appear as materialities, allotropic rather than oppositional. Working out from a tradition fractured along materialist-idealist lines clearly makes this very difficult to articulate fully rather than merely to assert. What I have to say about Pollock is based on a reading of her work as the beginnings of this kind of articulation. My point of departure was idealist; Pollock's was materialist. I see our positions now as conflicted but convergent. This is not in the cozily dangerous sense of settling all differences, but in being engaged in the same struggle of carving out the terms in which common problems may first be recognized as such, and then perhaps adequately be addressed.

To focus for a moment on the specifics within feminism, and the posi-tionalities adopted by so-called "second wave" thinkers since the 1960s. I want to ask why it is that even though a way forward exists that, far from being inimical to feminism, is crucial to it, it is resisted. Some combination of Modernism, post-Modernism, Subjectivity and Materialism are again central issues in this dispute which sometimes reads like a dialogue between people standing at a noisy city intersection: they pick up the gist, which will inevitably be more defined by their own pre-existing frameworks than if they could hear clearly, and as a result hear a distorted argument. This they reject. The interference of a traffic composed (at least) of disciplinary, pro-fessional, sexed, hegemonic and unconscious pathways is cacophonous indeed, and I do not mean that the answers are easy. But the reasons for it are worth looking at because it has become almost a received mode to adopt the voice of the alternative, to argue against (Modernism has even been posited as 'against' by definition): even reactionary critics often adopt the "alternative" stance. We are all revolutionaries now. The effect of this vocative mode is more than rhetorical; furthermore it is symptomatic of a simplified understanding of history that has cost the Left dear. The romance of revolution can be fatal both to any cause and to its supporters. The reasons why revolution cannot sustain its changes are material as well as psychoanalytic (for want of a better shorthand). The proletariat—whatever that now means, and I mean that—does not thrive on crisis.

To demonstrate this, let me quote from a recent and in many ways excellent article, which I have chosen precisely because it is good in some respects. The writer, Hemingway, is not being set up in the manner I have just described.

In rejecting epistemological realism, post-Marxist theory has tended to conflate or even deny the distinctions between the discursive and nondiscursive, with the result that ideology is not seen to represent any prior existing reality, and notions of objective interests deriving from different places in the social structure become untenable. However, as Terry Eagleton has argued, not only is this position ultimately idealist, it takes away the grounds for any meaningful collective politics, for interests become simply a matter of the values conferred within particular discursive frameworks, and no logical explanation can be given for the origination of those values in the first place. (Hemingway 1996, 24)

This is quite true of some post-Marxist theory, and Hemingway is right to emphasize the problems for collective politics—or indeed any kind of collectivity—and for an understanding of how values either intersect, collide or gain meaning at all. (I might take issue with "objective interests," but let that pass for now). What I want to ask is why such a writer, who is as well-informed of certain developments in feminism as he is in general, seems only to have taken up this element of "post-Marxist" theory and not those elements represented in this essay most importantly by Pollock, but also in often complementary ways by other important thinkers such as Rosi Braidotti, Carole Pateman, Drucilla Cornell and Teresa Brennan.

To move on from early Marxism is not necessarily to deny it. I would argue strongly that the -ismatic and post-ismatic habit is lethal to historical understanding. Marxism, like elements of Modernism, was a rationalist theory predicated on an optimistic belief in historical progress. But there is a time-lag between them: early Modernism was far more contradictory and complex either than Marxism in this (limited) sense, or than it (Modernism) became. There is currently a renewed awareness of the need to deal with supra-rational forces, both in the psyche and in historical and social change. It matters greatly that, *pace* the likes of Alain Minc, the metaphor of the Middle Ages is not allowed to obscure what is new in the current historical moment, because this way of conceptualizing the present through revisitation of earlier periods is all too often a conservative gesture of evasion. It is always less threatening to see change in terms of familiar paradigms than to recognize where it may be irrevocable. This is not at all to deny the importance of historical precedents. Of course any historicized theory must find ways tracking them. But these kinds of areas of the human psyche, of historical and social change, may be the Achilles heal of Marxism. And of the reduced movement Modernism became.

Without getting into arguments which are inevitably beyond the scope of this essay, I want to take a look at Pollock on class and its intersection with race and gender. I want to come at this by examining what I see as an invalid criticism of her work. It is, of course, a strategy open to misreading to quote unsympathetic or erroneous views of a writer, but I nevertheless think it is important here, because it exemplifies a widespread misconception and source of confusion. Pollock has been wrongly critiqued as failing to register that the structural relation of the working class to the means of production "expresses the fundamental asymmetrical relations of power locked into the capitalist system" (Roberts, 16). According to this view, assuming reciprocity between class, race and gender leads her to flatten out the "asymmetric causal relations between base and superstructure" (17). Why should acknowledging or even hypothesizing reciprocity between race, class and gender entail as a necessary consequence a distortion of power relations under capitalism? Even if this insistence on the primacy of what was a very specific constellation of class had considerable force in the nineteenth and earlier twentieth centuries, is it really an adequate description of late, virtual, multinational capitalism? Roberts's metaphor is static ("locked in"); capitalism has proved to be more and more protean. The effect of attempts like Pollock's to read the dynamics of art according to a more complex model is not necessarily to lose sight of the fundamental lessons of historical materialism. You only have to read

"Fetishism …" in this volume to see that it seriously misrepresents her work to remark in relation to it: "Modernism may have been made on the naked backs of women, but these were the backs largely of working class women" (17), and there are plenty of other examples. But at a more fundamental level still, this denies Pollock's attempted suturing of material relations of the art world, exclusion from the symbolic, relations between women as *outside* the capitalist model, a whole series of factors that have been articulated not only in separated discourses, but in opposed discourses. I have thought it worthwhile being specific about these misreadings because they indicate with some exactitude the kinds of difficulty entailed in her project of simultaneous critique and forging of the new—re-generation in its broadest sense.

The economic function of the sex-class-race force field has differed significantly between the USA and, say—because it is one of Pollock's examples—South Africa, as well as Europe and the UK, as have its meanings. Multi media technologies may be changing this beyond recognition, and in ways that are likely to discriminate still further against women in terms of visible economic activity.[1] Unless contemporary Marxism and its derivatives can develop ways out of economic masculinist monism—ways that are more nuanced than Bourdieu-style sociology, for example—it will lose explanatory power still further. Semiosis plays no small part in this economic change; it is information and its technologies that drive it as much as manufacturing or other forms of economic activity, and the movements of global capital have created a dynamic that escapes the categorizations of directly causal or teleological thinking. We are in the era of fuzzy logic; but even fuzz can be characterized (it usually is—as female), and the impossibility of definitive description may well apply far more broadly than is generally admitted. This moves the divisions as I have described them in cultural and related theories up the agenda for urgent attention. Very few thinkers indeed have tried to approach these questions, as Pollock has in essays such as "Fetishism …" or "Territories of Desire" (both in this volume) or *Avant-Garde Gambits*. Baudrillard at least attempts to address the relation between the sign and commodity, and while I would clearly have problems with his analysis—not least his romantic advocacy of "total revolution" or what I understand of his conceptualization of abstraction both in the economic cycle and in the sign—his attempt to address "semiological reduction" at a "global anthropological level"[2] should be followed through in art-historical practice far more than it currently is. Because Pollock's discursive frameworks and address are so far from Baudrillard's—and it is very tempting to sex their writing—it can be difficult to see the extent to which she is addressing the same underlying problematic, and the place/s of sex, gender and women within it.

At the risk of overemphasis, what I am arguing for is not to wish away what I see as a crucial engagement with the different positionalities around these issues. It is rather to advance the debate beyond what is becoming an entirely predictable set of arguments and positions, together with their theoretical support arranged in ranks; why is it perceived by many on both 'sides' as constructive to read any attempt to bring 'discursive materialism' into productive collision with Marxist-derived historical materialism as betrayal? Again, I put this not as a rhetorical question, but as a real and urgent one. The development of feminists such as Michele Barrett is characterized as substituting Foucault for Marx. Why is "the reunderstanding of materialist feminism coming out of the Marxist tradition" opposed to a "ludic" feminism whose materialism is merely idealism in disguise? (Ebert 24–5) Just like Michele Barrett, Pollock is seen by some as "abandoning Marx" for the post-Modern gurus such as Foucault, Derrida Lyotard, but this would adequately describe neither the provenance of her thinking nor its motivation. Why is the entire history of the twentieth century obliterated through the identification of all strands of post-Modern feminism, however conflicted, with Hegelianism and what Marx and Engels dismissed as its fight with "phrases"? (Ebert 42, quoting Marx) Those phrases have grown into transnational information and multimedia corporations, and if for no other reason require reconceptualizing in materialist terms.

Within explicitly feminist frameworks, both "sides" in this sometimes bitter debate may be accused of making a career out of trashing feminism, and of supporting the status quo. The caricature runs something like this: those seen to be post-Modernist evince an irresponsible hedonism, or, worse, sexual libertarianism which repeats masculinist oppression, the whole philosophy tantamount to indulging in privileged feminist fiddling while those who never even got to Rome burn; the straw socialist feminists supposedly dourly espouse a kind of antipleasure anti culturalism (productive work is "better than" art, which is not productive in any sense) in a backward-looking and unsophisticated literal-mindedness. These incomprehensions matter. We cannot afford to walk away from the arguments. Both "sides" are drawn into it because they need elements of what the other is saying. This ought to have been clear throughout the 1990s since the publication of serious texts like Lyndon Shanley and Carole Pateman's collection *Feminist Interpretations and Political Theory* (to name but one) at beginning of the decade (1991).

Such blockages and repetitions are produced by structural incomprehension deriving from divisions in the terms that anglophone cultural theorists of the 1990s have inherited and which necessarily form their starting points. To be more specific, they are symptomatic of the difficulty that has produced the social-psychic division which Pollock attempts to address. The way to understand the economics of the mind and of late capitalism may well be to start at opposite ends—the macro and micro—and to work towards each other. There are serious points being made on both "sides" but they are muddled by mistrust. Why go back to Lenin's critique of the Machians (Ebert 1996, 25–6) to ask questions about the way thinkers such as Butler, de Lauretis or Cornell are reformulating the relation between matter and thought, materialism and idealism? None of these thinkers is adequately described by saying they "evade materialism as simply a question of epistemology" (ibid). Nothing is "simply" a question of epistemology and interrogating the limits of discourse and of the material is not necessarily a claim to have "risen above" (25) materialism and idealism into liberal pluralism. Clearly a limply passive pluralism is a risk, and there are some who have retreated into it; but it is in no way adequate to describe the majority of feminists whose materialism is not Marxist as "guilty" of this kind of evasion. The relations of individuals to the means of production have changed—I do not say for the better—since Lenin. It is surely a materialist position to maintain that subjectivities and their epistemological relations will also have changed. Control over meaning—mass media, advertising and virtual communications as well as what used to be called culture—is historically a major element in this change. Why else did colonialists invariably outlaw indigenous languages and cultures? Why else were women marginalized in art alongside the peasantry (a source of modernist form in Eastern Europe) and the industrial working class?

The arguments are real; it is urgent that they be redirected into understanding an expanded materialism. To argue for the reality of epistemic violence is not to deny the reality of economics. It is to recognize their complicity, and, in the best thinkers, patiently to shift the terms so that they become analyzable.

"The neo-materialism of Foucault, the new materiality proposed by Deleuze are … a point of non-return for feminist theory" (Braidotti, 266). There are few—though, fortunately some—who have understood this and sought to work with it as well as Pollock, not only with regard to contemporary culture but also to art and its histories. In the next section, I shall look more closely at how it informs Pollock's negotiations of post-/and/Modernism.

neither from nor towards modernism or post-modernism

"My work is but another operation producing signifying space."
"What I am aiming at is historical knowledge."

Griselda Pollock

The late twentieth century was a period of transition. It moved out of a mindset driven by the categorical imperative, in which it was the category that dominated knowledge rather than serving it. A problem for anyone working as Pollock is towards another epistemology, especially in relation to the art of the last 150 years and its histories, is that even the artists themselves became so caught up in this way of seeing the world and their own production that their languages are encoded by it. It will require greater distance than we have as yet for this to be clearly visible by the majority. Meanwhile the forces of reaction try to intervene to reassert a view they could once assume as "natural." The most obvious symptom of this state of affairs is the habit of looking at art in terms of movements and more or less discrete groups, accepting the partial coherence this allows as whole. If only it were that simple.

It is in this context that I understand Pollock's self-positioning in relation to what she is careful to call "the modernist project" rather than Modernism. Viewed from the categorical point of view, some of her statements, like the two at the head of this section, may seem, at first, hard to reconcile. To aim at historical knowledge is to believe, at least up to a point, in something known (in the current shorthand) as Enlightenment principles which underlie contemporary notions of history and epistemology. Whether this is an adequate understanding of any of the eighteenth-century thinkers usually gestured towards in this way is another matter, but it is generally thought to be compatible with Modernism. To regard historical knowledge, however, as one operation among others productive of signifying space is neither the vocabulary nor the wider discourse of Modernism, traditionally defined. While Pollock's "modernist project" is clearly to be differentiated from the high Modernism now frequently signified by "Modernism," as well as from post-Modernism *tout court*, it is not contained by categorical thinking. Indeed Pollock's work implies other terms, and I would suggest it is best understood in that way, even while she is using those out of which she is moving. Her writing is sufficiently multivalent for it to do so, which is one of the reasons it is significant. While I recognize certain investments and political positionings at stake in insisting on the modernist project, my understanding of Pollock's work as an historian is that it not only implies something beyond the project of Modernism, but that any simple espousal of that project runs the risk of distorting some aspects of what needs to be done, and obstructing others. This is partly about the contradiction of dealing with culture and politics—Marxism, as much as feminism, is complexly implicated in revisioning Modernism—politics clearly must have a project, whereas culture will always exceed any such aim, inscribing a tension into politicized understandings of art to which it is necessary always to attend. But that it not all that it is about, as I hope to make clear. It is about the historical effects of rethinking subjectivities and collectivities. In so doing, I hope I shall also cast some light on current feminist thinking in the vexed and often unconstructive Modernism/post-Modernism debates.

It is not only because Pollock remains an avowed feminist, not at all swayed by the kinds of equivocation many of us are tempted into these embattled days, that any commitment to Modernism will by definition be conflicted and problematic; feminism is a challenge to the subject of Modernism not only as "the privileged male of the white race," in Spivak's phrase, but also, and more abstractly, as the ego which is complicit in the discourses of mastery. Modernism, like any historical telos including Hegelianism, could be said to be implicated at least in the unspeakable history of the Holocaust, though not in my way of thinking in any simple or direct causal sense. It might be hoist by its own petard, however, in that its own logic would implicate it more deeply. If feminism does not, according to Pollock, set itself against the "modernist project", it is inimical to the "Modernism", loosely associated with American Abstract Expressionism, and understood as a set of practices rather than a style or single practice. This is partly I think because instead of subverting mastery, such practices displaced the idea of the ego *evident* as mastery into that of the ego *as* mastery. Indeed, in a sense, the exact meaning of the more benign modernist project, which Pollock recognizes has been betrayed, remains open, although, perhaps surprisingly to some extent, she aligns herself with a Greenbergian position, at least insofar as it concerns historical legitimacy (1, 2). But she gives no succinct definition, and indeed this suggestiveness is part of the point. The writer on art is a Reader, a maker of meanings, engaged in and with a nexus of practices—which is one reason why she does not unequivocally call herself an historian; in her Barthesian definition (chapter 1), an array of cultural practices builds up a textuality, one which disperses authority but does not destroy it altogether. (In her text, she shifts from author to authority, which is all right as far as it goes. But it is not a necessary connection, that between author and authority, and it is perhaps a troublesome loose end to leave). Pollock uses Barthes's terms of reference to make a claim for the social production of meaning, a phrase which in her text indicates if not an equal emphasis on specificity, difference and materiality, then no hierarchy between them. This is an important detail which differentiates her usage from its customary traditional Materialist overtones.

So this modernist project is very much about the location of meaning in the processes of semiosis, as well as its production, implicitly in intersecting tensions between the social and the semiotic. One definition Pollock does offer is that of "a radical doubt about the possibility of meaning" (1, 3), and it is noteworthy that it is a definition that straddles the Modern/Post-Modernism notional divide. Rightly, in my view, she does not repress a radical fear of the actuality of meaninglessness—the void ("*le néant*")—in favor of the contemporary celebration of placelessness: the bottomless yielding to the depthless, to borrow from Jeremy Gilbert-Rolfe's insights into the contemporary sublime. Common to Modernism and Post-Modernism is the problematic of how to rework and assimilate knowledge of the mid-point of the pendulum-swing (temporal and spatial). It is a figure-ground strobe.

The issues concerning the temporal and ideological relation between Modernism and Post-Modernism, and indeed the shift in the roles of critic-painter-reader Pollock involves her readers in, go back well into the nineteenth century. It is symptomatic of the fragmentation that began with the immensely influential establishment in France, the crucible, of oppositional groups, both formal and informal. From Courbet's Pavilion, the Salon des Refusés, the Independants, the Impressionists, all set up in some relation to the official Salon, with its rules and hierarchies, the public groupings of artists proliferated, fostering a polarized and confrontational mode which we still inherit, another dimension to the adoption by the most conservative and reactionary critics of the "alternative" voice. The avant-garde prefigured the rebel without a cause: this voice is now the birthright of anyone who grew up after the last acknowledged Western world war, with a particular sexual spin: women had to find a way of adopting it to claim it. But does it signify the "ego with nothing to master" or a possibility of reconceptualizing the ego in terms other than mastery? Teresa Brennan has usefully commented on the power of the secondary source in today's academic institutions in terms of specific ego relations: this vocative mode is similarly symptomatic, and it begets a broken history, contributive on the one hand to current fantasies of the end of history, ahistoricism, and on the other to certain kinds of new historicism. It is a serious effect, because it produces the problems of articulation I have outlined, with one observation identified with one side of a polarized argument signifying a whole package, what is denoted being subordinated to what is currently connoted; this is symptomatic of a specific configuration and hierarchization of subjectivities in the sign, and of its rapid, staccato temporality. (Another good example is pornography: if you question the acceptability of censorship, you are "for" pornography, etc.)

The notion that one idea must necessarily signify a cultural position, even though it has no necessary connection in logic, is not trivial, nor are its formal and semiotic consequences. (I hope this is not oversimplified to the point of banality). At issue is a kind of paradox that results from this promotion of connotation as somehow better than denotation. There is no meaning without some kind of anchorage; a connection with the real is the condition of meaning. The varying nature/s of that connection and of the elements between which it creates a rapprochement are of course the difficult part, and the important and interesting one. In the caricature or extreme position that has been attributed to post-Modernism, erroneous in my view, one of the several effects of the attempted displacement of denotation is its return within connotation. Instead of the desired free play of meaning, meaning becomes mired. No hierarchy of form exists outside ideological intent: no specific form has inherent meaning or value. Denotation may be neither abolished nor fixed. Saussure may well have overplayed the arbitrary nature of the sign: even if arbitrary in origin, it is only so in highly developed systems if you believe in absolutes. This may well be clearer in the visual sign than in the linguistic or aural, because the nature of referentiality differs, as Pierce makes clear: the sign is not entirely arbitrary, even in origin. This is not to propose that it is simple in its relation.

I have suggested elsewhere (1992) that divisions between early modern movements may be analyzed outside this confrontational mode as positions in history through their relation to the sign-body across time (historical and historicized); they were all experimenting with the signification of space-time, and this is what produced the formal variation. That variation, moreover, may be linked to subjectivity, which I tentatively linked with pre-Renaissance painting and "the impossible synthesis," the attempt of the Scholastics to think of Man simultaneously in terms of the singular and the universal.[3] The importance of Pollock's insights into the application of Kristeva's essay "Women's Time"[4] and her discussion of the gendering of space in Modernism significantly take this kind of suggestion forward, and may be linked with Brennan's readings of the spatial implications of the "ego's era" in history as discussed below. The apparent contradictions in Pollock's position on Modernism derive from her recognition of its early multiplicity—part of what was "betrayed" in later reformulations. One element in that distortion is the re-description by many adherents and unconscious inheritors of high Modernism of metamorphic and transformative form as inherently inferior to an impossible "purity"; the problem is not "pure form," but rather its hierarchization. Bracha Lichtenberg Ettinger's restitutive work, promoted by Pollock, among others, begins to reinscribe (her "metramorphic") that formal potential, which has a profound connection with the real, with her personal re-membering, which is also that of a woman and that of an obscene chapter in the history of Modernism's quest for purity. This is not to make any simplistic link between individual artists work and the Holocaust; but it is to insist on the implications of the collective. Transformative form is not an absolute: what is transformative is as historicized as any adequate notion of the feminine; indeed in many ways, historicized—and thereby weakened—as the feminine. Thus it is not that abstraction is necessarily non-transformative when symbolism is (this would plainly be absurd, since the two meet in many artists like Klee or Kandinsky); the abstraction of Barbara Hepworth may be understood in terms analogous to the metramorphic (Florence 1995). It is the paradox, the irony, even, that the purity sought by Modernism rests on the connotative. This is implicit in Pollock's insistence on art as "complex and expanded textualities", by which she intends the whole social production of meaning, including the institutions of gallery and market, studio, productive practices, critic and historian. The "work of art" as formal presence in this nexus is mediator and commodity at the same time as "aesthetically vivid".

Pollock has strongly challenged the ways in which Gauguin's art is currently assessed. Gauguin's tendencies towards abstraction allied with his Symbolist affinities and Impressionist moments, the very rapidity of his absorption of major developments in the late nineteenth century make him an important case. Pollock contrasts his critical assessment with Manet's achievements to ask why the former's orientalizing has to an extent recuperated the earlier artist's "strategic dissonance." Feminism insists upon a re-examination of how ethics intersects with aesthetics, which makes authenticity, or its suspension, an issue. Following through this comparison between Manet and Gauguin (which was not the aim of Pollock's piece, but rather a matter raised by it) might cast light on these recalcitrant questions. They still matter, because the aesthetic and the attribution of supramaterial value are crucial components of semiotic and cultural power. With his customary equivocation, Mallarmé, the poet who has been made the arch-representative of art for art's sake, argued along these lines in the 1880s.

Feminism both exploits and is threatened by the degree of instability that exists within semiosis, a process which is inseparable from the subjectivities involved at any stage: initiating or responding, synchronically or historically. Gauguin was undoubtedly in many respects a repellant individual, and Pollock draws attention to the ways in which the banker's reinvention of himself as artist were played out across particular women. Their subjectivities, located in class and race, are extremely important to any understanding of the intersection between his subject-formation, the colonialism that produced him and the aesthetic values that have promoted his painting. Nor is bringing the question back to aesthetics a form of displacement: the connection is highly problematic, extremely uncomfortable and resistant to analysis—and inescapable. Aesthetic values cannot be argued away, as even Terry Eagleton admits; and even if the aesthetic were (or is) a bourgeois category, what that naming does is to shape the issues in a specific formation. It does not resolve them. To examine the aesthetic power of some of his work is not about "exculpating" Gaugin the man; as Pollock has eloquently argued in relation to van Gogh, the signifier "Gauguin" signifies more and other than the historical figure. The "conjunction of aesthetics, sexuality and colonialism" most certainly requires further and different examination from what little it has so far received, but that requirement does not abolish what has been called "the aesthetic." What is this excess allied to pleasure, where is it located (culturally, formally and in the Subject), and what are its meanings in history? Pollock may not answer such troublesome and insistent questions, of course not. But she is not halted or limited by them either in their specificity or their intractability. What really matters, though it sounds so easy, is that she does not evade them. Rather she works towards the elaboration of frameworks which might make the ceaseless revolving of question and answer move again.

In the last main section, I shall attempt to foreground one pathway of the unchartered territories all Readers have to negotiate if they are to be able to participate in the adventure.

knowledge and space

"In painting the rules of perspective decide the right place, but how will it be decided when it comes to truth and morality?"

Pascal (1670)
Cited by Lacan (1953)
Cited by Brennan (1993)

Emergent among the next significant moves in the theorization of culture and its truths, however provisional, is the rethinking of the nature of collectivities and of generalization. Clearly this will inflect how history as sexed is thought. I have commented above, as have many others, on the difficulty of moving between psychoanalytic readings of culture and analyses of the social or the collective—and Pollock herself is often rightly tentative in making moves of this kind. Nevertheless she makes them. It is a commonplace of the social history of art from T. J. Clark onward to connect historical analyses of Modernism with the city, quintessentially Haussman's Paris. Pollock is one of the few to attempt to bring this macro-environment down to the micro in terms of the complex transformations in the visual text of individual, gendered experience. The most obvious example is her essay on "Modernity and the Spaces of Femininity" in *Vision and Difference* (1988).

So the work on rethinking collectivities has begun. In order to elaborate this aspect of Pollock's work, I want to prepare the ground through Teresa Brennan who has also taken matters forward at the conjunction of history psychoanalysis and materialism. In *History after Lacan*, Brennan undertakes a complex reading of Lacan's theory of the ego's era and perspective on history, a relatively neglected side of his theory of the imaginary. There may of course be difficulties with the idea of an ego's era, but it should be noted that "ego" here is to be differentiated from the individual consciousness Freud set in contradistinction to the "id"; it is rather the rigidity of unconscious narcissism, among whose characteristics are negation, opposition and denial. It connects both with the Hegelian notion that history "finds a limit" and cultural ahistoricism (30–31). She makes what will be to many some surprising links between Lacan's theory, Adorno, Benjamin and the early Frankfurt School (8), and goes on to what is an extremely important part of her analysis, one which is implicit, sometimes latent but nevertheless a driving presence, in Pollock's work, which is the connection of the individual with the social *in the commodity* (10). Lacan has not fully worked his theory of history out, far from it, but by meticulously pursuing the hints and traces he has left, by making close readings of what he actually does say and seeking out its coherence rather than its contradictions, Brennan builds a powerful case for it in several respects. Chief among these for my purposes here are three features of her treatment of the Lacanian theory—and I think her generous sometimes in her attribution of some of the insights to Lacan. She sees it as "a lever for thinking out the trajectory of modernity": she notes that the fact that even while stressing the psychical, it does so in a way which makes the psychical into a material or, strictly, a physical force, which is at the same time cultural" (7); and the social ramifications of the master-slave dialectic link with "a dialectic working between space in the environment and the psyche" (8). Her understanding of the commodity as a point of convergence between the social and the psychical (see, especially, her Part II) may well stand further investigation in terms of the art-object as commodity, though it would be beyond the scope of the present discussion to go into it thoroughly. I want to signal its relevance with some emphasis to the synthesis I am arguing Pollock also works to effect.

Brennan points out that the way the ego and the environment affect each other in Lacan's thinking begins with the auto-competitiveness of the mirror stage, which importantly *prefigures* the aggressivity of territorializing and competitive social relations: there is a fundamental connection between the spatial dimension of the ego and the environment (42). This offers a particularly useful slant in support of Pollock's position on why the modernist city is both masculine and aggressive and how this is made manifest spatially, following the asymmetry of Oedipal resolution between the sexes. It also connects with the master-slave dialectic. Here again is Pollock's important emphasis on Ettinger's linkage between the feminine and racism and their location in the body and sign-body of an individual Jewish woman. Second-generation Holocaust survivors have borne witness to the physicality of the psychic transmission of trauma, further confirmation of the importance of establishing clearer understandings of psychosocial history.

Another site where history, the spatial and "the intimately inscribed processes of a particular subjectivity" come together for Pollock is in the work of Mary Kelly and Lubaina Himid, "at once case history and transforming analysis". In effect she says the same of Bracha Lichtenberg Ettinger's theory and practice of the Matrixial. As an analyst, theorist and artist, Ettinger creates a multiple textuality through which the matrixial is developed and embodied.

Lyotard observes about Bracha Lichtenberg Ettinger's use of the photo-copier as means of production, not reproduction, that it is a gesture ("*geste*") which challenges Benjamin's diagnosis of our era as "the age of mechanical reproduction," and a wager ("*gageure*") proving the suitability to art of such means (Lyotard et al. 1995, 7, 22). His exact words are what raises this above a fairly commonplace, if apposite, remark: gesture, diagnosis, wager. In these mutually imbricated terms, Ettinger's work takes risks—but with an exact aim; it seeks—but in spaces before and after that which is sought; it makes a gesture—but as it reaches beyond the originating body, it retains its connection. So that when Ettinger says, "Accomplish the mysterious gestures of painting in all that space now negatively feminized" (130) it may be understood in this expanded sense: the gesture is of the painter's body, of painting as a locus of practices capable of exceeding their physical generation and medium, and therefore of the sign-body.

This spatiality which Pollock finds to be enacted by Ettinger is also proposed in recent reconceptualization of a subjectivity neither severed from the maternal body nor understood in contradistinction to it. Brennan demonstrates how in the ego's era, it is possible to theorize time as replaced by space, which clearly impinges on the sense of history (11). Her analysis is of expansionist space, quite different from that under discussion. Perhaps I may clarify it with reference to a common art-historical move, which is to refer to earlier moments in Modernism (and sometimes in any period) as if it made no difference that there is a temporal gap. The structure and space of and in painting is then read in an essentialist manner as the same signifier, regardless of any other factor. Thus a recent commentary on Peter Greenaway's film *Pillow Book* refers to his metonymic use of screens as Cubist. Such a transfer of a term like this across medium and time usually goes unremarked. "We all know what he means." But it raises at least two main questions: if indeed this aspect of a brief moment in early Modernism is still so alive, why is it, and what does this mean for an embodied self which has been read as so radically changed? Spatial construction in painting the last century was revolutionized in no small part through contact with Japan, and before Cubism, the philosophical consequences of which have been resisted in myriad ways ever since, including *Pillow Book* itself. This connects with that materialism-idealism split discussed in the first part of this essay, not only in terms of culture, but in terms of a socioeconomics in which commodified culture plays an ever-growing part. Greenaway, of course, is probably among the most fine-art literate of well-funded filmmakers, but it should be remembered that his beginnings were as a minimally funded British Independent. The materiality of the screen, and its metaphoric configurations, has changed since Cubism. The silver screen is now the blank monitor, and Greenaway's "alternative voice" has been facilitated neither by old-style commodity capital nor by the artistic avant garde, but rather by the alliance between global capital and its understanding of the centrality of signification to its operations. The Sony corporation takes over from the British Film Institute. Anyone who thinks this does not impact on visual practice in painting and on its histories is mistaken. The same applies to assessing Pollock's position. This volume makes more widely available two of her essays on film which should alert the reader to her knowledge of film theory and its influence on her thinking, which is relatively underplayed. (See Part IV "Cinematic Moments")

It is in the light of these very far-reaching formal and historical issues that I suggest Pollock's claims for the strategic and formal importance of contemporary women practitioners are made. Pollock situates a work like Mary Kelly's *Interim* in a triangulated force-field: history painting, the recapitulation and supersession of "the high Modernist project" and the articulation of "the complexities of subjectivity in historical and social formations," this last understood as participatory also in critical culture. This may at first seem audacious. Pollock, of course, is being provocative in deliberately broadening the meaning of history painting in such a way as point up how limited its bureaucratic confinement in the nineteenth century had made it. Why do we need history painting and the high modernist project? Why their supersession rather than their abolition? Because (semiotic) abolition is a fantasy, and it is a fantasy of the ego's era. We need what it rendered impossible. The process is to "summon and redefine," it starts as feminist, but inevitably exceeds that "originating moment". Pollock sees this in Kristevan terms: "the resultant new significations—meanings and textualities—will not emerge from the repressed culture of women, or somewhere radically outside the system: they must be made by a specific kind of transgression within the system itself". Be that as it may, Pollock's underlying model for psychical processes is an energetic one, to some extent like Brennan's and like many since Deleuze (though I do not propose him and Guattari as origins). Brennan says that it has always been argued or assumed that in physical terms, it is the body that determines the social, and not the other way around. But it is in fact a process which works in both directions. The idea of a self-contained subjectivity which is an active agent within a passive environment is a fantasy, a projection of control, initially onto the mother (10–11).

Ettinger's work approaches these same crucial connections between subjective and social malady, starting from the mother's body. Pollock's readings placing it in the wider history of Modernism are important contributions to this broad project of thinking through the social implications of putting the subject's autonomy in art into question. Equally, Kelly's *Interim* is read as productive of new knowledge in precisely this area, that of a historical and individual restructuring of femininity through a/the symbolic mother.

Pollock herself is no stranger to the production of new knowledge in this area as well as others. This is legible in her account of the assumption of "whiteness" by the female child in the old Republic of South Africa that was herself is an attempt "to map the social and the psychic on to each other to extend both", and in so doing clarify through this specific example the intersection of class, race and sex. Her work is exemplary in its consistent engagement with this tripartite nexus, much cited by the radicals and ridiculed by the conservatives, but only slowly being seriously taken on in its difficulty, led by critics of color such as Gayatri Spivak. The depth of complexity is utterly belied by the ease with which anyone can plausibly and emptily list them: race, class and sex. Pollock foregrounds them here and in her detailed social reading of the Munby archive ("Fetishism, the laboring body and the color of its sex"). Race is not othered by her: it is taken on in personal and social history.

Her account in "Territories of Desire" rightly emphasizes the importance in the whole Oedipal scenario of "castration" and subsequent self-positioning through the individual's perception, or perhaps unconscious sensing and introjection, of the loci of power. That power translates into signification as both physical and socio-cultural. Thus she reveals the paradoxical shifts which mask the true physicality of the process; power is represented, as in one version of Freudian schema, as of natural origin because it is shifted away from the social and on to the sexed, racially specific body.

Yet there is a physical, spatial difference between the dominant bodies of the ego's era and the "passified" (in Brennan's terms). Freudian theory allows both for the recognition of the ego as corporeal projection and for the centrality of representation even in something as bodily as instinct (Grosz 1994). Pollock's insistence on "The question of white women's implication through the very fact of gender identification in the psychological formation and perpetuation of racism" makes it impossible to ignore the connection between her symbolic territories of the international women's movement and of desire.

I must confess that at first I regretted that Pollock's focus when she writes of sexual difference is on the mother and on femininity with relatively little probing of the detail of specific sexual formations: it is always unfair to ask a writer to take on matters outside those they choose. But this reader would still like to see a sequel to "Territories of Desire" which extends back into desire as sexual and explores it at the level of the social. I now see, however, the significance of displacing sex (gender and procreative desire), even if I still want to come full circle and return to them. The scenario Pollock depicts is of the white girl-child with two mothers of different race: one white and Oedipally positioned as the father, with power and leisure, one black, occupying the mother/feminine role of powerless Nanny ("the woman whose name was not really *Julia*). Her theoretical exploration of this relocated, re-spatialized feminine Oedipality (with males and sex displaced), both here and in her remarks on Kelly's *Interim*, exposes the maintenance of hystericized femininity—where all women are dismissed as invisible as "Dora's" mother was in Freud's case history-fragment-narrative of the woman whose name was not really *Dora* (1905). But how interesting it would be to re-pose the issues after traveling this route, to examine the question of how Frau K. , the equally discounted "other woman," Freud's rival, might relate to the white biological mother and to *Julia* in this articulation of what Ettinger calls the "matrixial space of the several" (86). Irigaray insists on the homosexuality of the archaic bond between mothers and daughters (1991). Neither female nor male homosexual desire has to be understood as limited to sexual practice for its impact on the social formation to be recognized: in fact I would probably go so far as to say there should be theoretical as well as actual spaces where it is not.

Pollock is of the generation of 1968, the first generation of women anywhere in history who have been able to make the choice to be heterosexually active and not to have children, certainly since the rise of the nuclear family, or to be homosexually active and to have "a family." This has had socio-economic consequences: women whose class prevented them taking such risks could now participate in post-industrial sexual experimentation without necessarily jeopardizing their economic independence. (This is still an issue: rightwing family values are a barely disguised attempt at recuperating women to the control of an individual male/father-substitute). The rise of a significant minority of sexual dissidents has brought that politico-personal positioning to bear in the analysis of culture. Both of these have been self-consciously put into discourse. It is important that other heterosexual thinkers take on board what this means historically, as Pollock tries to do, and not only by following her lead in acknowledging their positionings with regard to sexuality, and dealing with what may be threatening consequences. It is an irony that because the stakes can be very high indeed for lesbian and gay thinkers, so that such positions are necessarily highly politicized, they can be reduced to the political. As with women's view, or the "non-white," the non-heterosexual view becomes homogenized and contained as the specific instance rather seriously changing understandings of the generality.

Through Pollock's focus on the mother in "Territories of Desire," she hypothesizes that the mother-child dyad formed by the black nurse and her white charge is triangulated not by the father so much as by the economically and culturally empowered white mother". Pollock's argument here is important and insightful in relation to rethinking female desire without denial of the homoerotic. The spatiality of the sexed formation is radically altered, with intersecting and shifting geometries and dimensions. The sexual implications of this should be followed through not only in terms of social and economic power, so that the phallic is divested of its hold on sexuality. This is indeed as much implied by Ettinger as it is by Irigaray: "In the between-two of the sign and the figure, an uncertain space solicits the slippage from the visible to the readable, from the painted to the thought. The image beyond reference and context becomes an image-thought in which a multitude of signs and places melt into a kind of suspense—a gauze veil—or into a reflexive, musical mirror and its resonances" (Buci-Glucksmann in Lyotard et al. 1995, 59). It has long been my position that early Modernism opened on to these spaces (1986): it is prominent in what Mallarmé saw in Manet and in the other painters whose work he admired, those no longer in the modernist canon and difficult now to understand as co-extensive with it. But the intervening years have intervened and that position cannot be recovered. The idea of a "right to subjecthood" and access to the kinds of broadly cultural power wielded across the interlinked modernist-capitalist art establishment are major reasons why it cannot be abandoned either. Furthermore, the fact that feminism is a product of broad Enlightenment thinking—which has come to signify an extremely vague reference to a ragbag of definitions of a somehow achieved subjectivity—does not mean it has to be contained by it. This recalls to me the grounds on which Freud's work was othered: Freud was used as a signifier of impossibility, and still very often is, by some feminists as well as by others. Feminism as the structuring absence is indeed an "elsewhere within" as Pollock has put it, and the reality of that four-dimensional spatiality is inimical to the spatiality of what an irrecoverably diminished Modernism became.

The spaces of materialism and of psychoanalysis are already a kind of "elsewhere within" each other, even while they are indeed separate from each other and from art, and there are ways in which this will always mark any dialectical or otherwise dynamic move towards synthesis. Such growth will always involve a kind of catachresis. This makes the task, not definition (of post-Modernism or Modernism, or any of the abstractions Pollock moves to challenge through concretizing instances) but the patient reformulation of subjectivities in such a way as to render the distinction obsolete.

concluding note

The crisis over truth and morality with which I began is genuine, even if authenticity is in debate. Adherents to any position are in trouble, though few negotiate the hazardous consequences of this with greater honesty and skill than Pollock. The cultural phenomena called post-Modernism, materialism, feminism, etc. exist (the bottom line is that they have a name in circulation) and so require of the cultural commentator that they be understood before any idea of a "beyond" becomes possible. Entrenchment and/or attack is no answer.

There is an "ideal source" to which thought can have recourse, to borrow those now-impossible terms, "which never coincides with (its) real beginnings" (in Mallarmé's words). Pollock's contribution to the long-term reorientation within semiosis towards accommodating the dissolving geographies of the old orders and their accelerating histories deserves still wider attention. Feminism and much of the thinking called post-Modern derive philosophical inspiration, if not directly from an expanded understanding of Modernism, then from impulsions that are indicative of the need for a similar change of frame. All contemporary positions are mutually imbricated, or overlaid, and it is not easy to be clear about the different layers of a palimpsest, especially where they are paradoxical. But small differences matter, the manner of dealing with cultural disagreements matters, exemplifying as they do how I/not-I must be translated into I/non-I. Whether "we" agree matters far less than who is concealed in the first person plural and the power-syntax of the synergy that must underlie true agreement. The role of feminist thinkers such as Pollock must not be written out of the broader intellectual debate, as happened to women of earlier centuries. Accuracy, if not Truth, demands that the intellectual, social and cultural movements of any century should be assessed judiciously. This is perhaps more demanding of those who dissent than of those who agree.

notes

1   Demonstrated for example, in statistics published by the European Community in their occasional series *Women of Europe* (Dossier 44) Aug.–Oct. 1996.

2   See, for example, Baudrillard 1993, 57–98. Baudrillard at least gestures towards gender in his analysis. It may be slight, but it is at least there. His essay on "The

Art Auction" (1981 Chapter 5 112–122) is perhaps limited in the terms under discussion because he claims that his analysis is applicable to other knowledge-objects, or "knowledge" in general (122). It is the material specificity of painting that requires to be rethough in the economy of signs—and as *sexed.*

3   This takes up points made by Yves Bonnefoy: see p. 434.

4   This highly influential essay was first published in 1979 as "Le temps des femmes" *Cahiers des recherches de sciences des textes et documents* 33/34, 5, Hiver 5-19. It has since been made widely available.

references

Anon. (1990). "Can art history survive feminism?" *The New Criterion* vol. 8, April, 1–2.

Baudrillard, Jean (1981) *For a Critique of the Political Economy of Signs* St. louis: Telos Press.

Baudrillard, Jean (1993) *Symbolic Exchange and Death* (trans Grant, Ian) London/ Thousand Oaks: Sage.

Berger, John (1972) *Ways of Seeing* London: Penguin.

Braidotti, Rosi (1991) *Patterns of Dissonance* Cambridge: Polity.

Brennan, Teresa (1993) *History after Lacan* London: Routledge.

Ebert, Teresa (1996) *Ludic Feminism and After* Ann Arbor: University of Michigan Press.

Florence, Penny (1986) *Mallarmé, Manet and Redon: Visual and aural signs and the generation of meaning* Cambridge: Cambridge University Press.

Florence, Penny (1992) "Remembrance of Space-Time: Time and Perspective in nineteenth century poetry and painting" *Journal of the Institute of Romance Studies,* vol. 1, no. 1, 425–38.

Florence, Penny (1995) "Barbara Hepworth: the Odd Man Out" In *Barbara Hepworth Reconsidered* David Thistlewood (ed.) Liverpool: Tate Gallery/Liverpool University, 23–42.

Grosz, Elizabeth. (1994). *Volatile Bodies.* Bloomington: Indiana University Press.

Hemingway, Andrew and Vaughan, Williams (eds) (1997) *Art in Bourgeois Society 1790-1850* Cambridge: Cambridge University Press.

Kristeva, Julia (1971) 'Women's Time' *Signs* v. 7 no. 1 Autumn 13–35.

Lyotard, Jean-Francois, Buci-Glucksmann, Christine, Pollock, Griselda. (1995) *Bracha Lichtenberg Ettinger: Halala-Autistwork.* Catalogue. Cité due Livre, Aix en Provence and The Israel Museum. Jerusalem.

Parker, Roszika and Pollock, Griselda (1981) *Old Mistresses. Women, Art and Ideology* London: RKP.

Parker, Roszika and Pollock, Griselda (1987) *Framing Feminism. Art and the Women's Movement 1970-1985* London: Pandora.

Pollock, Griselda. (1988) *Vision and Difference* London: Routledge.

Pollock, Griselda. (1992) *Avant-garde Gambits* London: Thames & Hudson.

Roberts, John (1994) *Art has no History: the making and unmaking of modern art* London: Verso/NLB.

Shanley, Mary and Pateman, Carole (1991) *Feminist Interpretations and Political Theory* Cambridge: Polity.

Other forthcoming titles in the Critical Voices series

Practice: Architecture, Technique and Representation
Essays by Stan Allen. Commentary by Diana Agrest

Looking In: The Art of Viewing
Essays and Afterword by Mieke Bal. Edited and with an Introduction by Norman Bryson

The Information Subject
Essays by Mark Poster. Commentary by Stanley Aronowitz

Framing Formalism: Riegl's Work
Essays by Hans Sedlmayr, Julius von Schlosser, Richard Woodfield, Andrew Ballantyne, Joaquín Lorda, Stefan Muthesius, Joseph Masheck, Ivo Hlobil, Frauke Laarman, Benjamin Binstock, Matthew Rampley, Giles Peaker. Commentary by Richard Woodfield

Music Inside Out: Going Too Far in Musical Essays
Essays by John Rahn. Introduction and Commentary by Benjamin Boretz